Instructor's Manual

to accompany

Edwards ▪ Wattenberg ▪ Lineberry

Government in America

People, Politics, and Policy

Tenth Edition

Jan Leighley
Texas A & M University

New York Boston San Francisco
London Toronto Sydney Tokyo Singapore Madrid
Mexico City Munich Paris Cape Town Hong Kong Montreal

Instructor's Manual to accompany Edwards/Wattenberg/Lineberry, *Government in America: People, Politics, and Policy 10e*

ISBN: 0-321-09391-7

2 3 4 5 6 7 8 9 10-PHX-07 025 01 00

Contents

INTRODUCTION: TO THE INSTRUCTOR

Organization of the Textbook

Government in America provides a solid foundation for a course in American government and politics. In the Tenth Edition, the authors continue to adopt a policy approach to American government as a method of enabling students to understand the policies that governments produce. The themes of *democracy* and the *scope of government* provide a basic framework for analysis that students will find practical and worthwhile.

Government in America presents information in a format that challenges students to make policy choices. A variety of boxed features throughout the text provide background material and examples to supplement the contents of the chapter. The *You Are the Policymaker* sections present policy questions that have confronted policymakers. Students are invited to analyze each issue and reach their own conclusions. Chapter Four includes a series of special features entitled *You Are the Judge,* which describes a real case brought before the courts and asks the student to evaluate the case and render a judgment about it. *Making a Difference* highlights how individuals in the U.S. can sometimes dramatically affect government policies in various areas, introducing students to how individual citizens can have a dramatic effect on government policy. And a new feature, *How You Can Make a Difference*, suggests ways in which students might engage in political activity relevant to the chapter's topic.

While each of these features are included to sustain students' interest in reading the chapter text, they should also be considered important pedagogical devices, particularly as opportunities to enhance class discussion and debate.

Organization of the Instructor's Manual

This *Instructor's Manual* is intended as a comprehensive supplement to the textbook. For the most part, the words in the Manual are those of the authors of the textbook, and the outline parallels the organization of the text. **Bold print** identifies key terms and concepts the first time they appear in a chapter, as well as major divisions and subdivisions. *Italic print* has been used to highlight major concepts and explanations.

The *Instructor's Manual* contains an extensive chapter outline that should prove helpful in preparing lectures to accompany *Government in America.* In addition, a chapter overview provides highlights of the chapter in a shorter format. The textbook provides a foundation for each of the Class Discussion and Student Projects, most of which are based on material from the textbook, and many incorporate questions raised within the text. Some of these projects are designed to be done individually, and others in groups. But all of these exercises emphasize the development of students' independent research and analytical thinking skills.

Each chapter of the *Instructor's Manual* includes the following features:

* **Pedagogical Features** pinpoint special features included in each chapter that provide learning tools for both students and instructors.

* **Learning Objectives** point to important concepts and skills that the student should obtain from each chapter, provided in a brief "list" format.

* The **Chapter Overview** provides a summary of the chapter, with key terms and concepts highlighted with bold print or italics.

* The **Chapter Outline** contains a detailed outline of the chapter that parallels the presentation in the textbook.

* **Key Terms and Concepts** list major terms, principles, and political events, most of which appear in bold print in the textbook, along with definitions for each of these terms.

- **Teaching Ideas: Class Discussion and Student Projects** recommends questions for class discussion and for student research. Many of the topics augment questions that were raised within the body of the textbook.

- **Media Suggestions** include films that might be used to illustrate important principles or processes discussed in each chapter. These films might be shown during class periods, or even assigned for student viewing prior to coming to class.

Most of the videos and films included in the **Media Suggestions** section can be obtained from three sources. Information on PBS videos is available at www.pbs.org while information on videos from Films for the Humanities can be obtained at www.films.com. Insight Media can be reached at www.insight-media.com/Imhome.htm. Both the **Teaching Ideas** and **Media Suggestions** sections are "works in progress," and would benefit from any suggestions that instructors might have. They would also be enhanced by the addition of new ideas that others have found to be useful. I welcome your comments, criticisms and proposed additions, preferably by e-mail at leighley@polisci.tamu.edu.

Finally, instructors might want to consider a variety of other text supplements offered by Addison Wesley Longman, including a *Study Guide*, test item files, a computerized *Test Master* that contains the test bank questions and can be used to generate instructor-selected questions, student tutorial computer software, acetate transparencies, a *Politics in Action* video and an original laser disc.

Acknowledgments

I appreciate the efforts of Kelly Villella, Supplements Editor at Addison Wesley Longman, as well as the assistance of Jennifer Heath, who have helped with the development of this *Instructor's Manual*. I also greatly appreciate the unceasing support of my husband, Rick Johnson, to this on-going project.

JAN E. LEIGHLEY

CHAPTER ONE: INTRODUCING GOVERNMENT IN AMERICA

PEDAGOGICAL FEATURES

LEARNING OBJECTIVES

After studying this chapter, students should be able to:

- Distinguish among the fundamental concepts of *government*, *politics*, and *public policy*.
- Understand how *government*, *politics*, and *public policy* are interrelated.
- Ascertain how people can influence the government's *policy agenda*.
- Describe the basic concept of the *policymaking system*.
- Determine the essential principles of *traditional democratic theory*.
- Examine the three contemporary theories of American democracy: *pluralism*, *elite and class theory*, and *hyperpluralism*.
- Discuss and analyze the challenges to *democracy* presented in the text.

- Address the issue of the scope of government and explain how the scope of government is relevant to an understanding of *democracy*.
- Understand the importance of *individualism* in limiting the scope of American government.
- Begin to assess the two questions that are central to governing and that serve as themes for this textbook: *How should we govern?* and *What should government do?*

CHAPTER OVERVIEW

INTRODUCTION

Politics and government matter—that is the single most important message of this book. Despite the fact that government substantially affects each of our lives, youth today are especially apathetic about politics and government. The goal of *Government in America* is to assist students in becoming well-informed citizens by providing information and developing critical analytical skills.

GOVERNMENT AND POLITICS

This chapter introduces the fundamental concepts of government, politics, and public policy, and defines the ways in which the three are interrelated. **Government** consists of those *institutions that make authoritative public policies for society* as a whole. Regardless of how their leaders assume office, all governments have certain functions in common: they maintain national defense, provide public goods, use police powers to maintain order, furnish public services, socialize the young into the political culture, and collect taxes to pay for the services they provide.

Throughout *Government in America*, two fundamental questions about governing serve as themes: *How should we govern?* and *What should government do?* The chapters that follow acquaint students with the history of American democracy and ask important questions about the current state of democracy in the United States. One goal of the authors of *Government in America* is to familiarize students with the different ways to approach and answer these questions.

Politics determines whom we select as our governmental leaders and what policies they pursue. Political scientists still use the classic definition of politics offered by Harold D. Lasswell: *"Who gets what, when, and how."* The media usually focus on the *who* of politics. *What* refers to the substance of politics and government – benefits, such as medical care for the elderly, and burdens, such as new taxes. *How* people participate in politics is important, too. People *engage in politics* for a variety of reasons, and all of their activities in politics are collectively called **political participation.**

THE POLICYMAKING SYSTEM

A **policymaking system** is a set of institutions and activities that link together government, politics, and public policy. In a democratic society, parties, elections, interest groups, and the media are key **linkage institutions** between the preferences of citizens and the government's policy agenda. When people confront government officials with problems they expect them to solve, they are trying to influence the government's **policy agenda**. A government's policy agenda changes frequently: if public officials want to get elected, they must pay attention to the problems that concern the voters.

Three policymaking institutions—Congress, the presidency, courts, and the bureaucracy—stand at the *core* of the political system. They make **policies** concerning some of the issues on the policy agenda. Translating people's desires into public policy is crucial to the workings of democracy. **Public policy** is a choice that government makes in response to some issue on its agenda. Public policy includes all of the decisions *and nondecisions* of government: policymakers can establish a policy by doing *something* or by doing *nothing*, as can be seen by the government's original response of "inaction" to the AIDS crisis.

Policy impacts are the effects that policy has on people and on society's problems. The analysis of policy impacts carries the policymaking system *back to its point of origin* (often called *feedback*).

DEMOCRACY

Resounding demands for democracy have recently been heard in many corners of the world. In his famous Gettysburg Address, Abraham Lincoln referred to democracy as *"government of the people, by the people, and for the people."* Although Lincoln's definition imparts great emotional impact, such a definition is subject to many different interpretations. For example, what do we mean by *"people"*? No democracy permits government by literally every person in society. Throughout this textbook, the authors define **democracy** as *a means of selecting* *policymakers and of organizing government so that policy represents and responds to the public's preferences.*

Traditional democratic theory rests upon several principles that specify how a democratic government makes its decisions. Democratic theorist Robert Dahl lists five criteria that are essential for "an ideal democratic process": equality in voting, effective participation, enlightened understanding, citizen control of the agenda, and inclusion, which means that government must include (and extend rights to) all those subject to its laws.

Democracies must also practice **majority rule** and preserve **minority rights**. The relationship between the few leaders and the many followers is one of **representation**. *The closer the correspondence between representatives and their electoral majority, the closer the approximation to democracy.*

Theories of American democracy are essentially theories about who has power and influence. This chapter focuses on three contemporary theories of American democracy. **Pluralist theory** contends that many centers of influence compete for power and control over public policy, with no one group or set of groups dominating. Pluralists view bargaining and compromise as essential ingredients in our democracy. In sharp contrast to pluralist theory, **elite and class theory** contends that society is divided along class lines and that an upper-class elite rules. Wealth is seen as the basis of power, and a few powerful Americans are the policymakers. **Hyperpluralism** is "pluralism gone sour." Hyperpluralists contend that the existence of too many influential groups actually makes it impossible for government to act. When politicians try to placate every group, the result is confusing, contradictory, and muddled policy (or no policy at all). Both hyperpluralist theory and elite and class theory suggest that the public interest is rarely translated into public policy.

Regardless of which theory is most convincing, there are a number of continuing challenges to democracy: increased technical expertise, limited participation in government, escalating campaign costs and diverse political interests. Traditional democratic theory holds that ordinary citizens have the good sense to reach political judgments and that government has the capacity to act upon those judgments. However, it has become increasingly difficult to make knowledgeable decisions as human knowledge has expanded. There is evidence that Americans actually know very little about policy decisions or about who their leaders are. Today, the elite are likely to be those who command knowledge—the experts.

Many observers also worry about the close connection between money and politics. Candidates have become increasingly dependent on Political Action

Committees (PACs) to fund their campaigns. Critics charge that PACs have undue influence on members of Congress when it comes to the issues that the PACs care about.

The rapid rate of change of politics over the last three decades makes it more difficult for government to respond to demands. Some feel that this can lead to inefficient government that cannot adequately respond to challenges.

The large number and diversity of interest groups coupled with the decentralized nature of government makes it easy to prevent policy formulation and implementation, a condition known as **policy gridlock**.

Throughout *Government in America* students will be asked to evaluate American democracy.

- Are people knowledgeable about matters of public policy?
- Do they apply what knowledge they have to their voting choices?
- Are American elections designed to facilitate public participation?
- Does the interest group system allow for all points of view to be heard, or do significant biases give advantages to particular groups?
- Do political parties provide voters with clear choices, or do they intentionally obscure their stands on issues in order to get as many votes as possible?
- If there are choices, do the media help citizens understand them?
- Is the Congress representative of American society, and is it capable of reacting to changing times?
- Does the president look after the general welfare of the public, or has the office become too focused on the interests of the elite?

THE SCOPE OF GOVERNMENT IN AMERICA

One goal of *Government in America* is to familiarize the student with different ways to approach and answer the crucial questions that the authors raise. In particular, the text focuses on one of the most important questions facing modern American democracy: *Is the scope of government too broad, too narrow, or just about right?*

Our governments (national, state, and local) spend about one out of every three dollars of the **gross domestic product**. Our national government spends more than $1.7 trillion annually, employs nearly 5 million people, and owns one-third of the land in the United States. How does the American national government spend $1.7 trillion a year? National defense takes about one-sixth of the federal budget. Social Security consumes more than one-fifth of the budget. Medicare requires a little over one-tenth of the budget. The federal government helps fund highway and airport construction, police departments, school districts, and other state and local functions.

Most of the money in the federal budget goes to individuals or to state and local governments. If viewed in a comparative perspective, we find that *the United States devotes a smaller percentage of its resources to government* than do other economically developed nations. Moreover, the tax burden on Americans is also small, when compared to other democratic nations.

American **individualism**, which *developed from the desires of immigrants* to escape government oppression and from the *existence of a western frontier* with little government, helps account for the relatively small scope of government in America.

CHAPTER OUTLINE

I. POLITICS AND GOVERNMENT MATTER

- A. Many Americans – especially young people – are apathetic about politics and government.
  1. A tremendous gap has opened up between the young (defined as under age 25) and the elderly (defined as over 65) on measures of political interest, knowledge, and participation.
- B. It is the authors' hope that after reading this book, you will be persuaded that paying attention to politics and government is important.
  1. Government has a substantial impact on all our lives.
  2. We have the opportunity to have a substantial impact on government.

II. GOVERNMENT

- A. Government.
  1. **Government** consists of those institutions that *make authoritative public policies* for society as a whole.
  2. Four key institutions make policy at the national level: Congress, President, the Courts and the federal administrative agencies (bureaucracy).

B. This chapter raises *two fundamental questions about governing that will serve as themes for the text.*
   1. *How* should we govern?
   2. *What* should government do?

C. What governments do.
   1. Regardless of how they assumed power, *all governments have certain functions in common.*
      a. Governments maintain national defense.
      b. Governments provide **public goods** - things that everyone can share, such as clean air.
      c. Governments have police powers to provide order - as when Chinese security forces crushed the student protest in Tiananmen Square in 1989 and when the National Guard was called in to restore order in Los Angeles after the 1992 Rodney King verdict.
      d. Governments provide public services - such as schools and libraries.
      e. Governments socialize the young into the political culture - typically through practices such as reciting the Pledge of Allegiance in daily exercises at public schools.
      f. Governments collect taxes to pay for the services they provide.

III. POLITICS

A. **Politics** determines whom we select as governmental leaders and what policies they pursue.
   1. Harold D. Lasswell defined politics as "*who gets what, when, and how.*"

B. **Political participation** refers to the ways in which people get involved in politics.

C. **Single-issue groups** - interest groups whose members will vote on a single issue, such as pro-life and pro-choice groups that ignore a politician's stand on everything except abortion.

IV. THE POLICYMAKING SYSTEM

A. A **policymaking system** is a set of institutions and activities that link together government, politics, and public policy.
   1. In a democratic society, parties, elections, interest groups, and the media are key **linkage institutions** between the preferences of citizens and the government's policy agenda.
   2. The end product of government and politics is **public policy**. When people confront government officials with problems they expect

them to solve, they are trying to influence the government's **policy agenda**.

3. A **political issue** arises when people disagree about a problem or about a public policy choice.
4. The end product of government and politics is **public policy**.
5. Policymakers stand at the core of the political system, working within the three **policymaking institutions** established by the U.S. Constitution: the Congress, the presidency, and the courts.

B. **Policy impacts** are the *effects* policy has on people and on society's problems.

1. Having a policy implies a goal: people who raise a policy issue usually want a policy that *works*.
2. *Translating people's desires into public policy is crucial to the workings of democracy.*

V. DEMOCRACY

A. After the Russian Revolution (1917) and particularly when the Soviet Union expanded its sphere of influence throughout Eastern Europe after World War II, U.S. foreign policy was concerned with preventing the spread of communism.

B. Defining **democracy**.

1. The writers of the U.S. Constitution were suspicious of democracy.
2. In his Gettysburg Address, Abraham Lincoln defined democracy as *"government of the people, by the people, and for the people."*
3. The basic definition used throughout the *Government in America* textbook is: *democracy is a means of selecting policymakers and of organizing government so that policy represents and responds to the public's preferences.*

C. **Traditional democratic theory** rests upon several principles that specify how a democratic government makes its decisions.

1. Democratic theorist Robert Dahl refers to *five criteria that are essential for "an ideal democratic process"*:
   a. Equality in voting - the principle of *"one person, one vote"* is basic to democracy.
   b. Effective participation - political participation must be *representative*.
   c. Enlightened understanding - *free press and free speech are essential* to civic understanding.
   d. Citizen control of the agenda - citizens should have the *collective right to control* the government's policy agenda.
   e. Inclusion - *citizenship* must be open to all within a nation.

2. In addition, democracies must practice **majority rule** and preserve **minority rights**.
    a. The relationship between the *few leaders* and the *many followers* is one of **representation**: the closer the correspondence between representatives and their electoral majority, the closer the approximation to democracy.
    b. Most Americans also feel that it is vital to protect minority rights such as freedom of speech.

D. Three **contemporary theories** of American democracy.
1. **Pluralist theory** contends that many centers of influence compete for power and control.
    a. Groups compete with one another for control over public policy, with no one group or set of groups dominating.
    b. There are *multiple access points* to our government, with power dispersed among the various branches and levels of government.
    c. *Bargaining and compromise* are essential ingredients of our democracy.
    d. *Electoral majorities rarely rule*; rather, as Dahl puts it, "all active and legitimate groups in the population can make themselves heard at some crucial stage in the [policymaking] process."
    e. The *recent increase in interest group activity* is cited by pluralists as evidence for pluralism.
2. **Elite and class theory** contends that our society (like all societies) is *divided along class lines.*
    a. *An upper-class elite rules*, regardless of governmental organization.
    b. *Wealth is the basis of class power*: a few powerful Americans are the policymakers.
    c. *Big business* and its power is at the center of most elite and class theories.
    d. The Reagan Administration strongly promoted big business.
3. **Hyperpluralism** is *pluralism gone sour.*
    a. Many groups are so strong that *government is unable to act.*
    b. There are *too many groups* with access to the different levels and branches of government: these groups have multiple ways to both prevent policies they disagree with and promote those they support.
    c. When politicians try to placate every group, the result is confusing, contradictory, and muddled policy (or no policy at all).

E. Challenges to democracy.
   1. How can average citizens make decisions about complex issues?
   2. What if citizens know little about their leaders and policy decisions?
   3. Is American democracy too dependent on money?
   4. Does American diversity produce governmental gridlock?

F. Some key questions about Democracy.
   1. Are people knowledgeable about matters of public policy?
   2. Do they apply what knowledge they have to their voting choices?
   3. Are American elections designed to facilitate public participation?
   4. Does the interest group system allow for all points of view to be heard, or do significant biases give advantages to particular groups?
   5. Do political parties provide voters with clear choices, or do they intentionally obscure their stands on issues in order to get as many votes as possible?
   6. If there are choices, do the media help citizens understand them?
   7. Is the Congress representative of American society, and is it capable of reacting to changing times?
   8. Does the president look after the general welfare of the public, or has the office become too focused on the interests of the elite?

VI. THE SCOPE OF GOVERNMENT IN AMERICA

A. How active is American government?
   1. National, state, and local governments in America collectively spend about one out of every three dollars of our **gross domestic product** (the value of all goods and services produced annually by the United States).
   2. The national government alone spends more than $1.7 trillion annually, employs five million people, and owns one-third of the land in the United States.

B. A comparative perspective on the scope and size of government.
   1. The government of the United States actually *does less*—and is *small*—compared to the governments of similar countries.
   2. The *tax burden* on Americans is also small, compared to other democratic nations.

C. American **individualism** is a dominant theme in American political culture.
   1. It *developed from immigrants' desire* to escape government oppression.
   2. As Louis Hartz points out, it has helped *limit the scope of American government.*

3. *The existence of a western frontier* up until the early twentieth century allowed people to escape government almost entirely; this ethos still infuses American individualism.
4. Individualism remains highly valued in the United States, with the public policy consequences being a strong preference for free markets and limited government.

KEY TERMS AND CONCEPTS

Democracy: a means of selecting policy makers and of organizing government so that policy represents and responds to the public's preferences.

Elite and class theory: argues that society is divided along class lines and that an upper-class elite rules on the basis of their wealth.

Government: institutions that make public policy for a society.

Gross domestic product: the total value of all goods and services produced annually by the United States.

Hyperpluralism: argues that too many strong influential groups cripple the government's ability to make coherent policy by dividing government and its authority.

Individualism: a belief that individual problems can be solved by individual, not governmental, solutions.

Linkage institutions: institutions such as parties, elections, interest groups, and the media, which provide a linkage between the preferences of citizens and the government's policy agenda.

Majority rule: weighing the desires of the majority in choosing among policy alternatives.

Minority rights: protecting the rights and freedoms of the minority in choosing among policy alternatives.

Pluralist theory: argues that there are many centers of influence in which groups compete with one another for control over public policy through bargaining and compromise.

Policy agenda: the list of subjects or problems to which people inside and outside government are paying serious attention to at any given time.

Policy gridlock: where each interest uses its influence to thwart policies they oppose so that no coalition forms a majority to establish policy.

Policy impacts: the effects of a policy on people and society's problems.

Policymaking institutions: institutions such as Congress, the presidency and the Courts established by the Constitution to make policy.

Policymaking system: institutions of government designed to respond to each other and to the priorities of the people by governmental action.

Political issue: this arises when people disagree about a problem or about public policy choices made to combat a problem.

Political participation: the ways in which people get involved in politics.

Politics: determines whom we select as our government leaders and what policies they pursue; in other words who gets what; when, and how.

Public goods: things that everyone can share.

Public policy: a choice that government makes in response to some issue on its agenda.

Representation: the relationship between the leaders and the followers.

Single-issue groups: groups so concerned with one matter that their members cast their votes on the basis of that issue only.

Traditional democratic theory: a set of principles which specify how a democratic government makes its decisions including equality in voting, effective participation, enlightened understanding, citizen control of the agenda, inclusion, majority rule, minority rights, and representation.

TEACHING IDEAS: CLASS DISCUSSION AND STUDENT PROJECTS

- Today, large proportions of Americans believe that most or all politicians are corrupt, that government serves the interest of the few, and that government is dominated by the wealthy and powerful. Ask your students to evaluate these statements.

- Debate over the role and size of government is central to contemporary American politics, and it is a theme that is examined in each chapter of *Government in America.* The authors ask: is the scope of government too broad, too narrow, or just about right? Ask students to discuss, using contemporary examples, what is meant by government being "too big." Do students disagree as to what "too big" is? Why? Ask students to develop a set of criteria, or values, with which they could evaluate what is "too big" about government today.

- Discuss the importance of interest groups in politics today. Do students identify with any groups? Are they members of any groups? Are they represented by any groups, whether they are members or not?

- Have students use the Internet to visit some Web sites of civic groups devoted to encouraging political participation or providing election information. Discuss in class what students learned from these sites. Ask students if they think that the Internet can improve the quality of democracy in the United States. Why?

- Before starting your first lecture, or right after distributing the syllabus, ask students to take out a piece of paper. Have students briefly define what governments are, what governments do, what politics are, what democratic theory is, what liberals and conservatives believe, and why the size of government matters. This exercise serves to heighten students' awareness of how little they really know about the nature of American politics and government. By the end of the first lecture, have students compare what they wrote with the lecture material.

- This chapter discusses four challenges to democracy: increased technical expertise, limited participation in government, escalating campaign costs and diverse political interests. Ask students to identify which one of these challenges is most critical, and to discuss what might be done about it. This assignment could be a writing assignment or a debate format in class.

- For a reading and writing connection, have students keep a journal for three days detailing every instance where they have come into contact with government on the basis of the six duties of government outlined in the text under "What Do Governments Do." This exercise will serve to reinforce the role of government and separate democratic theory from functions of government.

- Use the beginning of the twenty-first century to stimulate a discussion on the text's theme of how we should be governed. What are the strengths of our democracy as we approach the millenium? Our weaknesses? Why? And what should we do about them? This topic could also be used for a reading and writing connection, asking students to keep a journal that focuses on these questions throughout the semester.

BACKGROUND READING

Bok, Derek. The State of the Nation: Government and the Quest for a Better Society. Cambridge: Harvard University Press. 1996.

Dahl, Robert. Democracy and Its Critics. New Haven: Yale University Press. 1989.

Domhoff, G. William. The Power Elite and the State: How Policy is Made in America. New York: Aldine de Gruyter. 1990.

Hartz, Louis. The Liberal Tradition in America. NY: Harcourt Brace, and World. 1955.

Huntington, Samuel P. American Politics: The Promise of Disharmony. Cambridge, MA: Harvard University Press. 1981.

Kingdon, John. Agendas, Alternatives, and Public Policies, 2nd ed. New York: Addison-Wesley. 1995.

MEDIA SUGGESTIONS

1984. A movie dramatization of George Orwell's classic novel depicting a grim perspective on a society where individualism is suppressed and information is distorted by government to achieve ultimate control over its population. The 1956 version is less haunting and grim than the 1984 remake, but not nearly as good.

Tocqueville's Europe: The Paradoxes of Tocqueville's Democracy in America. 1995. An analysis of Tocqueville's observations and criticisms of American democracy. Insight Media.

CHAPTER TWO: THE CONSTITUTION

PEDAGOGICAL FEATURES

LEARNING OBJECTIVES

After studying this chapter, students should be able to:

- Explain why the Constitution is sometimes called the "higher law."

- Outline the events that led early Americans to declare independence from Britain.
- Review the basic philosophy that underlies the Declaration of Independence.
- Summarize the parallels between Locke's writings and Jefferson's language in the Declaration of Independence.
- Explain how the weaknesses of the Articles of Confederation laid the groundwork for the Constitution.
- Describe what Madison meant by "factions" and how he proposed to solve the problems presented by factions.
- Evaluate how the Constitutional Convention dealt with issues of equality.
- Summarize the major compromises of the Constitutional Convention.
- Explain why economic issues were high on the agenda at the Constitutional Convention and how the framers tried to strengthen the economic powers of the new national government.
- Demonstrate what we mean by the "Madisonian model" and how it is incorporated within the Constitution.
- Understand why many critics claim that the Madisonian model actually reduces efficiency in the operations of government.
- Describe the major issues between the Federalists and the Anti-Federalists in the debates over ratification of the Constitution.
- Ascertain how constitutional changes—both formal and informal—continue to shape and alter the Madisonian system.
- Examine the Constitution in terms of the theme of democracy that runs throughout this chapter.
- Identify factors that have led to a gradual democratization of the Constitution.
- Understand how the Constitution affects the scope of government in America.

CHAPTER OVERVIEW

INTRODUCTION

A **constitution** is a nation's basic law. It creates political institutions, allocates power within government, and often provides guarantees to citizens. Constitutions thus establish who has power in society, and how that power is exercised. This chapter examines the background of the Constitution, and shows that the main principle guiding the writing of the Constitution was a concern for limited government and self-determination.

THE ORIGINS OF THE CONSTITUTION

The British king and Parliament originally left almost everything except foreign policy and trade to the discretion of individual colonial governments. However, Britain acquired a vast new territory in North America after the French and Indian War (1763). Parliament passed a series of taxes to raise revenue for colonial administration and defense of the new territory, and imposed the taxes on the colonists without their having direct representation in Parliament. The colonists protested, boycotted the taxed goods, and threw 342 chests of tea into Boston Harbor as a symbolic act of disobedience. Britain reacted by applying economic pressure through a naval blockade of the harbor, and the colonists responded by forming the First Continental Congress in September, 1774.

In May and June of 1776, the Continental Congress began debating resolutions about independence. Richard Henry Lee moved "that these United States are and of right ought to be free and independent states." On July 2, Lee's motion was formally approved. The **Declaration of Independence**—written primarily by Thomas Jefferson—was adopted two days later. The Declaration was a political polemic, announcing and justifying a revolution. Today, it is studied more as a statement of philosophy.

American political leaders were profoundly influenced by the writings of John Locke, especially ***The Second Treatise of Civil Government*** (1689). The foundation of Locke's philosophy was a belief in **natural rights**: before governments arise, people exist in a *state of nature* where they are governed only by the *laws of nature*. **Natural law** brings **natural rights**, including life, liberty, and property. According to Locke, the sole purpose of government was to protect natural rights. Government must be built on the **consent of the governed**, and it should be a **limited government**. In particular, governments must provide laws so that people know in advance whether or not their acts will be acceptable; government cannot take any person's property without his or her consent.

There are some remarkable parallels between Locke's thoughts and Jefferson's language in the Declaration of Independence. The sanctity of property was one of the few ideas absent in Jefferson's draft of the Declaration: he altered Locke's phrase *"life, liberty, and property"* to read *"life, liberty, and the pursuit of happiness."* Nevertheless, Locke's views on the importance of property figured prominently at the **Constitutional Convention**.

The **American Revolution** itself was essentially a conservative movement that did not drastically alter the colonists' way of life. Its primary goal was to restore rights that the colonists felt were already theirs as British subjects. They did not feel a need for great social, economic, or political changes. As a result, the revolution did not create class conflicts that would cause cleavages in society.

THE GOVERNMENT THAT FAILED: 1776-1787

In 1776, the Congress appointed a committee to draw up a plan for a permanent union of the states. That plan was the **Articles of Confederation**, which became the new nation's first governing document. The Articles established a government dominated by the states because the new nation's leaders feared that a strong central government would become as tyrannical as British rule. In general, the weak and ineffective national government could take little independent action. The Continental Congress had few powers outside of maintaining an army and navy, and had no power to tax or even to raise revenue to carry out that function. The weakness of the national government prevented it from dealing with the problems that faced the new nation.

Significant changes were occurring in the states—most significantly, a dramatic increase in democracy and liberty, at least for white males. Expanded political participation brought a new middle class to power. With expanded voting privileges, farmers and craftworkers became a decisive majority, and the old colonial elite saw its power shrink.

A postwar depression had left many small farmers unable to pay their debts and threatened with mortgage foreclosures. With some state legislatures now under the control of people more sympathetic to debtors, a few states adopted policies to help debtors (favoring them over creditors). In western Massachusetts, a small band of farmers led by Captain Daniel Shays undertook a series of armed attacks on courthouses to prevent judges from foreclosing on farms. **Shays' Rebellion** spurred the birth of the Constitution and reaffirmed the belief of the Philadelphia delegates that the new federal government needed to be a strong one.

MAKING A CONSTITUTION: THE PHILADELPHIA CONVENTION

The delegates who were sent to Philadelphia were instructed to meet *"for the sole and express purpose of revising the Articles of Confederation."* However, amendment of the Articles required unanimous consent of the states; so the delegates ignored their instructions and began writing a new constitution. Although the men held very different views, they agreed on questions of human nature, the causes of political conflict, and the object and nature of a republican government. James Madison of Virginia (who is often called *"the father of the Constitution"*) was perhaps the most influential member of the convention in translating political philosophy into governmental architecture. Pennsylvania delegate Gouverneur Morris was responsible for the style and wording of the Constitution.

The fifty-five delegates at the Constitutional Convention were the *postcolonial economic elite.* They were mostly wealthy planters, successful lawyers and merchants, and men of independent wealth. Many were creditors whose loans were being wiped out by cheap paper money. Many were college graduates. As a result, it is not surprising that they would seek to strengthen the economic powers of the new national government. As property holders, these leaders could not imagine a government that did not make its principal objective the preservation of individual rights to acquire and hold wealth. A few (like Gouverneur Morris) were even intent on shutting out the propertyless altogether.

James Madison claimed that **factions** arise from the unequal distribution of wealth. One faction is the majority, composed of the many who have little or no property. The other is the minority, composed of the few who hold much wealth. The delegates thought that, if left unchecked, either a majority or minority faction would become tyrannical. The founders believed that the secret of good government is *"balanced" government.* A limited government would have to contain checks on its own power. As long as no faction could seize the whole of government at once, tyranny could be avoided. In Madison's words, *"ambition must be made to counteract ambition."*

THE AGENDA IN PHILADELPHIA

Although the Constitution is silent on the issue of **equality**, some of the most important issues on the policy agenda at Philadelphia concerned the issue of equality. Three issues occupied more attention than almost any others: whether or not the states were to be equally represented, what to do about slavery, and whether or not to ensure political equality.

The delegates resolved the conflict over *representation for the states* with the **Connecticut Compromise**, under which a bicameral legislature would have equal representation for the states in the Senate and representation based on population in the House of Representatives. Although the Connecticut Compromise was intended to maximize equality among the states, it actually gives more power to states with small populations since it is the Senate that ratifies treaties, confirms presidential nominations, and hears trials of impeachment.

The delegates were bitterly divided over the issue of *slavery*. In the end, they agreed that Congress could limit future importing of slaves but did not forbid slavery itself in the Constitution. In fact, the Constitution stated that persons legally "held to service or labour" who escaped to free states must be returned to their owners. Northern and southern delegates also divided over the issue of how to *count* slaves. Under the **three-fifths compromise**, both representation and taxation were to be based upon the "number of free persons" plus three-fifths of the number of "all other persons."

The delegates dodged the issue of **political equality**. A few delegates favored universal manhood suffrage, while others wanted to place property qualifications on the right to vote. Ultimately, they left the issue to the states.

Economic issues were high on the policy agenda. The writers of the Constitution charged that the economy was in disarray. Virtually all of them thought a strong national government was needed to bring economic stability to the chaotic union of states that existed under the Articles of Confederation. The delegates made sure that the Constitution clearly spelled out the economic powers of the legislature. Consistent with the general allocation of power in the Constitution, Congress was to be the primary economic policymaker.

The delegates felt that they were constructing a limited government that could not threaten personal freedoms, and most believed that the various states were already doing an adequate job of protecting individual rights. As a result, the Constitution says little about personal freedoms. (It does prohibit suspension of the **writ of *habeas corpus***, prohibits **bills of attainder** and ***ex post facto* laws**, prohibits the imposition of religious qualifications for holding office in the national government, narrowly defines treason and outlines strict rules of evidence for conviction of treason, and upholds the right to trial by jury in criminal cases.) The absence of specific protections for individual rights led to widespread criticism during the debates over ratification.

THE MADISONIAN MODEL

The founders believed that human nature was self-interested and that inequalities of wealth were the principal source of political conflict. They also believed that protecting private property was a key purpose of government. Their experience with state governments under the Articles of Confederation reinforced their view that democracy was a threat to property. Thus, the delegates were faced with *the dilemma of reconciling economic inequality with political freedom.*

Madison and his colleagues feared both **majority** and **minority factions**. To thwart **tyranny by the majority**, Madison believed it was essential to keep most of the government beyond their power. Under Madison's plan, voters' electoral influence was limited and mostly indirect. Only the House of Representatives was to be directly elected. Senators were to be elected by state legislatures (modified by the Seventeenth Amendment in 1913), presidents were to be indirectly elected by an electoral college, and judges were to be nominated by the president.

The Madisonian plan also provided for a system of **separation of powers**, in which each of the three branches of government would be relatively independent so that no single branch could control the others. However, the powers were not completely separate: a system of **checks and balances** was established that reflected Madison's goal of setting *power against power* to constrain government actions.

The framers of the Constitution did not favor a direct democracy. They chose a **republic**, a system based on the consent of the governed in which power is exercised by *representatives* of the public.

RATIFYING THE CONSTITUTION

In the battle over ratification, the **Federalists** supported the Constitution and the **Anti-Federalists** opposed it. John Marshall (later chief justice) suggested, "It is scarcely to be doubted that in some of the adopting states, a majority of the people were in opposition."

The position of the Federalists was strengthened by the ***Federalist Papers***, written by James Madison, Alexander Hamilton, and John Jay as an explication and defense of the Constitution. Today, the *Federalist Papers* remain second only to the Constitution itself in symbolizing the ideas of the framers. The Anti-Federalists considered the Constitution to be a class-based document intended to ensure that a particular economic elite controlled the new government, and they believed that the Constitution would weaken the power of the states. They also feared that the new government would erode fundamental liberties. To allay fears that the Constitution would restrict personal freedoms, the Federalists promised to add amendments to the document specifically protecting individual liberties. James Madison did, indeed, introduce twelve constitutional amendments during the First Congress (1789); ten were ratified and have come to be known as the **Bill of Rights**.

The Constitution itself provided for ratification by special state conventions and required that nine states approve the document before it could be implemented. Delaware, the first, approved the Constitution on December 7, 1787. The ninth state (New Hampshire) approved only six months later.

CONSTITUTIONAL CHANGE

The Constitution may be modified either by formal amendment or by a number of informal processes. **Formal amendments** change the language of the Constitution in accordance with the procedures outlined in Article V. The Constitution may be **informally amended** in a variety of ways, such as through judicial interpretation or through custom and political practice. Political scientists often refer to the **unwritten constitution**—an unwritten body of tradition, practice, and procedure that, when altered, may change the *spirit of the Constitution*. For example, political parties and national conventions are not mentioned in the written document, but they are important parts of the unwritten constitution.

The Constitution was not intended to be static and unchanging. The founders created a *flexible system* of government, one that could *adapt to the needs of the times without sacrificing personal freedom*. The *brevity* of the Constitution also contributes to its flexibility: it is a very short document that does not attempt to prescribe the structure and functions of the national government in great detail. This flexibility has enabled the Constitution to survive for more than 200 years. Although the United States is young compared to other Western nations, it has the oldest functioning Constitution.

UNDERSTANDING THE CONSTITUTION

The theme of the *role of government* runs throughout this chapter. This section examines the Constitution in terms of the theme of *democracy*, and looks at the impact of the Constitution on policy-making. The Constitution created a *republic*, a *representative form of democracy* modeled after the Lockean tradition of *limited government.*

One of the central themes of American history is the *gradual democratization of the Constitution.* While eighteenth-century upper-class society feared and despised democratic government, today few people would share the founders' fear of democracy.

The systems of separation of powers and checks and balances established by the Constitution allow almost all groups some place in the political system where their demands for public policy can be heard. Because many institutions share power, a group can usually find at least one sympathetic ear. These systems also promote the politics of bargaining, compromise, and playing one institution against another—to such an extent that some scholars even suggest there is so much "checking" that effective government is almost impossible.

CHAPTER OUTLINE

I. THE ORIGINS OF THE CONSTITUTION

A. A **constitution** is a nation's basic law that:
   1. Creates political institutions
   2. Assigns or divides powers in government
   3. Often provides certain guarantees to citizens
   4. Includes an unwritten accumulation of traditions and precedents
   5. Sets the broad rules of the game of politics

B. The road to revolution.
   1. The King and Parliament originally left almost everything except foreign policy and trade to the discretion of individual colonial governments.
   2. Britain obtained a vast expanse of new territory in North America after the **French and Indian War** ended in 1763.
   3. The British Parliament passed a series of taxes to pay for the cost of defending the territory, and also began to tighten enforcement of its trade regulations.
   4. Americans resented the taxes, especially since they had no direct representation in Parliament.

5. The colonists responded by forming the First Continental Congress (September, 1774) and sent delegates from each colony to Philadelphia to discuss the future of relations with Britain.

C. Declaring independence.
   1. The Continental Congress met in almost continuous session during 1775 and 1776.
   2. In May and June of 1776, the Continental Congress began debating resolutions about independence; after two days of debate on the wording, the **Declaration of Independence** (written primarily by Thomas Jefferson) was adopted on July 4.

D. The English heritage: the power of ideas.
   1. John Locke's writings, especially *The Second Treatise of Civil Government*, profoundly influenced American political leaders.
   2. Locke's philosophy was based on a belief in **natural rights**, the belief that people exist in a state of nature before governments arise, where they are governed only by the *laws of nature*.
      a. **Natural law** brings natural rights, which include life, liberty, and property.
      b. Because natural law is superior to human law, natural law can justify even a challenge to the rule of a tyrannical king.
      c. Locke argued that government must be built on the **consent of the governed**—the people must agree on who their rulers will be.
      d. Government should also be a **limited government**, with clear restrictions on what rulers can do.
      e. According to Locke, the *sole purpose of government was to protect natural rights*.
      f. In an extreme case, people have a right to revolt against a government that no longer has their consent; but Locke stressed that people should not revolt *until injustices become deeply felt*.

E. Jefferson's handiwork: the American creed.
   1. There are a number of close parallels between Locke's thoughts and Jefferson's language in the Declaration of Independence.
   2. The sanctity of property was one of the few ideas absent in Jefferson's draft of the Declaration of Independence (but the Lockean concept of property figured prominently at the Constitutional Convention).
   3. Jefferson altered Locke's phrase *"life, liberty, and property"* to "*life, liberty, and the pursuit of happiness.*"

F. The "conservative" Revolution.
   1. The **Revolution** was essentially a conservative movement that did not drastically alter the colonists' way of life.

2. The primary goal of the Revolution was *to restore rights the colonists felt were already theirs* as British subjects.

II. The Government That Failed: 1776-1787

A. The **Articles of Confederation** established a government dominated by the states.
   1. The Articles established a national legislature (the **Continental Congress**) with one house.
      a. States could send up to seven delegates, but each state had only one vote.
      b. The Continental Congress had few powers outside of maintaining an army and navy (and little money to do even that); it had no power to tax; and could not regulate commerce (which inhibited foreign trade and the development of a strong national economy).
   2. There was no president and no national court.
   3. The weakness of the national government prevented it from dealing with the problems that faced the new nation.

B. Changes in the states.
   1. Important changes were occurring in the states, including a dramatic increase in democracy and liberty (for white males).
   2. Expanded political participation brought a new middle class to power, which included artisans and farmers who owned small homesteads.
   3. With expanded voting privileges, farmers and craftworkers became a decisive majority; members of the old colonial elite saw their power shrink, and they didn't like it.

C. Economic turmoil.
   1. A postwar depression had left many small farmers unable to pay their debts; many were threatened with mortgage foreclosures.
   2. State legislatures were now under the control of people more sympathetic to **debtors.**
   3. A few states (notably Rhode Island) adopted policies to help debtors, favoring them over **creditors**—some printed paper money and passed **"force acts"** requiring creditors to accept the almost worthless money.

D. Shays' Rebellion.
   1. In 1786, a small group of farmers in western Massachusetts led by Captain Daniel Shays rebelled at losing their land to creditors.
   2. **Shays' Rebellion** was a series of armed attacks on courthouses to prevent judges from foreclosing on farms.
   3. Shays' Rebellion spurred the birth of the Constitution.

E. The Aborted Annapolis Meeting.
   1. In September, 1786, a small group of continental leaders assembled at Annapolis, Maryland, to consider the problem of commercial conflicts that had arisen among the states.
   2. Only five states sent delegates, and they issued a call for a full-scale meeting of the states in Philadelphia the following May.

III. MAKING A CONSTITUTION: THE PHILADELPHIA CONVENTION

A. Delegates were given specific instructions to meet "*for the sole and express purpose of revising the Articles of Confederation.*"
   1. Amendment was not feasible since amending the Articles required the unanimous consent of the states.
   2. Twelve states sent representatives; Rhode Island refused to participate.
   3. The fifty-delegates ignored their instructions and began writing a new constitution.

B. Gentlemen in Philidelphia.
   1. A select group of economic and political notables.
   2. Men of wealth; many were college graduates.
   3. Most were coastal residents; a significant number were urbanites.

C. Philosophy Into Action.
   1. Although very different philosophical views were represented, the group *agreed on questions of human nature, the causes of political conflict, and the object and nature of a republican government.*
   2. The delegates were united in their belief that people were self-interested and that government should play a key role in *checking and containing the natural self-interest* of the people.
   3. James Madison, who is often called "*the father of the Constitution,*" was perhaps the most influential member of the Convention in translating political philosophy into governmental architecture.
      a. Madison believed that *the distribution of wealth* (property) *is the source of political conflict.*
      b. He claimed that **factions** arise from the unequal distribution of wealth: one faction is the majority (composed of the many who have little or no property); the other faction is the minority (composed of the few who hold wealth).
   4. The delegates believed that *either a majority or a minority faction will be tyrannical* if it goes unchecked and has too much power.
      a. Property must be protected against the tyrannical tendencies of faction.

   b. The secret of good government is *"balanced" government*: as long as no faction could seize complete control of government, tyranny could be avoided.

IV. THE AGENDA IN PHILADELPHIA

A. Although the *Constitution is silent on equality*, some of the most important issues on the policy agenda at Philadelphia concerned equality: representation of the states; what to do about slavery; and whether or not to ensure political equality.

B. Representation of the states.
   1. The **New Jersey Plan**, proposed by William Paterson of New Jersey, called for each state to be equally represented in the new Congress.
   2. The **Virginia Plan**, suggested by Edmund Randolph of Virginia, called for representation in Congress based on the state's share of the American population.
   3. The **Connecticut Compromise**, devised by Roger Sherman and William Johnson of Connecticut, was the solution adopted by the delegates that created a **bicameral legislature** in which the Senate would have two members from each state and the House of Representatives would have representation based on population.

C. Slavery.
   1. The delegates agreed that Congress could limit future *importing of slaves* (they prohibited it after 1808), but they *did not forbid slavery* itself.
   2. The Constitution stated that persons legally "held to service or labour" who escaped to free states had to be returned to their owners.
   3. Under the famous **three-fifths compromise**, both representation and taxation were to be based upon the "number of free persons" plus three-fifths of the number of "all other persons."

D. Political equality.
   1. Some delegates favored suffrage for all free, adult males; some wanted to put property qualifications on the right to vote.
   2. Ultimately, they decided to leave the issue to the states.

E. Economic issues.
   1. Economic issues played an important role at the Convention.
      a. Advocates of the Constitution (Federalists) stressed the economy's weaknesses.
      b. Opponents of the Constitution (Anti-Federalists, who opposed a strong national government) claimed that charges of economic weakness were exaggerated.
   2. It is not surprising that the framers of the Constitution would seek to strengthen the economic powers of the new national government

since delegates to the Constitutional Convention were the nation's postcolonial economic elite. Historian Charles Beard argued that the delegates primarily wanted these strong economic powers so that their own wealth would be protected; the best evidence does not support Beard's thesis.

3. The Constitution clearly spelled out the economic powers of Congress.
   a. Congress was to be the chief economic policymaker.
   b. Congress was granted power to tax and borrow, and to appropriate funds.
   c. Congress was also granted powers to protect property rights—powers to punish counterfeiters and pirates, ensure patents and copyrights, to legislate rules for bankruptcy, and to *regulate interstate and foreign commerce.*
4. The framers also prohibited practices in the states that they viewed as inhibiting economic development.
   a. State monetary systems.
   b. Placing duties on imports from other states.
   c. Interfering with lawfully contracted debts.
5. States were required to respect civil judgments and contracts made in other states, and to return runaway slaves to their owners (overturned by the Thirteenth Amendment).
6. The national government guaranteed the states "*a republican form of government*" to prevent a recurrence of Shays' Rebellion, and the new government was obligated to repay all the public debts incurred under the Continental Congress and the Articles of Confederation ($54 million).

F. Individual rights.
1. The delegates felt that preserving individual rights would be relatively easy.
   a. They were constructing a limited government that, by design, could not threaten personal freedoms.
   b. Powers were dispersed so that each branch or level of government could restrain the others.
   c. Most delegates believed that the various states were already protecting individual rights.
2. Although the Constitution says little about personal freedoms, it does include the following:
   a. The **writ of *habeas corpus*** may not be suspended except during invasion or rebellion.
   b. Congress and the states are prohibited from passing **bills of attainder** (which punish people without a judicial trial) and ***ex***

post facto **laws** (which punish people or increase the penalties for acts that were not illegal or were not as severely punished when the act was committed).

c. Religious qualifications may not be imposed for holding office in the national government.

d. Treason is narrowly defined, and strict rules of evidence for conviction of treason are specified.

e. The right to trial by jury in criminal cases is guaranteed.

3. The absence of specific protections for individual rights led to widespread criticism during the debates over ratification.

V. THE MADISONIAN MODEL

A. The delegates were faced with the dilemma of reconciling *economic inequality* with *political freedom.*

B. James Madison and his colleagues feared both majority and minority factions.

C. To prevent **tyranny by the majority**, Madison believed that it was essential to keep most of the government beyond their control.

1. Under Madison's plan that was incorporated in the Constitution, voters' electoral influence was limited and mostly indirect.
2. Only the House of Representatives was directly elected; senators and presidents were indirectly elected, and judges were nominated by the president (modified by the Seventeenth Amendment, which provides for direct popular election of senators).

D. Separation of powers and checks and balances.

1. The Madisonian scheme provided for a system of **separation of powers** in which each of the three branches of government would be relatively independent of the others so that no single branch could control the others.
2. Power was not separated absolutely, but was shared among the three institutions.
3. Since power was not completely separate, each branch required the consent of the others for many of its actions—thereby creating a system of **checks and balances** that reflected Madison's goal of setting *power against power* to constrain government actions.

a. The president checks Congress by holding the veto power.

b. Congress holds the "purse strings" of government, and the Senate has the power to approve presidential appointments.

c. **Judicial review** (the power of courts to hold executive and congressional policies unconstitutional) was not explicit in the Constitution, but was asserted by the Supreme Court under John Marshall in *Marbury v. Madison* (1803).

   d. Since the framers thought much government activity would take place in the states, federalism was considered an additional check on the power of the national government.

E. The constitutional republic.
   1. The framers of the Constitution established a **republic** (a system based on the consent of the governed in which power is exercised by representatives of the public).
   2. This *deliberative democracy* established an elaborate decision-making process.
   3. The system of checks and balances and separation of powers has a conservative bias because it favors the *status quo*; that is, people desiring change must usually have a *sizable majority* rather than a simple majority.
   4. The Madisonian system encourages moderation and compromise, and retards change.

VI. RATIFYING THE CONSTITUTION

A. Federalists and Anti-Federalists.
   1. A fierce battle erupted between the **Federalists** (who supported the Constitution) and the **Anti-Federalists** (who opposed it).
   2. Federalists:
      a. James Madison, Alexander Hamilton, and John Jay—writing under the name Publius—wrote a series of eighty-five articles (known as the ***Federalist Papers***) in defense of the Constitution.
      b. The *Federalist Papers* defended the Constitution detail by detail, but also represented *an important statement of political philosophy*.
   3. Anti-Federalists.
      a. The Anti-Federalists questioned the motives of the writers of the Constitution; they believed that the new government was an enemy of freedom.
      b. Anti-Federalists believed that the new Constitution was a *class-based document*, intended to ensure that a particular economic elite controlled the public policies of the national government.
      c. They feared that the new government would *erode fundamental liberties* and would *weaken the power of the states*.
   4. In a compromise to assure ratification, the Federalists promised to add amendments to the document specifically protecting individual liberties.
      a. James Madison introduced twelve constitutional amendments during the First Congress in 1789.

   b. Ten of the amendments—known as the **Bill of Rights**—were ratified by the states and took effect in 1791.

B. Ratification.
   1. The Federalists specified that the Constitution be ratified *by special conventions* in each of the states, not by state legislatures (a shrewd move since state legislatures were populated with political leaders who would lose power under the Constitution).
   2. The Constitution itself specified that nine states approve the document before it could be implemented.
   3. Delaware was the first state to ratify the Constitution (Dec. 7, 1787); New Hampshire became the ninth state six months later.
   4. George Washington was the electoral college's unanimous choice for president and he took office on April 30, 1789.

VII. CONSTITUTIONAL CHANGE

A. Constitutional changes may occur either by formal amendments or by a number of informal processes.

B. **Formal amendments** change the written language of the Constitution.
   1. Article V of the Constitution outlines procedures for formal amendment.
   2. There are two stages to the amendment process (proposal and ratification), each with two alternative routes.
      a. **Proposal** - an amendment may be proposed either by a two-thirds vote in each of Congress, or by a national convention called by Congress at the request of two-thirds of the state legislatures.
      b. **Ratification** - an amendment may be ratified either by the legislatures of three-fourths of the states, or by special state conventions called in three-fourths of the states.
   3. All of the amendments to the Constitution have been proposed by Congress (no constitutional convention has been convened since the original Constitutional Convention); all except one of the successful amendments have been ratified by the state legislatures.
   4. The president has no formal role in amending the Constitution.

C. Effects of formal amendment.
   1. Formal amendments have made the Constitution more egalitarian and democratic.
   2. The emphasis on economic issues in the original document is now balanced by amendments that stress equality and increase the ability of a popular majority to affect government.

3. The most important effect has been to *expand liberty and equality* in America.

D. **Informal amendment** - the Constitution changes *informally* as well as *formally*.
   1. The **unwritten constitution** refers to an *unwritten body of tradition, practice, and procedure* that—when altered—may change the *spirit of the Constitution*.
   2. The Constitution may change informally through judicial interpretation, through political practice, through demands on policymakers, or as a result of changes in technology.
      a. **Judicial interpretation** can profoundly affect how the Constitution is understood.
      b. *Changing political practice* can also change the meaning of the Constitution.
         (1) The development of political parties dramatically changed the form of American government.
         (2) Changing political practice has altered the role of the **electoral college**, which today is often seen as a "rubber stamp" in selecting the president.
      c. The Constitution has also been greatly changed by *technology*.
         (1) The *mass media* plays a role unimaginable in the eighteenth century.
         (2) The *bureaucracy* has grown in importance with the advent of technological developments such as computers.
         (3) *Electronic communications* and the development of *atomic weapons* have enhanced the president's role as commander in chief.
      d. The power of the presidency has grown as a result of *increased demands for new policies*.
         (1) The United States' growth to the status of a *superpower* in international affairs has located additional power in the hands of the chief executive.
         (2) Increased demands of domestic policy have placed the president in a more prominent role in preparing the federal budget and proposing a legislative program.

E. The importance of flexibility.
   1. The United States has the *oldest functioning constitution* in existence today.

2. The framers of the Constitution created a *flexible system of government* that could adapt to the needs of the times without sacrificing personal freedom.
3. Even with twenty-seven amendments, the Constitution is a very short document: it does not prescribe the structure and functioning of the national government in detail.

VIII. UNDERSTANDING THE CONSTITUTION

A. The Constitution and democracy.
   1. Democratic government was despised and feared among eighteenth-century upper-class society.
   2. The Constitution created a republic, a representative form of democracy modeled after the Lockean tradition of limited government.
   3. One of the *central themes of American history* is the *gradual democratization of the Constitution*, away from the elitist model of democracy and toward the pluralist one.
   4. Today, few people share the founders' fear of democracy.

B. The Constitution and the scope of government.
   1. Separation of powers and checks and balances allow almost all groups some place in the political system where their demands for public policy can be heard.
   2. Separation of powers and checks and balances also promote the politics of bargaining, compromise, playing one institution against another, and an increase of hyperpluralism.
      a. Some scholars suggest that so much "checking" was built into the American political system that effective government is almost impossible due to gridlock.
      b. The outcome may be nondecisions when hard decisions are needed.

KEY TERMS AND CONCEPTS

Anti-Federalists: opposed the new Constitution, feared the new Constitution would erode fundamental liberties, and argued that the new Constitution was a class-based document serving the economic elite.

Articles of Confederation: the document which outlines the voluntary agreement between states and was adopted as the first plan for a permanent union of the United States.

Bill of Rights: the first ten Amendments to the Constitution passed after ratification specifically protecting individual liberties to fulfill promises made by the Federalists to the Anti-Federalists in return for their support.

Checks and balances: each branch required the consent of the others for many of its decisions.

Connecticut Compromise: the plan adopted at the Constitutional Convention to provide for two chambers in Congress, one representing states equally and the other representing states on the basis of their share of the population.

Consent of the governed: people must agree on who their rulers will be.

Constitution: a nation's basic law creating institutions, dividing power, and providing guarantees to citizens.

Declaration of Independence: the document used by the signers to announce and justify the revolutionary war and which was specifically designed to enlist the aid of foreign nations in the revolt.

Equal Rights Amendment: was first proposed in 1923, passed by Congress in 1972, but was not ratified by three-fourths of the states; this amendment mandated equality of rights under the law regardless of gender.

Factions: groups of people, currently known as political parties or interest groups, who arise as a result of unequal distribution of wealth to seize the reins of government in their own interest.

Federalist Papers: articles written to convince others to support the new constitution.

Federalists: argued for ratification of the Constitution by writing the *Federalist Papers*; included Madison, Hamilton and Jay.

Judicial review: the courts have the power to decide whether the actions of the legislative and executive branches of state and national governments are in accordance with the Constitution.

Limited government: clear restrictions on what rulers could do and which safeguard natural rights.

Marbury v. Madison: Judicial review was established in this 1803 Supreme Court case.

Natural rights: these are rights to which people are entitled by natural law, including life, liberty, and property.

New Jersey Plan: a plan by some of the delegates to the Constitutional Convention to provide each state with equal representation in Congress.

Republic: a system based on the consent of the governed where power is exercised by representatives of the public.

Separation of powers: each branch of government would be independent of the other.

Shays' Rebellion: a series of armed attacks on courthouses to prevent judges from foreclosing on farms.

U.S. Constitution: the document where the foundations of U.S. government are written providing for national institutions each having separate but not absolute powers.

Virginia Plan: a plan by some of the delegates to the Constitutional Convention to provide each state with a share of Congressional seats based on its share of the population.

Writ of habeas corpus: this enables people who are detained by authorities to secure an immediate inquiry and reasons why they have been detained.

TEACHING IDEAS: CLASS DISCUSSION AND STUDENT PROJECTS

- The Constitution establishes the rules of the political game. These rules decentralize power rather than consolidating power in the hands of the executive or the legislature. Ask your students to debate the following questions: *Would American government be more efficient if power were concentrated within a single branch of government? Would it be more effective?*

- The delegates to the Constitutional Convention constituted an educational and economic elite, not the "common man." Ask your students to consider whether an elite can be representative of people from other strata in society. Expand the question to consider contemporary problems such as racism and poverty.

- Assign *Federalist #51* (in the Appendix of the text). Then ask for an evaluation of Madison's words: *"Ambition must be made to counteract ambition...."* How do these words fit into the constitutional framework that was adopted? How well do these words reflect the needs of the 1990s?

- It often surprises students to learn that Great Britain has no written constitution. Call for class discussion of how democracy can exist in a nation with no written constitution. Broaden the question to include unwritten aspects of the U.S. Constitution.

- Ask students to identify which features of the Constitution reflect a distrust of democracy. Who didn't the framers trust? Do we have similar beliefs today?

- *Government in America* points out that "one of the central themes of American history is the gradual democratization of the Constitution." Ask your class to evaluate this statement and to either substantiate or refute it.

- For a discussion question, ask students to interpret the modern meaning of the phrase "life, liberty, and pursuit of happiness." Using an overhead projector or the blackboard, list the various interpretations and how many times there is agreement as well as disagreement.

- For an extended discussion, ask students to compare the goals of the Declaration of Independence, especially the phrases "all men are created equal" and "life, liberty, and pursuit of happiness" to the goals of the failed Equal Rights Amendment. Ask students to debate whether the goals expressed in each are incompatible or similar.

- For an alternative discussion, ask students why minority rights are important. What type of minorities was Madison concerned about? Are minority rights still important in U.S. politics? Ask students to provide specific historical and contemporary examples of "minorities" seeking to protect their rights. How is the political system structured to "balance" minority and majority rights? What values are served by this balance: efficiency, equality, representation?

- For a short essay assignment, ask students to explain the relationship between separation of powers and the checks and balances contained in the Constitution to the framers' goal of establishing limited government.

- For an alternative essay assignment, have the student defend the importance of the Bill of Rights. In particular, they should explain why, if the Bill of Rights was so important, it was not contained in the original Constitution. Finally, ask them if the Bill of Rights would have been more or less powerful had it been included in the original document.

BACKGROUND READING

Beard, Charles. An Economic Interpretation of the Constitution. NY: Macmillan. 1941.

Jillson, Calvin C. Constitution Making: Conflict and Consensus in the Federal Convention of 1787. NY: Agathon. 1988.

Lipset, Seymour Martin. The First New Nation. NY: Basic Books. 1963.

Manley, J. F. and K. M. Dolbeare. Eds. The Case Against the Constitution. Armonk, NY: M.E. Sharpe. 1987.

Simmons, A. John. The Lockean Theory of Rights. Princeton, NJ: Princeton University Press. 1994.

Wood, Gordon S. The Creation of the American Republic. Chapel Hill: University of North Carolina Press. 1969.

MEDIA SUGGESTIONS

Bill of Rights. This program provides an overview of the importance of the Bill of Rights in contemporary politics, with special focus given to the First, Second and Fourth amendments. Edudex.com.

The Constitution of the United States. An Encyclopedia Britannica Educational Corporation film examining the various elements of the Constitution.

The Constitution: That Delicate Balance. A thirteen part series by Films Incorporated where panelists examine a variety of issues and constitutional interpretations.

The Government and You. 1989. Part of the Government by Consent Series distributed by Insight Media. Discusses and defines the philosophical basis of the Constitution.

In the Beginning. This film examines the intellectual origins of the U.S. Constitution and includes a discussion about those interests ignored by the framers. Available through Films for the Humanities and Sciences.

John Locke. This film provides a recreation of John Locke's conversations for an in-depth view of his principles. Available through Films for the Humanities and Sciences.

The Living Constitution. 1989. Part of the Government by Consent Series distributed by Insight Media. Examines how changes are made in the Constitution to adapt to changes in technology and the population.

Marbury v. Madison. Part of an Equal Justice Under Law Series presentation by National Audio Visual Center depicting a dramatic re-enactment of this historic case.

The Magna Carta. This film examines the origins of the Magna Carta and its contributions to the development of American democracy. Available through Films for the Humanities and Sciences.

Thomas Jefferson: The Pursuit of Liberty. An award winning examination of the philosophy and life of Thomas Jefferson. Available through Films for the Humanities and Sciences.

CHAPTER THREE: FEDERALISM

PEDAGOGICAL FEATURES

LEARNING OBJECTIVES

After studying this chapter, students should be able to:

- Describe the three basic forms of governmental structures: federalism, unitary, and confederacy.

- Explain why the relationship of local governments to the states is considered to be a unitary arrangement.

- Determine the significance of how the American federal system decentralizes our politics.
- Identify the ways in which the Constitution determines the powers of state and national governments.
- Evaluate how contrasting interpretations of the supremacy clause and the Tenth Amendment lead to divergent views of the scope of state and national powers.
- Describe how the Supreme Court set forth the principle of implied powers in the *McCulloch* v. *Maryland* case.
- Understand the relationship of implied powers to enumerated powers.
- Describe how the Civil War and the civil rights movement contributed to the development of national supremacy over the states.
- List and analyze the clauses in the Constitution that define the obligations that each state has to every other state.
- Trace the ways in which American federalism has changed over the past two centuries.
- Compare the contrasting forms of dual federalism and cooperative federalism.
- Describe what is meant by fiscal federalism and assess the role that federal money plays in state policies.
- Summarize the characteristics of categorical grants and block grants, and examine the effects they have on decision making at the state and local levels.
- Discuss how underfunded and unfunded mandates burden state governments.
- Analyze the ways in which American federalism has a positive effect on democracy.
- Analyze the ways in which American federalism has a negative effect on democracy.

CHAPTER OVERVIEW

INTRODUCTION

The relationships between the federal, state and local governments often confuse people, yet federalism is at the heart of critical battles over the nature and scope of public policy in the United States. While Republicans have sought to limit the scope of the national government in areas such as welfare and the environment, they have also expanded the scope of government in other areas such as immigration and crime. Understanding the scope and nature of local, state *and* national governments is thus critical to learning about the development of public policy in the United States.

DEFINING FEDERALISM

We generally speak of three forms of governmental structures—federalism, unitary, and confederate. **Federalism** is a way of organizing a nation so that two or more levels of government have formal authority *over the same area and people.* Chapter 3 explores the complex relationships between *different levels* of government in the United States. It describes the ways that the federal system has changed over two centuries of American government and why American federalism is at the center of important battles over policy.

Federalism is not the typical way by which nations organize their governments; there are only eleven countries with federal systems. Most governments in the world today are **unitary governments**, in which *all power resides in the central government.* Although American government operates under a federal system at the national level, the *states are unitary governments* with respect to their local governments. In the United States, local governments are legally *"creatures of the states"*: they are created by the states and can be changed (or even abolished) by the states.

In a **confederation**, the national government is weak and most or all of the power is in the hands of its components (such as states). The United States was organized as a confederacy after the American Revolution, with the **Articles of Confederation** as the governing document. Confederations are rare today except in international organizations.

The concept of **intergovernmental relations** refers to the *entire set of interactions among national, state, and local governments* in a federal system. The American federal system *decentralizes our politics.* For example, senators are elected as representatives of individual states and not of the nation. Moreover, with more layers of government, more opportunities exist for political participation; there are more points of access in government and more opportunities for interests to be heard and to have their demands for public policies satisfied.

The federal system not only decentralizes our politics; it also decentralizes our *policies.* The history of the federal system demonstrates the tensions that exist between the states and the national government about who controls policy and what it should be. Because of the overlapping powers of the two levels of government, most of our public policy debates are also debates about federalism.

The American states have always been policy innovators. Most policies that the national government has adopted had their beginnings in the states. In many ways, the states constitute a "national laboratory" to develop and test public policies.

THE CONSTITUTIONAL BASIS OF FEDERALISM

The Constitution does not refer directly to federalism, and little was said about it at the Constitutional Convention. However, the framers carefully defined the powers of state and national governments. The framers also dealt with a question that still evokes debate: Which level of government should prevail in a dispute between the states and the national government? Advocates of strong national powers generally emphasize the **supremacy clause**. In *Article VI* (the "supremacy clause"), three items are listed as *the supreme law of the land*: the Constitution; laws of the national government (when consistent with the Constitution); and treaties. However, the national government can only operate *within its appropriate sphere* and cannot usurp powers of the states. By contrast, advocates of states' rights believe that the **Tenth Amendment** means that the national government has only those powers *specifically assigned* by the Constitution.

In *United States* v. *Darby* (1941), the Supreme Court called the Tenth Amendment a *"constitutional truism"* (an assertion only that the states have independent powers of their own and not a statement that their powers are supreme over those of the national government). In 1976, the Court appeared to backtrack on this ruling in favor of national government supremacy (*National League of Cities* v. *Usery*), and then still later overturned the 1976 decision (*Garcia* v. *San Antonio Metro*, 1985).

Four key events have played a major role leading to the growth of federal powers relative to the states: the elaboration of the doctrine of implied powers, the definition of the commerce clause, the Civil War and the long struggle for racial equality. In ***McCulloch* v. *Maryland*** (1819), the Supreme Court ruled that

Congress has certain **implied powers** and that *national policies take precedence* over state policies. These two principles have been used to expand the national government's sphere of influence. Chief Justice John Marshall wrote that "...the government of the United States, though limited in its power, is supreme within its sphere of action." The **"necessary and proper"** clause (sometimes called the **elastic clause**) was interpreted to give Congress certain implied powers that go beyond its **enumerated powers**. National powers expanded after the Supreme Court defined commerce very broadly, encompassing virtually every form of commercial activity (***Gibbons* v. *Ogden***, 1824). The Supreme Court prohibited much federal regulation of business and the economy in the late nineteenth and early twentieth centuries, but had swung back to allowing broader federal powers by 1937.

The **Civil War** was a struggle over slavery, but it was also (and perhaps more importantly) a struggle between states and the national government. A century later, conflict erupted once again over states' rights and national power. In ***Brown* v. *Board of Education*** (1954), the Supreme Court held that school segregation was unconstitutional. Southern politicians responded with **"massive resistance"** to the decision. Throughout the 1960s the federal government enacted laws and policies to end segregation in schools, housing, public accommodations, voting, and jobs.

Federalism also involves *relationships among the states*. The Constitution outlines certain obligations that each state has to every other state. The Constitution requires states to give **full faith and credit** to the public acts, records, and civil judicial proceedings of every other state; states are required to return a person charged with a crime in another state for trial or imprisonment (**extradition**); and citizens of each state are entitled to all the **privileges and immunities** of any state in which they are located. The goal of the privileges and immunities clause is to prohibit states from discriminating against citizens of other states, but numerous exceptions have been made to this clause (such as higher tuition for out-of-state residents at state universities).

INTERGOVERNMENTAL RELATIONS TODAY

This section focuses on three important features: first, the gradual change from dual federalism to cooperative federalism; second, federal grants-in-aid as the cornerstone of the relationship between the national government and state governments; and third, the relative growth of the national government and state governments.

One way to understand the changes in American federalism is to contrast dual federalism with cooperative federalism. Before the national government began to assume a position of dominance, the American system leaned toward **dual federalism**, a system under which states and the national government each remain *supreme within their own spheres*. The analogy of **layer cake federalism** is often used to describe dual federalism because the powers and policy assignments of the layers of government are distinct (as in a layer cake), and proponents of dual federalism believe that the powers of the national government should be interpreted narrowly.

The national government took a direct interest in economic affairs from the very founding of the republic (see Chapter 2). As the United States changed from an agricultural to an industrial nation, new problems arose and with them new demands for governmental action. The United States moved from a system of dual federalism to one of **cooperative federalism**, in which the national and state governments share responsibility for public policies. Using the analogy of **marble cake federalism**, American federalism is portrayed as a system with *mingled responsibilities* and blurred distinctions between the levels of government. Cooperative federalism—which may be seen as a partnership between the national and state governments—began in earnest with the transformation of public attitudes toward the role of the national government during the Great Depression of the 1930s. For hundreds of programs, cooperative federalism involves shared costs, federal guidelines, and shared administration.

Fiscal federalism involves the pattern of spending, taxing, and providing grants in the federal system. **Grants-in-aid** are the main instrument the national government uses to both aid and influence states and localities. State and local aid from the national government amounts to about $240 billion per year. **Categorical grants** (accounting for nearly 90 percent of all federal aid to state and local governments) can be used only for *specific purposes (or **categories**)* of state and local spending. State and local agencies can obtain categorical grants only by meeting certain qualifications and by applying for the grants. Much federal regulation is accomplished by "strings" that are attached to categorical grants, such as nondiscrimination provisions. The most common type of categorical grant is a **project grant** (involving 419 of the 578 categories), awarded on the basis of *competitive applications*. **Formula grants** are distributed according to a formula based on factors such as population, per capita income, and percentage of rural population.

Complaints about the cumbersome paperwork and numerous federal requirements attached to categorical grants led to the adoption of **block grants**. Congress implemented block grants to support broad programs in areas such as community development and social services. Block grants provide more flexibility since states and communities have discretion in deciding how to spend the money. Another response to complaints from states and local communities culminated in the adoption of **revenue sharing** in 1976. Under revenue sharing, virtually no strings were attached to federal aid and payments could be used in almost any policy area. Budgetary policy of the Reagan administration later eliminated funds for revenue sharing.

In recent years states have been burdened by **underfunded mandates** and **unfunded mandates**. These require states to spend money to comply with a law of Congress (or, in some cases, a federal court order).

UNDERSTANDING FEDERALISM

Federalism was instituted largely to enhance democracy in America, and it strengthens democratic government in many ways. Different levels of government provide more opportunities for participation in politics and increase access to government. Since different citizens and interest groups will have access to the different levels, federalism also increases the opportunities for government to be responsive to demands for policies. Moreover, it is possible for the diversity of opinion within the country to be reflected in different public policies among the states. Different economic interests are concentrated in different states, and the federal system ensures that each state can establish a power base to promote its interests. By handling most disputes over policy at the state and local level, federalism also reduces decision making and conflict at the national level.

Conversely, diverse state policies and the large number of local governments also create some impediments to democracy. Since the states differ in the resources they devote to services like public education, the quality of such services varies greatly from one state to another. Diversity in policy can also discourage states from providing services that would otherwise be available—states are deterred from providing generous benefits to those in need when benefits attract poor people from states with lower benefits. Federalism may have a negative effect on democracy when local interests are able to thwart national majority support of certain policies, and having so many governments makes it difficult for many Americans to know which government is responsible for certain functions.

While the national government has grown in scope relative to state governments, it has not done so at the expense of state governments. The latter continue to carry out all the functions they have typically done. The national government has instead grown as it has taken on new responsibilities viewed as important by the public.

CHAPTER OUTLINE

I. DEFINING FEDERALISM

A. A system of *organizing governments.*

1. **Federalism** is a way of organizing a nation so that two or more levels of government have formal authority over the same area and people.
2. Only 11 (out of approximately 190 nations of the world) have federal systems.
3. Most governments in the world today have **unitary governments**, in which all power resides in the central government.
4. In a **confederation**, the national government is weak and most or all of the power is in the hands of its components.
5. The workings of the American system are sometimes called **intergovernmental relations**, which refers to interactions among national, state, and local governments.

B. Why federalism is important.

1. The federal system *decentralizes our politics.*
2. Federalism *decentralizes our policies* (in addition to our politics).

II. THE CONSTITUTIONAL BASIS OF FEDERALISM

A. The word *federalism is not mentioned in the Constitution.*

B. Eighteenth-century Americans had little experience in thinking of themselves as Americans first and state citizens second.

C. The **division of power**.

1. The writers of the Constitution carefully *defined the powers of state and national governments* [see Table 3.2].
2. Although favoring a stronger national government, states were retained as vital components of government.
3. The **supremacy clause** deals with the question of which government should prevail in disputes between the states and the national government; Article VI states that three items are the *supreme law of the land*:
   a. The Constitution
   b. Laws of the national government (when consistent with the Constitution)
   c. Treaties (which can only be made by the national government)
4. Judges in every state were specifically bound by the Constitution.

5. Questions remain concerning the boundaries of the national government's powers.
   a. The national government can only operate *within its appropriate sphere* and cannot usurp the states' powers.
   b. The **Tenth Amendment** states that "*powers not delegated to the United States by the Constitution, nor prohibited by it to the states, are reserved to the states respectively, or to the people.*"
   c. There have been variations in the Court's interpretation of the Tenth Amendment.

D. Establishing **national supremacy**.
   1. Four key events have largely settled the issue of how national and state powers are related: the *McCulloch* v. *Maryland* case, the Supreme Court's interpretation of the Commerce Clause, the Civil War, and the civil rights movement.
   2. ***McCulloch v. Maryland*** (1819) - the case that first brought the issue of *state versus national power* before the Supreme Court.
      a. In this case, the Supreme Court ruled that *national policies take precedence* over state policies: Chief Justice John Marshall wrote that "the government of the United States, though limited in its power, is supreme within its sphere of action."
      b. The Court also ruled that the Constitution gives Congress certain **implied powers** (based on the provision granting Congress the power to "make all laws necessary and proper for carrying into execution the foregoing powers") that go beyond the **enumerated powers** that are specifically listed in Article I, Section 8.
   3. The **Civil War** (1861-65) - settled militarily the issue that *McCulloch* had enunciated constitutionally.
   4. The **civil rights movement** - a century after the Civil War, the policy issue was *equality*.
      a. In 1954, the Supreme Court held that school segregation was unconstitutional (***Brown* v. *Board of Education***).
      b. The conflict between states and the national government over equality issues was *decided in favor of the national government*: throughout the 1960s, the federal government enacted laws and policies to end segregation in schools, housing, public accommodations, voting, and jobs.
   5. Federalism involves more than the relationships between the national government and state and local governments: Article IV of the Constitution outlines certain *obligations that each state has to every other state.*

a. **Full faith and credit** - States are required to give full faith and credit to the public acts, records, and civil judicial proceedings of every other state.
b. **Extradition** - States are required to return a person charged with a crime in another state to that state for trial or imprisonment.
c. **Privileges and immunities of citizens** - Citizens of each state receive all the privileges and immunities of any other state in which they happen to be.

III. INTERGOVERNMENTAL RELATIONS TODAY

A. From dual to cooperative federalism.
   1. **Dual federalism** ("*layer cake federalism*") - a form of federalism in which states and the national government each remain supreme within their own spheres.
   2. **Cooperative federalism** ("*marble cake federalism*") - a form of federalism with mingled responsibilities and blurred distinctions between the levels of government.
   3. The American federal system leaned toward dual federalism before the national government began to assert its dominance.

B. **Fiscal federalism** - the pattern of spending, taxing, and providing grants in the federal system.
   1. Fiscal federalism is the cornerstone of the national government's relations with state and local governments.
   2. **Grants-in-aid** are the main instrument the national government uses for *both aiding and influencing* states and localities.
   3. Federal aid to states and localities amounted to approximately $306 billion in 2001, despite cutbacks during the Reagan administration.

C. There are two major types of federal aid for states and localities: categorical grants and block grants.
   1. **Categorical grants** (the main source of federal aid) - grants that can be used only for *specific purposes, or categories*.
      a. State and local agencies can obtain categorical grants only by applying for them and by meeting certain qualifications.
      b. Categorical grants come with numerous "strings" (rules and requirements) attached, such as nondiscrimination provisions and punitive **cross-over sanctions** and **cross-cutting requirements** that reduce or deny federal funds if certain local or state laws are not passed or if federal guidelines are not met.
      c. There are two types of categorical grants:
         (1) **Project grants** - the most common type of categorical grant; awarded on the basis of *competitive applications* (such as grants to university professors from the National Science Foundation).

(2) **Formula grants** - distributed according to a formula; states and local governments automatically receive funds based on a formula developed from factors such as population, per capita income, or percentage of rural population (such as Medicare, Aid for Families with Dependent Children, public housing).

2. **Block grants** - used to support broad programs in areas like community development and social services.
   a. In response to complaints about the cumbersome paperwork and restrictive federal requirements attached to categorical grants, Congress established block grants to support broad programs.
   b. States have discretion in deciding how to spend the money.

D. On the whole, federal grant distribution follows the principle of *universalism*—that is, something for everybody, even though some money goes where it is not really needed.

E. There are some occasions when states would prefer *not* to receive some federal aid—such as when Congress extends a program that is administered by the states and only partly funded by the national government—an **underfunded mandate**. This means that the states have to budget more funds for the project in order to receive federal grant money.

F. Of even greater concern to states are **unfunded mandates**. These require state and local governments to spend money to comply with laws such as the Clean Air Act of 1970 and the Americans with Disabilities Act of 1990 with no financial help from the federal government that enacted the laws. In addition, federal courts create unfunded mandates for states regarding school desegregation, prison construction, and other policies. In 1995 Congress passed a law that will make it more difficult for Congress to impose new unfunded mandates.

IV. UNDERSTANDING FEDERALISM

A. By decentralizing the political system, federalism was *designed to contribute to the limited form of democracy* supported by the founders.

B. Advantages for democracy.
   1. Different levels of government provide more opportunities for participation in politics.
   2. Additional levels of government contribute to democracy by increasing access to government.
   3. Two levels of government increase the opportunities for government to be responsive to the demands for policies.
   4. A party that loses strength at the national level can rebuild and groom leaders at the state and local levels.
   5. It is possible for the diversity of opinion within the country to be reflected in different public policies among the different states.

6. By handling most disputes over policy at the state and local level, federalism reduces decision-making and conflict at the national level.

C. Disadvantages for democracy.
   1. The quality of services like education is heavily dependent on the state in which the service is provided; states differ greatly in the resources they can devote to public services.
   2. Diversity in policy can discourage states from providing services that would otherwise be available because poor people may be attracted from states with lower benefits.
   3. Federalism may have a negative effect on democracy when local interests are able to impede national majority support of certain policies.
   4. The vast number of local governments makes it difficult for many Americans to know which government is responsible for certain functions.

D. Federalism and the growth of the national government.
   1. The national government took a direct interest in economic affairs from the very founding of the republic [see Chapter 2].
   2. As the United States changed from an agricultural to an industrial nation, new problems arose and with them new demands for governmental action.
   3. The United States moved from a system of dual federalism to one of cooperative federalism, in which the national and state governments share responsibility for public policies [as seen above].

E. Federalism and the Scope of the National Government.
   1. The national government's share of expenditures has grown rapidly since 1929; today it spends about 20 percent of the GDP, while state and local governments spend about 9 percent today.
   2. The growth of the national government has not supplanted the states.

KEY TERMS AND CONCEPTS

Block grants: broad program grants given more or less automatically to states and communities which exercise discretion in how the money is spent.

Categorical grants: grants that can be used only for specific purposes or categories of state and local spending.

Cooperative federalism: where state and the national government responsibilities are mingled and blurred like a marble cake, powers and policies are shared.

Dual federalism: where states and the national government each remain supreme within their own spheres of power, much like a layer cake.

Elastic clause: the statement in the Constitution which says that Congress has the power to make all laws necessary and proper for carrying out its duties.

Enumerated powers: powers of Congress found in Article 1, Section 8 of the Constitution.

Extradition: the Constitution requires each state to return a person charged with a crime in another state to that state for trial or imprisonment.

Federalism: a system of shared power between two or more levels of government.

Fiscal federalism: the pattern of spending, taxing, and providing grants in the federal system.

Formula grants: a type of categorical grant where states and local governments do not apply for a grant but are given funds on the basis of a formula.

Full faith and credit: Article IV of the Constitution requires states to provide reciprocity toward other states' public acts, records, and civil judicial proceedings.

***Gibbons v. Ogden*:** the 1824 Supreme Court case which further expanded Congress' power to regulate interstate and international commerce by defining commerce very broadly to incorporate every form of commercial activity.

Implied powers: powers beyond Congress' enumerated powers which ensure that it can carry out its duties.

Intergovernmental relations: the term used to describe the entire set of interactions among national, state, and local governments.

***McCulloch v. Maryland*:** the 1819 Supreme Court case which established the supremacy of the national government over the states included both enumerated and implied powers of Congress.

Privileges and immunities: the Constitution prohibits states from discriminating against citizens of other states.

Project grants: categorical grants awarded on the basis of competitive applications.

Supremacy clause: Article VI of the Constitution states that the supreme law of the land is the Constitution, the laws of the national government, and treaties.

Tenth Amendment: specifies that powers not delegated to the national government are reserved for the state government or the people.

Unitary government: a system where all power resides in the central government.

TEACHING IDEAS: CLASS DISCUSSION AND STUDENT PROJECTS

- Identify a recent natural disaster—droughts in the Midwest, tornados in Oklahoma, hurricanes on the East coast or forest fires out West—and ask your students to discuss what the role of the federal government should be in response to the crisis. How much responsibility should the states assume? For what? Should the different levels of government react differently than they would in response to the loss of homes or businesses during a financial crisis? Suggest that your class read selections from news magazines from the time period of the crisis to prepare for this discussion. As a second part to the exercise, you might ask students to determine what actions the federal and state governments actually took and present a brief oral or written report.

- Assign two groups of students to serve as panels to debate the question: Does the American form of federalism increase democracy, or does it have a negative effect on democracy?

- Hold an in-class discussion on the following: How would politics and policies be different in America if there were a unitary system instead of a federal system? Or a confederation instead of a federal system?

- Ask students to study the budgets of the local school system, university, or city to determine the various proportions of revenue that the federal, state and local governments contribute. Would the school district, university, or city benefit from a change in how it is funded?

- For class discussion, ask students whether democracy in the U.S. would continue to exist without federalism. If it would, in what ways would it change? Be sure to remind them that unitary democratic systems exist in most European nations.

- Another class discussion should center around the role of the supremacy clause in defining the political and structural relationships between states and the national government. Be sure to note the Supreme Court's decision in the summer of 1999 that seemingly limits individuals from suing states under federal statutes.

- Assign students either individually or in groups to investigate the funding sources of a "local" project, encouraging them to use sources such as government documents, interviews with elected and appointed officials, and newspaper archives. Who was responsible for the project being funded? Were there any "strings" attached to federal or state monies?

- For a reading and writing connection, have students write an analytical essay concerning the changes which could reasonably occur if public education policy was fully nationalized. Ask them to comment about the advantages and disadvantages of having national educational policy goals funded solely by the federal government. For the most part, students may use the textbook as a source for their information by combining the discussion of funding for education with the advantages and disadvantages of federalism for democracy.

- Assign students to work in groups on different policy areas (e.g. transportation, agriculture, environment, welfare) by researching President George W. Bush's 2001 budget proposals. What types of grant programs are proposed for distributing funds to state and localities? Are the nature and funding levels of these programs different from Clinton's budgets in 1993 and 1997?

BACKGROUND READING

Anton, Thomas. American Federalism and Public Policy. Philadelphia: Temple University Press. 1989.

Beer, Samuel H. To Make A Nation: The Rediscovery of American Federalism. Cambridge, MA: Belknap Press of Harvard University Press. 1993.

Elazar, Daniel J. American Federalism: A View from the States. 3rd. ed. NY: Harper and Row. 1984.

Peterson, Paul A. The Price of Federalism. Washington, D.C.: Brookings Institution. 1995.

Walker, David B. The Rebirth of Federalism. New York: Chatham House Publishers. 2000.

Zimmerman, Joseph F. Contemporary American Federalism: The Growth of National Power. NY: Praeger. 1992.

MEDIA SUGGESTIONS

Federalism. Part of Government by Consent: A National Perspective. A 1989 Insight Media production examining the distribution of power between state and national governments.

Federalism: The National Government versus the States. Number thirteen in the series "The Constitution: That Delicate Balance," produced by the Corporation for Public Broadcasting. This program examines how much power the federal government can exert over state affairs.

CHAPTER FOUR: CIVIL LIBERTIES AND PUBLIC POLICY

PEDAGOGICAL FEATURES

LEARNING OBJECTIVES

After studying this chapter, students should be able to:

- Analyze why people who are advocates of rights in theory often hesitate when it comes time to put those rights into practice.

- Examine how decisions of the Supreme Court have extended specific provisions of the Bill of Rights to the states as part of the incorporation doctrine.

- Describe how the two constitutional statements about religion and government—the *establishment clause* and the *free exercise clause*—may sometimes conflict.

- Examine what the First Congress may have intended by the terms *establishment* and *free exercise* of religion.

- Establish why the Supreme Court will usually not permit prior restraint on speech and press.

- Explain why it has been so difficult for the courts to clearly define which types of materials are considered to be obscene.

- Differentiate between *freedom of speech* and related concepts like *symbolic speech* and *freedom of expression.*

- Understand the conflict that can occur between free speech and public order.

- Determine how essential rights such as the right to a fair trial can conflict with other rights such as the right to a free press.

- Identify the two facets of freedom of assembly and explain how they may conflict with other societal values.

- Explain how specific provisions of the Bill of Rights have been used to extend basic rights to defendants in criminal trials.

- Ascertain how concepts such as a *right to privacy* can be inferred or implied from the Bill of Rights.

- Explain why civil liberties are seen as an individual's protection against the *government.*

CHAPTER OVERVIEW

INTRODUCTION

Civil liberties are individual legal and constitutional *protections against the government.* Although Americans' civil liberties are established in the Bill of Rights, the courts determine what the Constitution actually means through the cases they decide. Disputes about civil liberties are frequent because the issues involved are complex and divisive. Throughout this chapter, students are introduced to the nuances of judicial decision making through special features called *You Are the Judge*. Students are asked to try to decide the outcome of these cases before turning to the actual court decisions, which are collected at the end of the chapter in a feature called *The Court Decides*.

THE BILL OF RIGHTS—THEN AND NOW

The **Bill of Rights** is fundamental to Americans' freedom. All of the state constitutions had bills of rights by the time of the 1787 convention, and the issue of adding a Bill of Rights to the proposed national constitution had become a condition of ratification. The Bill of Rights was passed as a group by the First Congress in 1789; the first ten amendments were ratified and became part of the Constitution in 1791.

Political scientists have discovered that people are advocates of rights *in theory*, but their support wavers when it comes time to put those rights into practice. Cases become particularly difficult when *liberties are in conflict*—such as free press versus a fair trial or free speech versus public order—or where the facts and interpretations are subtle and ambiguous.

The Bill of Rights was written to *restrict the powers of the new central government.* In ***Barron*** **v.** ***Baltimore*** (1833), the Supreme Court ruled that the Bill of Rights restrained *only* the national government and not states and cities. It was not until 1925 that the Court relied on the **Fourteenth Amendment** to find that a state government must respect some First Amendment rights (***Gitlow*** **v.** ***New York***). In *Gitlow*, the Court announced that freedoms of speech and press *"were fundamental personal rights and liberties protected by the due process clause of the Fourteenth Amendment from impairment by the states."*

The Supreme Court gradually applied most of the Bill of Rights to the states, particularly during the era of Chief Justice Earl Warren in the 1960s, developing the concept of the incorporation doctrine. At the present time, only the Second, Third, and Seventh Amendments and the grand jury requirement of the Fifth Amendment have not been applied specifically to the states. Not everyone agrees that the Fourteenth Amendment incorporated parts of the Bill of Rights into state laws; in 1985, Edwin Meese (then attorney general) strongly criticized *Gitlow* and called for "disincorporation" of the Bill of Rights.

FREEDOM OF RELIGION

The **First Amendment** makes two basic statements about religion and government, commonly referred to as the **establishment clause** and the **free exercise clause**. Sometimes these freedoms conflict, but cases involving these clauses usually raise different kinds of conflicts.

Some nations, like Great Britain, have an *established church* that is officially supported by the government. A few American colonies had official churches, but the religious persecutions that incited many colonists to move to America discouraged any desire for the First Congress to establish a national church in the United States. Debate still continues over what else the First Congress may have intended for the establishment clause. Some people believe that the establishment clause meant only that the government could not favor one religion over another. Thomas Jefferson argued that the First Amendment created a **"wall of separation"** between church and state that forbade any support for religion at all.

Debate has been especially intense over questions of aid to church-related schools and prayers or Bible reading in the public schools. School prayer is possibly the most controversial religious issue. In 1962 and 1963, the Court ruled that voluntary recitations of prayers or Bible passages, when done as part of classroom exercises in public schools, violated the establishment clause (***Engel* v. *Vitale*** and ***School District of Abington Township, Pennsylvania* v. *Schempp***). A majority of the public has never favored the Court's decisions on school prayer. Some religious groups pushed for a constitutional amendment permitting school prayer, and many school districts simply ignored the decision. In ***Employment Division* v. *Smith*** (1990) the Supreme Court ruled that states can prohibit certain religious practices, but not religion itself.

There is a fine line between aid to church-related schools that is permissible and aid that is not. In 1971, the Supreme Court declared that aid to church-related schools must have a secular legislative purpose, cannot be used to advance or inhibit religion, and should avoid excessive government "entanglement" with religion (***Lemon* v. *Kurtzman***).

Conservative religious groups have had an impact on the political agenda. They devoted much of their time and energies in recent years to the issues of *school prayer and creation science*; and while they lost some battles (such as the battle over teaching *creation science* in the public schools), they have won others (for example, the Court decision that religious scenes could be set up on public property).

The guarantee of *free exercise* of religion is also more complicated than it appears at first glance. The free exercise of religious beliefs sometimes clashes with society's other values and laws, as occurred when the Amish refused to send their children to public schools. The Supreme Court has consistently maintained that people have an absolute right to *believe* what they want, but the courts have been more cautious about the right to *practice* a belief (but in ***Wisconsin* v. *Yoder***, 1972, the Court did allow Amish parents to take their children out of school after the eighth grade).

FREEDOM OF EXPRESSION

The courts have frequently wrestled with the question of whether **freedom of expression** (like **freedom of conscience**) is an **absolute**. The courts have often ruled that there are instances when speech needs to be controlled, especially when the First Amendment conflicts with other rights. In their attempts to draw the line separating *permissible from impermissible speech*, judges have had to *balance* freedom of expression against competing values like public order, national security, and the right to a fair trial.

The courts have also had to decide what kinds of activities constitute *speech* (or press) within the meaning of the First Amendment. Certain forms of *nonverbal communication* (like picketing) are considered **symbolic speech** and are protected under the First Amendment. Other forms of expression are considered to be *action* and are not protected. The Court has generally struck down **prior restraint** of speech and press (censorship that prevents publication), although the writer or speaker could be punished for violating a law or someone's rights *after* publication (***Near* v. *Minnesota***, 1931).

Crises such as war often bring government efforts to enforce censorship. In ***Schenck* v. *United States*** (1919), Justice Oliver Wendell Holmes declared that government can limit speech if it provokes a **clear and present danger** of "substantive evils." Free speech advocates did little to stem the relentless persecution of *McCarthyism* during the "cold war" of the 1950s, when Senator Joseph McCarthy's unproven accusations that many public officials were Communists created an atmosphere in which the courts placed broad restrictions on freedom of expression. By the 1960s, the political climate had changed, and courts today are very supportive of the right to protest, pass out leaflets, or gather signatures on petitions (as long as it is done in public places).

The Bill of Rights is also a source of potential *conflicts between different types of freedoms*. The Constitution clearly meant to guarantee the right to a **fair trial** as well as the right to a **free press**, but a trial may not be fair if pretrial press coverage makes it impossible to select an impartial jury. Likewise, journalists seek full freedom to cover all trials (they argue that the public has a right to know), but they sometimes defend their right to keep some of their own files secret in order to protect a confidential source.

Efforts to define **obscenity** have perplexed the courts for years. Although the Supreme Court has held that *"obscenity is not within the area of constitutionally protected speech or press"* (***Roth*** **v.** ***United States***, 1957), it has proven difficult to determine what is legally obscene. The Court tried to clarify its doctrine by spelling out what could be classified as obscene and thus outside First Amendment protection in the 1973 case of ***Miller v. California***. Then Chief Justice Warren Burger wrote that materials were obscene if, taken as a whole, they appealed "to a prurient interest in sex"; showed "patently offensive" sexual conduct that was specifically defined by an obscenity law; and taken as a whole, lacked "serious literary, artistic, political, or scientific value." Advances in technology have created a new wrinkle in the obscenity issue. The Internet and the World Wide Web make it easier to distribute obscene material rapidly, and a number of online information services have taken advantage of this opportunity.

Libel and **slander** also raise *freedom of expression* issues that involve *competing values*. If public debate is not free, there can be no *democracy*. Conversely, some reputations will be unfairly damaged in the process if there are not limitations. Libel (the publication of statements known to be false that tend to damage a person's reputation) and slander (spoken defamation) are not protected by the First Amendment, but the Court has held that statements about **public figures** are libelous only if made with *malice* and *reckless disregard* for the truth (***New York Times*** v. ***Sullivan***, 1964) The right to criticize the government (which the Supreme Court termed "the central meaning of the First Amendment") is not libel or slander.

Wearing an armband, burning a flag, and marching in a parade are examples of **symbolic speech:** actions that do not consist of speaking or writing but that express an opinion. When Gregory Johnson set a flag on fire at the 1984 Republican National Convention in Dallas to protest nuclear arms buildup, the Supreme Court decided that the state law prohibiting flag desecration violated the First Amendment (***Texas v. Johnson,*** 1989). **Commercial speech** (such as advertising) is more restricted than are expressions of opinion on religious, political, or other matters. Similarly, radio and television stations are subject to more restrictions than the print media (justified by the fact that only a limited number of broadcast frequencies are available).

The Federal Communications Commission (FCC) regulates the content, nature, and very existence of radio and television broadcasting. Although newspapers do not need licenses, radio and television stations do. The state of Florida passed a law requiring newspapers in the state to provide space for political candidates to reply to newspaper criticisms. The Supreme Court, without hesitation, voided this law (***Miami Herald Publishing Company v. Tornillo,*** 1974). Earlier, in ***Red Lion Broadcasting Company v. Federal Communications Commission*** (1969), the Court upheld similar restrictions on radio and television stations, reasoning that such laws were justified because only a limited number of broadcast frequencies were available.

There are two facets to **freedom of assembly**. The *right to assemble* involves the right to gather together in order to make a statement, while the *right to associate* is the freedom to associate with people who share a common interest. The Supreme Court has generally upheld the right of any group—no matter how controversial or offensive—to *peaceably* assemble on public property. The *balance between freedom and order* is tested when protest verges on harassment.

DEFENDANTS' RIGHTS

The First Amendment guarantees the freedoms of religion, speech, press, and assembly. Most of the remaining rights in the Bill of Rights concern the rights of people accused of crimes. These rights were originally intended to protect the accused in *political* arrests and trials. Today, the protections in the Fourth, Fifth, Sixth, and Eighth Amendments are primarily applied in criminal justice cases. Moreover, the Supreme Court's decisions have *extended most provisions of the Bill of Rights to the states* as part of the *general process of incorporation.*

The Bill of Rights covers every stage of the criminal justice system. The **Fourth Amendment** is quite specific in forbidding **unreasonable searches and seizures.** No court may issue a **search warrant** unless **probable cause** exists to believe that a crime has occurred or is about to occur, and warrants must describe the area to be searched and the material sought in the search. Since 1914, the courts have used the **exclusionary rule** to prevent illegally seized evidence from being introduced in federal courts. In 1961, the Supreme Court incorporated the exclusionary rule within the rights that restrict the states as well as the federal government (***Mapp* v. *Ohio***). The Burger Court made a number of exceptions to the exclusionary rule, including the **good-faith exception** (***United States* v. *Leon***, 1984).

Under the **Fifth Amendment** prohibition against forced **self-incrimination,** suspects cannot be compelled to provide evidence that can be used against them. The burden of proof rests on the police and the prosecutors, not the defendant. ***Miranda* v. *Arizona*** (1966) set guidelines for police questioning of suspects, whereby suspects must be informed of their constitutional rights. The more conservative Rehnquist Court made some *exceptions* to the *Miranda* rulings, including a ruling in 1991 that a *coerced confession* is a *"harmless error"* if other evidence is sufficient for conviction (***Arizona* v. *Fulminante***).

Although the **Sixth Amendment** has always ensured the **right to counsel** in *federal courts*, this right was not *incorporated* to state courts until recently. In 1932, the Supreme Court ordered states to provide an attorney for indigent defendants accused of a *capital crime* (***Powell* v. *Alabama***), and in 1963, the Court extended the same right to everyone accused of a *felony* (***Gideon* v. *Wainwright***). The Court later ruled that a lawyer must be provided for the accused *whenever imprisonment could be imposed* (***Argersinger* v. *Hamlin***, 1972). The Sixth Amendment also ensures the right to a **speedy trial** and an **impartial jury**, but most cases are settled through **plea bargaining** rather than through trial by jury.

The **Eighth Amendment** forbids **cruel and unusual punishment**, but it *does not define* the phrase. Most of the constitutional debate over cruel and unusual punishment has centered on the *death penalty*. In ***Furman* v. *Georgia*** (1972), the Court first confronted the question of whether the death penalty is inherently cruel and unusual punishment. A divided Court overturned Georgia's death penalty law because its imposition was "freakish" and "random" in the way it was arbitrarily applied (particularly with regard to factors such as race and income). Thirty-five states passed new laws that were intended to be less arbitrary. In recent years, the Court has come down more clearly on the side of the death penalty. A divided Court rebuffed the last major challenge to the death penalty in ***McCleskey v. Kemp*** (1987) when it refused to rule that the penalty violated the equal protection of the law guaranteed by the Fourteenth Amendment.

THE RIGHT TO PRIVACY

Today's technologies raise key questions about *ethics* and the Constitution. Although the Constitution does not specifically mention a **right to privacy**, the Supreme Court has said that it is implied by several guarantees in the Bill of Rights. Questions involving a right to privacy have centered on such diverse issues as abortion rights, the drafting of state laws to define death, technological developments like in-vitro fertilization, and the right to die. Supporters of privacy rights argue that the Fourth Amendment was intended to protect privacy.

Opponents claim that the Supreme Court was inventing protections not specified by the Constitution when it ruled on constitutionally protected "rights of privacy."

The Supreme Court first referred to the idea that the Constitution guarantees a right to privacy in a 1965 case involving a Connecticut law that forbade contraceptives (***Griswold* v. *Connecticut***), but the *most important application of privacy rights* came in the area of *abortion.* Americans are deeply divided on abortion: the positions of "pro-choice" and "pro-life" are irreconcilable.

Justice Harry Blackmun's majority opinion in ***Roe* v. *Wade*** (1973) followed the practice of medical authorities in dividing pregnancy into three equal *trimesters. Roe* forbade any state control of abortions during the first trimester; permitted states to allow regulated abortions to protect the mother's health in the second trimester; and allowed the states to ban abortion during the third trimester except when the mother's life was in danger. In 1989, a clinic in St. Louis challenged the constitutionality of a Missouri law that forbade the use of state funds or state employees to perform abortions, but the Court upheld the law in ***Webster* v. *Reproductive Health Services*** (1989). In 1992, the Court changed its *standard for evaluating restrictions on abortion* from one of *"strict scrutiny"* of any restraints on a *"fundamental right"* to one of *"undue burden"* that permits considerably more regulation (***Planned Parenthood* v. *Casey***). Beginning in 1994, the Supreme Court strengthened women's access to health clinics, while Congress passed the Freedom of Access to Clinic Entrances Act, which made it a federal crime to intimidate abortion providers or women seeking abortions.

Technology has also created political issues out of the "right" to live or to die. In-vitro fertilization, frozen embryos, and artificial insemination complicate efforts to define birth by separating reproduction from sexual intercourse and the parent-child relationship. Several of these issues crystallized in two "Baby Doe" cases, where parents requested that medical treatment be withheld from their newborn babies. The Supreme Court affirmed parents' rights to make medical decisions for their children. In ***Cruzan* v. *Director, Missouri Department of Health*** (1990) the Supreme Court recognized a limited constitutional right for patients to refuse unwanted medical treatment, a form of suicide. However, in 1997, the Supreme Court ruled in ***Vacco* v. *Quill*** and ***Washington* v. *Glucksberg*** that there is no consitutional right to physician-assisted suicide and that states may prohibit it if they wish.

UNDERSTANDING CIVIL LIBERTIES

American government is both *democratic* (because it is governed by officials elected by the people and answerable to them) and *constitutional* (because it has a fundamental organic law, the Constitution, that limits the things government can do). The democratic and constitutional components of government can produce conflicts, but they also reinforce one another. One task that government must perform is to resolve conflicts between rights.

The rights guaranteed by the First Amendment are essential to a democracy. Likewise, the rights guaranteed by the Fourth, Fifth, Sixth, and Eighth Amendments protect all Americans; but they also make it harder to punish criminals. Ultimately, it is the courts that decide what constitutional guarantees mean in practice: although the federal courts are the *branch of government least subject to majority rule*, the courts *enhance democracy by protecting liberty and equality from the excesses of majority rule.*

CHAPTER OUTLINE

I. THE BILL OF RIGHTS—THEN AND NOW

A. **Civil liberties** are individual legal and constitutional protections against the government. They are essential for democracy.
   1. Americans' civil liberties are set down in the **Bill of Rights**, but the courts are the arbiters of these liberties because they determine what the Constitution means in the cases that they decide.
      a. Although the original Constitution had no bill of rights, the states made it clear that adding one was a condition of ratification.
      b. The first ten amendments (ratified in 1791) comprise the Bill of Rights.
      c. The Bill of Rights was passed at a period of history when British abuses of the colonists' civil liberties were still a recent and bitter memory.
   2. Political scientists have found that people are supporters of rights in theory, but their support often falters when it comes time to put those rights into practice.
   3. Cases become particularly difficult *when liberties are in conflict* (such as free press versus a fair trial or free speech versus public order) or where the facts and interpretations are subtle and ambiguous.

B. The Bill of Rights was written to *restrict the powers* of the new central government (every state constitution had its own bill of rights).
   1. In ***Barron* v. *Baltimore*** (1833), the Court ruled that the Bill of Rights restrained only the national government, not states and cities.

2. **Incorporation doctrine** provides the rationale for the process by which fundamental freedoms have been applied against state action through interpretation of the Fourteenth Amendment.
   a. The **Fourteenth Amendment** (ratified in 1868) included guarantees of *privileges and immunities of citizens*, *due process of law*, and *equal protection of the law*, and explicitly applied these guarantees against the *states*.
   b. It was not until 1925 that the Court relied on the Fourteenth Amendment to find that a state government must respect some First Amendment rights (***Gitlow* v. *New York***); in *Gitlow*, the Court announced that freedoms of speech and press "*were fundamental personal rights and liberties protected by the due process clause of the Fourteenth Amendment from impairment by the states.*"
   c. The Supreme Court gradually applied most of the Bill of Rights to the states, particularly during the era of chief Justice Earl Warren in the 1960s.
   d. At the present time, only the Second, Third, and Seventh Amendments and the grand jury requirement of the Fifth Amendment have not been applied specifically to the states.
3. Not everyone agrees that the Fourteenth Amendment incorporated parts of the Bill of Rights into state laws; in 1985, Edwin Meese (then U.S. Attorney General) strongly criticized *Gitlow* and called for "disincorporation" of the Bill of Rights.

II. FREEDOM OF RELIGION

A. The **First Amendment** includes *two* statements about religion and government, commonly referred to as the *establishment clause* and the *free exercise clause.*

B. These freedoms sometimes conflict, but establishment and free exercise cases usually raise different kinds of conflict.

C. The **establishment clause** states that "Congress shall make no law respecting an establishment of religion."
   1. This clause clearly prohibits an establishment of a national church in the United States (a reaction to the religious persecutions that had convinced many colonists to move to America).
   2. Debate still continues over what else the First Congress may have intended for the establishment clause.
      a. Thomas Jefferson argued that the First Amendment created a **"wall of separation"** between church and states, which would prohibit not only favoritism but any support for religion at all.

b. Proponents of aid to parochial schools (known as **parochiaid**) argue that it does not favor any particular religion; opponents claim that the Roman Catholic church gets most of the aid.

c. In ***Lemon* v. *Kurtzman*** (1971), the Supreme Court declared that aid to church-related schools must have a secular purpose, cannot be used to advance or inhibit religion, and should avoid excessive government "entanglement" with religion.

d. In ***Westside Community Schools v. Mergens*** (1990), the Supreme Court upheld the 1984 Equal Access Act, which made it unlawful for any public high school receiving federal funds to keep student groups from using school facilities for religious worship if the school opens its facilities for other student meetings.

e. School prayer is possibly the most controversial religious issue.

(1) In 1962 and 1963, the Court ruled that voluntary recitations of prayers or Bible passages, when done as part of classroom exercises in public schools, violated the establishment clause (***Engel* v. *Vitale*** and ***School District of Abington Township, Pennsylvania* v. *Schempp***).

(2) In *Engel* and *Abington*, the Court observed that "the place of religion in our society is an exalted one, but in the relationship between man and religion, the State is firmly committed to a position of neutrality."

(3) A majority of the public has never favored the Court's decisions on school prayer.

D. Fundamentalist Christians.

1. Conservative religious groups devote much of their time and energies to the issues of *school prayer and creation science*.

2. They lost some court battles to create a more conservative agenda, but won others.

a. The Supreme Court rejected attempts to legalize school prayer by making it voluntary (*Wallace* v. *Jaffree*, 1985) and to mandate the teaching of **creation science** as an alternative to Darwinian theories of evolution (*Edwards* v. *Aguillard*, 1987).

b. Recent Supreme Court rulings brought some lowering of the "wall of separation," as when the Court held that religious scenes could be set up on public property (*Lynch* v. *Donelly*, 1984 and *County of Allegheny* v. *American Civil Liberties Union*, 1992).

E. The First Amendment also guarantees the **free exercise** of religion.

1. The free exercise of religious beliefs sometimes clashes with society's other values or laws, as occurred when the Amish refused to send their children to public schools.

2. The Supreme Court has consistently maintained that people have an absolute right to *believe* what they want, but the courts have been more cautious about the right to *practice* a belief (but in ***Wisconsin* v. *Yoder***, 1972, the Court did allow Amish parents to take their children out of school after the eighth grade).
3. In the Religious Freedom Restoration Act of 1993 Congress attempted to overcome this ruling, but the law was found unconstitutional by the Supreme Court in 1997 (*Boerne v. Flores*).

III. FREEDOM OF EXPRESSION

A. Does "no law" in the First Amendment really mean "*no law*"? The courts have frequently wrestled with the question of whether **freedom of expression** (like **freedom of conscience**) is an **absolute**.
   1. Supreme Court Justice Hugo Black believed that the words *no law* literally meant that Congress shall make *no* laws abridging the fundamental rights of the First Amendment.
      a. The courts have often ruled that there are instances when speech needs to be controlled, especially when the First Amendment conflicts with other rights (as when Justice Oliver Wendell Holmes wrote in 1919 that "*the most stringent protection of free speech would not protect a man in falsely shouting 'fire' in a theater and causing a panic.*")
      b. In their attempts to draw the line separating *permissible from impermissible speech*, judges have had to *balance* freedom of expression against competing values like public order, national security, and the right to a fair trial.
   2. The courts have also had to decide what kinds of activities constitute *speech* (or press) within the meaning of the first Amendment.
      a. Certain forms of *nonverbal communication* (like picketing) are considered **symbolic speech**, and are protected under the First Amendment.
      b. Other forms of expression are considered to be *action*, and are not protected.

B. **Prior restraint** - a government's actions that *prevent* material from being published.
   1. The Supreme Court has generally struck down prior restraint of speech and press (***Near* v. *Minnesota***, 1931), although the writer or speaker could be punished for violating a law or someone's rights *after* publication.
   2. There are exceptions to the general doctrine that prohibits prior restraint.

a. In *Hazelwood School District* v. *Kuhlmeier* (1988), the Court ruled that a high school newspaper was not a public forum and could be regulated in "any reasonable manner" by school officials.
b. Many argue that government should sometimes limit individual behavior on the grounds of *national security*.
   (1) The courts have been reluctant to issue injunctions prohibiting the publication of material even in the area of national security.
   (2) In the famous ***"Pentagon Papers"*** case (*New York Times* v. *United States*, 1971), the Nixon administration was unable to obtain an injunction against the *Times* that would have prohibited publication of secret documents pertaining to American involvement in the Vietnam War.

C. Free speech and public order.
1. War often brings government efforts to enforce censorship.
   a. In ***Schenck* v. *United States*** (1919), Justice Oliver Wendell Holmes declared that government can limit speech if it provokes a **clear and present danger** of "substantive evils that Congress has a right to prevent."
   b. The **Smith Act** of 1940 forbade the *advocacy* of violent overthrow of the American government.
   c. Free speech advocates did little to stem the relentless persecution known as *McCarthyism* during the "cold war" of the 1950s, when Senator Joseph McCarthy's unproven accusations that many public officials were Communists created an atmosphere in which broad restrictions were placed on freedom of expression.
   d. By the 1960s, the political climate had changed.
      (1) The Court narrowed the interpretation of the Smith Act so that the government could no longer use it to prosecute dissenters.
      (2) Waves of protest over the Vietnam War and unrest over political, economic, racial, and social issues expanded the constitutional meaning of free speech.
2. Today, courts are very supportive of the right to protest, pass out leaflets, or gather signatures on petitions (as long as it is done in public places).

D. Free press versus free trial.
1. The Bill of Rights is a source of potential *conflicts between different types of freedoms*: the Constitution clearly meant to guarantee the right to a **fair trial** as well as the right to a **free press**, but a trial may

not be fair if pretrial press coverage makes it impossible to select an impartial jury.

2. Journalists seek full freedom to cover all trials: they argue that the public has a *right to know*.
   a. Although reporters want *trials to be open to them*, they sometimes defend their right to keep some of their own files secret in order to protect a *confidential source*.
   b. A few states have passed **shield laws** to protect reporters in situations where they need to protect a confidential source; but in most states, reporters have no more rights than other citizens once a case has come to trial.
   c. The Supreme Court has ruled that (in the absence of shield laws) *the right to a fair trial preempts* the reporter's right to protect sources (*Branzburg* v. *Hayes*, 1972) and has sustained the right of police to obtain a search warrant to search the files of a student newspaper (***Zurcher* v. *Stanford Daily***, 1976).
   d. The Court has revoked *gag orders* imposed by lower courts (forbidding the press to report details of a case), but a 1979 case also permitted a *closed hearing* on the grounds that pretrial publicity might compromise the defendant's right to a fair trial.

E. Efforts to define **obscenity** have perplexed the courts for years.
   1. Public standards vary from time to time, place to place, and person to person.
   2. Work that some call "obscene" may be "art" to others.
   3. No nationwide consensus exists that offensive material should be banned.
   4. The newest issue in the obscenity controversy involves the claim of some women's groups that pornography degrades and dehumanizes women.
   5. The courts have consistently ruled that states may protect *children* from obscenity (*Osborne* v. *Ohio*, 1991); *adults* often have legal access to the same material.
   6. Although the Supreme Court has held that *"obscenity is not within the area of constitutionally protected speech or press"* (***Roth* v. *United States***, 1957), it has proven difficult to determine just what is obscene.
   7. In ***Miller* v. *California*** (1973), the Court tried to clarify what could be classified as obscene, and therefore outside First Amendment protection.
      a. Chief Justice Warren Burger wrote that materials were obscene if the work, *taken as a whole*, appealed to a *"prurient interest"* in

sex; *and* if it showed *"patently offensive sexual contact"*; *and* if it *"lacked serious artistic, literary, political, or scientific merit."*

b. In *Miller*, the Court also ruled that decisions should be made by *local* (not national) communities.

F. **Libel** (the publication of statements known to be false that tend to damage a person's reputation) and **slander** (spoken defamation) are *not protected* by the first Amendment.

1. Libel and slander involve *freedom of expression* issues that involve *competing values*.
    a. If public debate is not free, there can be no *democracy*.
    b. Conversely, some reputations will be unfairly damaged in the process.
2. The Court has held that statements about **public figures** are libelous only if made with *malice* and *reckless disregard* for the truth (***New York Times*** **v.** ***Sullivan***, 1964).
    a. The right to criticize the government (which the Supreme court termed "the central meaning of the First Amendment") is not libel or slander.
    b. In 1984, General William Westmoreland dropped his suit against CBS in return for a mild apology; he realized that it would be impossible to prove that the network had been *intentionally malicious*, even though he was able to show that CBS had knowingly made factual errors.
3. **Private persons** only need to show that statements about them were *defamatory falsehoods* and that the author was *negligent*.

G. **Symbolic speech** refers to *actions that do not consist of speaking or writing but that express an opinion.*

1. Broadly interpreted, *freedom of speech* is a guarantee of *freedom of expression.*
2. The doctrine of symbolic speech *is not precise*: burning a flag is protected speech, but burning a draft card is not (***Texas*** **v.** ***Johnson***, 1989, and ***U.S.*** **v.** ***O'Brien***, 1968).

H. **Commercial speech** (such as advertising) is more restricted than are expressions of opinion on religious, political, or other matters.

1. The **Federal Trade Commission (FTC)** decides what kinds of materials may be advertised on radio and television, and regulates the content of advertising.
2. Although commercial speech is regulated more rigidly than the other types of speech, the courts have been broadening its protection under the Constitution; in recent years, the courts have struck down many restrictions (including restraints against advertising for professional

services and for certain products such as condoms) as violations of freedom of speech.

I. *Radio and television stations* are subject to more restrictions than the print media (justified by the fact that only a limited number of broadcast frequencies are available).
   1. The **Federal Communications Commission (FCC)** regulates the content and nature (and the very existence) of radio and television broadcasting.
   2. A licensed station must comply with regulations that include provisions for a certain percentage of broadcast time for public service, news, children's programming, political candidates, or views other than those its owners support.

J. **Freedom of assembly** - the basis for forming interest groups and political parties, for picketing and protesting in groups.
   1. *Two facets* of the freedom of assembly.
      a. **Right to assemble** - the right to gather together in order to make a statement.
         (1) Within reasonable limits (called *time, place, and manner restrictions*), freedom of assembly includes the rights to parade, picket, and protest.
         (2) The Supreme Court has generally upheld the right of any group—no matter how controversial or offensive—to peaceably assemble *on public property*.
         (3) The *balance between freedom and order* is tested when protest verges on harassment (as illustrated by the dispute over protesters lined up outside abortion clinics).
      b. **Right to associate** - freedom to associate with people who share a common interest.
         (1) The right to associate includes the right to meet with people who want to create political change.
         (2) In 1958, the Court found Alabama's attempt to require the NAACP to turn over its membership list to be an unconstitutional restriction of freedom of association (***NAACP* v. *Alabama***).

IV. DEFENDANTS' RIGHTS

A. Interpreting defendants' rights.
   1. The **First Amendment** guarantees the *freedoms of religion, speech, press, and assembly.*
   2. Most of the remaining rights in the Bill of Rights concern the rights of people accused of crimes.

    a. These rights were originally intended to protect the accused in *political* arrests and trials.
    b. Today, the protections in the *Fourth, Fifth, Sixth, and Eighth Amendments* are primarily applied in *criminal justice cases.*
  3. The language of the Bill of Rights is vague, and defendants' rights are not well defined.
  4. The Supreme Court's decisions have *extended most provisions of the Bill of Rights to the states* as part of the *general process of incorporation.*

B. The **Fourth Amendment** is quite specific in forbidding **unreasonable searches and seizures.**
  1. No court may issue a **search warrant** unless **probable cause** exists to believe that a crime has occurred or is about to occur.
  2. Warrants must specify the area to be searched and the material sought in the search.
  3. Since 1914, the courts have used the **exclusionary rule** to prevent illegally seized evidence from being introduced in the courtroom.
    a. In ***Mapp* v. *Ohio*** (1961), the Supreme Court incorporated the exclusionary rule within the rights that restrict the states as well as the federal government.
    b. *Critics of the exclusionary rule* argue that its strict application may permit guilty persons to go free because of police carelessness or innocent errors (or "technicalities").
    c. *Supporters of the exclusionary rule* respond that the Constitution is not a technicality; defendants' rights protect the accused in a system whereby everyone is presumed to be innocent until proven guilty.
    d. The Burger Court made some *exceptions to the exclusionary rule.*
    e. Warrantless searches are valid if probable cause exists, if the search is necessary to protect an officer's safety, or if the search is limited to material relevant to the suspected crime or within the suspect's immediate control.

C. The **Fifth Amendment** prohibits forced **self-incrimination.**
  1. Suspects cannot be compelled to provide evidence that can be used against them.
    a. The burden of proof rests on the police and the prosecutors, not the defendant.
    b. This right applies to congressional hearings and police stations, as well as to courtrooms.
    c. Suspects *must testify* if the government guarantees **immunity** from prosecution.

2. ***Miranda* v. *Arizona*** (1966) set guidelines for police questioning of suspects.
   a. Suspects must be *informed* of their constitutional right to remain silent.
   b. Suspects must be warned that what they say can be used against them in a court of law.
   c. Suspects must be told that they have a right to have a lawyer present during questioning, and that a lawyer will be provided if the accused cannot afford one.
3. The more conservative Supreme Court under Chief Justice Burger did not weaken the *Miranda* rulings, but the Rehnquist Court did begin to make exceptions: in 1991, the Court held that a *coerced confession* is *"harmless error"* if other evidence is sufficient for conviction (*Arizona* v. *Fulminante*).
4. If law enforcement officials encourage persons to commit crimes (such as accepting bribes or purchasing illicit drugs) that they otherwise would not commit, convictions for these crimes will be overturned by the courts.

D. Although the **Sixth Amendment** has always ensured the **right to counsel** in *federal courts*, this right was not extended (*incorporated*) to state courts until recently.
   1. In 1932, the Supreme Court ordered states to provide an attorney for indigent defendants accused of a *capital crime* (*Powell* v. *Alabama*).
   2. In 1963, the Court extended the same right to everyone accused of a *felony* (***Gideon* v. *Wainwright*,** which was heard by the Court only after Clarence Gideon wrote a *pauper's petition* with the help of the prison's law books).
   3. The Court later ruled that a lawyer must be provided for the accused *whenever imprisonment could be imposed* (*Argersinger* v. *Hamlin*, 1972).

E. The Sixth Amendment also ensures the right to a **speedy trial** and an **impartial jury**.
   1. Most cases (90 percent) are settled through **plea bargaining** rather than through trial by jury.
      a. In plea bargaining, an agreement is made between a defendant's lawyer and a prosecutor to the effect that a defendant will plead guilty to a lesser crime or to fewer crimes and often results in greatly reduced punishment.
      b. Critics believe that plea bargaining permits many criminals to avoid deserved punishment; however, it also saves the state time and money.

2. The Constitution does not specify the size of a jury; tradition has set jury size at twelve, but six jurors are sometimes used in petty cases.
3. Juries traditionally had to be unanimous in order to convict, but the Burger Court *permitted states to use fewer than twelve jurors* and to *convict with less than a unanimous vote.* Federal courts still employ juries of twelve persons and require unanimous votes for a criminal conviction.

F. The **Eighth Amendment** forbids **cruel and unusual punishment**, but it *does not define* the phrase.
   1. Most of the constitutional debate over cruel and unusual punishment has centered on the *death penalty*.
      a. ***Witherspoon*** **v.** ***Illinois*** (1968) - overturned a death sentence because opponents of the death penalty had been excluded from the jury at sentencing.
      b. ***Furman*** **v.** ***Georgia*** (1972) - overturned Georgia's death penalty law because its imposition was "freakish" and "random" in the way it was arbitrarily applied (particularly with regard to factors such as race and income).
      c. ***Woodson*** **v.** ***North Carolina*** (1976) - ruled against mandatory death penalties.
      d. ***Gregg*** **v.** ***Georgia*** (1976) - found that the death penalty is "an extreme sanction, suitable to the most extreme of crimes".
      e. ***McCleskey*** **v.** ***Kemp*** (1987) – upheld the constitutionality of the death penalty against charges that it violated the **Fourteenth Amendment** because minority defendants were more likely to receive the death penalty than were white defendants.
   2. The Supreme Court has recently held that it was constitutionally acceptable to execute 16- or 17-years-olds or mentally retarded persons; has made it more difficult for death row inmates to force legal delays through *habeas corpus* petitions; and has allowed *"victim impact" statements* detailing the character of murder victims and their families' suffering to be used against a defendant.

V. THE RIGHT TO PRIVACY

A. Today's technologies raise key questions about *ethics* and the Constitution.
   1. Although the Constitution does not specifically mention a **right to privacy**, the Supreme Court has said that it is implied by several guarantees in the Bill of Rights.
   2. In 1928, Justice Brandeis called privacy "the right to be left alone."
   3. Questions involving a right to privacy have centered on such diverse issues as abortion rights; the drafting of state laws to define death;

technological developments like in-vitro fertilization, frozen embryos, and artificial insemination; and even the right to die (a patient's right to refuse treatment, or the right of families of a guardian to exercise the patient's right when a patient is no longer able to communicate).

B. The Supreme Court first referred to the idea that the constitution guarantees a right to privacy in a 1965 case involving a Connecticut law that forbade contraceptives.
   1. In *Griswold* v. *Connecticut*, the Court found that various portions of the Bill of Rights cast *"penumbras"*—unstated liberties implied by the explicitly stated rights—that protected a right to privacy.
   2. Supporters of privacy rights argued that the Fourth Amendment was intended to protect privacy.
   3. Critics of the ruling claimed that the Supreme Court was inventing protections not specified by the Constitution.

C. The *most important application of privacy rights* came in the area of *abortion*.
   1. Americans are deeply divided on abortion: the positions of "pro-choice" and "pro-life" are irreconcilable (making abortion a politician's nightmare).
   2. Supreme Court Justice Harry Blackmun's opinion in ***Roe* v. *Wade*** (1973) followed that of medical authorities in dividing pregnancy into three equal *trimesters*.
   3. *Roe* forbade any state control of abortions during the first trimester, permitted states to allow regulated abortions to protect the mother's health in the second trimester, and allowed the states to ban abortion during the third trimester except when the mother's life was in danger.
   4. *Roe* caused a furor that has never subsided, and numerous state and federal regulations were passed which prohibited the use of funds for abortions.
      a. A clinic in St. Louis challenged the constitutionality of a Missouri law that forbade the use of state funds or state employees to perform abortions, but the Court upheld the law in ***Webster* v. *Reproductive Health Services*** (1989).
      b. The Court has also upheld laws requiring minors to obtain the permission of one or both parents or a judge before obtaining an abortion; and in *Rust* v. *Sullivan* (1991), the Court upheld a Department of Health and Human Services ruling that provided that family planning services that received federal funds could not provide women with *any* counseling regarding abortions.

(President Clinton lifted the ban on abortion counseling on his third day in office.)

5. In 1992, the Court changed its *standard for evaluating restrictions on abortion* from one of *"strict scrutiny"* of any restraints on a *"fundamental right"* to one of *"undue burden"* that permits considerably more regulation (***Planned Parenthood* v. *Casey***).
6. In *Madsen v. Women's Health Center* (1994), the Court upheld a Florida state court's order of a 36-foot buffer zone around an abortion clinic to allow people to enter abortion clinics. In another 1994 case, the Court decided that abortion clinics can invoke the federal racketeering law to sue violent anti-abortion protest groups for damages. In 1994, Congress passed a law making it a federal crime to intimidate abortion providers or women seeking abortions.
7. In 1997, the Court also upheld a 15-foot buffer zone. In another case, the Court decided that abortion clinics can invoke the federal racketeering law to sue violent anti-abortion protest groups for damages.

D. One of the most difficult issues facing our high-tech society is whether there is a right to *choose to die* or a right for parents to choose to allow their children to die.
   1. Many of the issues surrounding birth and death were crystallized in two "Baby Doe" cases in the early 1980's; both involved seriously ill babies that needed surgery to survive.
   2. Eventually, the Supreme Court affirmed parents' rights to make medical decisions for their children.

E. Other difficult issues facing society include who has custody of children produced by in-vitro fertilization and artificial insemination, and who has custody of frozen embryos.

F. In 1997, the Supreme Court ruled in *Vacco v. Quill* and *Washington v. Glucksberg* that there is no constitutional right to physician-assisted suicide and that states may prohibit it if they wish.

VI. UNDERSTANDING CIVIL LIBERTIES

A. American government is both *democratic* (because it is governed by officials elected by the people and answerable to them) and *constitutional* (because it has a fundamental organic law, the Constitution, that limits the things government can do).

B. The democratic and constitutional components of government can produce conflicts, but they also reinforce one another.

C. Civil liberties and democracy
   1. Individual rights may conflict with other values.

a. The rights guaranteed by the First Amendment are essential to a democracy.
b. Individual participation and the expression of ideas are crucial components of democracy, but so is majority rule, which can conflict with individual rights.
c. The rights guaranteed by the Fourth, Fifth, Sixth, and Eighth Amendments protect all Americans; but they also make it harder to punish criminals.

2. Ultimately, the courts decide what constitutional guarantees mean in practice: although the federal courts are the *branch of government least subject to majority rule*, the courts *enhance democracy by protecting liberty and equality from the excesses of majority rule.*

D. Civil liberties and the scope of government.
1. Today's government is huge and commands vast, powerful technologies.
2. Since Americans can no longer avoid the attention of government, strict limitations on governmental power are essential—limitations that are provided by the Bill of Rights.
3. In general, civil liberties limit the scope of government. However, in some instances, such as protecting the right to abortion, an expansion of freedom may require simultaneous expansion of government to protect those freedoms.

KEY TERMS AND CONCEPTS

Bill of Rights: The first ten amendments to the Constitution.

Civil Liberties: legal and constitutional protections against government infringement of political liberties and criminal rights.

Commercial Speech: communication in the form of advertising.

Cruel and unusual punishment: Eighth Amendment prohibits such punishment.

Eighth Amendment: forbids cruel and unusual punishment, although it does not define this phrase.

Establishment clause: First Amendment prohibits government from establishing a religion; is the basis for separation of church and state.

Exclusionary rule: prohibits government from including illegally obtained evidence in a trial.

Fifth Amendment: prohibits government from forcing individuals to testify against themselves.

First Amendment: establishes freedom of religion, press, speech, and assembly.

Fourteenth Amendment: prohibits states from denying equal protection of the laws.

Free exercise clause: government is prohibited in the First Amendment from interfering in the practice of religion.

Incorporation Doctrine: legal concept under which the Supreme Court has nationalized the Bill of Rights by making most of its provisions applicable to the states through the Fourteenth Amendment.

Libel: publication of false or malicious statements that damage someone's reputation.

Plea Bargaining: an actual bargain struck between the defendant's lawyer and the prosecutor to the effect that the defendant will plead guilty to a lesser crime (or fewer crimes) in exchange for the state's promise not to prosecute the defendant for a more serious (or additional) crime.

Prior restraint: government instrument to prevent material from being published.

Probable cause: police must have a good reason to arrest someone.

Right to privacy: a contrived right from unstated liberties in the Bill of Rights.

Search warrant: written authorization from a court specifying the area to be searched and what the police are searching for.

Self-incrimination: testifying against oneself.

Sixth Amendment: designed to protect individuals accused of crimes; includes the right to counsel, the right to confront witnesses, and the right to a speedy and public trial.

Symbolic Speech: political actions instead of words.

Unreasonable searches and seizures: obtaining evidence without a good reason.

KEY CASES

Barron v. Baltimore (1833)
Engel v. Vitale (1962)
Gideon v. Wainwright (1963)
Gitlow v. New York (1925)
Gregg v. Georgia (1976)
Lemon v. Kurtzman (1971)
Mapp v. Ohio (1961)
McCleskey v. Kemp (1987)
Miami Herald Publishing Co. v. Tornillo (1974)
Miller v. California (1973)
Miranda v. Arizona (1966)
NAACP v. Alabama (1954)
Near v. Minnesota (1931)
New York Times v. Sullivan (1964)
Planned Parenthood v. Casey (1992)
Red Lion Broadcasting Co. v. Federal Communications Commission (1969)
Roe v. Wade (1973)
Roth v. United States (1957)
Schenck v. United States (1919)
School District of Abington Township, Pennsylvaia v. Schempp (1963)
Texas v. Johnson (1989)
Zurcher v. Stanford (1976)

TEACHING IDEAS: CLASS DISCUSSION AND STUDENT PROJECTS

- Special features entitled *You Are the Judge* are dispersed throughout this chapter. Each feature describes an actual case brought before the courts and asks students to evaluate the case and render a judgment about it. Interesting class discussions could be based on these cases, particularly if you ask students to try to evaluate the reasoning behind the decisions. Take an informal survey to see how your class would have voted, then turn to the end of the chapter and review the actual court decisions, which are collected in a feature entitled *The Court Decides*.

- We know that people often support rights in theory, but their support may disappear when it comes time to put those rights into practice. Set aside part of one class period for students to list both supports and objections to extending rights to controversial and unpopular groups. You could "set the stage" by first introducing your class to one or two famous incidents, such as the demands of the American Nazi Party in 1977 to march through a Jewish neighborhood in Skokie, Illinois.

- The most famous case in recent years involving prior restraint and national security rose out of the release of the *Pentagon Papers*. Ask your class to envision themselves as a jury in the trial of Daniel Ellsberg. Did his actions constitute theft of government property, or were his actions justifiable since he was giving information to the American people? How would they vote?

- Although the Supreme Court has ruled that obscenity is not protected by the First Amendment, it has been difficult to determine precisely what is obscene. Ask your students to "try their hands" at writing a definition that could be used by a court or a censorship panel to distinguish *obscenity* from legally protected *art.*

- The textbook points out that libel is a freedom of expression that involves competing values. If public debate is not free, there can be no democracy; but with free public debate, some reputations will be unfairly damaged. Ask your class to consider the way in which the courts distinguish between *public persons* and *private persons*, and ask them to evaluate whether it is fair (or appropriate) to use this distinction. How would they change the process to make it more equitable? Would the public lose its ability to evaluate candidates for public office if candidates could sue for libel or slander as readily as persons who are not in the public eye? What rights of privacy should public figures retain?

- Ask your class to consider the problem of crime control, both from the position of protecting individual liberties for "unsavory" people in order to protect rights for everyone, and from the perspective of protecting the rights of "society" and of victims.

- One task that government must perform is to resolve conflicts between rights. Class participation can be animated if you will encourage your students to think about potential conflicts within the Bill of Rights, such as possible conflicts between public order and free speech. Ask your class to consider the nature of individual rights from the perspective of a victim's family and from the outlook of a defendant's family.

- Ask students to find the facts of a current conflict over civil liberties, either using the Internet or the daily newspaper and to lead a class discussion over these facts. What rights or values are in conflict? Ask students to explain how, and why, they would decide the case. Also encourage the students to follow the case over the course of the semester or quarter, and to write a brief essay describing the issues involved and their final position in the conflict.

  Each of the following exercises may be modified to be either class participation/debate assignments or writing assignments. In either case, they may also be modified to ask students to locate a particular case that serves as an example of the conflicting rights. Ask students to use Lexis/Nexis, the Internet, or other records to brief the class on the particular case (rather than discussing these rights in the abstract).

- There is a fine line between aid to parochial schools that is permissible and aid that is not. Divide the class into panels, and ask them to debate the merits and problems of government aid to church-related schools. Ask members of the panels to prepare for the debate by reading summaries of cases that are used in the textbook to illustrate the establishment clause of the Constitution. Also encourage panelists to research how recent decisions of the Supreme Court have modified these policies.

- A majority of the public has never favored the Court's decisions on school prayer. Assign short essays, in which each student would take one of the following positions: (1) The school prayer decisions demonstrate the Court's important role in protecting minority rights in the face of majority opinion; *or* (2) The school prayer decisions demonstrate how the Court has lost sight of the traditional values that were favored by the framers of the Constitution.

- Reporters argue that freedom of the press guarantees them certain rights that other potential witnesses cannot claim, such as the right to protect confidential sources, even in criminal trials. Divide the class in sections, with one section assigned the task of defending the right of journalists to shield confidential sources and the other section assigned the task of showing that reporters have no more rights than other citizens. Each section should select a spokesperson to present the group's analysis.

- Ask students to debate whether it is always preferable to support First Amendment rights over all others. In particular, should government limit religious practices which include such activities as dancing with snakes or the taking of illegal drugs? Should government limit the right of the press to publish the names of victims of violent sex crimes? Such questions will reinforce the difficulty of protecting liberties when two or more come into conflict.

- Have students do a clipping file of current or recent events involving violations of civil liberties and the expansion of government. Ask them to write an essay identifying the violations and to describe how government has expanded as a result of efforts to provide protections.

BACKGROUND READING

Amar, Akhil Reed. The Bill of Rights: Construction and Reconstruction. New Haven: Yale University Press. 1998.

Amar, Akhil Reed. For the People: What the Constitution Really Says About Your Rights. New York: Free Press. 1998.

Carpenter, Ted Galen. The Captive Press: Foreign Policy Crises and the First Amendment. Washington DC: Cato Institute. 1995

Devins, Neal. Shaping Constitutional Values: Elected Government, the Supreme Court and the Abortion Debate. Baltimore: Johns Hopkins University Press. 1996.

Domino, John C. Civil Rights and Liberties: Toward the Twenty-first Century. New York: Addison-Wesley. 1994.

Leo, Richard A., and George C. Thomas III, eds. The Miranda Debate: Law, Justice and Policing. Boston: Northeastern University Press. 1998.

Levy, Leonard W., ed. Freedom of the Press from Zenger to Jefferson. 1996.

Levy, Leonard W. Origins of the Bill of Rights. New Haven and London: Yale University Press. 1999.

Lewis, Anthony. Gideon's Trumpet. New York: Vintage Books. 1989.

MEDIA SUGGESTIONS

The American Civil Liberties Union: A History. Provides an overview of the development of the ACLU, highlighting the major civil rights and liberties cases and issues in which it has been involved since its inception. Films for the Humanities & Sciences.

Bill of Rights: Bill of Responsibilities. 1995. This film provides a practical example of the impact of the Bill of Rights on the daily lives of individuals using current events and pop culture. Insight Media.

Bill of Rights: Bill of Responsibility. This program, hosted by Bill Maher of television's "Politically Incorrect," considers the meaning of the Constitution and the Bill of Rights in the context of current political issues and controversies. Films for the Humanities & Sciences.

First Amendment Freedoms. Part of the "Government by Consent" series produced by Insight Media. This 1989 video examines the current status of the First Amendment in American political culture.

For Which It Stands: Flag Burning and the First Amendment. 1992. Features a debate between supporters and opponents of flag burning as a First Amendment right. Close Up Publishing.

Keeping the Faith: Religion and Democracy. 1996. This film examines the role of religion in the U.S. and examines the issue of separation between church and state. Films for the Humanities and Sciences.

Politics in Action. Chapter 7: Political Debate, Civil Rights and the Judicial Process. Includes sections on a variety of issues relating to abortion, such as Roe v. Wade, regulating abortion, counseling about abortion and protesting abortion.

CHAPTER FIVE: CIVIL RIGHTS AND PUBLIC POLICY

PEDAGOGICAL FEATURES

LEARNING OBJECTIVES

After studying this chapter, students should be able to:

- Understand how civil rights have been used to extend more equality to groups that historically have been subject to discrimination.

- Analyze different interpretations of *equality*, such as equality of opportunity contrasted with equality of results.
- Identify provisions of the Bill of Rights that have implications for equality.
- Explain how the Fourteenth Amendment guarantee of "equal protection of the laws" has been applied to the idea of equality.
- Examine how the Supreme Court has used different levels of judicial scrutiny for racial, ethnic, and gender classifications.
- Explain how the Supreme Court provided a constitutional justification for segregation in the 1896 case of *Plessy* v. *Ferguson.*
- Summarize the reasoning of the Court in the 1954 case of *Brown* v. *Board of Education* and use this case to show how the Court set aside its earlier precedent in *Plessy* v. *Ferguson.*
- Determine how the distinction between *de jure* and *de facto* segregation has sometimes been blurred by past practices.
- Explain how sit-ins, marches, and civil disobedience were used as key strategies of the civil rights movement of the 1950s and 1960s.
- Show the significance of the Civil Rights Act of 1964 and explain why efforts for civil rights legislation were finally successful in the mid-1960s.
- Trace the attempts of southern states to deny African Americans the right to vote even after the passage of the Fifteenth Amendment.
- Identify the major public policy milestones in the movement toward gender equality.
- Determine the ways in which Americans with disabilities have become the successors to the civil rights movement.
- Explain why gay and lesbian activists may face the toughest battle for equality of any of America's minority groups.
- Evaluate the opposing positions of those who favor affirmative action and those who claim that these policies simply create reverse discrimination.

- Analyze how the important democratic principles of *equality* and *individual liberty* may actually conflict with each other.

- Determine how civil rights laws increase the scope and power of government.

CHAPTER OVERVIEW

INTRODUCTION

When the value of equality conflicts with the value of liberty—when individuals in privileged positions are challenged to give them up—citizens often look to the government to resolve the issue. This chapter examines what the Constitution says about equality and how constitutional rights to equality have been interpreted. It also reviews the development of civil rights in the United States, highlighting the important role of the court system in expanding equality over the past three decades.

RACIAL EQUALITY: TWO CENTURIES OF STRUGGLE

The real meaning of equality is both elusive and divisive. Most Americans favor **equality** in the abstract, but the concrete struggle for equal rights has been our nation's most bitter battle. The rallying call for groups demanding more equality has been **civil rights**, which are policies that extend basic rights to groups historically subject to discrimination. Philosophically, the struggle for equality involves defining the term; constitutionally, it involves interpreting laws; politically, it often involves power.

American society does not emphasize equal results or equal rewards. A belief in equal rights has often led to a belief in equality of opportunity. Today's debates over inequality in America center on racial discrimination, gender discrimination, and discrimination based on factors such as age, disability, and sexual preference.

The delegates to the Constitutional Convention came up with a plan for government rather than guarantees of individual rights, and the word *equality* does not even appear in the original Constitution. The only place in which the idea of equality clearly appears in the Constitution is in the **Fourteenth Amendment**, which prohibits the states from denying *"equal protection of the laws"* to any person. It was not until the mid-twentieth century that the Fourteenth Amendment was used to assure rights for disadvantaged groups, but the equal protection clause gradually became the vehicle for more expansive constitutional interpretations.

The Court has developed three levels of *judicial scrutiny* (or *classifications*). Most classifications that are **reasonable** (that bear a rational relationship to some legitimate governmental purpose) are constitutional. Racial and ethnic classifications are **inherently suspect**—they are presumed to be invalid and are upheld only if they serve a *"compelling public interest"* that cannot be accomplished in some other way. Classifications based on gender fall somewhere between *reasonable* and *inherently suspect*—gender classifications must bear a **substantial** relationship to an *important legislative purpose.*

RACE, THE CONSTITUTION, AND PUBLIC POLICY

African Americans have been the most visible minority group in the United States, and the civil rights laws that African-American groups pushed for have also benefited members of other minority groups. Three eras define African Americans' struggle for equality in America: the era of slavery, from the beginnings of colonization until the end of the Civil War; the era of Reconstruction and resegregation, from the end of the Civil War until 1954; and the era of civil rights, from 1954 to the present.

The delegates to the Constitutional Convention did their best to avoid facing the divergence between slavery and the principles of the Declaration of Independence. During the slavery era, any public policy of the slave states or the federal government had to accommodate the property interests of slave owners. The Union victory in the Civil War and the ratification of the **Thirteenth Amendment** ended slavery. After the Civil War ended, Congress imposed strict conditions on the former Confederate states before they could be readmitted to the Union. Many African-American men held state and federal offices during the ten years following the war. As soon as they regained control following Reconstruction, white Southerners imposed a code of **"Jim Crow laws"** that required African Americans to use separate public facilities and school systems.

The early Republic limited **suffrage** primarily to property-holding white males. The **Fifteenth Amendment** (1870) guaranteed African Americans the right to vote, but full *implementation* did not occur for another century. States used various methods to circumvent the Fifteenth Amendment, including literacy tests with grandfather clauses, white primaries, and poll taxes. During this period, segregation was legally required in the South (***de jure***) and sanctioned in the North (***de facto***). The Supreme Court provided constitutional justification for segregation in ***Plessy* v. *Ferguson*** (1896) when it held that segregation in public facilities was not unconstitutional as long as the facilities were *substantially equal* (a principle that was commonly referred to as the **"separate but equal"** doctrine, though subsequent decisions paid more attention to the "separate" than to the "equal" part).

Although some limited progress was made in the first half of the twentieth century, the Supreme Court decision in ***Brown* v. *Board of Education*** (1954) really marks the beginning of the era of civil rights. In a landmark decision, the Court held that school segregation was *inherently unconstitutional* because it violated the Fourteenth Amendment's guarantee of *equal protection*. The modern **civil rights movement** began in 1955 when Rosa Parks refused to give up her seat in the front of a Montgomery, Alabama, bus (where only whites were permitted to sit). The boycott that followed her arrest is often seen as the beginning of the African-American civil rights movement. Sit-ins, marches, and civil disobedience were key strategies of the civil rights movement.

Desegregation proceeded slowly in the South, and some federal judges ordered the *busing* of students to achieve *racially balanced schools*. The **Civil Rights Act of 1964** made racial discrimination illegal in hotels, motels, restaurants, and other places of public accommodation. The Act also forbade many forms of job discrimination, and Congress cut off federal aid to schools that remained segregated. The **Voting Rights Act of 1965** prohibited any government from using voting procedures that denied a person the vote on the basis of race or color. Poll taxes in federal elections were prohibited by the **Twenty-fourth Amendment** (1964), and poll taxes in state elections were invalidated by the Supreme Court two years later (*Harper* v. *Virginia State Board of Elections*).

The civil rights laws that African-American groups pushed for have benefited members of other minority groups such as American Indians, Asians, and Hispanics. The United States is heading toward a *minority majority* status, when minority groups will outnumber Caucasians of European descent. Hispanic Americans will soon displace African Americans as the largest minority group.

WOMEN, THE CONSTITUTION, AND PUBLIC POLICY

The first women's rights activists were products of the abolitionist movement. The legal doctrine of **coverture** deprived married women of any identity separate from that of their husbands. Lucretia Mott and Elizabeth Cady Stanton organized a meeting at Seneca Falls, New York, to discuss women's rights. The *Seneca Falls Declaration of Sentiments and Resolutions* (signed on July 19, 1848) was the beginning of the movement that would culminate in the ratification of the **Nineteenth Amendment** (1920), which gave women the right to vote.

The feminist movement seemed to lose momentum after winning the vote, possibly because the vote was about the only goal on which all feminists agreed. Public policy toward women continued to be dominated by *protectionism* (which also protected male workers from female competition), and state laws tended to reflect and reinforce the traditional family roles.

Before the advent of the contemporary feminist movement, the Supreme Court upheld virtually all cases of sex-based discrimination. In ***Reed* v. *Reed*** (1971), the Court ruled that any "arbitrary" sex-based classification violated the equal protection clause of the Fourteenth Amendment (marking the first time the Court applied the Fourteenth Amendment to a case involving classification by sex). Five years later, ***Craig* v. *Boren*** established a "medium scrutiny" standard: Gender discrimination would be presumed to be neither valid nor invalid. The courts were to show less deference to gender classifications than to more routine classifications, but more deference than to racial classifications. The Supreme Court has now ruled on many occasions against gender discrimination in employment and business activity. Some of the litigants have been *men seeking equality with women* in their treatment under the law.

Some important progress was made through congressional legislation. The *Civil Rights Act of 1964* banned sex discrimination in employment; in 1972, the *Equal Employment Opportunity Commission (EEOC)* was given the power to sue employers suspected of illegal discrimination; and *Title IX of the Education Act of 1972* forbade sex discrimination in federally subsidized education programs, including athletics. The Court has remained silent so far on the issue of **"comparable worth"** (which refers to the fact that traditional women's jobs often pay much less than men's jobs that demand comparable skill).

Women now comprise 11 percent of the armed forces and compete directly with men for promotion. Statutes and regulations prohibit women from serving in combat, but the Persian Gulf War demonstrates that policy and practice are not always the same, since women piloted helicopters at the front and some were taken as prisoners of war.

Many women are now making claims for their civil rights. In the 1990s, national attention has focused on issues of **sexual harassment.** For example, the Supreme Court again spoke expansively about sexual harassment in the workplace in *Faragher v. City of Boca Raton*. The Court made it clear that employers are responsible for preventing and eliminating harassment at work. They can be held liable for even those harassing acts of supervisory employees that violate clear policies and of which top management has no knowledge.

NEWLY ACTIVE GROUPS UNDER THE CIVIL RIGHTS UMBRELLA

New activist groups now realize that policies that were enacted to protect racial minorities and women can also be applied to other groups. Aging Americans, young Americans, the disabled, and homosexuals have begun to exert their own demands for civil rights.

People in their eighties comprise the fastest growing age group in this country. It is not clear what the fate of the **gray liberation movement** will be as its members approach the status of a *minority majority.*

Young people have also suffered from inferior treatment under the law. There are obvious difficulties in organizing a "children's rights movement," but there have been instances of young people who were successful in asserting their rights (including a youth who "divorced" his parents).

Americans with disabilities have suffered from both direct and indirect discrimination. The **Americans with Disabilities Act of 1990** requires employers and public facilities to provide *"reasonable accommodations"* and prohibits employment discrimination against the disabled.

Gay activists *may face the toughest battle for equality.* Homosexual activity is illegal in some states, and homosexuals often face prejudice in hiring, education, access to public accommodations, and housing. A substantial percentage of the American public express opposition to homosexuals entering many common occupations. However, gay activists have won some important victories. Seven states and more than 100 communities have passed laws protecting homosexuals against some forms of discrimination.

AFFIRMATIVE ACTION

The interests of women and minorities have converged on the issue of **affirmative action** (policies requiring special efforts in employment, promotion or school admissions on behalf of disadvantaged groups). The goal of affirmative action is to *move beyond equal opportunity* toward *equal results.*

Some groups have claimed that affirmative action programs constitute **"reverse discrimination."** In ***Regents of the University of California* v. *Bakke*** (1978), the Supreme Court rejected a plan at the University of California at Davis that set aside 16 out of a total of 100 places in the entering class for "disadvantaged groups." The Court objected to the use of a quota of positions for particular groups, but the Court said that a university could use race or ethnic background as one component in the admissions procedure. The Court has also permitted a special training program that was intended to rectify years of past discrimination (*United Steelworkers of America, AFL-CIO* v. *Weber*, 1979). However, in 1995, in ***Adarand Constructors* v. *Pena***, the Court held that federal programs that classify people by race, even for an ostensibly benign purpose such as expanding opportunities for minorities, should be presumed to be unconstitutional.

In 1996, California voters passed Proposition 209, which banned state affirmative action programs based on race, ethnicity, or gender in public hiring, contracting, and education admissions. Opponents immediately filed a lawsuit in federal court to block enforcement of the law, claiming that it violated the Fourteenth Amendment. Ultimately, the U.S. Supreme Court will have to resolve the issue, but there is little question that support for Proposition 209 represents a widespread skepticism about affirmative action programs.

Surveys find that most Americans oppose affirmative action programs, even though Americans in general support nondiscrimination in employment and education. Opposition is especially strong when people view affirmative action as *reverse discrimination* where less qualified individuals get hired or admitted to educational or training programs.

Affirmative action supporters believe that increasing the number of women and minorities in desirable jobs is such an important social goal that it should be considered when determining an individual's qualifications. They claim that what white males lose from affirmative action programs are privileges to which they were never entitled in the first place; after all, nobody has the right to be a doctor or a road dispatcher.

UNDERSTANDING CIVIL RIGHTS AND PUBLIC POLICY

Democracy is often in conflict with itself—both *equality* and *individual liberty* are important democratic principles, but they *may conflict with each other.* For example, equality tends to favor majority rule, but equality threatens individual liberty in situations where the majority may want to deprive the minority of its rights.

Civil rights laws increase the *scope and power of government* since these laws place both restrictions and obligations on individuals and institutions. Libertarians and those conservatives who want to reduce the size of government are uneasy with civil rights laws (and sometimes hostile to them).

CHAPTER OUTLINE

I. TWO CENTURIES OF STRUGGLE

A. Most Americans favor **equality** in the *abstract*, but the *concrete struggle for equal rights* has been our nation's most bitter battle.

B. The real meaning of equality is both elusive and divisive.

1. **Civil rights** are the policies that extend basic rights to groups historically subject to discrimination.
2. The modern **civil rights movement** began in 1965 when Rosa Parks refused to give up her seat in the front of a Montgomery, Alabama, bus (where only whites were permitted to sit); the boycott that followed her arrest is often seen as the beginning of the African-American civil rights movement.

C. Today's debates over inequality in America center on racial discrimination, gender discrimination, and factors such as discrimination based on age, disability, and sexual preference.

D. Conceptions of equality.

1. Philosophically, the struggle for equality involves defining the term; constitutionally, it involves interpreting laws; politically, it often involves power.
2. American society does not emphasize equal results or equal rewards—a belief in equal rights has often led to a belief in equality of *opportunity*.

E. Early American views of equality.

1. Jefferson's statement in the Declaration of Independence that "all men are created equal" did not mean that he thought there were no differences among people.
2. Few colonists were eager to defend slavery, and the delegates to the Constitutional Convention *did their best to avoid* facing the divergence between slavery and the principles of the Declaration of Independence.
3. Women's rights received even less attention than did slavery at the Convention.

F. The Constitution and inequality.

1. The delegates to the Constitutional Convention came up with *a plan for government*, not guarantees of individual rights: the word *equality* does not even appear in the original Constitution.

a. Even the Bill of Rights does not directly mention equality, but it does have implications for the principle of equality since it does not limit the scope of its guarantees to any specified groups.
b. The only place in which the idea of equality clearly appears in the Constitution is in the **Fourteenth Amendment**, which prohibits the states from denying "*equal protection of the laws*" to any person.

2. What does **equal protection of the laws** mean?
   a. It was not until the mid-twentieth century that the Fourteenth Amendment was used to assure rights for disadvantaged groups.
   b. Over the last one hundred years, the equal protection clause has become the vehicle for more expansive constitutional interpretations.
3. The Court has developed three levels of *judicial scrutiny* (or *classifications*).
   a. Most classifications that are **reasonable** (that bear a rational relationship to some legitimate governmental purpose) are constitutional.
   b. Racial and ethnic classifications are **inherently suspect**: they are presumed to be invalid and are upheld only if they serve a *"compelling public interest"* that cannot be accomplished in some other way.
   c. Classifications based on gender fit somewhere between *reasonable* and *inherently suspect*: gender classifications must bear a **substantial** relationship to an *important legislative purpose* (and is sometimes called "*medium scrutiny*").

II. RACE, THE CONSTITUTION, AND PUBLIC POLICY

A. The civil rights laws that African American groups pushed for have also benefited members of other minority groups.

B. Three eras define African Americans' struggle for equality in America: the era of slavery, from the beginnings of colonization until the end of the Civil War; the era of reconstruction and resegregation, from the end of the Civil War until 1954; and the era of civil rights, from 1954 to the present.

C. The era of slavery (1600s-1865).
   1. During the slavery era, any public policy of the slave states or the federal government had to accommodate the property interests of slave owners.
   2. The most infamous statement in defense of slavery occurred in ***Dred Scott* v. *Sandford*** (1857), in which Chief Justice Taney declared that an African-American man was "chattel" and had no rights under a white man's government; Congress had no power to ban slavery in

the western territories (thereby effectively invalidating the *Missouri Compromise*).

3. The Union victory in the Civil War and the ratification of the **Thirteenth Amendment** ended slavery.

D. The era of reconstruction and resegregation (end of Civil War to 1954).

1. After the Civil War ended, Congress imposed strict conditions on the former Confederate States before they could be readmitted to the Union.
2. As soon as they regained power, white Southerners imposed a code of **"Jim Crow laws,"** or *Black Codes* (segregation laws that required African-Americans to use separate public facilities and school systems); although not required *by law*, segregation was also *common practice* in the North.
3. In the era of segregation, housing, schools, and jobs were—in one way or another—classified as "white" or "colored."
4. The Supreme Court provided constitutional justification for segregation in ***Plessy* v. *Ferguson*** (1896) when it held that segregation in public facilities was not unconstitutional as long as the facilities were *substantially equal* (a principle that was commonly referred to as the **"separate but equal"** doctrine, though subsequent decisions paid more attention to the "separate" than to the "equal" part).
5. Some limited progress was made in the first half of the twentieth century, including executive orders (such as desegregation of the armed forces) and court decisions (including ***Guinn* v. *United States***, 1915, which banned the grandfather clause in voting; ***Smith* v. *Allwright***, 1944, overturning all-white primaries; and ***Sweatt* v. *Painter***, 1950, which held that blacks are entitled to the same professional and graduate education as students of other races).

E. The era of civil rights (1954-present).

1. During the period leading up to the civil rights movement, segregation was legally required in the South (***de jure***) and sanctioned in the North (***de facto***).
2. ***Brown* v. *Board of Education*** (1954) marks the *beginning of the era of civil rights*.
    a. The Supreme Court used *Brown* to set aside its earlier precedent of *Plessy* v. *Ferguson* (1896).
    b. In a landmark decision, the Court held that school segregation was *inherently unconstitutional* because it violated the Fourteenth Amendment's guarantee of *equal protection*.
    c. In 1955, the Court ordered lower courts to proceed with "all deliberate speed" to desegregate public schools; however,

desegregation moved very slowly until the passage of the **Civil Rights Act of 1964**, which denied federal funds to segregated schools.

3. The **civil rights movement** organized both African Americans and whites to end the policies and practices of segregation.
   a. The movement began in 1955 when Rosa Parks refused to give up her seat in the front of a Montgomery, Alabama, bus (where only whites were allowed to sit); her arrest led to a boycott led by Rev. Martin Luther King, Jr.
   b. *Sit-ins, marches, and civil disobedience* were key strategies of the civil rights movement, which sought to establish *equal opportunities* in the *political and economic sectors* and to bring an end to policies that put up barriers against people because of race.
4. The 1950s and 1960s saw a marked increase in public policies designed to foster racial equality.
   a. The Civil Rights Act of 1964 made racial discrimination illegal in hotels, motels, restaurants, and other places of public accommodation; it also forbade many forms of job discrimination, and Congress cut off federal aid to schools that remained segregated.
   b. Desegregation proceeded slowly in the South and some federal judges ordered the *busing* of students to achieve *racially balanced schools* (upheld by the Supreme Court in ***Swann* v. *Charlotte-Mecklenberg County Schools***, 1971).

F. Getting and using the right to vote.
   1. The early Republic limited **suffrage** (the legal right to vote) primarily to property-holding white males.
   2. The **Fifteenth Amendment** (1870) guaranteed African Americans the right to vote, but full *implementation* did not occur for another century.
   3. States used various methods to circumvent the Fifteenth Amendment:
      a. **Grandfather clause** - exempted persons whose grandfathers were eligible to vote in 1860 from taking *literacy tests* in order to vote; the exemption obviously did not apply to grandchildren of slaves (declared unconstitutional in *Guinn* v. *U.S.*, 1915).
      b. **Poll tax** - small taxes levied on the right to vote; the taxes often fell due at a time of year when poor sharecroppers had the least amount of cash available.
      c. **White primary** - permitted political parties in the heavily Democratic south to exclude blacks from primary elections, on the pretext that political parties (and primaries) were private and

not public institutions; this device deprived blacks of a voice in the primaries, where the *real contest* occurred (declared unconstitutional in *Smith* v. *Allwright*, 1944).

   d. Many areas in the South employed **voter registration** tests (sometimes called **voter literacy tests**) in a discriminatory manner; some of the tests checked for an understanding of the Constitution.

4. The civil rights movement put suffrage high on its political agenda, and many barriers to African-American voting fell during the 1960s.
   a. Poll taxes in federal elections were prohibited by the **Twenty-fourth Amendment** (1964); poll taxes in state elections were invalidated two years later in *Harper* v. *Virginia State Board of Elections*.
   b. The **Voting Rights Act of 1965** prohibited any government from using voting procedures that denied a person the vote on the basis of race or color.
      (1) Federal election registrars were sent to areas that had long *histories of discrimination*, and many African-Americans were registered in southern states as a direct result.
      (2) The Voting Rights Act produced a major increase in the number of African-Americans registered to vote in the southern states, and in the number of African-Americans who held public office.

G. The civil rights laws that African-American groups pushed for have benefited members of other minority groups such as American Indians, Asians, and Hispanics. The United States is heading toward a *minority majority* status, when minority groups will outnumber Caucasians of European descent.

1. Native Americans:
   a. The oldest minority group in America, but they were not made U.S. citizens until 1924.
   b. The *Indian Claims Act* was enacted in 1946 to settle financial disputes arising from land taken from the Indians.
2. Hispanic Americans:
   a. Will *soon displace* African Americans *as the largest minority group*.
3. Asian Americans:
   a. The *fastest growing minority group*.
   b. During World War II, the U.S. government rounded up more than 100,000 Americans of Japanese descent and placed them in *internment encampments* known as "war relocation centers."

c. The Supreme Court upheld the internment as constitutional in ***Korematsu* v. *United States*** (1944), but Congress later provided benefits for the former internees (which still have not been distributed).

III. WOMEN, THE CONSTITUTION, AND PUBLIC POLICY

A. The struggle for women's equality has *emphasized legislation over litigation.*

B. The battle for the vote.
1. The *first women's rights activists* were products of the *abolition* movement.
2. The legal doctrine of **coverture** deprived married women of any identity separate from that of their husbands.
3. Lucretia Mott and Elizabeth Cady Stanton organized a meeting at Seneca Falls, New York, to discuss women's rights.
4. The *Seneca Falls Declaration of Sentiments and Resolutions* (signed on July 19, 1848) was the beginning of the movement that would culminate in the ratification of the **Nineteenth Amendment** (1920), which gave women the right to vote.

C. The "doldrums": 1920-1960.
1. The feminist movement seemed to lose momentum after winning the vote, possibly because the vote was about the only goal on which all feminists agreed.
2. Alice Paul, the author of the **Equal Rights Amendment (ERA),** claimed that the real result of protectionist law was to perpetuate *sexual inequality*; but most people in the 1920s saw the ERA as a *threat to the family.*

D. The second feminist wave.
1. The civil rights movement of the 1950s and 1960s attracted many women activists.
2. Groups like the *National Organization for Women (NOW)* and the *National Women's Political Caucus* were organized in the 1960s and 1970s.
3. Judicial development.
   a. Before the advent of the contemporary feminist movement, the Supreme Court upheld virtually all cases of sex-based discrimination.
   b. In ***Reed* v. *Reed*** (1971), the Court ruled that any "arbitrary" sex-based classification violated the equal protection clause of the Fourteenth Amendment (marking the first time the Court applied the Fourteenth Amendment to a case involving classification by sex).

   c. In ***Craig* v. *Boren*** (1976), the Court established a "*medium scrutiny" standard,* under which sex discrimination would be presumed to be neither valid nor invalid.
   d. The Supreme Court has now struck down many laws and rules for discriminating on the basis of gender; some of the litigants have been *men seeking equality with women* in their treatment under the law.
4. The ERA was revived when Congress passed it in 1972 and granted a three-year extension six years later; the ERA fell three states short of ratification, but losing the ERA battle has stimulated vigorous feminist activity.

E. Women in the Workplace.
1. As conditions have changed, public opinion and public policy demands have also changed.
   a. The traditional family role of father at work/mother at home is becoming a thing of the past.
   b. The civilian labor force includes 64 million women (74 million males).
   c. There are 30 million female-headed households; about two-thirds of American mothers who have children below school age are in the labor force.
2. Some important progress was made through congressional legislation:
   a. The *Civil Rights Act of 1964* banned sex discrimination in employment.
   b. In 1972, the *Equal Employment Opportunity Commission (EEOC)* was given the power to sue employers suspected of illegal discrimination.
   c. *Title IX of the Education Act of 1972* forbade sex discrimination in federally subsidized education programs, including athletics.
   d. Three of the most controversial issues that legislators will continue to face are wage discrimination, the role of women in the military, and sexual harassment.
3. The Supreme Court has frequently ruled against gender discrimination in employment and business activity.

F. Wage discrimination and comparable worth.
1. The U.S. Supreme Court has remained silent so far on the issue of **"comparable worth,"** which refers to the fact that traditional women's jobs often pay much less than men's jobs that demand comparable skill.
2. Median annual earnings for full-time women workers are only about two-thirds those of men.

G. Women in the military.
   1. Women have served in every branch of the armed services since World War II (originally in separate units, but now part of the regular service).
   2. Women comprise 11 percent of the armed forces, and compete directly with men for promotion.
   3. There are still two important differences between the treatment of men and women in military service:
      a. Only men must register for the draft when they turn age eighteen (upheld in *Rostker* v. *Goldberg*, 1981).
      b. Statutes and regulations prohibit women from serving in combat.

H. **Sexual harassment** can occur anywhere, but may be especially prevalent in male-dominated occupations such as the military. Sexual harassment violates federal policies against sexual discrimination in the workplace (although it was not a violation of federal policy when Anita Hill worked for Clarence Thomas).
   1. In ***Harris v. Forklift Systems*** (1993), the Supreme Court held that no single factor is required to win a sexual harassment case under Title VII of the 1964 Civil Rights Act. The law is violated when the workplace environment "would reasonably be perceived, and is perceived, as hostile or abusive."
   2. In 1996 and 1997, a number of army officers and noncommissioned officers had their careers ended, and some went to prison, for sexual harassment of female soldiers in training situations.
   3. In ***Faragher v. City of Boca Raton*** (1998), the Supreme Court stated that employers can be held liable for even those harassing acts of supervisory employees that violate clear policies and of which top management has no knowledge.

IV. NEWLY ACTIVE GROUPS UNDER THE CIVIL RIGHTS UMBRELLA

A. New activist groups began to realize that policies that were enacted to protect racial minorities and women can also be applied to other groups, such as aging Americans, young Americans, the disabled, and homosexuals.

B. Civil rights and the graying of America.
   1. People in their eighties comprise the fastest growing age group in this country.
   2. Since 1967, Congress has passed several laws that ban various types of age discrimination.
   3. It is not clear what the fate of the **gray liberation movement** will be as its members approach the status of a *minority majority*.

C. Are the young a disadvantaged group, too?
   1. Young people have also suffered from inferior treatment under the law.
   2. There are obvious difficulties in organizing a "children's rights movement," but there have been instances of young people who were successful in asserting their rights (illustrated by Walter Polovchak, who refused to return to the Ukraine with his parents, and a 12-year-old boy in Florida who "divorced" his family so he could be adopted by foster parents).
D. Civil rights and people with disabilities.
   1. Americans with disabilities have suffered from both direct and indirect discrimination.
   2. The first rehabilitation laws were passed in the late 1920s; the *Rehabilitation Act of 1973* (twice vetoed by President Nixon as "too costly") added disabled people to the list of Americans protected from discrimination.
   3. The **Americans with Disabilities Act of 1990** requires employers and public facilities to provide *"reasonable accommodations,"* and prohibits employment discrimination against the disabled.
   4. Questions have been raised over whether AIDS victims are handicapped and thus entitled to protection. So far, no case dealing with AIDS victims has reached the Supreme Court.
E. Gay and lesbian rights.
   1. Gay (or homosexual) activists *may face the toughest battle for equality*.
      a. Homosexual activity is illegal in some states, and homosexuals often face prejudice in hiring, education, access to public accommodations, and housing.
      b. There are no positive stereotypes commonly associated with homosexuality.
      c. *Homophobia* (fear and hatred of homosexuals) has many causes, and homosexuals are often seen as safe targets for public hostility.
      d. A substantial percentage of the American public express opposition to homosexuals entering many common occupations.
      e. In 1993, President Clinton announced a new policy that barred the Pentagon from asking recruits or service personnel to disclose their sexual orientation. Popularly known as the "don't ask, don't tell" policy, it also reaffirmed the Defense Department's strict prohibition against homosexual conduct.
   2. Despite some setbacks, gay activists have won some important victories.

a. Seven states and more than one-hundred communities have passed laws protecting homosexuals against some forms of discrimination.
b. Most colleges and universities now have gay rights organizations on campus.

V. AFFIRMATIVE ACTION
A. The interests of women and minorities have converged on the issue of **affirmative action** (policies requiring special efforts on behalf of disadvantaged groups).
1. Affirmative action involves efforts to bring about increased employment, promotion, or admission for members of such groups.
2. The goal of affirmative action is to *move beyond equal opportunity* toward *equal results*.
3. The federal government has mandated that all state and local governments—together with each institution receiving aid from or contracting with the federal government—adopt an affirmative action program.
B. Some groups have claimed that affirmative action programs constitute **"reverse discrimination."**
1. In ***Regents of the University of California* v. *Bakke*** (1978), the Court rejected a plan at the University of California at Davis that set aside 16 of a total of 100 places in the entering medical school class for "disadvantaged groups."
a. The Court said a university could not set aside a *quota* of spots for particular groups.
b. However, the Court said that a university could adopt an "admissions program where race or ethnic background is simply one element in the selection process."
2. The following year, the Court ruled that a voluntary union-and-management-sponsored program was *not* discriminatory because the Kaiser Aluminum Company's special training program was intended to rectify years of past employment discrimination at Kaiser (*United Steelworkers of America, AFL-CIO* v. *Weber*, 1979).
C. In other cases, the Court has ruled that public employers may use affirmative action plans to counter under-representation of women and minorities, but the Court has also ruled that affirmative action does not exempt recently hired minorities from traditional work rules specifying the "last hired, first fired" order of layoffs.
D. Opposition to affirmative action policies.

1. Surveys find that most Americans oppose affirmative action programs, even though Americans in general support nondiscrimination in employment and education.
2. Opposition is especially strong when people view affirmative action as reverse discrimination where less qualified individuals get hired or admitted to educational or training programs.
3. In 1996, California voters passed Proposition 209, which banned state affirmative action programs based on race, ethnicity, or gender in public hiring, contracting, and educational admissions. Ultimately the U.S. Supreme Court will decide the issue.

VI. UNDERSTANDING CIVIL RIGHTS AND THE CONSTITUTION

A. Civil rights and democracy.
   1. Democracy is often in conflict with itself: both *equality* and *individual liberty* are important democratic principles, but they *may conflict with each other.*
      a. Equality tends to favor *majority rule*, but *equality threatens individual liberty* in situations where the majority wants to deprive the minority of its rights.
      b. Majority rule is not the only threat to liberty: *minorities* have suppressed majorities as well as other minorities.
   2. Even when they lacked the power of the vote, both African Americans and women made many gains by using other rights (such as the First Amendment freedoms) to fight for equality.

B. Civil rights and the scope of government.
   1. Civil rights laws increase the *scope and power of government.*
      a. These laws place both restrictions and obligations on individuals and institutions—they tell individuals and institutions that there are things they must do and other things they cannot do.
      b. Libertarians and those conservatives who want to reduce the size of government are uneasy with these laws (and sometimes hostile to them).
   2. Civil rights is an area in which *increased government activity in protecting basic rights* can lead to *greater checks on the government* by those who benefit from such protections.

KEY TERMS AND CONCEPTS

Affirmative action: a policy designed to give special consideration to those previously discriminated against.

Americans with Disabilities Act of 1990: strengthened protections of individuals with disabilities by requiring employers and public facilities to make "reasonable accommodations" and prohibiting employment discrimination against people with disabilities.

Civil rights: extending citizenship rights to participate to those previously denied them.

Civil Rights Act of 1964: forbids discrimination in public accommodations and facilities.

Comparable worth: equal pay for equal worth.

Equal Protection of the Laws: provided by the Fourteenth Amendment mandating that all people be protected by the law.

Equal rights amendment: proposal that equality of rights under the law not be denied on the account of sex.

Fifteenth Amendment: provides the right to vote for blacks.

Fourteenth Amendment: prohibits states from denying equal protection of the laws.

Nineteenth Amendment: provided women with the right to vote.

Poll Taxes: taxes levied on the right to vote designed to hurt poor blacks.

Suffrage: the legal right to vote.

Thirteenth Amendment: abolished slavery and involuntary servitude.

Twenty-fourth Amendment: prohibited poll taxes in federal elections.

Voting Rights Act of 1965: a policy designed to reduce the barriers to voting for those suffering discrimination.

White Primary: practice where only whites could vote in primaries.

KEY CASES

Adarand Constructors v. Pena (1995)
Brown v. *Board of Education* (1954)
Craig v. *Boren* (1976)
Dred Scott v. *Sandford* (1857)
Korematsu v. *United States* (1944)
Plessy v. *Ferguson* (1896)
Reed v. *Reed* (1971)
Regents of the University of California v. *Bakke* (1978)

TEACHING IDEAS: CLASS DISCUSSION AND STUDENT PROJECTS

- Have your students select a court case that is currently in the news or being discussed on the Internet that has implications for civil rights. The class should follow the case as it develops and try to evaluate how well it fits within the framework of what they have been reading in the textbook.

- As a class project, have your class look up magazine and newspaper articles from the World War II era when Americans of Japanese descent were sent to war relocation centers. In your students' opinions, did the fear of a Japanese invasion of the Pacific Coast adequately explain what happened? Or is this an example of racism, as many have charged? Ask one group of students to review the Court decision (and public reaction) in *Korematsu* v. *United States*, as well as the recent decision to pay families sent to relocation centers for damages incurred. Do you agree with this decision?

- Suggest that your students compare the Equal Rights Amendment with the Fourteenth Amendment. Did the ERA cover some of the same ground as the Fourteenth Amendment, or did they deal with completely separate concepts?

- Divide your class into panels to discuss the role that women and homosexuals should play in the military. One team should be assigned to examine the congressional hearings that were conducted after the Persian

Gulf War which led to a congressional decision to permit women to serve as combat pilots; another team should be given an assignment to look at coverage in the media of public reaction to the 1993 compromise concerning gays in the military ("don't ask, don't tell, don't pursue").

- Americans with disabilities have suffered from both direct and indirect discrimination. The Americans with Disabilities Act of 1990 requires employers and public facilities to provide "reasonable accommodations" and prohibits employment discrimination against the disabled. Ask your class to consider who is "disabled" within the meaning of this act. For example, is a person with a terminal illness disabled? What rights do employers have in the equation? Compare students' assessments of these issues with the Supreme Court's decision in 1999.

- Surveys show that most Americans oppose affirmative action programs, even though Americans in general support nondiscrimination in employment and education. Ask students to research the legal rationale behind affirmative action policies, and how the Courts have evaluated various affirmative action programs. Have several members of your class debate the concepts of affirmative action and reverse discrimination. Can one group be protected without discriminating against another? Where would your students place their priorities?

- It can be instructive to show a segment of *Eyes on the Prize* in a classroom setting. The civil rights era is recreated through newsreel footage and interviews, and the era is "brought to life" for students who otherwise view the 1950s and 1960s only as "history." This award-winning series is available on videocassette.

- Using recent news events, perhaps the Rodney King verdict, ask students to identify civil rights and civil liberties violations which have occurred. Other recent cases might be the slaying of a black man in Texas by three whites who dragged him behind their pickup truck until his body was dismembered, or incidents of church bombings. In what ways were these violations of civil liberties? Civil rights? Class discussion can focus on the difficulty of maintaining limited government when the facts are subject to interpretation and when "conflicting" rights are at issue.

- Ask students to document historical and contemporary civil rights issues in South Africa to assess whether there is anything familiar about the problems of citizenship and discrimination. In general, the discussion should focus on disenfranchisement and dual citizenship problems, which blacks and women have especially suffered both there and in the United States.

- Have students do a clipping file of current or recent events involving violations of civil rights and the expansion of government. Ask them to write an essay identifying the violations and to describe how government has expanded as a result of efforts to provide protections.

- For a reading and writing connection, have students choose one of the key conflicts of the 1960's civil rights movements (e.g., Selma, Montgomery). Ask students to write a brief description of the events, explaining why blacks and whites engaged in the behaviors they did. Who won? Who lost? Why?

BACKGROUND READING

Chong, Dennis. Collective Action and the Civil Rights Movement. Chicago: University of Chicago Press. 1991.

Hampton, Henry and Steve Fayer. Voices of Freedom. New York: Bantam. 1990.

Klein, Ethel. Gender Politics. Cambridge, MA: Harvard University Press. 1974.

McAdam, Doug. Freedom Summer. New York: Oxford University Press. 1988.

McGlen, Nancy E. and Karen O'Conner. Women, Politics, and American Society, 2nd ed. Englewood Cliffs, NJ: Prentice Hall. 1998.

Steele, Shelby. The Content of Our Character: A New Vision of Race in America. NY: St. Martin's Press. 1990.

MEDIA SUGGESTIONS

Affirmative Action: The History of an Idea. This program considers the historical development of affirmative action policies and highlights current debates over its usefulness. Films for the Humanities and Sciences.

American Civil Liberties Union: A History. This program reviews the history of the ACLU, highlighting its contributions to protecting minorities. Films for the Humanities.

Bill of Rights: Bill of Responsibilities. 1995. This film provides a practical example of the impact of the Bill of Rights on the daily lives of individuals using current events and pop culture. Insight Media.

Eyes on the Prize. A Public Broadcasting Service series chronicling the civil rights movement in America. Excerpts are especially useful for visual effect.

Figures of the Civil Rights Movement: Sit-Ins and the Little Rock Nine. This show highlights the 1960 Nashville sit-ins and the desegregation of Little Rock's Central High School in 1957. Includes archival footage. Films for the Humanities & Sciences.

For Which It Stands: Flag Burning and the First Amendment. 1992. Features a debate between supporters and opponents of flag burning as a First Amendment right. Close Up Publishing.

Gideon's Trumpet. A 1979 production on Goodtimes Home Video. A dramatic recreation of the events leading up to the case Gideon v. Wainwright (1963).

Murder in Mississippi: The Price for Freedom. 1996. This film provides an in-depth examination of the murders of three civil rights workers during Freedom Summer in Mississippi. Films for the Humanities and Sciences.

Politics in Action, Chapter 8: A History of the Women's Movement. Provides a history of the women's movement, noting its successes and failures.

Racism in Theory and Practice. 1995. A historical examination of racism. Insight Media.

Religion and Race in America: Martin Luther King's Lament. 1996. This film provides an analysis of the different roles churches play in shaping a nation's political culture. Films for the Humanities and Sciences.

Rights of the Accused. 1989. An examination of the rights at the bar of justice using landmark cases.

Walk a Mile in My Shoes: The 90-Year History of the NAACP. This program, hosted by Julian Bond, provides a historical overview of the NAACP and the issues that it has worked on since 1920. Edudex.com.

CHAPTER SIX: PUBLIC OPINION AND POLITICAL ACTION

PEDAGOGICAL FEATURES

LEARNING OBJECTIVES

After studying this chapter, students should be able to:

- Understand the implications for political change of the movement toward a new *minority majority*.

- Contrast the relative positions of African Americans, Hispanic Americans, Asian Americans, and Native Americans in the American political and economic spheres.

- Identify the political implications of an increasingly elderly population.

- Describe the process of political socialization and identify the primary agents of socialization.

- Explain why an understanding of the content and dynamics of public opinion is important in evaluating the extent to which the people rule in a democracy.

- Outline the components that are essential if one wants to obtain accuracy in public opinion polling.

- Evaluate the role of polls in American democracy.

- Ascertain how the American political system works as well as it does given the lack of public knowledge about politics.

- Identify the political beliefs that are likely to be preferred by liberals and conservatives.

- Identify the activities that encompass political participation in the United States.

- Distinguish between conventional and unconventional types of political participation.

- Show how nonviolent civil disobedience was one of the most effective techniques of the civil rights movement in the American South.

- Explain what political scientists mean when they conclude that Americans are ideological conservatives but operational liberals.

CHAPTER OVERVIEW

INTRODUCTION

In a representative democracy citizens' preferences are supposed to guide policymakers. Yet the American people are amazingly diverse, which means that there are many groups with many opinions rather than a single public opinion. And most citizens know very little about politics. This chapter focuses on the nature of these "public opinions," how citizens learn about politics, and the extent to which these opinions are conveyed to government officials through various types of political participation.

THE AMERICAN PEOPLE

One way of looking at the American public is through **demography** – the science of human populations. The most valuable tool for understanding demographic changes in America is the **census**.

With its long history of immigration, the United States has often been called a **melting pot**; but policymakers now speak of a new **minority majority** because it is estimated that all the minority groups combined should pass the 50 percent mark by the year 2060. The largest component of the minority majority currently is the *African-American population.* A legacy of racism and discrimination has left the African-American population economically and politically disadvantaged, but African-Americans have recently been exercising a good deal of political power. If current immigration and birth rates continue, the *Hispanic population* will outnumber the black population early in the twenty-first century. Hispanics are rapidly gaining power in the Southwest. The problem of what to do about *illegal immigration* is of particular concern to the Hispanic community. The recent influx of *Asians* has been headed by a new class of professional workers. Asian Americans are the most highly skilled immigrant group in American history, and they are the best off of America's minority groups. *Native Americans* are by far the worst off of America's minority groups. Statistics show that they are the least healthy, the poorest, and the least educated group. Most remain economically and politically disadvantaged.

Americans live in an increasingly multicultural and multilingual society. Yet, regardless of ethnic background most Americans share a common **political culture** – an overall set of values widely shared within a society. Over the last sixty years, much of America's population growth has been centered in the West and South, particularly with movement *to* the **"sunbelt"** states of Florida, California, and Texas *from* **"rust belt"** states like Pennsylvania, Ohio, and Michigan. This demographic change is associated with political change, as the process of **reapportionment** brings with it gains or losses of congressional representation as the states' population balance changes. The *fastest growing age group* in America is composed of citizens over age sixty-five. The new political interests of the elderly have been mobilized under the umbrella of **"gray power."**

HOW AMERICANS LEARN ABOUT POLITICS: POLITICAL SOCIALIZATION

Richard Dawson notes that **political socialization** is "the process through which an individual acquires his or her own political orientations." **Agents of socialization** are numerous, including the family, the media, and schools. Only a small portion of Americans' political learning is formal; *informal learning* is much more important.

Politics is a lifelong activity, and political behavior is to some degree *learned behavior*. The family's role is central because of its monopoly on time and emotional commitment in the early years. Although most students like to think of themselves as independent thinkers, one can accurately predict how the majority of young people will vote simply by knowing the political leanings of their parents.

The mass media has been referred to as "the new parent." Television now displaces parents as the chief source of information as children get older. Governments throughout the world use the schools in their attempt to instill a commitment to the basic values of the system. Both democratic and authoritarian governments want students to learn positive features about their political system because it helps ensure that youth will grow up to be supportive citizens. Governments largely aim their socialization efforts at the young because one's *political orientations grow firmer* as one becomes more socialized with age.

MEASURING PUBLIC OPINION AND POLITICAL INFORMATION

Public opinion is the distribution of people's beliefs about politics and policy issues. There is *rarely a single public opinion*: with so many people and such diversity of populations, there are also many opinions. Public opinion is one of the products of political learning.

Public opinion **polling** was first developed by George Gallup in 1932. Polls rely on a **sample** of the population (a relatively small proportion of people who are chosen as *representative* of the whole) to measure public opinion. The key to the accuracy of opinion polls is **random sampling**, which operates on the principle that everyone should have an equal probability of being selected. However, there is always a certain amount of risk of inaccuracy involved, known as the **sampling error**. Proper sampling techniques must be followed in order to remain within the **margin of error**.

Sophisticated technology is now available for measuring public opinion. Most polling is now done on the telephone with samples selected through **random digit dialing**, in which calls are placed to telephone numbers within randomly chosen exchanges. Supporters of polling consider that it is a *tool for democracy* by which policymakers can keep in touch with changing opinions on issues. Critics of polling think polls can weaken democracy by *distorting the election process*. Polls are often accused of creating a **"bandwagon effect,"** in which voters may support a candidate only because they see that others are doing so. Moreover, emphasis on poll results sometimes has drowned out the *issues* of recent presidential campaigns. The election day **exit poll** is probably the most criticized type of poll. In the 1980, 1984, and 1988 presidential elections, the networks declared a winner while millions on the West Coast still had hours to vote (but analysis of survey data show that few voters have actually been influenced by exit poll results). Perhaps the most pervasive criticism of polling is that by altering the *wording* of questions, pollsters can get pretty much the results they want.

Polls have revealed again and again that the average American has a low level of political knowledge. Likewise, surveys show that citizens around the globe lack a basic awareness of the world around them. Increased levels of education over the last four decades have scarcely raised public knowledge about politics. Part of the reason the American political system works as well as it does is that people do know what *basic values* they want upheld, even when they do not have information on policy questions or decision makers. Sadly, the American public has become increasingly dissatisfied with government over the last three decades.

WHAT AMERICANS VALUE: POLITICAL IDEOLOGIES

Generally, Americans tend to identify themselves as conservatives more than moderates or liberals—which helps to account for the relatively limited scope of government in the United States. But who identifies as a liberal or conservative often varies according to age, gender, race and socioeconomic status. Ideological thinking is not widespread in the American public, nor are people necessarily consistent in their attitudes. For most people, the terms *liberal* and *conservative* are not as important as they are for the political elite. Thus, the authors of the classic study *The American Voter* (Angus Campbell, et al.) concluded that to speak of election results as indicating a movement of the public to either the "left" or "right" is a misnomer because most voters do not think in such terms.

President Reagan led what he proclaimed to be a conservative revolution in the 1980s. However, scholarly analyses showed that people liked Reagan more than his specific policies. He was elected twice because voters (especially **swing voters**) care more about results than ideology. Consistent with this, support for Bill Clinton reflects more on his policies than on his personal popularity. Thus, it is difficult to conclude that there has been an enduring shift toward conservatism.

HOW AMERICANS PARTICIPATE IN POLITICS

Political participation encompasses the many activities used by citizens to influence the selection of political leaders or the policies they pursue. Paradoxically, the United States has a *participatory political culture*; but only 51 percent of Americans voted in the 2000 presidential election, and the numbers are even lower for state and local elections. Political scientists generally distinguish between two broad types of participation, conventional and unconventional. **Conventional participation** includes many widely accepted modes of influencing government, such as voting, trying to persuade others, ringing doorbells for a petition, and running for office. Although the decline of voter turnout is a development Americans should rightly be concerned about, a broader look at political participation reveals some positive developments for participatory democracy. **Unconventional participation** includes activities that are often dramatic, such as protesting, civil disobedience, and even violence.

Protest is a form of political participation designed to achieve policy change through dramatic and unconventional tactics, and protests today are often orchestrated to provide television cameras with vivid images. Throughout American history, individuals and groups have sometimes used **civil disobedience,** in which they consciously break laws that they think are unjust. Nonviolent civil disobedience was one of the most effective techniques of the civil rights movement in the American South. Although political participation can also be violent (as in some of the Vietnam War protests of the 1960s), perhaps the best indicator of *how well socialized Americans are to democracy* is that protest typically is aimed at *getting the attention of government* rather than at overthrowing it.

In the United States, participation is a *class-biased activity*, with citizens of higher socioeconomic status participating more than others. Minority groups like Hispanics and African-Americans are below average in terms of political participation. However, the participation differences between these groups and the national average has been declining. When blacks, Hispanics, and whites *of equal incomes and educations* are compared, it is the *minorities who participate more* in politics.

UNDERSTANDING PUBLIC OPINION AND POLITICAL ACTION

While more people today think the government is too big rather than too small, a plurality has consistently called for spending on programs like education, health care, aid to big cities, protecting the environment, and fighting crime. Many political scientists have looked at these contradictory findings and concluded that Americans are *ideological conservatives* but *operational liberals*.

Americans often take for granted the opportunity to replace our leaders at the next election. Even if they are only voting according to the nature of the times, voters are being heard—which holds elected officials accountable for their actions.

CHAPTER OUTLINE

I. **THE AMERICAN PEOPLE**
   A. Public opinion
      1. The United States remains *one of the most diverse countries* in the world today.
      2. The study of American **public opinion** aims to understand the distribution of the population's belief about politics and policy issues.
      3. Such diversity *makes the study of American public opinion especially complex*, for there are many groups with a great variety of opinions.
      4. The task is further complicated by the fact that people are often not well informed about the issues, and they may have contradictory attitudes.
      5. There are also *consequences for democracy*: the least informed are also the least likely to participate in the political process, thereby leading to inequalities in who takes part in political action.
   B. One way of looking at the American public is through **demography** (the science of population changes).
      1. The most valuable tool for understanding demographic changes in America is the **census**, which was first conducted in 1790 to comply with the constitutional requirement that the government conduct an "actual enumeration" of the population every ten years.

2. Once a group can establish its numbers, it can then ask for federal aid in proportion to its size.

C. The United States has always been a nation of immigrants.
   1. Americans live in a *multicultural and multilingual society* that is becoming more diverse all the time.
   2. Despite this diversity, minority groups have *assimilated many basic American values*, such as the principle of equality.
   3. Today, federal law allows up to 800,000 new immigrants to be legally admitted every year (which is the equivalent of adding a city with the population of Washington, D.C., every year).
   4. There have been three great waves of immigration to the United States:
      a. Before the Civil War - northwestern Europeans.
      b. After the Civil War (reaching its high point in the first decade of the twentieth century) - southern and eastern Europeans.
      c. After World War II (the 1980s saw the largest number of immigrants of any decade in American history) - Hispanics and Asians.

D. With its long history of immigration, the United States has often been called a **melting pot** (a mixture of cultures, ideas, and peoples), but policymakers now speak of a new **minority majority** (a phrase meaning that America will eventually cease to have a white, generally Anglo-Saxon majority).
   1. The *largest component* of the minority majority currently is the *African-American population* (one in eight Americans).
      a. A legacy of racism and discrimination has left the African-American population economically and politically disadvantaged, but African-Americans have recently been exercising a good deal of political power.
      b. Nearly 27 percent of African-Americans currently live under the poverty line, compared to about 11 percent for whites.
   2. If current immigration and birth rates continue, the *Hispanic population will outnumber the black population* early in the twenty-first century.
      a. Hispanics are rapidly gaining power in the Southwest, and cities like San Antonio and Denver have elected mayors of Hispanic heritage.
      b. The problem of what to do about *illegal immigration* is of particular concern to the Hispanic community.
      c. The Simpson-Mazzoli Act required all employers to *document the citizenship* of their employees (as of June 1987).

3. Unlike Hispanics who have come to America to escape poverty and African-Americans who were brought as slaves, the recent influx of *Asians* has been headed by a *new class of professional workers* looking for greater opportunity.
   a. Asian Americans are the *most highly skilled* immigrant group in American history, and they are the *best off of America's minority groups*.
   b. Forty-two percent of Asian Americans over the age of twenty-five hold a college degree (almost twice the national average).
4. The *Native American* population declined from an estimated twelve to fifteen million American Indians before the Europeans arrived in America to 210,000 by 1910; as of the 1990 census, approximately 1.8 million Americans listed themselves as being of Indian heritage.
   a. Native Americans are by far *the worst off* of America's minority groups.
   b. Statistics show that they are the least healthy, the poorest, and the least educated group.
   c. Most remain economically and politically disadvantaged—the 1990 census found that over half of the Indians in the Dakotas (site of the largest Sioux reservations) lived below the poverty line.
5. It is estimated that all the minority groups combined should pass the 50 percent mark by the middle of the next century.

E. *Demographic changes* are associated with *political changes*.
   1. Over the last fifty years, much of America's population growth has been centered in the West and South, particularly with *movement to* the **"sunbelt"** states of Florida, California, and Texas *from* **"rust belt"** states like Pennsylvania, Ohio, and Michigan.
   2. The process of **reapportionment** occurs every ten years following the census, and brings with it gains or losses of congressional representation as the states' population balance changes (New York has lost about one-third of its delegation over the last fifty years).
   3. The *fastest growing age group* in America is composed of citizens *over age sixty-five:* people are living longer as a result of medical advances, and the birth rate has dropped.
      a. The *Social Security system* is second only to national defense as America's most costly public policy; the growing demands to care for the elderly will almost certainly become more acute in the decades ahead.
   4. New political interests have been mobilized under the umbrella of **"gray power;"** in Florida, the state's senior citizens typically vote

against referenda for school taxes, and they have secured tax breaks and service benefits for older people.

II. HOW AMERICANS LEARN ABOUT POLITICS: POLITICAL SOCIALIZATION

A. How Americans learn: the process of political socialization.

1. **Political socialization** is "the process through which an individual acquires his or her own political orientations."
2. Only a small portion of Americans' political learning is formal; *informal learning* is much more important.
3. **Agents of socialization** are numerous; they include family, the media, and schools.
   a. *The family*'s role is central because of its monopoly on two crucial resources in the early years—time and emotional commitment.
   b. The *mass media* has been referred to as "the new parent."
   c. Governments throughout the world use the *schools* in their attempt to instill a commitment to the basic values of the system.

B. *Politics is a lifelong activity.*

1. *Aging increases* one's *political participation* and the strength of one's *party attachment.*
2. Political behavior is to some degree *learned behavior.*
3. Governments largely aim their socialization efforts at the young (not the old) because one's *political orientations grow firmer* as one becomes more socialized with age.

III. MEASURING PUBLIC OPINION AND POLITICAL INFORMATION

A. Public opinion.

1. What Americans believe (and believe they know) is **public opinion**—the distribution of people's beliefs about politics and policy issues.
2. There is *rarely a single public opinion*: with so many people and such diversity of populations, there are also many opinions.
3. Public opinion is one of the products of political learning.

B. Measuring public opinion.

1. Public opinion **polling** was first developed by George Gallup in 1932.
2. Polls rely on a **sample** of the population (a relatively small proportion of people who are chosen as *representative* of the whole) to measure public opinion.

a. A sample of about 1500 to 2000 people can be representative of the **"universe"** (the larger group whose opinion is being measured) of potential voters.
b. The key to the accuracy of opinion polls is **random sampling**, which operates on the principle that everyone should have *an equal probability of being selected.*
c. There is always a certain amount of risk of inaccuracy involved, known as the **sampling error**.

3. Sophisticated technology is now available for measuring public opinion.
   a. Computer and telephone technology have made surveying less expensive and more commonplace.
   b. Most polling is now done on the telephone with samples selected through **random digit dialing**, in which calls are placed to telephone numbers within randomly chosen exchanges.

C. The role of polls in American democracy.

1. *Supporters* of polling believe it is a *tool for democracy* by which policymakers can keep in touch with changing opinions on issues.
2. *Critics* of polling think it makes politicians *more concerned with following than leading* and may thus discourage bold leadership.
3. Political scientist Benjamin Ginsberg argues that polls actually *weaken democracy* because polls permit government to think that it has taken public opinion into account when only passive (often ill-informed) opinions have been counted.
4. Polls can weaken democracy by *distorting the election process*; polls are often accused of creating a **"bandwagon effect,"** in which voters may support a candidate only because they see that others are doing so.
5. Emphasis on poll results sometimes has drowned out the *issues* of recent presidential campaigns.
6. The election day **exit poll** is probably the most-criticized *type* of poll.
7. Perhaps the most pervasive criticism of polling is that pollsters can get pretty much the results they want by altering the *wording* of questions. Although the *bias* in such questions may be easy to detect, the ethical problem is that *an organization may not report how the survey questions were worded.*

D. What polls reveal about Americans' political information.

1. Polls have revealed again and again that the average American has a low level of political knowledge.
   a. In the 1996 National Election Study, only 88 percent knew that Al Gore was vice-president; 66 percent knew that Boris Yeltsin was president of Russia; 59 percent knew that Newt Gingrich was

the speaker of the house; and 10 percent knew that William Rehnquist was chief justice of the Supreme Court.

b. Surveys also show that citizens around the globe lack a basic awareness of the world around them.

2. Part of the reason the American political system works as well as it does is that people do know what *basic values* they want upheld, even when they do not have information on policy questions or decision makers.
3. Increased levels of education over the last four decades have scarcely raised public knowledge about politics.

IV. WHAT AMERICANS VALUE: POLITICAL IDEOLOGIES

A. Who are the liberals and conservatives?

1. A **political ideology** is a *coherent set of values and beliefs about public policy.*
2. Overall, more Americans consistently choose the ideological label of conservative over liberal.
3. Some groups are more liberal than others, and want to see government do more; this includes people under the age of 30, minorities and women.

B. Do people think in ideological terms?

1. Ideological thinking is not widespread in the American public, nor are people necessarily consistent in their attitudes.
2. The authors of the classic study *The American Voter* (Angus Campbell, et al.) first looked carefully at the ideological sophistication of the American electorate in the 1950s. They divided the public into four groups, according to ideological sophistication.
   a. **Ideologues** - Only 12 percent could connect their opinions and beliefs with broad policy positions taken by parties or candidates.
   b. **Group benefits voters** - Forty-two percent of Americans thought of politics mainly by the groups they liked or disliked.
   c. **Nature of the times voters** - The "handle on politics" of 24 percent of the population was limited to whether the times seemed good or bad to them.
   d. **No issue content voters** - Twenty-two percent of the voters were devoid of any ideological or issue content in their political evaluations; most simply voted routinely for a party or judged the candidates by their personalities.
3. If the same methods are used to update the analysis of *The American Voter* through the 1980s, one finds some increase in the proportion of ideologues, but the overall picture looks much the same.

B. Has there been a turn toward conservatism? Why or why not?

1. Despite Reagan's victories throughout the 1980s, scholarly analyses included the common theme that people liked Reagan but not his policies (in practice, they support increased government spending and intervention for most domestic programs)—which runs contrary to the notion of a swing toward conservatism.
2. President Clinton's centrist policies remain popular, again counter to claims that public opinion has shifted to conservatism.
3. Why no shift to conservatism?
   a. Many **swing voters** (those classified as *nature of the times* voters by *The American Voter*) care more about results than ideology.
   b. The 1980 election was more about voting Carter out of office than voting Reagan into it.
   c. With the economic downturn in 1992, these same swing voters propelled Bill Clinton into the White House, who has pursued centrist policies and enjoyed a good economy.

V. HOW AMERICANS PARTICIPATE IN POLITICS

A. **Political participation** encompasses the many activities used by citizens to influence the selection of political leaders or the policies they pursue.
   1. Americans have many avenues of political participation open to them.
   2. Paradoxically, the United State has a *participatory political culture*, but only 49 percent of Americans voted in the 1996 presidential election, 38 percent turned out for the 1998 mid-term elections, and the numbers get even smaller for state and local elections.

B. Political scientists generally distinguish between two broad types of participation—*conventional* and *unconventional.*
   1. **Conventional participation** includes many widely accepted modes of influencing government, such as voting, trying to persuade others, ringing doorbells for a petition, and running for office.
   2. **Unconventional participation** includes activities that are often dramatic, such as protesting, civil disobedience, and even violence.
      a. **Protest** is a form of political participation designed to achieve policy change through dramatic and unconventional tactics, and protests today are often orchestrated to provide television cameras with vivid images.
      b. Throughout American history, individuals and groups have sometimes used **civil disobedience** (consciously breaking a law that they think is unjust), illustrated in different eras by people like Henry David Thoreau in the 1840s and the Rev. Martin Luther King, Jr. in the 1950s and 1960s.

c. Nonviolent civil disobedience was one of the most effective techniques of the civil rights movement in the American South. Rev. King's *Letter from a Birmingham Jail* is a classic defense of civil disobedience.
d. Political participation can also be violent (as in some of the Vietnam war protests of the 1960s).

C. Class, inequality, and participation.
1. In the United States, participation is a *class-biased activity*, with citizens of higher socioeconomic status participating more than others.
2. *Minority groups* like Hispanics and African Americans are *below average* in terms of political participation.
a. The participation differences between these groups and the national average has been declining.
b. When blacks, Hispanics, and whites *of equal incomes and educations* are compared, it is *minorities who participate more* in politics.

VI. UNDERSTANDING PUBLIC OPINION AND POLITICAL ACTION

A. Public attitudes toward the scope of government.
1. The question of government power is a complex one, but it is one of the key controversies in American politics today.
a. Public opinions on different aspects of the same issue do not always hold together well: while more people today think the government is too big rather than too small, a plurality has consistently called for spending on programs like education, health care, aid to big cities, protecting the environment, and fighting crime.
b. Many political scientists have looked at these contradictory findings and concluded that Americans are *ideological conservatives* but *operational liberals*.

B. Democracy, public opinion, and political action.
1. Americans often take for granted the opportunity to replace our leaders at the next election.
2. Perhaps the best indicator of *how well socialized Americans are to democracy* is that protest typically is aimed at *getting the attention of government*, not at overthrowing it.
3. Even if they are only voting according to the nature of the times, voters are clearly being heard, which holds elected officials accountable for their actions.

KEY TERMS AND CONCEPTS

Census: a count of the American population conducted every ten years.

Civil disobedience: a form of unconventional participation designed to consciously break a law thought to be unjust.

Conservatism: a set of beliefs about politics, public policy, and public purpose, emphasizing maintaining peace through strength, supporting right-to-life and prayer in school, opposing affirmative action and favoring free-market rather than government solutions.

Demography: the science of human populations.

Exit poll: a poll taken at randomly selected polling places after the citizens have placed their votes.

Gender gap: a consistent attitudinal pattern where women are more likely than men to express liberal attitudes and to support Democratic candidates.

Liberalism: a set of beliefs about politics, public policy, and public purpose, emphasizing less spending on the military, free choice on abortion, opposition to prayer in school and viewing the government as a regulator in the public interest.

Melting pot: the mixture of cultures, ideas, and peoples in the United States.

Minority majority: a reference to the impending status of white, Anglo-Saxon Americans, currently holding majority status.

Political culture: an overall set of values widely shared within a society.

Political ideology: a coherent set of values and beliefs about public policy.

Political participation: the activities used by citizens to influence political outcomes.

Political socialization: the process by which citizens acquire their knowledge, feelings, and evaluations of the political world.

Protest: a form of political participation designed to change policy through unconventional tactics.

Public opinion: the distribution of the population's beliefs about politics and issues.

Random digit dialing: phone numbers are dialed at random around the country.

Random sampling: a polling technique which is based on the principle that everyone has an equal probability of being selected as part of the sample.

Reapportionment: the reallocation of 435 seats in the House of Representatives based on changes in residency and population found in the census.

Sample: a small proportion of the population chosen as representative of the whole population.

Sampling error: the level of confidence involved in a sample result—the level is dependent on the size of the sample.

TEACHING IDEAS: CLASS DISCUSSION AND STUDENT PROJECTS

- Public opinion surveys consistently reveal an astounding lack of public knowledge about politics. Give students a "pop quiz" on several major political issues and have them grade their own quiz. Alternatively, administer to them a subset of questions from the exam that the Immigration and Naturalization Service administers to immigrants applying for citizenship. Briefly discuss their performance, and possible reasons for it. Then ask your students to discuss whether the American political system is affected by such a low level of public information.

- The textbook points out that the diversity of the American public and its opinions must be faithfully channeled through the political process in order for the American government to work efficiently and effectively. At the same time, the least informed among the public are also the least likely to participate in the political process. Ask your class to evaluate the effect that this inequality of participation has on the democratic process.

- The textbook points out that the elderly now exercise "gray power." In Florida, the state's senior citizens typically vote against referenda for school taxes, and they have secured tax breaks and service benefits for older people. Ask your class to think about the potential for divisiveness between the aged (who have been promised benefits that they expect to collect) and younger workers (who may resent "gray power" votes that deny benefits to their children).

- Select a controversial topic (such as flag burning). Call for each student to devise a survey to measure attitudes on this issue and administer it to a group of friends. Their surveys will not be representative, so they should obtain very different results. Use the results to discuss the problems that may arise with improperly administered surveys, particularly if the public relies on the results.

- Table 6.3 tells *How to Tell a Liberal from a Conservative.* Before assigning the chapter to be read, have students write down whether they are strongly conservative, conservative, weakly conservative, moderate, weakly liberal, liberal, or strongly liberal. Then devise a point system based on the criteria in Table 6.3 and have students rank themselves on each criteria. After adding up their criteria points, have students discuss whether their numerical score might differ from their self-identification.

- The authors of the textbook point out that more people today think the government is too big rather than too small, yet a plurality has consistently called for increased spending on domestic programs. Many political scientists have looked at these contradictory findings and concluded that Americans are ideological conservatives but operational liberals. Ask your class to examine this theory with reference to public debate over President Clinton's budget proposals in 1993.

- Have students visit the Internet site operated by Gallup, the National Election Study, or the General Social Survey to find public opinion data on a question of interest. Have each student write up, or present orally in class, what the question wording was, the response distribution, and how to interpret the data.

- One very effective way to reinforce the problems of public opinion measurement, especially in regard to attitude stability, is to examine a policy proposal currently before Congress or awaiting the President's signature. Any policy proposal from the previous two weeks which has been covered by the media is sufficient. Take a simple poll asking students whether they support implementation or not. After each set has expressed either a yes, no, or no opinion response, count or estimate the percentage of the class for each category. Then choose students from each group to tell briefly why they gave their answers. After no more than ten minutes of debate and discussion about the bill, take the poll again. Using the same question format, ask which students are for, against, or have no opinion. Count or estimate the percentage of students in each category again. Discuss the implications of any shift in the percentage answering for, against, and no opinion. In particular, emphasize the role of information and group consciousness in creating the shift. Finally, remind students that if public opinion can shift in ten minutes, to consider the effect of information for determining the accuracy of public attitudes in polls taken in one week, one month, six months, and one year intervals. This exercise reinforces the problems using public opinion polls to guide public policy making.

- The concept of political socialization is difficult for students to grasp without examples and discussion. Ask students to think about the role of political symbols in society. In particular, ask students to list these symbols and where they are most often seen. For example, the flag, the constitution, Uncle Sam, etc. Discuss the pledge of allegiance as a socializing agent for young children as well as activities during Fourth of July celebrations which are often used to reinforce public values of nationalism, patriotism, and reverence for the Constitution. Once they have listed a variety of these, then ask them to explain why the national anthem is sung at baseball games. Ask how many know all of the words, how many have stood but did not sing, and how many did not sing or stand while the national anthem was being sung at a baseball game. This exercise provides an unintimidating yet thoughtful way of emphasizing just how pervasive political socialization has been used to instill principles, values, and beliefs in citizens. A follow-up exercise may include a short essay debating whether the reciting of pledge of allegiance or the singing of the national anthem is more appropriate for baseball games, given that most people can say the pledge without hesitation, but have trouble singing the national anthem.

- Ask students to watch criminal justice entertainment shows from the 1970's compared to those in the 1990's. Then have students write brief essays on the political value or information conveyed in these shows, and the implications of these for individuals' political beliefs.

- Using newspaper archives and/or the Internet, ask students to research recent protests at the World Trade Organization meetings, or other international summits or other more "local" protests. Who were the protestors, and what were they protesting? What response did they receive?

BACKGROUND READING

Asher, Herbert. Polling and the Public: What Every Citizen Should Know. Washington, DC: Congressional Quarterly. 1998.

Asher, Herbert. Polling and the Public: What Every Citizen Should Know, 4th ed. Washington, D.C.: CQ Press. 1998.

Campbell, Angus et. al. The American Voter. NY: John Wiley. 1960.

Delli Carpini, Michael X. and Scott Keeter. What Americans Know about Politics and Why It Matters. New Haven: Yale University Press. 1996.

Key, V. O. Public Opinion and American Democracy. NY: Alfred A. Knopf. 1964.

Page, Benjamin I. and Robert Y. Shapiro. The Rational Public. Chicago: University of Chicago Press. 1992.

Verba, Sidney, Kay Lehman Schlozman and Henry E. Brady. Voice and Equality. Cambridge: Harvard University Press. 1995.

Zaller, John R. The Nature and Origins of Mass Opinion. Cambridge: University of Cambridge Press. 1992.

MEDIA SUGGESTIONS

Leading Questions. Part of the Public Mind series distributed by Films for the Humanities and Sciences. This program examines public opinion polling and marketing techniques used in campaigns.

CHAPTER SEVEN: THE MASS MEDIA AND THE POLITICAL AGENDA

PEDAGOGICAL FEATURES

LEARNING OBJECTIVES

After studying this chapter, students should be able to:

- Trace the development of the mass media and the way in which presidents have used the media in different periods of our history.
- Analyze the impact that investigative journalism has had on public cynicism and negativism about politics.
- Ascertain the major sources that people rely on for their information about politics.

- Determine how journalists define what is newsworthy, where they get their information, and how they present it.
- Explain the role that the profit motive plays in decisions by the mass media on how to report the news.
- Examine and analyze the charge that the media have a liberal bias.
- Identify factors that would explain why the news is typically characterized by political *neutrality*.
- Determine methods used by political activists to get their ideas placed high on the governmental agenda.
- Clarify how the media act as *key linkage institutions* between the people and the policymakers.
- Indicate how functions of the media may help to keep government small.
- Identify functions of the media that may encourage the growth of government.
- Describe how the rise of television broadcasting has encouraged individualism in the American political system.
- Explain why the rise of the "information society" has not brought about a corresponding rise of an "informed society."
- Summarize how the news and its presentation are important influences in shaping public opinion on political issues.

CHAPTER OVERVIEW

INTRODUCTION

The American political system has entered a new period of **high-tech politics** in which the behavior of citizens and policymakers, as well as the political agenda itself, is increasingly shaped by technology. The **mass media** are a key part of that technology. Television, radio, newspapers, magazines, and other means of popular communication are called mass media because they reach out and profoundly influence not only the elites but the masses. This chapter describes the historical development of the mass media as it relates to news coverage of government and politics. Questions regarding how news is defined, how it is presented and what impact it has in politics are also addressed.

THE MASS MEDIA TODAY

Modern political success depends upon control of the mass media. Image making does not stop with the campaign. It is also a critical element in day-to-day governing since politicians' images in the press are seen as good indicators of their clout. A large part of today's so-called *30-second presidency* is the slickly produced TV commercial.

THE DEVELOPMENT OF THE MASS MEDIA

The daily newspaper is largely a product of the late nineteenth century, while radio and television have been around only since the first half of the twentieth century. As recently as the presidency of Herbert Hoover (1929-1933), reporters submitted their questions to the president in writing, and he responded in writing (if at all). Franklin D. Roosevelt (1933-1945) was the first president to use the media effectively. Roosevelt held about *1000 press conferences* in his twelve years in the White House and broadcast a series of *"fireside chats"* over the radio to reassure the nation during the Great Depression.

At the time of Roosevelt's administration, the press had not yet started to report on a political leader's public life. The events of the Vietnam War and the Watergate scandal soured the press on government. Today's newspeople work in an environment of cynicism; the press sees ferreting out the truth as their job since they believe that politicians rarely tell the whole story. **Investigative journalism**—the use of detective-like reporting methods to unearth scandals—pits reporters against political leaders. There is evidence that TV's fondness for investigative journalism has contributed to greater public cynicism and negativism about politics.

Scholars distinguish between two kinds of media: the **print media**, which include newspapers and magazines, and the **broadcast media**, which consist of television and radio. Each has reshaped political communication at different points in American history.

The first American daily newspaper was printed in Philadelphia in 1783, but daily newspapers did not become common until the technological advances of the mid-nineteenth century. Newspapers consolidated into **chains** during the early part of the twentieth century. Today's massive media conglomerates control newspapers with 78 percent of the nation's daily circulation. These chains often control television and radio stations as well. Ever since the rise of TV news, however, newspaper circulation rates have been declining.

The broadcast media have gradually displaced the print media as Americans' principal source of news and information. As a form of technology, television is almost as old as radio; the first television station appeared in 1931. Nevertheless, the 1950s and 1960s were the developmental years for American television. The first televised **presidential debates** were the 1960 Kennedy-Nixon debates. The poll results from this debate illustrate the visual power of television in American politics: whereas people listening to the radio gave the edge to Nixon, those who saw it on television thought Kennedy won.

Television took the nation to the war in Vietnam during the 1960s, and TV exposed governmental naïveté (some said it was outright lying) about the progress of the war. With the growth of *cable TV*, particularly the Cable News Network (CNN), television has entered a new era of bringing news to people (and to political leaders) *as it happens*. Since 1963, surveys have consistently shown that more people rely on TV for the news than any other medium; and by a regular two-to-one margin, people think television reports are more believable than newspaper stories.

With the increase in cable channels and Internet usage, a recent trend has been the increase in "broadcast" channels that are oriented toward particularly narrow audiences, often referred to as **narrowcasting**. With so many readily available sources of information for so many specific interests, it will also be extremely easy for those who are not very interested in politics to completely avoid news and public affairs. The result could well be a growing inequality of political information, with the politically interested becoming more knowledgeable while the rest of the public slips further into political apathy.

REPORTING THE NEWS

News reporting is a *business* in America in which *profits shape how journalists define what is newsworthy, where they get their information, and how they present it.* To a large extent, TV networks define *news* as what is entertaining to the average viewer.

A surprising amount of news comes from *well-established sources.* Most news organizations assign their best reporters to particular **beats**—specific locations where news frequently emanates from, such as Congress. Very little of the news is generated by spontaneous events or a reporter's own analysis. Most stories are drawn from situations over which *newsmakers have substantial control.* For example, those who make the news depend on the media to spread certain information and ideas to the general public. Sometimes they feed stories to reporters in the form of **trial balloons**: information leaked to see what the political reaction will be.

TV news is little more than a headline service. With exceptions like the *MacNeil-Lehrer Newshour* (PBS) and *Nightline* (ABC), analysis of news events rarely lasts more than a minute. At the same time, complex issues—like nuclear power, the nation's money supply, and pollution—are difficult to treat in a short news clip.

The charge that the media have a *liberal bias* has become a familiar one in American politics, and there is some limited evidence to support it. Reporters are more likely to call themselves liberal than the general public, and more journalists identify themselves as Democrats than Republicans. However, there is little reason to believe that journalists' personal attitudes sway their reporting of the news. Most stories are presented in a "point/counterpoint" format in which two opposing points of view are presented.

A conclusion that news reporting contains little explicit *partisan or ideological* bias is *not* to argue that it does not *distort reality* in its coverage. Ideally, the news should mirror reality. In practice, there are too many potential stories for this to be the case. Journalists must select which stories to cover and to what degree. Due to economic pressures, the media are biased in favor of stories with high drama that will attract people's interest (rather than extended analyses of complex issues). Television is particularly biased toward stories that generate good pictures.

THE NEWS AND PUBLIC OPINION

For many years, students of the subject tended to doubt that the media had more than a marginal effect on public opinion. The "minimal effects hypothesis" stemmed from the fact that early scholars were looking for direct impacts – for example, whether the media affected how people voted. When the focus turned to how the media affect *what Americans think about,* more positive results were uncovered. The decision to cover or to ignore certain issues can affect public opinion. By focusing public attention on specific problems, the media influence the criteria by which the public evaluates political leaders.

THE MEDIA'S AGENDA-SETTING FUNCTION

As was explained in chapter 1, people are trying to influence the government's **policy agenda** when they confront government officials with problems they expect them to solve. Interest groups, political parties, politicians, public relations firms, and bureaucratic agencies are all pushing for their priorities to take precedence over others. *Political activists* (often called **policy entrepreneurs**—people who invest their political "capital" in an issue) depend heavily upon the *media* to get their ideas placed high on the governmental agenda.

The *staging of political events to attract media attention* is a political art form. Important political events are orchestrated minute by minute with an eye on American TV audiences. Moreover, it is not only the elites who have successfully used the media. Civil rights groups in the 1960s relied heavily on the media to tell their stories of unjust treatment. Many believe that the introduction of television helped to accelerate the movement by graphically showing Americans (in both North and South) what the situation was.

UNDERSTANDING THE MASS MEDIA

The media act as *key linkage institutions* between the people and the policymakers and have a profound impact on the political policy agenda. The media are so crucial in today's society that they are often referred to as the **"fourth branch of government."**

The **watchdog function** of the media *helps to keep government small.* Many observers feel that the press is *biased against whoever holds office* and that reporters want to expose them in the media. With every new proposal being met with skepticism, regular constraints are placed on the growth of government. Conversely, when they focus on injustice in society, the media inevitably *encourage the growth of government.* The media *portray government as responsible for handling* almost every major problem.

The rise of television has furthered individualism in the American political process. Candidates are now much more capable of running for office on their own by appealing to people directly through television.

The rise of the "information society" has not brought about a corresponding rise of an "informed society." With the media's superficial treatment of important policy issues, it is not surprising that the incredible amount of information available to Americans today has not visibly increased their political awareness or participation. The media's defense is to say that this is what the people want. Since they are in business to make a profit, they have to appeal to the maximum number of people.

CHAPTER OUTLINE

I. THE MASS MEDIA TODAY

A. The American political system has entered a new period of **high-tech politics** in which the behavior of citizens and policy makers, as well as the political agenda itself, is increasingly shaped by technology.

B. The **mass media** are a key part of that technology. Television, radio, newspapers, magazines, and other means of popular communication are called mass media because they reach out and profoundly influence not only the elites but the masses.

C. Modern political success depends upon control of the mass media.

1. Candidates have learned that one way to *guide the media's focus* is to limit what they report on to carefully *scripted events*—a strategy that both Bush and Clinton used effectively in 1992. These events are known as **media events**, that is, an event that is staged primarily for the purpose of being covered.
2. Image making does not stop with the campaign. It is also a critical element in day-to-day governing since politicians' images in the press are seen as good indicators of their clout. For example, the Reagan administration was particularly effective in controlling the president's image as presented by the media. A large part of today's so-called *30-second presidency* (a reference to 30-second sound bites on TV) is the slickly produced TV commercial.

II. THE DEVELOPMENT OF THE MASS MEDIA

A. The daily newspaper is largely a product of the late nineteenth century, while radio and television have been around only since the first half of the twentieth.

B. As recently as the presidency of Herbert Hoover (1929-1933), reporters submitted their questions to the president in writing, and he responded in writing (if at all).

C. Franklin D. Roosevelt (1933-1945) was the first president to use the media effectively. To Roosevelt, the media were a potential ally, and he promised reporters two **press conferences** (presidential meetings with reporters) a week.

D. At the time of Roosevelt's administration, the press had not yet started to report on a political leader's private life: the press *never even reported to the American public that the President was confined to a wheelchair.*

   1. The events of the Vietnam War and the Watergate scandal soured the press on government. Today's newspeople work in an environment of cynicism; the press sees *ferreting out the truth* as their job since they believe that politicians rarely tell the whole story.
   2. **Investigative journalism**—the use of detective-like reporting methods to unearth scandals—pits reporters against political leaders. There is evidence that TV's fondness for investigative journalism has contributed to greater public cynicism and negativism about politics.

E. The **print media**.

   1. Newspapers
      a. The first American daily newspaper was printed in Philadelphia in 1783, but daily newspapers did not become common until the technological advances of the mid-nineteenth century. Rapid printing and cheap paper made the "*penny press*" possible—a paper that could be bought for a penny and read at home.
      b. By the 1840s, the telegraph permitted a primitive "*wire service,*" which relayed news stories from city to city faster than ever before. The Associated Press, founded in 1849, depended heavily on this new technology.
      c. Two newspaper magnates, Joseph Pulitzer and William Randolph Hearst, enlivened journalism around the turn of the century. This was the era of **yellow journalism**, where the main topics were sensationalized accounts of violence, corruption, wars, and gossip.
      d. Newspapers consolidated into **chains** during the early part of the twentieth century. Today's massive media conglomerates control newspapers with 78 percent of the nation's daily circulation; these chains often control television and radio stations as well.
      e. Among the most influential newspapers today are *The New York Times* (a cut above most newspapers in its influence and impact almost from the beginning), *The Washington Post* (perhaps the best coverage inside Washington), and papers from a few major

cities (*The Chicago Tribune*, *The Los Angeles Times*, and others). For most newspapers in medium-sized and small towns, the main source of national and world news is the Associated Press wire service.

2. Magazines.
   a. The political content of leading magazines is pretty slim. Newsweeklies such as *Time*, *Newsweek*, and *U.S. News and World Report* rank well behind popular favorites such as *Reader's Digest*, *TV Guide*, and *National Geographic*.
   b. Serious magazines of political news and opinion (such as the *New Republic*, the *National Review*, and *Commentary*) are primarily read by the educated elite.

F. The **broadcast media**.

1. The broadcast media have gradually displaced the print media as Americans' principal source of news and information.
   a. Radio was invented in 1903; the first modern commercial radio station was Pittsburgh's KDKA, whose first broadcast was of the 1920 Harding-Cox presidential election returns.
   b. As a form of technology, television is almost as old as radio; the first television station appeared in 1931.
2. The 1950s and 1960s were the adolescent years for American television.
   a. The first televised **presidential debate** was the 1960 Kennedy-Nixon debate. The poll results from this debate illustrate the visual power of television in American politics: whereas people listening to the radio gave the edge to Nixon, those who saw it on television thought Kennedy won.
   b. Television took the nation to the war in Vietnam during the 1960s, and TV exposed governmental naïveté (some said it was outright lying) about the progress of the war. President Johnson soon had two wars on his hands, one in Vietnam and the other at home with antiwar protesters—both covered in detail by the media.
3. With the growth of *cable TV*, particularly the Cable News Network (CNN), television has entered a new era of bringing news to people (and to political leaders) *as it happens*.
4. Since 1963, surveys have consistently shown that more people rely on TV for the news than any other medium; and by a regular two-to-one margin, people think television reports are more believable than newspaper stories.

5. Another trend associated with the growth of cable TV and the Internet is the development of **narrowcasting**, where "broadcast" stations target particularly narrow audiences.

III. REPORTING THE NEWS

A. Defining news.

1. News reporting is a *business* in America in which *profits shape how journalists define what is newsworthy, where they get their information, and how they present it.*
2. Edward J. Epstein found that to a large extent, TV networks define *news* as what is entertaining to the average viewer.

B. Finding the news.

1. A surprising amount of news comes from *well-established sources.* Most news organizations assign their best reporters to particular **beats**—specific locations where news frequently emanates from, such as Congress.
   a. Numerous studies of both the electronic and print media have found that journalists rely almost exclusively on such established sources to get their information.
   b. Those who make the news depend on the media to spread certain information and ideas to the general public (sometimes via stories fed to reporters in the form of **trial balloons**—information leaked to see what the political reaction will be).
   c. In turn, reporters rely on public officials to keep them informed. Official sources who have the information (such as knowledge about movements during the Gulf War) usually have the upper hand over those who merely report it.
   d. Very little of the news is generated by spontaneous events or a reporter's own analysis. Most stories are drawn from situations over which *newsmakers have substantial control.*
2. Despite this dependence on familiar sources, reporters occasionally have an opportunity to live up to the image of the "crusading truth-seeker."
   a. Local reporters Carl Bernstein and Bob Woodward of *The Washington Post* uncovered important evidence in the Watergate case.
   b. Columnists like Jack Anderson regularly expose government corruption and inefficiency.
3. The **Watergate** scandal signaled *a new era in the relationship between journalists and politicians.* Journalists began to assume that politicians had something to hide, and politicians assumed that reporters were out to embarrass them.

C. Presenting the news.
   1. Once the news has been "found," it has to be compressed into a 30-second news segment or fit in among the advertisements in a newspaper.
   2. TV news is little more than a headline service. With exceptions like the *MacNeil-Lehrer Newshour* (PBS) and *Nightline* (ABC), analysis of news events rarely lasts more than a minute. At the same time, complex issues—like nuclear power, the nation's money supply, and pollution—are difficult to treat in a short news clip.
   3. Paradoxically, as technology has enabled the media to pass along information with greater speed, news coverage has become less complete. Americans now hear **sound bites** of fifteen seconds or less on TV.

D. Bias in the news.
   1. The charge that the media have a *liberal bias* has become a familiar one in American politics, and there is some limited evidence to support it.
      a. Reporters are more likely to call themselves liberal than the general public, and a 1992 survey of 1400 journalists found that 44 percent identified themselves as Democrats compared to 16 percent who said they were Republicans.
      b. However, there is little reason to believe that journalists' personal attitudes sway their reporting of the news. Most stories are presented in a "point/counterpoint" format in which two opposing points of view are presented.
   2. The news is typically characterized by political neutrality.
      a. Most reporters strongly believe in journalistic objectivity.
      b. Those who are best at objective reporting are usually rewarded by their editors.
      c. Media outlets have a direct financial stake in attracting viewers and subscribers.
   3. A conclusion that news reporting contains little explicit *partisan or ideological* bias is *not* to argue that it does not *distort reality* in its coverage.
      a. Ideally, the news should mirror reality. In practice, there are too many potential stories for this to be the case.
      b. Journalists must select which stories to cover and to what degree. Due to economic pressures, the media are biased in favor of stories with high drama that will attract people's interest (rather than extended analyses of complex issues).
      c. Television is particularly biased toward stories that generate good pictures; seeing a **talking head** (a shot of a person's face talking

directly to the camera) is boring, and viewers will switch channels in search of more interesting visual stimulation.

IV. THE NEWS AND PUBLIC OPINION

A. It is difficult to study the effects of the news media on people's opinions and behavior. One reason is that it is hard to separate the media from other influences. In addition, the effect of one news story on public opinion may be negligible, while the cumulative effect of dozens of news stories may be quite important.

B. There is evidence that the news and its presentation are important in shaping public opinion about political issues.
   1. The decision to cover or to ignore certain issues can affect public opinion.
   2. By focusing public attention on specific problems, the media influence the criteria by which the public evaluates political leaders.
   3. There is also some evidence that people's opinions shift with the tone of the news coverage. Popular presidents prompt the public to support policies, but the most powerful influence is that of news commentators on public opinion change.

C. Much remains unknown about the effects of the media and the news on American political behavior. Enough is known, however, to conclude that the media are a *key political institution.*

V. THE MEDIA'S AGENDA-SETTING FUNCTION

A. As was explained in Chapter 1, people are trying to influence the government's **policy agenda** when they confront government officials with problems they expect them to solve.
   1. Interest groups, political parties, politicians (including the president and Congress), public relations firms, and bureaucratic agencies are all pushing for their priorities to take precedence over others.
   2. *Political activists* (often called **policy entrepreneurs**—people who invest their political "capital" in an issue) depend heavily upon the *media* to get their ideas placed high on the governmental agenda.
      a. Policy entrepreneurs' weapons include press releases, press conferences, letter writing, buttonholing reporters and columnists, and trading on personal contacts.
      b. People in power can also use a **leak**, a carefully placed bit of inside information that is given to a friendly reporter.

B. The *staging of political events to attract media attention* is a political art form.

1. Important political events (such as Nixon's famous trip to China) are orchestrated minute by minute with an eye on American TV audiences.
2. It is not only the elites who have successfully used the media. Civil rights groups in the 1960s relied heavily on the media to tell their stories of unjust treatment. Many believe that the introduction of television helped to accelerate the movement by graphically showing Americans (in both North and South) what the situation was.
3. Conveying a *long-term, positive image* via the media is *more important than a few dramatic events.* Policy entrepreneurs depend on goodwill and good images. Public relations firms may be hired to improve a group's (or individual's) image and their ability to sell their policy positions.

VI. UNDERSTANDING THE MASS MEDIA

A. The media are so crucial in today's society that they are often referred to as the **"fourth branch of government"** (an appellation that has also been applied to other institutions such as the bureaucracy).
   1. The media act as *key linkage institutions* between the people and the policymakers.
   2. The media have a profound impact on the political policy agenda.

B. The media and the scope of government.
   1. The **watchdog function** of the media *helps to keep government small.*
      a. Many observers feel that the press is *biased against whoever holds office* and that reporters want to expose them in the media. With every new proposal being met with skepticism, regular constraints are placed on the growth of government.
      b. The watchdog orientation of the press can be characterized as *neither liberal nor conservative*, but *reformist.*
   2. When they focus on injustice in society, the media inevitably *encourage the growth of government.*
      a. Once the media identify a problem in society, reporters usually begin to ask what the government is doing about the problem.
      b. The media *portray government as responsible for handling* almost every major problem.

C. Individualism and the media.
   1. The rise of television has furthered individualism in the American political process.
      a. Candidates are now much more capable of running for office on their own by appealing to people directly through television.

   b. Congress is difficult to cover on television because there are 535 members, but there is only one president, so the presidency has increasingly received more exposure vis-à-vis the Congress.

D. Democracy and the media.
   1. The rise of the "information society" has not brought about the rise of the "informed society."
      a. The media do a much better job of covering the "horse race" aspects of politics than of covering substantive issues.
      b. With the media's superficial treatment of important policy issues, it is not surprising that the incredible amount of information available to Americans today has not visibly increased their political awareness or participation.
   2. The media's defense is to say that this is what the people want. Network executives claim that they are in business to make a profit, and to do so they have to appeal to the maximum number of people.

KEY TERMS AND CONCEPTS

Beats: specific locations where news frequently occurs.

Broadcast media: one of two kinds of media, includes television and radio.

Chains: media conglomerates which control a large percentage of daily newspaper circulation and some television and radio stations as well.

High-tech politics: politics where technology has shaped political behavior and the political agenda.

Investigative journalism: the use of detective-like reporting methods to unearth scandals.

Mass media: media which reaches and influences both elites and the masses.

Media event: an event staged primarily for the purpose of being covered.

Narrowcasting: strategy of some broadcast channels that appeal to a narrow, rather than a broad, audience.

Policy agenda: the list of subjects or problems to which government officials and people outside of government closely associated with those officials are paying some serious attention at any given time.

Policy entrepreneurs: political activists who invest their political capital in an issue.

Press conferences: presidential meetings with the press.

Print media: one of two kinds of media, includes newspapers and magazines.

Sound bites: a portion of a speech aired on TV of fifteen seconds or less.

Talking head: a shot of a person's face talking directly into the camera.

Trial balloons: information leaked to the media to see what the political reaction will be.

TEACHING IDEAS: CLASS DISCUSSION AND STUDENT PROJECTS

- We frequently complain about bias by the media in reporting the policies and activities of the president and Congress, but officeholders also manipulate the media. In fact, modern political success depends upon control of the mass media. Have your class try to determine how each manipulates the other.

- *You Are the Policymaker: Should Networks Have to Provide Free Air Time to Candidates?* examines a proposal for free air time—scheduled at the same time on all networks and interested cable outlets one month prior to presidential elections. Ask your class to read this selection and be prepared to discuss the proposal in class. Who would such a policy advantage? Disadvantage? Would our democracy be stronger if in fact we adopted such a proposal?

- Assign students to debate the question as to whether—or in what ways—the mass media are biased. Require that they develop working definitions of bias and gather evidence regarding characteristics of reporters and editors; chain ownership and advertising; and actual media content.

- Ask your students to discuss the role that the *profit motive* plays in how journalists report the news. What would be their reactions to proposals to have a *publicly funded* information service?

- If there is a local newspaper in your town, contact the editor and ask if one of the reporters would be willing to speak to your class. This is often seen as good public relations for the newspaper, and can enliven a class by bringing in the "real world" of reporting.

- For class discussion, ask students to evaluate whether American mass media has become too powerful. In particular, ask students to debate whether mass media's impact on public opinion and political outcomes is consistent with the concepts of limited government and balanced power. Is there any democratic way to hold mass media organizations accountable for their behavior?

- For class discussion, ask students to discuss the ways in which mass media influences the political thought and behavior of citizens. In particular, have students evaluate the media's role in creating an informed citizenry, which is vital to the successful functioning of democratic government.

- For a reading and writing connection, have students prepare a content analysis of the following news media including a local newspaper, the New York Times, the local television news, a national television news, the MacNeil-Lehrer Newshour on PBS television, a local radio station's news, and the local NPR radio station's news. Using a coding sheet, have them code the content of the headline news reports for one week. The coding sheet should include the date/time of the media presentations, the subject, the length of time the item was discussed, and an evaluation of the amount of detail provided for each news story. Then have students write an essay comparing and contrasting the differences in information acquired from each medium in terms of quality, depth, breadth, originality, and timeliness.

- Divide your class into five groups: network television, daily local newspapers, daily national newspapers, cable news, and radio. Ask that they watch, read, or listen to the news only from their arranged source for one or two weeks, and then quiz them in terms of their knowledge of current events.

- Alternatively, have students compare the topics and amount of information presented in traditional media sources versus the Internet. Allow students to debate which news source is better.

BACKGROUND READING

Bennett, W. Lance. News: The Politics of Illusion. 3rd ed. NY: Longman. 1995.

Cook, Timothy E. Governing with the News: The News Media as a Political Institution. Chicago: University of Chicago Press. 1998.

Epstein, Edward J. News From Nowhere: Television and the News. NY: Random House. 1973.

Graber, Doris A. Mass Media and American Politics. 5th ed. Washington, DC: Congressional Quarterly Press. 1996.

Graber, Doris A., Denis McQuail and Pippa Norris, eds. The Politics of News, The News of Politics. Washington, D.C.: CQ Press. 1998.

Iyengar, Shanto and Donald R. Kinder. News That Matters. Chicago: University of Chicago Press. 1987.

Linsky. Martin. Impact: How the Press Affects Federal Policy Making. NY: Morrow. 1986.

Neuman, W. Russell, Marion R. Just and Ann N. Crigler. Common Knowledge: News and the Construction of Political Meaning. Chicago: University of Chicago Press. 1992.

Patterson, Thomas E. Out of Order. NY: Knopf. 1993.

West, Darrell M. Air Wars: Television Advertising in Election Campaigns, 1952-1992. Washington, DC: Congressional Quarterly Press. 1993.

MEDIA SUGGESTIONS

All the President's Men. A 1976 movie dramatization of Woodward and Bernstein's investigation of the Watergate scandal.

Cost of Free Speech. This film analyzes the effect of freedom of the press, especially examining the possible harm from media having too much freedom. Films for the Humanities and Sciences.

Disconnected: Politics, the Press and the Public. This program focuses on the extent to which the media, with its emphasis on profit, deadlines and entertainment, compromise media coverage of elections and disconnect the public from the political system. Films for the Humanities & Sciences.

Free Speech for Sale: A Bill Moyers Special. Moyers, along with various public advocates, discuss the ability of well-funded interests to dominate public debate, largely due to their access to the mass media. Films for the Humanities & Sciences.

Politics in Action, Chapter 9: Media at War. Contrasts the style of media coverage of wars across five decades, highlighting the changing nature of reporting norms in covering political events.

CHAPTER EIGHT: POLITICAL PARTIES

PEDAGOGICAL FEATURES

LEARNING OBJECTIVES

After studying this chapter, students should be able to:

- Understand the roles of the party-in-the-electorate, the party as an organization, and the party-in-government.

- Examine how political parties in a democracy serve as key linkage institutions to translate inputs from the public into outputs from the policymakers.

- Describe Anthony Downs' *rational-choice theory* as a working model of the relationship among citizens, parties, and policy.
- Trace the historical development of the American two-party system.
- Describe what is meant by *party eras*, *critical elections*, and *party realignment*.
- Examine the significance of *divided government* and explain how the recent pattern of divided government may explain party *dealignment*.
- Differentiate between the ideology or party philosophy of the Democratic and Republican parties.
- Explain why it is rational in the American two-party system for both Democrats and Republicans to stay near the center of public opinion.
- Explain how electoral rules such as the "winner-take-all" plurality system have helped to maintain a two-party system in the United States.
- Evaluate the impact of third parties on American politics and the American party system.
- Determine the consequences or effects of the American two-party system as contrasted with a multi-party system.
- Understand the significance of the weak and decentralized character of the American party system.
- Evaluate proposals that call for a "more *responsible* two-party system."

CHAPTER OVERVIEW

INTRODUCTION

Although political parties may not be highly regarded by all, many observers of politics agree that political parties are central to representative government because they provide meaning to citizens' choices between competing candidates in elections. The alternating of power and influence between the two major parties is one of the most important elements in American politics. **Party competition** is the battle between Democrats and Republicans for the control of public offices. Historically, changes in party control of government have been associated with substantial changes in the nature and scope of government. The recent trend toward divided government—where Congress is controlled by one party and the President represents the other—seems to have blocked any major changes in the scope of government.

THE MEANING OF PARTY

In a large democracy, **linkage institutions** *translate inputs from the public* into *outputs from the policymakers.* Linkage institutions help ensure that public preferences are heard. The *four main linkage institutions* in the United States are *parties*, *elections*, *interest groups*, and the *media.*

As linkage institutions, **political parties** nominate candidates for office, coordinate campaigns, provide cues for voters, articulate policies, and coordinate policy making. It is not always easy to distinguish between the parties since each rationally chooses to stay near the center of public opinion.

Political scientists often view parties as *"three-headed political giants"*—the party-in-the-electorate, the party as an organization, and the party-in-government. The **party-in-the-electorate** are voters who identify with a political party. Unlike many European political parties, American parties do not require dues or membership cards to distinguish members from nonmembers. One needs only to *claim to be a member* to be a member of a party in the United States. The **party as an organization** has a national office, a full-time staff, rules and bylaws, and budgets. These are the people who keep the party running between elections and make its rules. The **party-in-government** consists of elected officials who call themselves members of the party, such as the president and Congress. These leaders are the main spokespersons of the party.

Economist Anthony Downs has provided a working model of *the relationship among citizens, parties, and policy*, employing a rational-choice perspective. **Rational choice theory** assumes that parties and political actors have pragmatic goals (such as winning elections) that are more important to the party than ideology. A party that wants to win office will pursue policies that have broad public appeal.

THE PARTY IN THE ELECTORATE

The *party in the electorate* consists largely of symbolic images. There is no formal "membership" in American parties, and the party is a psychological label for most people. Party images help shape people's **party identification**—the *self-proclaimed preference* for one of the parties. The clearest trend in party identification over the last five decades has been *the decline of both parties* and the resultant *upsurge of Independents* (mostly at the expense of the Democrats). Party identification still remains strongly linked to the voter's choice, but **ticket-splitting** is near an all-time high, with many people voting with one party for one office and another for other offices. *Divided government* has often been the result (frequently with Republican control of the White House and Democratic control of Congress).

THE PARTY ORGANIZATIONS: FROM THE GRASS ROOTS TO WASHINGTON

American political parties are *decentralized and fragmented.* Unlike many European parties, formal party organizations in America have little power to enforce their decisions by offering rewards to officeholders who follow the party line and punishing those who do not. American national parties are a loose aggregation of state parties, which in turn are a fluid association of individuals, groups, and local organizations. There are fifty state party systems, no two exactly alike.

At one time, the urban political party was the basis of political party organization in America; but urban party organizations are no longer very active. From the late nineteenth century through the New Deal of the 1930s, scores of cities were dominated by **party machines** (a party organization that depends on material inducements such as **patronage**, in which jobs were awarded for political reasons rather than for merit or competence). Urban party organizations are also no longer very active as a rule. Progressive reforms that placed jobs under the merit system rather than at the machine's discretion weakened the machines' power. Party filling in the void created by the decline of the inner-city machines has been a revitalization of party organization at the county level – particularly in affluent suburbs.

Organizationally, state parties are on the upswing throughout the country. Though no study of state parties has been conducted recently, it is almost certain that their financial resources have increased. In the 1996 case of *Colorado Republican Campaign Committee v. Federal Election Commission*, the Supreme Court ruled that the government may not restrict the amount that the state or national parties spend on behalf of candidates through independent expenditures.

The **national convention** of each party meets every four years to write the party's platform and nominate its candidates for president and vice president. The **national committee**, composed of representatives from the states and territories, keeps the party operating between conventions. Day-to-day activities of the national party are the responsibility of the **national chairperson**, who hires the staff, raises the money, pays the bills, and attends to the daily duties of the party.

THE PARTY-IN-GOVERNMENT: PROMISES AND POLICY

Party control *does matter* because each party and the elected officials who represent it generally try to turn campaign promises into action. Voters and coalitions of voters are attracted to different parties largely (though not entirely) by their performance and policies. The parties have done a fairly good job over the years of *translating their platform promises into public policy*; the impression that politicians and parties never produce policy out of promises is largely erroneous.

PARTY ERAS IN AMERICAN HISTORY

America has always had two parties, in contrast to most democratic nations. Throughout American history, one party has been the dominant majority party for long periods of time (referred to as **party eras**). Party eras were punctuated by **critical elections**—in which new issues appeared that divided the electorate—and *party coalitions underwent realignment*. A **party realignment** (a rare event) is typically associated with a major crisis or trauma in the nation's history, such as the Civil War and the Great Depression, both of which led to realignments. A new coalition is formed for each party, and the coalition endures for many years.

Alexander Hamilton was probably the person most instrumental in establishing the first party system. The foundation of the **Federalist** party developed from his politicking and coalition building while he tried to get congressional support for policies he favored (particularly a national bank). The **Democratic-Republicans** (also known as *Jeffersonians*), which replaced the Federalists, were based on a coalition derived from agrarian interests. This made the party popular in the rural South, but the coalition was torn apart by *factionalism*.

General Andrew Jackson founded the modern American political party when he forged a new coalition in 1828. Jackson was originally a Democratic-Republican, but soon after his election his party became known simply as the **Democratic** party (which continues to this day). Jackson's successor, Martin Van Buren, was a realist who argued that a governing party needed a loyal opposition to represent other parts of society. This opposition was provided by the **Whigs**, but the Whig party was only able to win the presidency when it nominated popular military heroes such as William Henry Harrison (1840) and Zachary Taylor (1848).

The **Republican** party rose in the late 1850s as the antislavery party. The Republicans forged a coalition out of the remnants of several minor parties and elected Abraham Lincoln as president in 1860. The Civil War brought a *party realignment*, and the Republican party was in ascendancy for more than sixty years (though the Democrats controlled the South). The election of 1896 was a watershed event during this era—a period when party coalitions shifted and the Republicans were entrenched for another generation.

The Republicans continued as the nation's majority party until the stock market crash of 1929 and the ensuing Great Depression. President Herbert Hoover's handling of the Great Depression was disastrous for the Republican party. Franklin D. Roosevelt promised a *New Deal* and easily defeated Hoover in 1932. Congress passed scores of Roosevelt's anti-Depression measures during his *first hundred days* in office. Party realignment began in earnest after the Roosevelt administration got the country moving again, and Roosevelt forged the **New Deal coalition** from such diverse groups as union members, southerners, intellectuals, liberals, the poor, and African Americans.

Although the Democrats have been the majority party since Roosevelt's time, the coalition has steadily weakened since the mid-1960s. An unprecedented period of **divided government** (when the executive and legislative branches are controlled by different parties) has existed since that time.

Many political scientists believe that the recent pattern of divided government means that the party system has **dealigned**, with people gradually moving away from *both* political parties. Many scholars fear that the parties are becoming useless and ineffective through the pattern of divided government and dealignment. However, the recent dealignment has been characterized by a growing **party neutrality**; those who do identify with a party are more likely to belong to *the party that matches their ideology*; and *party organizations have become more energetic and effective* even though party loyalty has declined.

THIRD PARTIES: THEIR IMPACT ON AMERICAN POLITICS

Although the United States has a two-party system, **third parties** have controlled enough votes in one-third of the last thirty-six presidential elections to have decisively tipped the electoral college vote. Third parties have brought new groups into the electorate, have served as "safety valves" for popular discontent, and have brought new issues to the political agenda.

The *most obvious consequence of two-party governance* is the *moderation of political conflict*. With just two parties, both will cling to a centrist position to maximize their appeal to voters. The result is often political ambiguity—parties will not want to risk taking a strong stand on a controversial policy if doing so will only antagonize many voters.

Election rules in the United States tend to favor a two party system. For example, the **winner-take-all system** has meant that the party that receives a plurality is declared the winner and the other parties get nothing. By contrast, in a system that uses **proportional representation** (used in most European countries), legislative seats are allocated according to each party's percentage of the nationwide vote. A small party may use its seats to combine with one of the larger parties to form a coalition government.

UNDERSTANDING POLITICAL PARTIES

Political parties are essential components of democratic government. Ideally, candidates in a democracy should say what they mean to do if elected and be able to carry out what they promised once they are elected. Critics of the American party system complain that this is all too often not the case, and have called for a more **responsible party** system. The responsible party model calls for each party to present distinct, comprehensive programs; carry out its program if elected; implement its programs if it is the majority party or state what it would do if it were in power; and accept responsibility for the performance of the government. American parties do not meet the criteria of the responsible party model. They are too *decentralized* to take a single national position and then enforce it; parties *do not have control* over those who run under their labels; and there is no mechanism for a party to discipline officeholders and ensure cohesion in policy making.

There are also supporters of America's two-party system who criticize the responsible party model. They argue that the complexity and diversity of American society needs a different form of representation, and that local differences need an outlet for expression. Advocates of America's decentralized parties consider them appropriate for the type of *limited government* the founders sought to create and most Americans wish to maintain.

Because no single party in the United States can ever be said to have firm control over the government, the hard choices necessary to limit the growth of government are rarely addressed. Divided government has meant that neither party is really in charge, and each tries to blame the other for failures and limitations of government.

Parties are no longer the main source of political information. More and more political communication is through the mass media rather than face-to-face. However, there are indications that the parties are beginning to adapt to the high-tech age. State and national party organizations have become more visible and active. Although more people than ever before call themselves Independent and split their tickets, the majority still identify with a party (and this percentage seems to have stabilized).

CHAPTER OUTLINE

I. INTRODUCTION

A. **Party competition** is the battle between Democrats and Republicans for control of public office.

B. Without this competition there would be no choice, and without choice there would be no democracy.

II. THE MEANING OF PARTY

A. **Political parties** endorse candidates for public office and *try to win elections*.

B. Party leaders often disagree about policy, and between elections the parties are nearly invisible.

C. Political scientists often view parties as "*three-headed political giants*"—the *party-in-the-electorate*, the *party as an organization*, and the *party-in-government.*

1. The **party-in-the-electorate** are individuals who perceive themselves as party members; many voters have a party identification that guides and influences their votes. Unlike many European political parties, American parties do not require dues or membership cards to distinguish members from nonmembers. To be a *member of a party*, one needs only to claim to be a member.
2. The **party as an organization** has a national office, a full-time staff, rules and bylaws, and budgets. Party activists *keep the party running* between elections and *make its rules*. Although American parties are loosely organized at the national, state, and local levels, the party organization *pursues electoral victory*.
3. The **party-in-government** consists of *elected officials* who call themselves members of the party (such as President and Congress). These leaders *do not always agree on policy*; but they are the main spokespersons of the party.

D. Tasks of the parties.
   1. In a large democracy, **linkage institutions** *translate inputs from the public* into *outputs from the policymakers*.
   2. Tasks performed by parties as linkage institutions:
      a. Parties pick policymakers; a **nomination** is the party's endorsement of a candidate.
      b. Parties run campaigns; although parties *coordinate the campaigns*, recent technology has made it easier for candidates to campaign on their own.
      c. Parties give **cues** to voters; even though party ties have weakened, most voters have a **party image** of each party; and many voters still rely on a party to give them cues for voting.
      d. Parties *articulate policies*; within the electorate and in the government, each political party advocates specific policy alternatives.
      e. Parties *coordinate policy-making*; each office holder is also a member of a party, and the first place they look for support is to their fellow partisans.

E. Parties, voters, and policy: The **Downs Model**.
   1. Anthony Downs has provided a working model of *the relationship among citizens, parties, and policy*, employing a *rational-choice perspective*.
   2. **Rational-choice theory** assumes that parties and political actors have goals (such as winning elections) that are more important to the party than ideology.
      a. If both parties and voters are rational, both will try to select the best way to achieve their goals.
      b. In order to win an office, the wise party pursues policies that have broad public appeal.
      c. The majority of the American electorate are in the middle, and successful parties in the U.S. rarely stray far from the midpoint of public opinion.
      d. Although we frequently hear criticism that there is not much difference between the Democrats and Republicans, the two parties have little choice (given the nature of the American political market).
      e. From a rational-choice perspective, one should expect the parties to *differentiate* themselves to some extent. The two parties have to forge different identities in order to build voter loyalty.

III. THE PARTY IN THE ELECTORATE

A. The *party in the electorate* consists largely of symbolic images.

1. There is no formal "membership" in American parties.
2. For most people, the party is a psychological label.

B. Party images help shape people's **party identification**—the *self-proclaimed preference* for one of the parties.
1. The clearest trend in party identification over the last four decades has been *the decline of both parties* and the resultant *upsurge of Independents* (mostly at the expense of the Democrats).
2. Virtually every major social group (except African-American voters) has moved toward a position of increased independence.
3. By contrast, African-Americans have moved even more solidly into the Democratic party (currently only 5 percent of African-Americans identify themselves as Republicans).

C. Party identification remains strongly linked to the voter's choice, but **ticket-splitting** (voting with one party for one office and another for other offices) is near an all-time high.
1. Not only are there more Independents now, but those who still identify with a party are no longer as loyal in the voting booth as they once were.
2. *Divided government* has frequently been the result (often with Republican control of the White House and Democratic control of Congress).

IV. THE PARTY ORGANIZATIONS: FROM THE GRASS ROOTS TO WASHINGTON

A. American political parties are *decentralized and fragmented.*
1. Unlike many European parties, formal party organizations in America have little power to enforce their decisions by offering rewards (like campaign funds and appointments) to officeholders who follow the party line and punishing those who do not.
2. Candidates in the United States can get elected on their own, and the party organization is relegated to a relatively limited role.

B. Local parties: the dying urban machines.
1. Urban party organizations are no longer very active.
2. At one time, the urban political party was the basis of political party organization in America.
    a. From the late nineteenth century through the New Deal of the 1930s, scores of cities were dominated by **party machines** (a party organization that depends on material inducements such as **patronage**, in which jobs were awarded for political reasons rather than for merit or competence).

C. The fifty state party systems.

1. American national parties are a loose aggregation of state parties, which in turn are a fluid association of individuals, groups, and local organizations.
2. There are fifty state party systems, no two exactly alike. Parties in some states (such as Pennsylvania) are well organized, have sizable staffs, and spend a lot of money, while parties in other states (such as California) are very weak.
3. The states are allowed great discretion in the regulation of party activities, and how they choose to organize elections influences the strength of the parties profoundly. States determine how easy it is to participate in nomination contests by their adoption of **closed primaries, open primaries or blanket primaries.**

D. The national party organizations.
1. The **national convention** of each party meets every four years to *write the party's platform* and *nominate its candidates for president and vice president.*
2. The **national committee**, composed of representatives from the states and territories, keeps the party operating between conventions.
3. Day-to-day activities of the national party are the responsibility of the **national chairperson.**

V. THE PARTY IN GOVERNMENT: PROMISES AND POLICY

A. Party control *does matter* because each party and the elected officials who represent it generally try to turn campaign promises into action.
B. Since candidates are now much less dependent upon parties to get nominated and elected, party control has weakened. In addition, presidents are now less likely to play the role of party leader, and members of Congress are less amenable to being led.
C. Voters and coalitions of voters are attracted to different parties largely (though not entirely) by their performance and policies.
D. The parties have done a fairly good job over the years of *translating their platform promises into public policy*—the impression that politicians and parties never produce policy out of promises is largely erroneous.

VI. PARTY ERAS IN AMERICAN HISTORY

A. In contrast to the United States, most democratic nations have more than two parties represented in their national legislature.
B. Throughout American history, one party has been the dominant majority party for long periods of time (referred to as **party eras**).
1. Party eras were punctuated by **critical elections**, in which new issues appeared that divided the electorate and *party coalitions underwent realignment.*

2. A **party realignment** (a rare event) is typically associated with a major crisis or trauma in the nation's history (such as the Civil War and the great Depression, both of which led to realignments).
3. A new **coalition** (a set of individuals or groups supporting the party) is formed for each party, and the coalition endures for many years.
4. A critical election period may require more than one election before change is apparent, but the party system will be transformed in such a period.

C. 1796-1824: The first party system.
1. Alexander Hamilton was probably the person most instrumental in establishing the first party system.
2. Hamilton needed congressional support for policies he favored (particularly a national bank), and the foundation of the **Federalist** party came from his politicking and coalition building.
3. The Federalists were America's shortest-lived major party: they were poorly organized, they faded after John Adams was defeated in his reelection bid of 1800, and they no longer even had a candidate for president after 1820.
4. The **Democratic-Republicans** (also known as *Jeffersonians*) replaced the Federalists. The Democratic-Republican coalition was derived from agrarian interests—which made the party popular in the rural South—but the coalition was torn apart by *factionalism*.

D. 1828-1856: Jackson and the Democrats versus the Whigs.
1. General Andrew Jackson founded the modern American political party when he forged a new coalition in 1828.
2. Jackson was originally a Democratic-Republican, but soon after his election his party became known simply as the **Democratic** party (which continues to this day).
3. Jackson's successor, Martin Van Buren, was a realist who argued that a governing party needed a loyal opposition to represent other parts of society. This opposition was provided by the **Whigs**, but the Whig party was only able to win the presidency when it nominated popular military heroes such as William Henry Harrison (1840) and Zachary Taylor (1848).
4. The Whigs had two distinct wings—northern industrialists and southern planters—who were brought together more by the Democratic policies they opposed than by issues on which they agreed.

E. 1860-1928: The Republican Era.
1. The issue of slavery dominated American politics and split both the Whigs and the Democrats in the 1850s.
2. The **Republican** party rose in the late 1850s as the antislavery party.

3. The Republicans forged a coalition out of the remnants of several minor parties and elected Abraham Lincoln as president in 1860.
4. The Civil War brought a *party realignment*, and the Republican party was in ascendancy for more than sixty years (though the Democrats controlled the South).
5. The election of 1896 was a watershed during this era—a period when party coalitions shifted and the Republicans were entrenched for another generation.
6. The Republicans continued as the nation's majority party until the *stock market crash of 1929* and the ensuing *Great Depression.*

F. 1932-1964: The New Deal coalition.
1. President Herbert Hoover's handling of the Great Depression was disastrous for the Republicans. He took the position that "economic depression cannot be cured by legislative action."
2. Franklin D. Roosevelt promised a *New Deal* and easily defeated Hoover in 1932.
3. Congress passed scores of Roosevelt's anti-Depression measures during his *first hundred days* in office.
4. Party realignment began in earnest after the Roosevelt administration got the country moving again, and Roosevelt forged the **New Deal coalition** from such diverse groups as union members, southerners, intellectuals, liberals, the poor, and African-Americans.

G. 1968-present: The era of divided government.
1. Although the Democrats have been the majority party ever since Roosevelt's time, the coalition has steadily weakened since the mid-1960s.
2. An unprecedented period of **divided government** (when the executive and legislative branches are controlled by different parties) has existed since 1968.
3. It is likely that divided party government will be a regular phenomenon at both the federal and state levels.

H. **Party dealignment** means that people are gradually moving away from *both* political parties.
1. Many political scientists believe that the recent pattern of *divided government* means that the party system has dealigned rather than realigned.
2. Many scholars fear that the parties are becoming useless and ineffective through the pattern of divided government and dealignment.
3. Conversely, there are also some signs of party renewal, such as the increase in the regular Washington staff of the national party organizations.

4. The recent dealignment has been characterized by a growing **party neutrality**; many voters are aware of the candidates but lack any party anchoring (and are often referred as "*the floating voters*").
5. Those who do identify with a party are *more likely to belong to the party that matches their* ideology—the parties have become ideologically differentiated, and people who call themselves conservatives are more likely to be in the Republican party while liberals are concentrated in the Democratic party.
6. *Even though party loyalty has lagged, party organizations have become more energetic and effective*—the parties learned the secrets of high-tech fund-raising; the parties' national, congressional, and senatorial campaign committees are now wealthier, more stable, better organized, and better staffed.

VII. THIRD PARTIES: THEIR IMPACT ON AMERICAN POLITICS

A. There are three basic varieties of **third parties.**
   1. Parties that promote certain causes—either a controversial single issue such as prohibition of alcoholic beverages or an extreme ideological position such as socialism or libertarianism;
   2. *Splinter parties* that are offshoots of a major party—such as Teddy Roosevelt's Progressives (1912), Strom Thurmond's States' Righters (1948), and George Wallace's American Independents (1968);
   3. Parties that are an extension of a popular individual with presidential aspirations—including John Anderson (1980) and Ross Perot (1992 and 1996).

B. Importance of third parties.
   1. Third parties have controlled enough votes in one-third of the last thirty-six presidential elections to have decisively tipped the electoral college vote.
   2. They have brought new groups into the electorate and have served as "safety valves" for popular discontent.
   3. They have brought new issues to the political agenda.

C. Consequences of the two-party system.
   1. The *most obvious consequence of two-party governance* is the *moderation of political conflict.*
      a. With just two parties, both will cling to a centrist position to maximize their appeal to voters.
      b. The result is often political ambiguity—parties will not want to risk taking a strong stand on a controversial policy if doing so will only antagonize many voters (as with Goldwater in 1964 and McGovern in 1972).

2. One of the major reasons the United States has only two parties represented in government is structural—America has a **winner-take-all system.**
   a. In this system, the party that receives a plurality (more votes than anyone else, even though it may be less than a majority) is declared the winner; the other parties get nothing.
   b. This system *discourages small parties.*
3. In a system that uses **proportional representation** (used in most European countries), legislative seats are allocated according to each party's percentage of the nationwide vote.
   a. A party must achieve a certain percentage of votes to be awarded seats in the legislature.
   b. A small party may use its seats to combine with one of the larger parties to form a coalition government.
4. A **coalition government** is created when two or more parties join together to form a majority in a national legislature. This form of government is quite common in the multiparty systems of Europe.

VIII. UNDERSTANDING POLITICAL PARTIES

A. Political parties are considered *essential elements of democratic government.*
B. Democracy and responsible party government.
   1. Ideally, in a democracy candidates should say what they mean to do if elected and be able to do what they promised once they are elected.
   2. Critics of the American party system complain that this is all too often not the case, and have called for a more disciplined, **responsible party** system.
      a. The responsible party model calls for each party to present distinct, comprehensive programs; carry out its program if elected; implement its programs if it is the majority party or state what it would do if it were in power; and accept responsibility for the performance of the government.
      b. Under this model, a party's officeholders would have firm control of the government, and they would be *collectively* (rather than individually) *responsible* for their actions.
   3. American parties do not meet the criteria of the responsible party model.
      a. They are too *decentralized* to take a single national position and then enforce it.
      b. Because virtually anyone can vote in party primaries, parties *do not have control* over those who run under their labels.

c. In America's loosely organized party system, there is no mechanism for a party to discipline officeholders and ensure cohesion in policymaking.

4. There are supporters of America's two-party system who criticize the responsible party model.
   a. They argue that the complexity and diversity of American society needs a different form of representation; local differences need an outlet for expression.
   b. America's decentralized parties are appropriate for the type of *limited government* the founders sought to create and most Americans wish to maintain.

C. Individualism and gridlock.
1. The Founding Fathers wanted to preserve individual freedom of action by elected officials.
   a. With America's weak party system, this is certainly the case.
2. Weak parties make it easier for politicians to avoid tough decisions; this creates *gridlock.*

D. American political parties and the scope of government.
1. Weak parties limit the scope of government in America because the President cannot command party discipline to pass important legislation, such as health care.
2. Because no single party can ever be said to have firm control over government, the hard choices necessary to cut back on existing government spending are rarely addressed.
3. *Divided government* has meant that neither party is really in charge, and each points the finger at the other.

E. Is the party over?
1. Parties are no longer the main source of political information.
   a. More and more political communication is not face-to-face but rather through the mass media.
   b. The technology of campaigning—television, polls, computers, political consultants, media specialists, and the like—can be bought by candidates for themselves, and they therefore do not need to be dependent on the party.
   c. With the advent of television, *voters* no longer need the party to find out what the candidates are like and what they stand for.
   d. The power of *interest groups* has grown enormously in recent years; they pioneered much of the technology of modern politics, including mass mailings and sophisticated fund-raising.

2. There are indications that the parties are beginning to adapt to the high-tech age.
   a. State and national party organizations have become more visible and active.
   b. Although more people than ever before call themselves Independent and split their tickets, the majority still identify with a party (and this percentage seems to have stabilized).

KEY TERMS AND CONCEPTS

Blanket primaries: nomination contest where voters are presented with a list of the candidates from all the parties and allow them to pick candidates from all parties.

Coalition: a set of individuals and groups supporting a political party.

Coalition government: governments where smaller parties combine with larger parties to control half of the seats in the legislature.

Closed primaries: nomination contest where only people who have registered in advance with the party can vote.

Critical election: an election where each party's coalition of support begins to break up and a new coalition of forces is formed for each party.

Linkage institutions: institutions such as parties, elections, interest groups, and the media translate inputs from the public into outputs from policy makers.

National chairperson: the person responsible for taking care of the day to day activities and daily duties of the party.

National committee: a coalition of representatives from the states and territories charged with maintaining the party between elections.

National convention: the supreme power within each party which meets every four years, writes the party platform, and nominates candidates for president and vice-president.

New Deal coalition: the new coalition of forces (urban, unions, Catholics, Jews, the poor, Southerners, African-Americans, and intellectuals) in the Democratic party which was forged as a result of national economic crisis associated with the Great Depression.

Open primaries: nomination contest where voters can decide on election day whether they want to participate in the Democratic or Republican contest.

Party competition: the battle between the two dominant parties in the American system.

Party dealignment: when voters move away from both parties.

Party eras: occasions where there has been a dominant majority party for long periods of time.

Party identification: the self-proclaimed preference for one or the other party.

Party image: is what voters know or think they know about what each party stands for.

Party machines: a particular kind of party organization that depends on both specific and material inducements for rewarding loyal party members.

Party neutrality: when voters have an indifferent attitude toward both parties.

Party realignment: process whereby the major political parties form new support coalitions that endure for a long period.

Patronage: one of the key inducements used by machines whereby jobs are given for political reasons rather than for merit or competence alone.

Political party: a team of men and women seeking to control the governing apparatus by gaining office in a duly constituted election.

Proportional representation: an electoral system where legislative seats are allocated on the basis of each party's percentage of the national vote.

Rational-choice theory: a theory that seeks to explain political processes and outcomes as consequences of purposive behavior, where political actors are assumed to have goals and who pursue those goals rationally.

Responsible party model: an ideal model of party organization recommending that parties provide distinct programs, encourage candidates to be committed to the party platform, intend to implement their programs, and accept responsibility for the performance of government.

Third parties: minor parties which either promote narrow ideological issues or are splinter groups from the major parties.

Ticket-splitting: voting with one party for one office and another for other offices.

Winner-take-all system: an electoral system where whoever gets the most votes wins the election.

TEACHING IDEAS: CLASS DISCUSSION AND STUDENT PROJECTS

- We frequently hear criticism that there is not much difference between the Democrats and Republicans. Have your class summarize the contents of the front section of the newspaper for one or two weeks. Students should pay particular attention to whether there are differences between Republicans and Democrats on issues that make the front page. At the end of the week, compare the number of issues on which there appears to be party differences compared to those on which there is little difference. Have students then reassess their beliefs about differences between Republicans and Democrats.

- Although few people actually read party platforms, they are one of the best written sources for what the parties believe in. A brief summary of the 1996 Democratic and Republican platforms is given in Table 8.3 in the textbook. Ask your class to read the summaries and then discuss whether the perception that there is "no difference" between Democrats and Republicans is correct.

- As a library project, ask students to read editorials for a period of several days following Ronald Reagan's 1980 and 1984 elections. They should have no difficulty in finding a number of articles that speculated on whether this was a *realigning* election. Ask them to write "follow-up" essays reflecting on Bill Clinton's victories in 1992 and 1996. Were the journalists correct in describing the early 1980s as a realigning period? Why or why not?

- For an interesting class discussion, first ask students if they believe there is any difference between Republicans and Democrats. Then repeat the question, focusing on specific political issues (e.g., abortion, obscenity, environment, tax policy) and which social groups identify with each party.

- To reinforce the lecture material, have students debate the reasons why parties have declined in popularity. In particular, have them draw comparisons between the benefits of membership in an interest group versus the benefits of membership in a political party.

- For a reading and writing connection, give students a research assignment where they compare and contrast the role of the parties and their platforms in the 1996 and 1998 elections and in the 1948 election of Harry Truman. In particular, ask students to pay special attention to how media, especially television, was used to promote party goals. Because television was still very new in 1948 and was used strategically in 1996 and 1998, the comparisons should result in starkly different images of parties. In addition, students should see the difference between party-centered and candidate-centered campaigns.

- Invite representatives from the two mainstream parties (as well as any others organized on campus) to present brief talks to your class regarding their parties, and why identifying with their party, or getting involved with it, is a good thing. After the representatives leave, have your students discuss whether they were persuaded in any way (that parties are good, or involvement is good, for example) and why: what incentives became apparent in the lectures and subsequent discussion?

- Assign students to research the party platforms and organizational characteristics of state-level parties, with each student taking a different party in a different state. How much diversity is there across the states? How do the state parties compare with the national parties?

BACKGROUND READING

Aldrich, John H. Why Parties? The Origin and Transformation of Political Parties in America. Chicago: University of Chicago Press. 1995.

Burnham, Walter Dean. Critical Elections and the Mainsprings of American Politics. NY: W. W. Norton. 1970.

Maisel, L. Sandy, ed. The Parties Respond. Boulder, CO: Westview Press, 1990.

Rosenstone, Steven J., Roy L. Behr, and Edward H. Lazarus. Third Parties in America, 2nd ed. Princeton, NJ: Princeton University Press. 1996.

Sabato, Larry. The Party's Just Begun: Shaping Political Parties for America's Future. Glenview, IL: Scott, Foresman/Little Brown. 1988.

Sundquist, James L. Dynamics of the Party System. Rev. ed. Washington, DC: Brookings Institution. 1983.

MEDIA SUGGESTIONS

A Third Choice. This program examines third parties in the U.S., including interviews with academic experts, campaign memorabilia and rare archival footage. Films for the Humanities & Sciences.

The Candidate. A 1972 Warner Brothers film about packaging a political candidate. In an expose style, this movie provides a dramatic portrayal of high-tech political campaigning and public manipulation. In particular, it shows how a party-centered campaign can easily turn into a candidate-centered campaign with the help of professional campaign consultants.

Third Parties in American Politics. 1996. This film examines the impact of third parties on presidential elections. Films for the Humanities and Sciences.

CHAPTER NINE: NOMINATIONS AND CAMPAIGNS

PEDAGOGICAL FEATURES

LEARNING OBJECTIVES

After studying this chapter, students should be able to:

- Review the two types of campaigns in American politics—*nomination* campaigns and *election* campaigns.

- Describe the role of *campaign strategy* in winning a nomination to elective office.

- Identify the general characteristics of presidential candidates.
- Describe and evaluate the *caucus* and *primary* methods of delegate selection.
- Contrast the American primary system of nomination with those of other nations such as Great Britain.
- Trace the historical evolution of national party conventions as nominating vehicles for presidential candidates.
- Consider the ways that high-tech campaigning has changed the nature of American politics.
- Identify the key actions that candidates must accomplish in order to effectively organize their campaigns.
- Examine the growth of PACs and their impact on modern campaigning.
- Assess the crucial role of money and technology in American campaign organizations.
- Analyze the role the media play in influencing the style and substance of presidential campaigns.
- Discuss the three effects that campaigns have on voters: *reinforcement*, *activation*, and *conversion*.
- Evaluate whether the "openness" of the American style of campaigning leads to a more democratic system or a less democratic system of government.
- Assess whether or not American presidential elections lead to an increased scope of government.

CHAPTER OVERVIEW

INTRODUCTION

The long and arduous campaign required of campaign hopefuls is unique to the United States. While some argue that this extended period is a useful testing ground, others question its effectiveness in helping citizens choose the best candidate. This chapter discusses the structure and dynamics of presidential election campaigns, with special attention given to the role of money in campaigns.

THE NOMINATION GAME

There are two types of campaigns in American politics: campaigns for party nominations and campaigns between the two nominees. A **nomination** is a party's official endorsement of a candidate for office. Success in the nomination game generally requires money, media attention, and momentum. Candidates attempt to manipulate each of these elements through **campaign strategy**.

From February through June of election year, the individual *state parties* choose their delegates to the national convention through caucuses or primaries. At one time, all states selected their delegates to the national convention in a meeting of state party leaders, called a **caucus**. Today, caucuses are open to all voters who are registered with the party. The Democrats also require strict adherence to complex rules of representation. Only a minority of states hold caucuses today, with the earliest caucus traditionally held in Iowa.

Today, most of the delegates to the national conventions are selected in **presidential primaries**, in which voters in a state go to the polls and vote for a candidate or for delegates pledged to a candidate.

The most recent restructuring of Democratic party primaries began in 1968. Riots at the Democratic National Convention that year led to the creation of the **McGovern-Fraser Commission**, which established open procedures and quota requirements for delegate selection. The party has since replaced most of its quota requirements with affirmative action guidelines, with the exception that each delegation must be half male and half female. Many believe that the divisiveness of the Democrats' open procedures has hurt their ability to unite for the fall campaign, and the party has tried to restore a role for its party leaders by setting aside a portion of delegate slots for party leaders and elected officials (known as **superdelegates**).

The primary season begins in the winter in New Hampshire. At this early stage, the campaign is not for delegates but for *images*. In 1988, the southern states (feeling that northern states like New Hampshire had disproportionate influence in the choice of the Democratic nominees) created **Super Tuesday** by moving all of their primaries to the same day in early March. **Frontloading** refers to the recent tendency of states to hold primaries early in the calendar in order to capitalize on media attention. A wide variety of different procedures are used because *state* *laws* (not federal) determine when primaries are held, and each state party sets up its own rules for how delegates are allocated.

There are a number of criticisms of the primary system, including the disproportionate amount of attention that is given to the early caucuses and primaries. Running for the presidency has become a full-time job, and prominent politicians find it difficult to take time out from their duties to run. Money plays too big a role in the caucuses and primaries. Participation is low and is not representative of the voting population. There are also numerous defenders of the system, including most of the candidates—many of whom feel that the primary contest keeps candidates in touch with the public.

The idea of holding a **national primary** to select party nominees has been discussed virtually ever since state primaries were introduced. According to its proponents, a national primary would bring directness and simplicity to the process for the voters as well as the candidates. The length of the campaign would be shortened, and no longer would votes in one state have more political impact than votes in another. Critics claim that because Americans would not want a candidate nominated with 25 percent of the vote from among a field of six candidates, in most primaries a runoff election between the top two finishers in each party would have to be held. Another common criticism of a national primary is that only well-established politicians would have a shot at breaking through in such a system.

Perhaps more feasible than a national primary is holding a series of **regional primaries** in which, say, states in the eastern time zone would vote one week, those in the central time zone the next, and so on. Recently, the National Association of Secretaries of State – the organization of the leading election officials of the states – endorsed a plan to establish regional primaries for the 2004 campaign. The major problem with the regional primary proposal, however, is the advantage gained by whichever region goes first.

The winners of presidential nominations are usually a foregone conclusion by the time of the national party conventions. The preferences of delegates selected in primaries and open caucuses are known before the conventions begin. Nevertheless, conventions are *a significant rallying point* for the parties and they are important in *developing the party's policy positions* and in *promoting political representation.*

THE CAMPAIGN GAME

Modern campaigning is *heavily dependent on technology.* As one of its most important uses, computer technology targets mailings to prospective supporters.

The technique of **direct mail** involves locating potential supporters by sending information and a request for money to huge lists of people who have supported candidates of similar views in the past. Direct mail induces millions of people each year to contribute to various candidates and political causes, totaling over $1 billion. The accumulation of mailing lists enables a candidate to pick almost any issue and write to a list of people concerned about it.

Once nominated, candidates concentrate on **campaigning** for the **general election** in November. Three ingredients are needed to project the right image to the voters: a campaign organization, money, and media attention.

MONEY AND CAMPAIGNING

Campaigns are expensive, and they are growing more so in America's high-tech political arena. Candidates need money to build a campaign organization and to get the message out. There is a common *perception that money buys votes* and influence.

In the early 1970s, momentum developed for *campaign financing reform.* Several public interest lobbies (particularly Common Cause and the National Committee for an Effective Congress) led the drive for reform. Congress subsequently passed the **Federal Election Campaign Act** in 1974 with the goals of *tightening reporting requirements for contributions* and *limiting overall expenditures.* A bipartisan **Federal Election Commission (FEC)** was created to administer campaign finance laws and enforce compliance with their requirements. Among other provisions, the act provided public financing for presidential primaries and general elections, and limits were established for presidential campaign spending. An amendment to the original act (FECA) was added that made it easier for political parties to raise money for voter registration drives and the distribution of campaign material at the grass roots level or for generic party advertising. Money raised for such purposes is known as **soft money** and is not subject to any contribution limits.

Campaign spending reforms have made campaigns more open and honest. All contribution and expenditure records are open, and FEC auditors try to make sure that the regulations are enforced. However, campaign reforms also encouraged the spread of **Political Action Committees (PACs).** A PAC is formed when a business association, or some other interest group, decides to contribute to candidates whom it believes will be favorable toward its goals. Any interest group can now form its own PAC to directly channel contributions of up to $5,000 per candidate.

PACs have proliferated in recent years and play a major role in paying for expensive campaigns. Critics of the PAC system believe that this has led to a system of open graft. They fear that the large amount of money controlled by PACs leads to PAC control over what the winners do once they are in office. On the other hand, this chapter notes that the perception that PACs control officeholders may be misleading since *most PACs give money to candidates who already agree with them.* The impact of PAC money on presidents is even more doubtful since presidential campaigns are partly subsidized by the public and presidents have well-articulated positions on most important issues.

Money is critical to electoral victory. In this era of high-tech politics, pollsters, public relations people, direct-mail consultants, and many other specialists are crucial to a campaign. Every four years, Americans spend over $2 billion on national, state, and local elections. Although this seems like a tremendous amount of money, campaigns are actually relatively inexpensive when compared with the amount of money Americans spend on items of much less importance. (The cost per voter is about as much as an audio CD.) Perhaps the most basic complaint about money and politics is that there may be a direct *link between dollars spent and votes received.*

THE IMPACT OF CAMPAIGNS

Political scientists have found that campaigns have three major *effects on voters*: **reinforcement**, **activation**, and **conversion**. Campaigns can reinforce voters' preferences for candidates; they can activate voters, getting them to contribute money or become active in campaigns; and they can convert by changing voters' minds. However, campaigns rarely convert; they *primarily reinforce and activate.* Political scientists' emphasis on reinforcement and activation reflects the fact that most people pay relatively little attention to campaigns in the first place. People have a remarkable capacity for **selective perception** – paying most attention to things they already agree with and interpreting events according to their own predispositions.

UNDERSTANDING NOMINATIONS AND CAMPAIGNS

The American political system *allows citizens a voice at almost every point* of the election process, unlike many countries where a political elite controls nominations and elections. As a result, party outsiders can get elected in a way that is virtually unknown outside the United States. The process has also led to what some call "the permanent campaign" and what Martin Wattenberg has termed the "candidate-centered age." Some analysts believe the process of openness places numerous demands on citizens; many are overwhelmed by the process and do not participate.

States are the key battlegrounds of presidential campaigns. To secure votes from each region of the country, candidates end up supporting a variety of local interests. The way modern campaigns are conducted is thus one of many reasons why politicians usually find it easier to expand the scope of American government than to limit it.

CHAPTER OUTLINE

I. THE NOMINATION GAME

A. A **nomination** is a party's official endorsement of a candidate for office.

B. Success in the nomination game generally requires money, media attention, and momentum. Candidates attempt to manipulate each of these elements through **campaign strategy**.

C. Deciding to run.
   1. Campaigns are more strenuous than ever, and many strong (perhaps electable) candidates decide not to run.
   2. Unlike Britain—where campaigns are limited by law to five weeks—a presidential candidacy in the United States needs to be either announced or an "open secret" for at least a year before the election.
   3. Presidential candidates need to be risk-takers; they need enough self-confidence to put everything on the line in pursuit of the presidency.

D. Competing for delegates.
   1. The goal of the nomination game is to win the majority of delegates' support at the **national party convention**.
   2. From February through June of election year, the individual *state parties* choose their delegates to the national convention through *caucuses* or *primaries*.
   3. Party caucuses.
      a. At one time, all states selected their delegates to the national convention in a meeting of state party leaders, called a **caucus**.
      b. Today, caucuses are open to all voters who are registered with the party. The Democrats also require strict adherence to complex rules of representation.
      c. Only a minority of states hold caucuses today, and the earliest caucus is traditionally held in Iowa.
      d. Caucuses are usually *organized like a pyramid.*
   4. Presidential primaries.

a. Today, most of the delegates to the national conventions are selected in **presidential primaries**, in which voters in a state go to the polls and vote for a candidate or for delegates pledged to a candidate.
b. The primary season begins in the winter in New Hampshire. At this early stage, the campaign is not for delegates but for *images*.
c. The Democratic Party began to reform its delegate selection procedures after a high conflictual national convention in 1968; these reforms were proposed by the **McGovern-Fraser Commission.**
d. In 1988, the southern states (feeling that northern states like New Hampshire had disproportionate influence in the choice of the Democratic nominees) created **Super Tuesday** by moving all of their primaries to the same day in early March.

5. Political scientists and commentators have a number of *criticisms* of the primary and caucus system:
   a. A disproportionate amount of attention goes to the early caucuses and primaries. Critics think America's media-dominated campaigns are distorted by early primaries and caucuses.
   b. Running for the presidency has become a full-time job, and prominent politicians find it difficult to take time out from their duties to run.
   c. Money plays too big a role in the caucuses and primaries.
   d. Participation is low and is not representative of the voting population. Although about 50 percent of the population votes in the November presidential election, only about 20 percent cast ballots in presidential primaries. Voters in primaries and caucuses also tend to be better educated and more affluent than voters in general.
   e. Primaries and caucuses exaggerate regional factors in decision making.
   f. The system gives too much power to the media.
6. The current system also has powerful *defenders*, including many of the candidates themselves.
   a. George Bush has written that the system "brings presidential candidates into contact with the flesh-and-blood world."
   b. Even losing candidates usually support the process. Senator Paul Simon argues that it is best to start the race in small states where people can meet the candidates face-to-face.
7. Proposals for national and regional presidential primaries.
   a. Proponents of a **national primary** to select party nominees believe that this would bring directness and simplicity to the

process for both the voters and the candidates. The length and cost of the campaign would be reduced, and concentration of media coverage on this one event would increase political interest and public understanding of the issues involved.

b. Critics of a national primary respond that a national primary would almost inevitably require a runoff election between the top two finishers to avoid having a candidate win with only a plurality of the vote. Big money and intense attention from the national media would become more crucial than ever, and obscure candidates would never have a chance.

c. There have also been proposals for **regional primaries** in which groups of states (such as those in a particular time zone) would vote one week, then another the following week, and so on. The major problem with the regional primary proposal is the advantage gained by whichever region goes first.

8. The convention send-off.
   a. The "drama" has now been largely drained from conventions, as the winner is usually a foregone conclusion. The preferences of delegates selected in primaries and open caucuses are known before the conventions begin.
   b. The last time there was any doubt as to who would win at the convention was in 1976, when Gerald Ford barely defeated Ronald Reagan for the Republican nomination.
   c. The parties have also learned that it is not in their best interest to provide high drama—the raucous conventions held by the Republicans in 1964 and the Democrats in 1968 and 1972 exposed such divisiveness that the parties were unable to unite for the fall campaign.
   d. Today's conventions are carefully scripted to present the party in its best light. With little news to be made at conventions, fewer people watch them; and the networks have substantially reduced the number of hours of coverage in recent years.
   e. Although conventions are no longer very interesting, they are *a significant rallying point* for the parties.
   f. Conventions are also important in *developing the party's policy positions* and in *promoting political representation.* Party reformers—especially among the Democrats—have worked hard to make the conventions far more demographically representative than they were in the past.

II. THE CAMPAIGN GAME

A. Campaigning today is *heavily dependent on technology.*

1. Television is the most prevalent means used by candidates to reach voters.
2. As one of its most important uses, computer technology targets mailings to prospective supporters.
   a. The technique of **direct mail** involves sending information and a request for money to names obtained from lists of people who have supported candidates of similar views in the past.
   b. The accumulation of mailing lists enables a candidate to pick almost any issue and write to a list of people concerned about it.

B. Once nominated, candidates concentrate on **campaigning** for the **general election** in November.

C. Three ingredients are needed to project the right *image* to the voters: a campaign organization, money, and media attention.

D. To effectively *organize* their campaigns, candidates must succeed in numerous key areas:
1. Line up a campaign manager.
2. Get a fund-raiser.
3. Get a campaign counsel.
4. Hire media and campaign consultants.
5. Assemble a campaign staff.
6. Plan the logistics.
7. Get a research staff and policy advisors.
8. Hire a pollster.
9. Get a good press secretary.

III. MONEY IN CAMPAIGNS

A. Campaigns are *expensive*, and they are growing more so in America's high-tech political arena.
1. Candidates need money to build a campaign organization and to get the message out.
2. There is a common *perception that money buys votes* and influence. This chapter examines the *role of money in campaigns.*
3. In the early 1970s, momentum developed for *campaign financing reform.*
   a. Several *public interest lobbies* (particularly Common Cause and the National Committee for an Effective Congress) led the drive for reform.

B. Congress passed the **Federal Election Campaign Act** in 1974 with the goals of *tightening reporting requirements for contributions* and *limiting overall expenditures*. Provisions of the act (with subsequent amendments) included:

1. A bipartisan **Federal Election Commission (FEC)** was created to administer campaign finance laws and enforce compliance with their requirements.
2. It provided public financing for presidential primaries and general elections.
3. Limits were established for presidential campaign spending.
4. All candidates must file periodic financial disclosure reports with the FEC, listing who contributed funds and how the money was spent.
5. It limited contributions, with individual contributions restricted to one thousand dollars.

C. Impact of the act.
   1. Campaign spending reforms have made campaigns more open and honest.
   2. Small donors are encouraged, and the rich are restricted in terms of the money they can give directly to a candidate.
   3. All contribution and expenditure records are open, and FEC auditors try to make sure that the regulations are enforced.

D. A 1979 amendment to the original FECA which made it easier for political parties to raise money for voter registration drives and the distribution of campaign material at the grass roots level.
   1. Money used for these purposes is referred to as **soft money**.

E. Campaign reforms also encouraged the spread of **Political Action Committees (PACs)**.
   1. The 1974 reforms created a new way for interest groups like business and labor to contribute to campaigns. Any interest group can now form its own PAC to directly channel contributions of up to $5,000 per candidate.
   2. A PAC is formed when a business association—or some other interest group—decides to contribute to candidates they believe will be favorable toward their goals. After the group registers with the FEC as a PAC, the PAC can collect money from interested parties and contribute money to candidates. (All expenditures must be accounted for to the FEC.)
   3. PACs have proliferated in recent years and play a major role in paying for expensive campaigns. PACs contributed $178 million to congressional candidates for the 1992 campaign.
   4. Critics of the PAC system believe that this has led to a system of open graft. They fear that the large amount of money controlled by PACs leads to PAC control over what the winners do once they are in office.
   5. However, the perception that PACs control office holders may be misleading since *most PACs give money to candidates who already*

agree with them. The impact of PAC money on presidents is even more doubtful since presidential campaigns are partly subsidized by the public and presidents have well-articulated positions on most important issues.

F. Are campaigns too expensive?
   1. Every four years, Americans spend over $2 billion on national, state, and local elections. Although this seems like a tremendous amount of money, campaigns are actually relatively inexpensive when compared with the amount of money Americans spend on items of much less importance.
   2. Many officeholders feel that the need for continuous fund-raising distracts them from their jobs as legislators.
   3. Although some lawmakers support public financing reform, it is felt that **incumbents** (current office holders) will not readily give up the advantage they have in raising money.

G. Does money buy victory?
   1. Money is crucial to electoral victory. In this era of *high-tech politics*, pollsters, public relations people, direct-mail consultants, and many other specialists are crucial to a campaign.
   2. Perhaps the most basic complaint about money and politics is that there may be a direct *link between dollars spent and votes received.*
   3. Herbert Alexander refers to "*the doctrine of sufficiency*" to describe the idea that it is more important to have "enough" money than to have "more" money—enough to compete effectively but not necessarily more money than the opponent.

IV. THE IMPACT OF CAMPAIGNS

A. Politicians tend to overestimate the impact of campaigns. Political scientists have found that campaigns have three major *effects on voters*: **reinforcement**, **activation**, and **conversion**. Campaigns can *reinforce* voters' preferences for candidates; they can *activate* voters, getting them to contribute money or become active in campaigns; and they can *convert* by changing voters' minds.

B. Campaigns *primarily reinforce and activate*. Only rarely do campaigns convert because several factors tend to weaken campaigns' impact on voters:
   1. People have a remarkable capacity for **selective perception**—paying most attention to positions they already agree with and interpreting events according to their own predispositions.
   2. Although party identification is not as important as it once was, such factors still influence voting behavior.

3. Incumbents start with a substantial advantage in terms of name recognition and an established record.

V. UNDERSTANDING NOMINATIONS AND CAMPAIGNS

A. Impact of nominations and campaigns on democracy.
   1. The American political system *allows citizens a voice at almost every point* of the election process, unlike many countries where a political elite controls nominations and elections. As a result, party outsiders can get elected in a way that is virtually unknown outside the United States.
   2. The process has also led to what some call "the permanent campaign." Some analysts believe the process of openness places numerous demands on citizens; many are overwhelmed by the process and do not participate.
   3. The burdens of the modern campaign can also discourage good candidates from entering the fray.
   4. The current system of running for office has been labeled by Wattenberg as the "candidate-centered age." It allows for politicians to decide on their own to run, to raise their own campaign funds, to build their own personal organizations, and to make promises as to how they specifically will act in office.

B. Do big campaigns lead to an increased scope of government?
   1. Because states are the key battlegrounds of presidential campaigns, candidates must tailor their appeals to the particular interests of each major state.
   2. Candidates end up supporting a variety of local interests in order to secure votes from each region of the country.
   3. The way modern campaigns are conducted is thus one of the many reasons why politicians always find it easier to *expand the scope of American government* than to limit it.

KEY TERMS AND CONCEPTS

Campaign strategy: the way candidates use scarce resources to achieve the nomination or win office.

Caucus: a meeting to determine which candidate delegates from a state party will support.

Direct mail: the use of targeted mailings to prospective supporters, usually compiled from lists of those who have contributed to candidates and parties in the past.

Federal Election Campaign Act: 1974 legislation designed to regulate campaign contributions and limit campaign expenditures.

Federal Election Commission: A bipartisan body charged with administering campaign finance laws.

Frontloading: states' decisions to move their presidential primaries and caucuses to earlier in the nomination season in order to capitalize on media attention.

McGovern-Fraser Commission: a committee in the Democratic party charged with recommending changes in party rules to promote more representation of women and minorities in the delegate selection process.

National party convention: a meeting of the delegates from each state to determine the party's nominee for president.

National primaries: a proposal by critics of the caucuses and presidential primaries systems who would replace these electoral methods with a nationwide primary held early in the election year.

Nomination: a party's official endorsement of a candidate for office.

Party platform: the party's statement of its goals and policies for the next four years.

Political action committees: a legal entity formed expressly for the purpose of contributing money to candidates and influencing electoral outcomes.

Presidential primaries: a state-level election to determine which candidate the state's delegates will support.

Regional primaries: a proposal by critics of the caucuses and presidential primaries to replace these electoral methods with a series of primaries held in each geographic region.

Selective perception: the act of paying the most attention to things that one already agrees with or has a predisposition towards.

Soft money: money raised by political parties for voter registration drives and the distribution of campaign material at the grass-roots level.

Superdelegates: delegates to the Democratic party's national convention who obtain their seats on the basis of their positions within the party structure.

TEACHING IDEAS: CLASS DISCUSSION AND STUDENT PROJECTS

- The great length and cost of American campaigns is unusual when compared to the systems used in other nations. Refer to the systems used in other Western democracies for comparison and contrast. Ask students to reflect on what changes (such as types of candidates) might occur if the United States adopted a shorter campaign period. Preface the assignment with a reminder that reforms often are accompanied by unintended (and unforeseen) consequences, and ask your class to consider the implications of this possibility. Brief reading selections could be placed on reserve in the library to supplement this section.

- If student body officer elections attract a lot of attention on your campus (and are currently being held), have your students interview the various candidates regarding their campaign strategies. Have students write brief essays re: how "their" candidate could improve their campaign.

- Critics believe that a disproportionate amount of attention is paid to the early caucuses and primaries. Refer your students to Figure 9.1 (which shows how critics think America's media-dominated campaigns are distorted by early primaries and caucuses) and *You Are the Policymaker: National and Regional Presidential Primary Proposals* (which describes proposals for a national primary or a series of regional primaries). Divide the class into three groups, and have each group defend one system—a single national primary, a series of regional primaries, and the current system of state primaries held on various dates from February through June.

- As a class project, have each student interview a recent candidate for a local office to get the candidate's reaction to questions of ethics in campaigning. (If your class is large, consider dividing the class into teams to avoid overwhelming local candidates with requests for interviews!) What is the candidate's views on the nature of the campaign process? Are there any concerns with possible invasion of privacy? Is "mud-slinging" becoming more of a problem? Is there a link between campaign expenditures and the number of votes received?

- If this is an election year, have students gather campaign material from both the Democratic and Republican local headquarters. Compare both the style and content of the literature. Suggest that students volunteer to work for a few hours for one of the parties, then compare notes in class about their experiences.

- The textbook says this: *Reformers in the nineteenth and twentieth centuries held that the solution to democratic problems was more democracy.... In principle, more democracy always sounds better than less, but it is not such a simple issue in practice."* This statement could be the basis for a provocative class discussion and analysis.

- Review and discuss the issue of "soft money" raised in congressional hearings during the summer of 1996. What allegations were made against the Democrats? The Republicans? How and why has soft money become so important in elections? What do we know about soft money in the 1998 Congressional elections? The 2000 Presidential election? Ask students to research current proposals for campaign finance reform, using either government documents or the Internet. Will the proposed reforms improve the campaign finance system?

- What issues are raised by current proposals to conduct voting on-line?

- For a reading and writing connection (and if the course is being taught in an election year), have students keep a clipping file on candidate for an office of their choice. Using broadcast and print media sources and descriptive journal entries for each item, have students identify the policy positions of the candidate from these sources. In a short analytical essay, have them compare the information they obtained through news coverage of their candidates with information they obtained in campaign advertisements about the candidates' issue positions. Alternatively, students could compare media images between competing candidates using the same format.

BACKGROUND READING

Asher, Herbert B. Presidential Elections and American Politics. 5th ed. Pacific Grove, CA: Brooks/Cole. 1992.

Bartels, Larry M. Presidential Primaries and the Dynamics of Public Choice. Princeton, NJ: Princeton University Press. 1988.

Corrado, Anthony. Campaign Finance Reform: Beyond the Basics. Washington, D.C.: Brookings. 2000.

Corrado, Anthony, Thomas Mann, Daniel Ortiz and Trevor Potter. The New Campaign Finance Sourcebook. Washington, D.C.: Brookings. 2000.

Hess, Stephen. The Presidential Campaign. 3rd. ed. Washington, DC: Brookings Institution. 1988.

Kahn, Kim Fridkin and Patrick J. Kenney. The Spectacle of U.S. Senate Campaigns. Princeton: Princeton University Press. 1999.

Lavrakas, Paul J. and Michael W. Traugott. Election Polls, the News Media and Democracy. New York: Chatham House. 2000.

Orren, Gary R. and Nelson W. Polsby. Media and Momentum: The New Hampshire Primary and Nomination Politics. Chatham, New Jersey: Chatham House Publishers. 1987.

Polsby, Nelson W. and Aaron Wildavsky. Presidential Elections. 7th ed. NY: Free Press. 1992.

Wayne, Stephen H. The Road to the White House 1996: The Politics of Presidential Elections. NY: St. Martin's Press. 1997.

MEDIA SUGGESTIONS

Campaign Finance: Abuses and Reforms. This show provides an overview of campaign finance reform, including interviews with Senator John McCain, Bill Bradley and Jack Kemp. The broad political issues are discussed, as are several case studies of campaign finance in Florida and Maine. Films for the Humanities & Sciences.

Campaigning for the Presidency. A 1992 PBS production examining campaigning techniques and negative advertising.

The Candidate. A 1972 Warner Brothers film about packaging a political candidate. In an expose style, this movie provides a dramatic portrayal of high-tech political campaigning and public manipulation. In particular, it shows how a party-centered campaign can easily turn into a candidate-centered campaign with the help of professional campaign consultants.

The Decline of Politics: The Superficial Democracy. 1996. This program analyzes the influence of modern campaigns which are characterized by form over substance in American democracy. Films for the Humanities and Sciences.

Electing Women. A 1993 video by Insight Media which examines gender bias in the electoral process.

Modern Campaign Techniques. An excellent 1993 documentary by Insight Media which chronicles the evolution of campaign technology.

Politics in Action, Chapter 1: Conducting a Campaign. Provides an overview of the 1993 New York Mayoral Campaign.

Politics in Action, Chapter 2: Political Commercials and Debates. Includes clips of famous political ads from Eisenhower through Clinton, as well as clips of the Kennedy/Nixon and Bush/Clinton/Perot debates.

Price of Power: Money in Politics. A 1993 program by Insight Media which examines the role of money in influencing electoral outcomes.

CHAPTER TEN: ELECTIONS AND VOTING BEHAVIOR

PEDAGOGICAL FEATURES

LEARNING OBJECTIVES

After studying this chapter, students should be able to:

- Explain how elections provide regular access to political power and how the process is related to the level of political *legitimacy*.

- Describe procedures that permit voters to enact legislation directly, such as the initiative, petition and referendum.

- Trace the historical evolution of the American style of campaigning from 1800 to 2000.

- Identify the characteristics of voters and nonvoters.

- Explore the reasons why voter turnout has actually declined as the right to vote was extended to new groups.
- Ascertain the role that voter registration procedures and requirements have played in structuring voter turnout.
- Compare voter turnout in the United States with that of other democracies.
- Determine how *policy differences* and *civic duty* affect a person's decision to vote or not to vote.
- Explain why *party identification* is crucial for many voters and review the decline of party affiliation since the 1950s.
- Identify the conditions that must be present for true *policy voting* to occur.
- Outline the procedures of the electoral college and compare the present system with the process that was envisioned by the framers of the Constitution.
- Understand the tasks that elections accomplish, according to democratic theory.
- Establish how elections may affect public policy and how public policy may affect elections.
- Analyze how elections influence the scope of government in a democracy.

CHAPTER OVERVIEW

INTRODUCTION

Elections *socialize* and *institutionalize* political activity, making it possible for most political participation to be peacefully channeled through the electoral process. Because elections provide regular access to political power, leaders can be replaced without being overthrown. American voters rarely question the fairness of election results, allowing officeholders to govern with a **legitimacy** they can take for granted. This chapter focuses on how elections work in the United States, who votes and how individuals make their voting decisions.

HOW AMERICAN ELECTIONS WORK

Unlike most other democracies, the United States has *three kinds of elections*: those which select *party nominees*, those which select *officeholders* from among the nominees, and those in which voters engage in *making or ratifying legislation*. Elections in most other countries perform only the function of selecting officeholders.

A TALE OF THREE ELECTIONS

Elections have changed dramatically since 1800 when Adams ran against Jefferson. In 1800, there were no primaries, no nominating conventions, no candidate speeches, and no entourage of reporters. Both incumbent President John Adams and challenger Thomas Jefferson were nominated by their parties' elected representatives in Congress (caucuses). Once nominated, the candidates did not campaign; they let their state and local organizations promote their cause. Although the election had to be decided in the House of Representatives, the transition from Adams to Jefferson marked *the first peaceful transfer of power between parties via the electoral process* in the history of the world.

By 1896, **national nominating conventions** had become well established. William Jennings Bryan broke with tradition and actively campaigned in person, traveling through twenty-six states. William McKinley ran a front-porch campaign from his home in Ohio, and managed to label the Democrats as the party of depression. The *Republicans* won overwhelmingly in the industrial Northeast and Midwest, and became firmly entrenched as *the nation's majority party for the next several decades.*

The 2000 presidential election will no doubt go into the history books as one of the most memorable finishes in the history of democracy. The election coverage on television provided a wild night of entertainment, full of ups and downs for everyone. Because Bush's lead over Gore in the initial count was less than one-tenth of one percent, Florida law mandated an automatic recount. Ultimately, with the margin between Bush and Gore down to 537 votes, the election hinged on whether or not the undervotes (ballots that showed no vote for president) would be examined by hand or not. As with any dispute, this one ended up in the courts, which played a pivotal role in a presidential election for the first time ever. The U.S. Supreme Court in *Bush v. Gore* (2000) overruled the Florida Supreme Court and held that although a recount was legal, the same (and more precise) standards for evaluating ballots would have to be applied in all counties. Most importantly, they ruled that there was not enough time to recount all the ballots in an orderly fashion by the time the electors were to vote on December 12. Thus, the U.S. Supreme Court ultimately determined that George W. Bush would emerge the winner. The 2000 election, however, showed that how candidates present themselves to the American people really matters. Had Gore been able to keep the focus on past performance, he no doubt would have done better. Instead, at the Democratic Convention he announced that he was running as his own man. George W. Bush sought to take advantage of concerns over presidential character raised during the Clinton Administration by repeatedly promising to "restore dignity and honor to the White House." While Bush and Gore debated the crucial theme of the scope of government, Green Party candidate Ralph Nader raised issues neglected by the major parties.

WHETHER TO VOTE: A CITIZEN'S FIRST CHOICE

Nearly two centuries of American electoral history include greatly expanded **suffrage** (the right to vote). Ironically, *proportionately fewer of those eligible* have chosen to exercise that right. The highest turnout of the past 100 years was the 80 percent turnout in 1896; in 2000, only 51 percent of the adult population voted for president.

Individuals with high levels of political efficacy and civic duty are more likely to vote, as are individuals who see policy differences between the two parties. Before voting, citizens in most states must register to vote, often a cumbersome procedure. The Motor Voter Act—which allows individuals to register to vote when they receive or renew their drivers' license—has made registration a little easier since 1993. Another reason why many people vote is that they have a high sense of **political efficacy** – the belief that ordinary people can influence the government.

There are several distinguishing demographic *characteristics of voters and nonvoters*: education, age, race, gender, marital status, mobility, and union membership.

Research suggests that some political outcomes would change if this class bias in turnout did not exist. Accordingly, it is likely that little further will be done to modify voter registration requirements and encourage turnout, as many Republicans believe that increased turnout will be to their disadvantage.

HOW AMERICANS VOTE: EXPLAINING CITIZENS' DECISIONS

Many journalists and politicians believe the winner of an election has a **mandate** from the people to carry out the policies they promised during the campaign. Conversely, political scientists know that different kinds of people vote a certain way for different reasons. Political scientists focus instead on *three major elements of voters' decisions*: voters' party identification, voters' evaluations of the candidates, and the match between voters' policy positions and those of the candidates and parties (known as policy voting).

Because of the importance of **party identification** in deciding how to vote, the parties tended to rely on groups that lean heavily in their favor to form their basic coalition. Scholars singled out party affiliation as the *single best predictor of a voter's decision* in the 1950s. With the emergence of television and candidate-centered politics, the hold of the party on the voter eroded substantially during the 1960s and 1970s, and then *stabilized at a new and lower level* during the 1980s.

Political psychologists Shawn Rosenberg and Patrick McCafferty show that it is possible to manipulate a candidate's appearance in a way that affects voters' choices. Other research has shown that the three most *important components of candidate image are integrity, reliability, and competence.*

Policy voting occurs when people base their choices in an election on *their own issue preferences*. True policy voting can take place only when several conditions are met: voters must have a clear view of their own policy positions; voters must know where the candidates stand on policy issues; voters must see a difference between candidates on these issues; and voters must actually cast a vote for the candidate whose policy positions coincide with their own. One recurrent problem is that candidates often decide that the best way to handle a controversial issue is to cloud their positions in rhetoric; *both* candidates may be deliberately ambiguous. The problem is further complicated by the fact that the media typically focus more on the "horse race" aspects of the campaign than on the policy stands of the candidates.

THE LAST BATTLE: THE ELECTORAL COLLEGE

It is the **electoral vote** that actually determines the outcome of the presidential election. The founders created the **electoral college** because they wanted the president to be selected by the nation's elite. Nevertheless, it has been customary since 1828 for electors to vote for *the candidate who won their state's popular vote.*

The electoral vote may *distort* the popular vote. All states except Maine and Nebraska have a **winner-take-all** system in which electors vote as a bloc for the candidate who received the most votes in the states. Furthermore, big states are likely to have big cities; thus, the big-state bias produces an urban bias in the electoral college.

UNDERSTANDING ELECTIONS AND VOTING BEHAVIOR

According to democratic theory, elections accomplish two tasks: they *select the policymakers*, and they are supposed to *help shape public policy*. In the hypothetical world of *rational choice theory* and the Downs model (see chapter 8), elections do in fact guide public policy. Social science research on the question has produced mixed findings. Elections do affect public policy to some degree, and public policy decisions also partly affect electoral outcomes.

The greater the policy differences between the candidates, the more likely voters will be able to steer government policies by their choices. If elections can affect policies, then policies can also affect elections. Most policies have consequences for the well-being of certain groups or the society as a whole. Those who feel better off as a result of certain policies are likely to support candidates who pledge to continue those policies, whereas those who feel worse off are inclined to support opposition candidates. This is known as the theory of **retrospective voting**.

While the threat of election defeat constrains policymakers, it also helps to increase generalized support for government and its powers. Elections *legitimize the power of the state*, thereby making it easier to expand the size of the government. When people have the power to dole out electoral reward and punishment, they are more likely to see government as their servant instead of their master. As a result, citizens in a democracy often *seek to benefit from government* (rather than to be protected from it). As democracy has spread, government has come to do more and more, and its size has grown.

CHAPTER OUTLINE

I. HOW AMERICAN ELECTIONS WORK

A. Elections serve many important functions in American society, including legitimizing the actions of elected officials.

1. They *socialize* and *institutionalize* political activity, making it possible for most political participation to be peacefully channeled through the electoral process.
2. Political **legitimacy** means that the people within a nation accept the procedures by which rules and transfers of power are made.
3. American voters rarely question the fairness of election results, allowing officeholders to govern with a legitimacy they can take for granted.

B. Some unique American electoral features.
1. Unlike most other democracies, the United States has *three kinds of elections*: those which select *party nominees*, those which select *officeholders* from among the nominees, and those in which voters engage in *making or ratifying legislation.*
2. Elections held for the purpose of picking party nominees are called **primaries.**
3. The **initiative petition** enables voters in twenty-three states to place proposed legislation on the ballot if they gather the required number of signatures on a petition (usually a number equaling 10 percent of the voters in the previous election).
4. The **referendum** is a form of direct legislation in which voters are given the chance to approve or disapprove some legislative act (such as school bonds) or constitutional amendment.

II. A TALE OF THREE ELECTIONS

A. Elections have changed dramatically since 1800 when Adams ran against Jefferson.
1. By 1896, it was acceptable for candidates to campaign in person, as William Jennings Bryan did.
2. Today, campaigns are slick, high-tech affairs.

B. 1800: The first electoral transition of power.
1. In 1800, there were no primaries, no nominating conventions, no candidate speeches, and no entourage of reporters.
2. Both incumbent President John Adams and challenger Thomas Jefferson were nominated by their parties' elected representatives in Congress (caucuses).
3. Once nominated, the candidates did not campaign; they let their state and local organizations promote their cause.
4. The focus of the campaign was on state legislatures (not the voters), which had the responsibility for choosing members of the electoral college.
5. Most newspapers of that time were openly partisan and made no attempt to be objective.

6. The election was thrown into the House of Representatives through an error when all of Jefferson's electors also voted for Aaron Burr. At that period of history, each elector cast two ballots; the winner would be president and the runner-up would be named vice president. The result in 1800 was a tie vote, and the Federalist-controlled House of Representatives took thirty-six ballots before electing Thomas Jefferson.
7. The transition from Adams to Jefferson marked *the first peaceful transfer of power between parties via the electoral process* in the history of the world.

C. 1896: A bitter fight over economic interests.
   1. By 1896, **national nominating conventions** had become well established.
   2. The election was fought primarily over economics.
   3. Bryan broke with tradition and actively campaigned in person, traveling through twenty-six states. McKinley ran a front-porch campaign from his home in Ohio, and managed to label the Democrats as the party of depression.
   4. The *Republicans* won overwhelmingly in the industrial Northeast and Midwest, and became firmly entrenched as *the nation's majority party for the next several decades.*

III. 2000: WHAT A MESS!

A. The 2000 presidential election will no doubt go into the history books as one of the most memorable finishes in the history of democracy.
   1. Because Bush's lead over Gore in the initial count was less than one-tenth of one percent, Florida law mandated an automatic recount.
   2. Ultimately, with the margin between Bush and Gore down to 537 votes, the election hinged on whether or not the undervotes (ballots that showed no vote for president) would be examined by hand or not.
   3. As with any legal dispute, this one ended up in the courts, which played a pivotal role in a presidential election for the first time ever.
      a. The U.S. Supreme Court in *Bush v. Gore* (2000) overruled the Florida Supreme Court and held that although a recount was legal, the same (and more precise) standards for evaluating ballots would have to be applied in all counties. Most importantly, they ruled that there was not enough time to recount all the ballots in an orderly fashion by the time the electors were to vote on December 12. Thus, the U.S. Supreme Court ultimately determined that George W. Bush would emerge the winner.

B. For academic voting behavior specialists, Bush's election came as quite a surprise.
   1. With the economy rolling along, and with Bill Clinton's job approval rating hovering around 60 percent, it seemed like a no-brainer for them to project that the Democrats would retain the White House.
   2. The 2000 election, however, showed that how candidates present themselves to the American people really matters.
      a. Had Gore been able to keep the focus on past performance he no doubt would have done better. Instead, at the Democratic Convention he proudly announced that he was running as his own man.
      b. George W. Bush sought to take advantage of concerns over presidential character raised during the Clinton Administration by repeatedly promising to "restore dignity and honor to the White House."
   3. While Bush and Gore debated the crucial theme of the scope of government, Green Party candidate Ralph Nader raised issues neglected by the major parties.

C. There were sharp regional divisions in the vote in 2000.
   1. Bush ran strong in the South and Mountain West, whereas Gore turned in a good showing in the Northeast and the Pacific Coast states.

D. Although Bush won in the Electoral College by 271 to 266 (one elector from Washington, D.C. abstained in protest), Gore narrowly won the popular vote by 48.4 to 47.9 percent.
   1. This marked the first time since 1888 that the winner of the popular vote lost the decisive electoral college count.
   2. As a result, serious discussion is now being given to changing the electoral college system, but it is likely that reform proposals will encounter strong opposition from senators who represent small states.

IV. WHETHER TO VOTE: A CITIZEN'S FIRST CHOICE

A. Who votes and who stays home?
   1. Nearly two centuries of American electoral history include greatly expanded **suffrage** (the right to vote).
      a. As the right to vote has been extended, *proportionately fewer of those eligible* have chosen to exercise that right.
      b. The highest turnout of the past hundred years was the 80 percent turnout in 1896; in 2000, only 51 percent of the adult population voted for president.
   2. A policy approach to deciding whether to vote.

   a. In his model of democracy, economist Anthony Downs argues that people who see **policy differences** between the parties are more likely to join the ranks of voters.
3. Another reason why many people vote is that they have a high sense of **political efficacy** – the belief that ordinary people can influence the government.
4. Those who vote out of a sense of **civic duty** are people who vote simply to support democratic government (even if they are indifferent about the outcome).

B. The registration system.
   1. States adopted **voter registration** around the turn of the century, largely to prevent corruption associated with stuffing the ballot boxes.
   2. Registration procedures differ greatly from one state to another.
      a. States in the upper Great Plains and the Northwest make it easiest to register; there is no registration at all in North Dakota; and four states permit registration on election day.
      b. States in the South still face the most difficult forms of registration (and they also record lower voter turnout rates).
      c. This changed somewhat when the 1993 **Motor Voter Act** went into effect in 1996. The act requires states to permit people to register to vote at the same time citizens apply for driver's licenses. The Motor Voter Act *makes voter registration much easier* by allowing eligible voters to simply check a box on their driver's license application or renewal form.

C. Social science research points to several characteristics of voters and nonvoters:
   1. Voting is a class-biased activity. People with higher than average education and income levels have a higher rate of voting. This is *the most important factor affecting turnout.*
   2. Young people have the lowest turnout rate.
   3. Whites vote with greater frequency than members of minority groups (but blacks and other minority groups with high levels of income and education have a higher turnout rate than whites with comparable socioeconomic status).
   4. Southerners are less likely to vote than northerners.
   5. Government employees are heavy participators in the electoral process.
   6. Voting is not very strongly related to gender.

D. The political consequences of class bias in turnout.
   1. Research suggests that some political outcomes would be different if there was no class bias in turnout.

2. Future reforms oriented toward increasing turnout will likely be minimal, because Republicans will likely block such changes, believing they will be disadvantaged by them.

V. HOW AMERICANS VOTE: EXPLAINING CITIZENS' DECISIONS

A. Mandate theory of elections.
   1. Many journalists and politicians believe the winner of an election has a **mandate** from the people to carry out the policies they promised during the campaign.
   2. Conversely, political scientists know that people rarely vote a certain way for the same reasons. Political scientists focus instead on *three major elements of voters' decisions*: voters' party identification, voters' evaluations of the candidates, and the match between voters' policy positions and those of the candidates and parties (known as policy voting).

B. Party identification.
   1. Because of the importance of **party identification** in deciding how to vote, the parties tended to rely on groups that lean heavily in their favor to form their basic coalition.
   2. With the emergence of television and candidate-centered politics, the *hold of the party on the voter* eroded substantially during the 1960s and 1970s, and then *stabilized at a new and lower level* during the 1980s.
   3. Scholars singled out *party affiliation* as the *single best predictor of a voter's decision* in the 1950s. Voting along party lines is less common today, particularly in elections for the House of Representatives, where *incumbency* is now of paramount importance.

C. Candidate evaluations.
   1. Political psychologists Shawn Rosenberg and Patrick McCafferty show that it is possible to manipulate a candidate's appearance in a way that affects voters' choices (even by substituting a good picture for a bad one).
   2. Research by Miller, Wattenberg, and Malanchuk shows that the three most important components of candidate image are integrity, reliability, and competence. However, *integrity* (where Jimmy Carter scored high) is not enough; a candidate must also be seen as being dependable and decisive. (George Bush's image of *reliability* suffered when he broke his "no new taxes" pledge prior to the 1992 campaign.) The personal traits most often mentioned by voters involve *competence* (which played a major role in 1988 when a majority of voters were more impressed with Bush's wide experience in office than with Michael Dukakis' stance).

D. Policy voting.
   1. **Policy voting** occurs when people base their choices in an election on *their own issue preferences.*
   2. True policy voting can take place only when several conditions are met.
      a. Voters must have a clear view of their own policy positions.
      b. Voters must know where the candidates stand on policy issues.
      c. Voters must see a difference between candidates on these issues.
      d. Voters must actually cast a vote for the candidate whose policy positions coincide with their own.
   3. One recurrent problem is that *candidates* often decide that the best way to handle a controversial issue is to cloud their positions in rhetoric; *both* candidates may be deliberately ambiguous.
   4. The *media* also may not be helpful, as they typically focus more on the "horse race" aspects of the campaign than on the policy stands of the candidates.
   5. Although it is questionable whether voters are really much more sophisticated now about issues, policy voting has become somewhat easier than in the past. Today's candidates are compelled to take clear stands to appeal to their own party's *primary* voters. Thus, it is the *electoral process* that has changed rather than the voters.

VI. THE LAST BATTLE: THE ELECTORAL COLLEGE

A. It is the **electoral vote** rather than the popular vote that actually determines the outcome of the presidential election.
   1. Because the founders wanted the president to be selected by the nation's elite—and not directly by the people—they created the electoral college.
   2. *Political practice* since 1828 has been for electors to vote for *the candidate who won their state's popular vote.*

B. Mechanics of the electoral college system.
   1. Each state has as many electoral votes as it has U.S. senators and representatives. Today, state parties nominate slates of electors.
   2. All states except Maine and Nebraska have a **winner-take-all** system in which electors vote as a bloc for the candidate who received the most popular votes in the states.
   3. Electors meet in their respective states in December and mail their votes to the president of the Senate (vice president of the U.S.). The vote is counted when the new congressional session opens in January, and the result is reported by the president of the Senate.
   4. If no candidate receives an electoral college majority, the election is thrown into the House of Representatives, which must choose from

among the top three electoral vote winners. The *unit rule* is used, which means that each state delegation has one vote (not each member).

5. If the election is not thrown into the House, the system gives extra clout to big states. The *big-state bias* also produces an *urban bias* in the electoral college.

VII. UNDERSTANDING ELECTIONS AND VOTING BEHAVIOR

A. According to democratic theory, *elections* accomplish two tasks: they *select the policymakers*, and they are supposed to *help shape public policy.*
   1. In the hypothetical world of *rational choice theory* and the Downs model [see Chapter 8], elections do in fact guide public policy.
   2. Social science research on the question has produced mixed findings. Elections do affect public policy to some degree, and public policy decisions also partly affect electoral outcomes.

B. Democracy and elections.
   1. The greater the policy differences between the candidates, the more likely it is that voters will be able to influence government policies by their choices.
   2. As long as politicians can take refuge in ambiguity, the possibility of democratic control of policy is lessened.
   3. When individual candidates offer a clear choice, voters are more able to guide the government's policy direction.
   4. Most policies have consequences for the well-being of certain groups or for society as a whole. According to the theory of **retrospective voting**, voters essentially ask the question, "What have you done for me lately?"
   5. Public policy—especially the *perception of economic policy impacts*—can affect elections. In presidential elections, people who are unhappy with the state of the economy tend to blame the incumbent.

C. Elections and the scope of government.
   1. While the threat of election defeat constrains policymakers, it also helps to increase generalized support for government and its powers. Elections *legitimize the power of the state*, thereby making it easier to *expand the scope* of the government.
   2. When people have the power to dole out electoral reward and punishment, they are more likely to see government as their servant instead of their master. As a result, citizens in a democracy often *seek to benefit from government* (rather than to

be protected from it). As democracy has spread, government has come to do more and more, and its scope has grown.

KEY TERMS AND CONCEPTS

Civic duty: a belief in the obligation to vote.

Electoral college: the institution designated in the Constitution whereby a body of electors select the president and vice president.

Initiative petition: direct democracy technique that allows proposed legislative items to be placed on a statewide ballot when enough signatures are obtained.

Legitimacy: widely-shared belief that a democratic government was elected fairly and freely.

Mandate theory of elections: the belief that the election winner has a mandate to implement policy promises.

Motor Voter Act (1993): this legislation requires states to let people register to vote at the same time they apply for a driver's license.

Policy voting: occurs when people base their choices on how close a candidate's issues positions are to their own issue preferences.

Political efficacy: the belief that ordinary people can influence government.

Referendum: direct democracy technique that allows citizens to approve or disapprove some legislative act, bond, issue, or constitutional amendment proposed by a state legislature.

Retrospective voting: voting theory that suggests that individuals who feel that they are better off as a result of certain policies are likely to support candidates who pledge to continue those policies, and those who feel worse off are inclined to support opposition candidates.

Suffrage: the legal right to vote.

Voter registration: a requirement that citizen register to vote before the election is held.

TEACHING IDEAS: CLASS DISCUSSION AND STUDENT PROJECTS

- It is common to hear people in public life say, "Vote any way you want, but VOTE." Have your class consider the following question: Do people in an election campaign organization really want to increase voter turnout, or are they interested in types of people who they think will vote for their party or candidate? Small groups of students could interview local officeholders and ask for their "realistic" opinions. Are "get out the vote" campaigns geared primarily to a party's (or candidate's) supporters? Compare their responses to similar questions asked of campus student leaders.

- Divide your class into two sections and ask them to take opposing positions on the following question: *Is it reasonable for a voter to look at personality and "character" traits as a basis for judging candidates for public office?* Class discussion on this topic is often animated and responsive.

- Ask students to research the legislative history of the Motor Voter Act. Who supported the act? Who opposed it? Why? Has "motor voter" had any effect on voter registration? Turnout?

- Bring information to class on procedures for voter registration. Consider using your class as the basis for a voter registration drive on campus. Information, publicity, and transportation are often problems for students who would like to vote.

- Ask students to debate the relative value of voter registration. Although voter registration is designed to minimize corruption or cheating in the election, what other possible reasons could be underlying the voter registration system? How do other democratic countries control corruption without voter registration? What other possible mechanisms exist which could control corruption and cheating equally well or better? What issues are raised by current proposals for on-line voting?

- For a reading and writing connection (and if the course is being taught in an election year), have students keep a clipping file on candidates for an office of their choice. Using broadcast and print media sources and descriptive journal entries for each item, have students identify the policy positions of the candidate from these sources. In a short analytical essay, have them compare the information they obtained through news coverage of their candidates with information they obtained in campaign advertisements about the candidates' issue positions. Alternatively, students could compare media images between competing candidates using the same format.

- Ask students to debate (or write an analytical essay) on the desirability of having a tax on non-voting. What would be the benefits? What would be the costs? Does the Constitution protect citizens' right to abstain from voting?

- For a lively and entertaining classroom activity, announce that students must elect an official notetaker. Advise students that this official notetaker will provide you with a copy of the class notes so that you can weigh your exam on the basis of what students are able to glean from the lecture. The election should be held with a primary, if necessary, for nominations. Then have each nominee give an election speech, complete with issue positions and qualifications. This exercise addresses a variety of concepts. It addresses democratic decision making by allowing students to inform you as a policy maker. It addresses problems of selective perception in individual attention to details. It provides a practical example of policy voting. Do not be surprised if students pick someone who is not the best student in class. Because students will compare their capacity for notetaking with the nominee's, students often will pick the least qualified or an average student to minimize the chance that they will miss something important in the lecture. Thus the exercise reinforces the problem that elections do not always result in the best, most qualified person winning.

BACKGROUND READING

Aldrich, John H., David W. Rohde and Paul R. Abramson. Change and Continuity in the 1996 and 1998 Elections. Washington, D.C.: CQ Press. 1999.

Alvarez, R. Michael. Information and Elections. Ann Arbor, MI: University of Michigan Press. 1999.

Hart, Roderick P. Campaign Talk: Why Elections Are Good For Us. Princeton: Princeton University Press. 2000.

Longley, Lawrence D. and Neal R. Peirce. The Electoral College Primer 2000. New Haven: Yale University Press. 1999.

Miller, Warren and J. Merrill Shanks. The New American Voter. Cambridge: Harvard University Press. 1996.

Niemi, Richard G. and Herbert F. Weisberg, eds. Controversies in Voting Behavior. 3rd ed. Washington, DC: Congressional Quarterly Press. 1993.

Rosenstone, Steven J. and John Mark Hansen. Mobilization, Participation and Democracy in America. NY: MacMillan. 1993.

Wolfinger, Raymond. E. and Steven J. Rosenstone. Who Votes? New Haven, CT: Yale University Press. 1980.

MEDIA SUGGESTIONS

Politics in Action, Chapter 3: The Electoral College. A brief animated film explaining the origin and procedures followed in the Electoral College.

Price of Power: Money in Politics. A 1993 program by Insight Media which examines the role of money in influencing electoral outcomes.

Vote: A Right and Responsibility. 1995. This film examines the fundamentals and structure of voting in America, including information on registration, filing an absentee ballot, and opportunities for voting at each level of government. Insight Media.

Voting: A Right and a Responsibility. This show demonstrates how elections are central to democracy in the U.S. and beyond; includes discussions on candidate evaluation, and direct democracy mechanisms such as the initiative and referendum. Films for the Humanities & Sciences.

CHAPTER ELEVEN: INTEREST GROUPS

PEDAGOGICAL FEATURES

LEARNING OBJECTIVES

After studying this chapter, students should be able to:

- Distinguish the essential differences between *interest groups* and *political parties.*

- Understand three basic theories of interest group politics: *pluralist* theory, *elite* theory, and *hyperpluralist* theory.

- Examine how *interest group liberalism* may be promoted by the network of *subgovernments* (or *"iron triangles"*) in the American political system.

- Determine the factors that tend to make an interest group successful.
- Differentiate between a *potential group* and an *actual group*, and determine how the *free-rider problem* applies.
- Explain how interest groups try to shape public policy.
- Determine how lobbyists represent interest groups in influencing the legislative agenda.
- Distinguish among the various forms of interest groups, such as economic interests and public interest groups.
- Explain why the authors of the textbook say that the problems of honest lobbying now appear to outweigh the traditional problems of dishonest lobbying.
- Summarize the implications for the size of government that are generated by the power of PACs and special interest groups.
- Analyze the appropriate role of interest groups within a democratic environment.

CHAPTER OVERVIEW

INTRODUCTION

Although voter turnout has declined substantially in the U.S. since the 1960s, the number of interest groups active in lobbying the government has increased dramatically. This chapter examines this growth and the activities of interest groups, why individuals join groups and what groups get for their efforts.

THE ROLE AND REPUTATION OF INTEREST GROUPS

An **interest group** is *an organization of people with similar policy goals* that tries to influence the political process to try to achieve those goals. In so doing, interest groups try to influence every branch and every level of government. This *multiplicity of policy arenas* helps distinguish interest groups from political parties.

Interest groups may also support candidates for office, but American interest groups *do not run their own slate of candidates*. Interest groups are often *policy specialists*, whereas parties are policy generalists. Thus, interest groups do not face the constraint imposed by trying to appeal to everyone (unlike political parties).

Despite their importance to democratic government, interest groups traditionally have had a negative image in America. Even Madison's term **faction** was general enough to include both parties and groups. There is little doubt that honest lobbying outpaces dishonest lobbying by a wide margin. Ironically, many political scientists now believe that *honest lobbying* poses *greater problems for democracy* than dishonest lobbying.

THEORIES OF INTEREST GROUP POLITICS

Understanding the debate over whether honest lobbying creates problems requires an examination of three important theories: (1) **pluralist theory** argues that interest group activity brings representation to all as groups *compete and counterbalance one another*; (2) **elite theory** argues that *a few groups (mostly the wealthy) have most of the power*; (3) **hyperpluralist theory** asserts that *too many groups are getting too much of what they want*, resulting in a *government policy that is often contradictory and lacking in direction.*

According to pluralist theory, groups win some and lose some, but *no group wins or loses all the time.* Pluralists do not deny that some groups are stronger than others or that competing interests do not always get an equal hearing, but they argue that *lobbying is open to all* and should not be regarded as a problem. No one group is likely to become too dominant, and *all legitimate groups are able to affect public policy.*

Elite theorists maintain that *real power is held by relatively few people, key groups, and institutions.* Government is run by *a few big interests* looking out for themselves. Interest groups are extremely unequal in power; thus the preponderance of power held by elites means that *pluralist theory does not accurately describe the reality of American politics.*

This chapter also explores *hyperpluralism and interest group liberalism.* Theodore Lowi coined the phrase **interest group liberalism** to refer to the government's *excessive deference to groups.* Interest group liberalism holds that virtually all pressure group demands are legitimate and that the job of the government is to advance them all. In an effort to appease every interest, government agencies proliferate, conflicting regulations expand, programs multiply, and the budget skyrockets.

Interest group liberalism is promoted by the network of **subgovernments** (also known as **iron triangles**). These subgovernments are composed of key interest groups interested in a particular policy, the government agency in charge of administering the policy, and the members of congressional committees and subcommittees handling the policy. Relations between groups and the government become too cozy. Hard choices about national policy rarely get made as the government tries to favor all groups, leading to *policy paralysis*. Hyperpluralist theorists often point to the government's contradictory tobacco-related policies as an example of interest group liberalism.

WHAT MAKES AN INTEREST GROUP SUCCESSFUL?

Many factors affect the success of an interest group, including the *size of the group*, the *intensity*, and its *financial resources*. Small groups actually have *organizational advantages over large groups*. A **potential group** is composed of all people who might be group members because they share some common interest. An **actual group** is composed of those in the potential group who choose to join. Groups vary enormously in the degree to which they enroll their potential membership.

A **collective good** is something of value (such as clean air or a higher minimum wage) that cannot be withheld from a potential group member. Members of the potential group share in benefits that members of the actual group work to secure. The **free-rider problem** occurs when potential members decide not to join but to sit back and let other people do the work (from which they will nevertheless benefit). According to **Olson's law of large groups**, *the bigger the group, the more serious the free-rider problem.*

One way a large potential group may be mobilized is through an issue that *people feel intensely* about, such as abortion. Both small and large groups enjoy a psychological advantage when intensity is involved. Politicians are more likely to listen when a group shows that it cares deeply about an issue, and many votes may be won or lost on a single issue. One of the biggest indictments of the interest group system is that it is biased toward the wealthy.

THE INTEREST GROUP EXPLOSION

Although *turnout in elections has declined* since 1960, *participation in interest groups has mushroomed.* There are an enormous number of highly specialized and seemingly trivial groups, usually with a staff and publications. One of the major factors in the explosion in the number of interest groups in the United States has been the development of sophisticated technology such as computerized mail lists.

HOW GROUPS TRY TO SHAPE POLICY

The three *traditional strategies* of interest groups are *lobbying*, *electioneering*, and *litigation*. In addition, groups have recently developed *a variety of sophisticated techniques* to appeal to the public for widespread support.

Lobbyists are political persuaders who are the representatives of organized groups. They normally work in Washington, handling groups' legislative business. Although lobbyists primarily try to *influence* members of Congress, they can also be of *help* to them. For example, lobbyists are an important source of specialized information.

Political scientists are *not in agreement* about the *effectiveness of lobbying*. Much evidence suggests that lobbyists' power over policy is often exaggerated, but plenty of evidence to the contrary suggests that lobbying can sometimes persuade legislators to support a certain policy. It is difficult to evaluate the specific effects of lobbying because it is hard to isolate its effects from other influences. Like campaigning, lobbying is directed primarily toward *activating and reinforcing* one's supporters.

Getting the right people into office or keeping them there is another key strategy of interest groups. Many groups therefore get involved in **electioneering**—aiding candidates financially and getting their members to support them. **Political Action Committees (PACs)** have provided a means for groups to participate in electioneering more than ever before.

Today, **litigation** is often used if an interest group fails in Congress or gets only a vague piece of legislation. Environmental legislation, such as the Clean Air Act, typically includes written provisions allowing ordinary citizens to sue for enforcement. Possibly the most famous interest group victories in court were by civil rights groups in the 1950s. These groups won major victories in court cases concerning school desegregation, equal housing, and labor market equality. Consumer groups have also used suits against businesses and federal agencies as a means of enforcing consumer regulations.

The practice of interest groups *appealing to the public for support* has a long tradition in American politics. Public opinion ultimately makes its way to policymakers, so interest groups carefully cultivate their public image.

TYPES OF INTEREST GROUPS

Political scientists loosely *categorize interest groups* into four main policy areas: some deal primarily with *economic issues*, others with issues of *the environment*, others with *equality* issues, and still others with the interests of all consumers. **Economic groups** are ultimately concerned with wages, prices, and profits. In the American economy, government does not directly determine these factors. More commonly, public policy in America has economic *effects* through regulations, tax advantages, subsidies and contracts, and international trade policy. Business, labor, and farmers all worry about government regulations. Every economic group wants to get its share of direct aid and government contracts.

Environmental interests have exerted a great deal of influence on Congress and state legislatures. Group politics intensifies when two public interests clash, such as environmental protection and an ensured supply of energy.

Interest groups representing minorities and women have made *equal rights* their main policy goal. Equality at the polls, in housing, on the job, in education, and in all other facets of American life has long been the dominant goal of African-American groups, the oldest of which is the National Association for the Advancement of Colored People (NAACP). The Nineteenth Amendment (1920) guaranteed women the right to vote, but other guarantees of equal protection for women remain absent from the Constitution. More recently, women's rights groups such as the National Organization for Women (NOW) have lobbied for an end to sexual discrimination.

Some groups cannot be easily molded into the four policy areas. **Public interest groups** like Common Cause and **ideological groups** like the now-disbanded Moral Majority involve themselves in a wide range of issues.

Public interest lobbies (representing groups that champion causes or ideas "in the public interest") are organizations that seek a "collective good," by which everyone should be better off—regardless of whether they joined in the lobbying. Consumer groups have won many legislative victories in recent years, including the creation in 1973 of the Consumer Product Safety Commission (authorized to regulate all consumer products and to ban particularly dangerous ones). Other public interest groups include groups that speak for those who cannot speak for themselves, such as children, animals, and the mentally ill; good-government groups such as Common Cause; religious groups; and environmental groups.

UNDERSTANDING INTEREST GROUPS

The problem of interest groups in America today remains much the same as James Madison defined it over 200 years ago. A free society must allow for the representation of all groups, yet groups are usually more concerned with their own self-interest than with the needs of society as a whole. For democracy to work well, it is important that self-interested groups not be allowed to assume a dominant position.

Madison's solution was to create an open system in which many groups would be able to participate. Groups with opposing interests would *counterbalance* each other. *Pluralist theorists* believe that a rough approximation of the public interest emerges from this competition. *Elite theorists* point to the proliferation of business PACs as evidence of more interest group corruption in American politics than ever. They particularly note that wealthier interests are greatly advantaged by the PAC system. *Hyperpluralist theorists* feel that government attempts to accommodate all major interest groups lead to policy gridlock and the inability for government to initiate major policies.

The power of special interest groups through PACs and other means has implications for the *scope of government.* Most special interest groups strive to maintain established programs that benefit them—and thus promote larger government. Conversely, one can make the argument that the growth of the scope of government in recent decades accounts for a good portion of the proliferation of interest groups. As the federal government has become involved in more areas, more interest groups have risen to influence policy.

CHAPTER OUTLINE

I. THE ROLE AND REPUTATION OF INTEREST GROUPS

A. Although turnout in elections has declined since 1960, participation in interest groups has mushroomed.

B. The *freedom to organize* (the right "peaceably to assemble, and to petition" guaranteed by the First Amendment) is as fundamental to democratic government as freedom of speech or of the press.

C. Distinguishing interest groups from political parties.

1. An **interest group** is an organization of people with similar policy goals that tries to influence the political process to try to achieve those goals. In so doing, interest groups try to influence every branch and every level of government.
2. This *multiplicity of policy arenas* helps *distinguish interest groups from political parties.*
3. Interest groups may support candidates for office, but American interest groups *do not run their own slate of candidates*. By contrast, interest groups in many countries with *multiparty systems* often form their own political parties to push for their demands.
4. Interest groups are often *policy specialists*, whereas *parties are policy generalists.*
5. Unlike political parties, interest groups do not face the constraint imposed by trying to appeal to everyone.

D. Why interest groups get bad press.
   1. Despite their importance to democratic government, interest groups traditionally have had a negative image in America. Even Madison's term **faction** was general enough to include both parties and groups.
   2. There is little doubt that *honest lobbying outpaces dishonest lobbying* by a wide margin. However, many political scientists now believe that *honest lobbying* poses *greater problems for democracy* than dishonest lobbying.

II. THEORIES OF INTEREST GROUP POLITICS

A. Understanding the debate over whether honest lobbying creates problems requires an examination of three important theories.
   1. **Pluralist theory** argues that interest group activity brings representation to all; groups *compete and counterbalance one another.*
   2. **Elite theory** argues that *a few groups (mostly the wealthy) have most of the power.*
   3. **Hyperpluralist theory** asserts that *too many groups are getting too much of what they want*, resulting in a *government policy that is often contradictory and lacking in direction.*

B. Pluralism and group theory.
   1. In pluralist theory, the extensive organization of competing groups is seen as evidence that influence is widely dispersed among them. *Groups win some and lose some, but no group wins or loses all the time.*
   2. A *group theory of politics* contains several essential arguments.

   a. Groups provide a key link between people and government whereby all legitimate interests in the political system can get a hearing from government.
   b. Groups compete, and interests constantly make claims on one another.
   c. No one group is likely to become too dominant. When one group grows too powerful, its opponents are likely to intensify their organization and thus restore balance to the system.
   d. Groups usually play by the "rules of the game," with few groups lying, cheating, stealing, or engaging in violence.
   e. Groups weak in one resource can use another. All legitimate groups are able to affect public policy.
3. Pluralists do not deny that some groups are stronger than others or that competing interests do not always get an equal hearing, but they argue that *lobbying is open to all and should not be regarded as a problem.*

C. Elites and the denial of pluralism.
   1. Elite theorists maintain that *real power is held by relatively few people, key groups, and institutions.* Government is run by a few big interests looking out for themselves.
   2. Elitists point to *interlocking and concentrated power centers.* About one-third of top institutional positions are occupied by people who hold more than one such position.
   3. The fact that there are numerous groups proves nothing because *groups are extremely unequal in power.* When confronted with the power of multinational corporations, consumer interests are easily pushed aside.
   4. Honest lobbying is a problem because it benefits the few at the expense of the many.

D. Hyperpluralism and interest group liberalism.
   1. Hyperpluralists argue that *the pluralist system is out of control.*
   2. Theodore Lowi coined the phrase **interest group liberalism** to refer to the government's *excessive deference to groups.*
   3. Interest group liberalism holds that virtually all pressure group demands are legitimate and that the job of the government is to advance them all. In an effort to appease every interest, government agencies proliferate, conflicting regulations expand, programs multiply, and the budget skyrockets.
   4. Interest group liberalism is promoted by the network of **subgovernments** (also known as **iron triangles**). These subgovernments are composed of key interest groups interested in a particular policy, the government agency in charge of administering

the policy, and the members of congressional committees and subcommittees handling the policy.

5. Relations between groups and the government become too cozy. Hard choices about national policy rarely get made as the government tries to favor all groups, leading to *policy paralysis*. Hyperpluralist theorists often point to the government's contradictory tobacco-related policies as an example of interest group liberalism.
6. Ironically, the recent interest group explosion is seen by some as *weakening the power of subgovernments*. With so many more interest groups to satisfy and with many of them competing against one another, a cozy relationship between groups and the government is more difficult to sustain.

III. WHAT MAKES AN INTEREST GROUP SUCCESSFUL?

A. The surprising ineffectiveness of large groups.

1. Many factors affect the success of an interest group, including the *size of the group*, the *intensity*, and its *financial resources*. Small groups actually have *organizational advantages over large groups*.
2. A **potential group** is composed of all people who might be group members because they share some common interest.
3. An **actual group** is composed of those in the potential group who choose to join. Groups vary enormously in the degree to which they enroll their potential membership.
4. A **collective good** is something of value (such as clean air or a higher minimum wage) that cannot be withheld from a potential group member. Members of the potential group share in benefits that members of the actual group work to secure.
    a. Economist Mancur Olson points that all groups—as opposed to individuals—are in the business of providing collective goods. The **free-rider problem** occurs when potential members decide not to join, but rather to sit back and let other people do the work (from which they will nevertheless benefit).
    b. According to **Olson's law of large groups**, *the bigger the group, the more serious the free-rider problem.*
        (1) It is easier to organize a small group with clear economic goals than it is to organize a large group with broader goals.
        (2) Small groups have an organizational advantage over large ones because a given member's share of the collective good in a small group may be great enough that he or she will try to secure it; but in the largest groups, each member can only expect to get a tiny share of the policy gains.

c. This advantage of small groups helps to explain why public interest groups have a hard time financially. In contrast, the lobbying costs and benefits for business are concentrated. Large corporations also enjoy an inherent size advantage. Small potential groups like business have an easier time organizing themselves for political action than large potential groups, such as consumers.

d. The primary way for large potential groups to overcome Olson's law is to provide **selective benefits**. These are goods that a group can restrict to those who pay their yearly dues, such as information publications, travel discounts, and group insurance rates.

B. Intensity.

1. One way a large potential group may be mobilized is through an issue that *people feel intensely* about, such as abortion.

   a. Both small and large groups enjoy a psychological advantage when intensity is involved. Politicians are more likely to listen when a group shows that it cares deeply about an issue, and many votes may be won or lost on a single issue.

   b. A **single-issue group**—which has a narrow interest, dislikes compromise, and single-mindedly pursues its goal—characteristically deals with issues that evoke strong emotions (such as nuclear power plants, gun control, and abortion).

2. Perhaps the most emotional issue of all in recent years has been that of abortion. Regardless of which side candidates for political office are on, they will be taking heat on the abortion issue for years to come.

C. Financial resources.

1. Critics charge that PACs—as the source of so much money in today's expensive high-tech campaigns—distort the governmental process in favor of those that can raise the most money.

2. Conversely, the big interests do not always win, even on some of the most important issues (such as the Tax Reform Act of 1986).

IV. THE INTEREST GROUP EXPLOSION

A. One of the major factors in the explosion in the number of interest groups in the United States has been the development of sophisticated technology such as computerized mail lists.

1. Over 90% of groups have their headquarters in Washington, D.C.
2. There are an enormous number of highly specialized and seemingly trivial groups.
3. Almost every group has a staff and publications.

B. The interests of many groups are primarily economic. Eighty percent of the groups originated from occupational, industrial, or professional memberships.

V. HOW GROUPS TRY TO SHAPE POLICY

A. The three *traditional strategies* of interest groups are *lobbying*, *electioneering*, and *litigation*. In addition, groups have recently developed *a variety of sophisticated techniques* to appeal to the public for widespread support.

B. Lobbying.
   1. **Lobbyists** are political persuaders who are the representatives of organized groups. They normally work in Washington, handling groups' legislative business.
   2. Basically, there are two types of lobbyists: regular, paid employees of a corporation, union, or association, and lobbyists for hire on a temporary basis.
   3. Although lobbyists primarily try to *influence* members of Congress, they can also be of *help* to them. Ornstein and Elder list four ways lobbyists can help a member of Congress:
      a. They are an important source of information. Lobbyists can confine themselves to a single policy area, and thus can provide specialized expertise.
      b. They can help a member with political strategy. In effect, they are free consultants.
      c. They can help formulate campaign strategy and get the group's members behind a politician's reelection campaign.
      d. They are a source of ideas and innovations.
   4. Political scientists are *not in agreement* about the *effectiveness of lobbying*.
      a. Much evidence suggests that lobbyists' power over policy is often exaggerated.
      b. Plenty of evidence to the contrary suggests that lobbying can sometimes persuade legislators to support a certain policy. Examples include opposition to gun control legislation by the National Rifle Association and intensive lobbying against the 1988 Catastrophic Health Care Act conducted by the nation's most wealthy senior citizens.
      c. It is difficult to evaluate the specific effects of lobbying because it is hard to isolate its effects from other influences. Like campaigning, lobbying is directed primarily toward *activating and reinforcing* one's supporters.

C. Electioneering.

1. Getting the right people into office or keeping them there is a key strategy of interest groups. Many groups therefore get involved in **electioneering**—aiding candidates financially and getting their members to support them.
2. **Political Action Committees (PACs)** have provided a means for groups to participate in electioneering more than ever before. In recent years, nearly half of the candidates running for reelection to the House of Representatives have received the majority of their campaign funds from PACs. Most funds from PACs go to incumbents ($99 million to House incumbents during the 1991-1992 election cycle contrasted with $12 million to challengers) because *incumbents are the most likely to provide a return the PACs' investment.*

D. Litigation.
   1. Today, **litigation** is often used if an interest group fails in Congress or gets only a vague piece of legislation.
      a. Environmental legislation, such as the Clean Air Act, typically includes written provisions allowing ordinary citizens to sue for enforcement. The constant threat of a lawsuit increases the likelihood that businesses will consider the environmental impact of what they do.
      b. Possibly the most famous interest group victories in court were by civil rights groups in the 1950s. These groups won major victories in court cases concerning school desegregation, equal housing, and labor market equality.
      c. Consumer groups have used suits against businesses and federal agencies as a means of enforcing consumer regulations.
   2. Tactics and strategies.
      a. One tactic that lawyers employ to make the views of interest groups heard by the judiciary is the filing of ***amicus curiae*** **("friend of the court") briefs**, which consist of written arguments submitted to the courts in support of one side of a case.
      b. A more direct judicial strategy employed by interest groups is the filing of **class action lawsuits**, which enables a group of similarly situated plaintiffs to combine similar grievances into a single suit.

E. Going public.
   1. Many interest groups find it important to shape a good *image*, employing public relations techniques to present themselves in the most favorable manner.
   2. The practice of interest groups appealing to the public for support has a long tradition in American politics.

VI. TYPES OF INTEREST GROUPS

A. Political scientists loosely *categorize interest groups* into four main policy areas: some deal primarily with *economic issues*, others with issues of *the environment*, others with *equality* issues, and still others with the interests of all consumers.

B. Some groups cannot be easily molded into the four policy arenas. **Public interest groups** like Common Cause and **ideological groups** like the now-disbanded Moral Majority involve themselves in a wide range of issues. However, most groups concern themselves with a *limited range of issues*.

C. Economic groups.
   1. All economic interests are ultimately concerned with wages, prices, and profits.
   2. In the American economy, government does not directly determine these factors. More commonly, public policy in America has economic *effects* though regulations, tax advantages, subsidies and contracts, and international trade policy.
      a. Business, labor, and farmers all worry about government regulations. Every economic group wants to get its share of direct aid and government contracts.
      b. Business executives, factory workers, and farmers seek to influence government because regulations, taxes, subsidies, and international economic policy affect their economic livelihoods.

D. Labor.
   1. Labor has more affiliated members than any other interest group except the American Association for Retired Persons (AARP). The AFL-CIO is itself a union of unions.
   2. Unions press for policies to ensure better working conditions and higher wages.
      a. Unions have fought hard to establish the **union shop,** which requires new employees to join the union representing them.
      b. Business groups have supported **right-to-work laws,** which outlaw union membership as a condition of employment. In 1947, Congress passed the **Taft-Hartley Act** permitting states to adopt right-to-work laws.
   3. The American labor movement reached its peak in 1956 when 33 percent of the non-agricultural work force belonged to a union; the percentage has declined since then to about 16 percent.

a. One factor behind the decline is that low wages in other countries have diminished the American job market in a number of key manufacturing areas.
b. Unions have had difficulty in getting today's workers to believe that they will benefit from unionization. Paul Johnson argues that this task has become more difficult in recent years due to the efforts of employers to make nonunion jobs satisfying.

E. Agriculture.
1. The "family farm" has given way to massive **agribusinesses**, often heavily involved with exports. Only 3 percent of Americans now make their living as farmers.
2. There are several broad-based agricultural groups, but equally important are the *commodity associations* such as peanut farmers, potato growers, dairy farmers, and other producers. The U.S. Department of Agriculture and the agricultural subcommittees in Congress are organized along commodity lines.

F. Business.
1. Seventy percent of all interest group organizations having a Washington presence represent business, and business PACs have increased more dramatically than any other category of PACs. Most large firms now have offices in Washington that monitor legislative activity.
2. Business interests are generally unified when it comes to promoting greater profits, but are often fragmented when policy choices have to be made. Two umbrella organizations—the National Association of Manufacturers (NAM) and the Chamber of Commerce—include most corporations and business and speak for them when general business interests are at stake.
3. The hundreds of trade and product associations fight regulations that would reduce their profits. They seek preferential tax treatment as well as government subsidies and contracts.
4. It is not only American trade associations that are concerned with policies such as tariffs and preferential tax treatment; foreign corporations and governments are also concerned.

G. Environmental interests.
1. Environmentalists have exerted a great deal of influence on Congress and state legislatures. A few environmentalist groups—like the Sierra Club and the Audubon Society—have been around since the nineteenth century, but many others trace their origins to the first *Earth Day* in 1970, when ecology-minded people marched to symbolize their support for environmental protection.

2. Group politics intensifies when two public interests clash, such as environmental protection and an ensured supply of energy.
   a. Environmentalists insist that, in the long run, energy supplies can be ensured without harming the environment or risking radiation exposure from nuclear plants.
   b. Energy producers argue that environmentalists oppose nearly all new energy projects. They argue that some limited risks have to be taken to fulfill energy demands.

H. Equality interests.
1. Racial and ethnic minorities.
   a. Interest groups representing women and minorities have made equal rights their main policy goal.
   b. Equality at the polls, in housing, on the job, in education, and in all other facets of American life has long been the dominant goal of African American groups, the oldest of which is the National Association for the Advancement of Colored People (NAACP). Although they have won many victories in principle, *equality in practice* has been much slower in coming.
   c. Today, civil rights groups continue to push for more effective affirmative action programs to ensure that minority groups are given educational and employment opportunities. In recent years, the NAACP's main vehicle has been the *Fair Share program*, which negotiates agreements with national and regional businesses to increase minority hiring and the use of minority contractors.
2. Women.
   a. The Nineteenth Amendment (1920) guaranteed women the right to vote, but other guarantees of equal protection for women remained absent from the Constitution.
   b. More recently, women's rights groups such as the National Organization for Women (NOW) have lobbied for an end to sexual discrimination.
      (1) Their primary goal has been the passage of the *Equal Rights Amendment (ERA)*. The ERA was approved by Congress in 1972 but fell three states short of the thirty-eight necessary for ratification. Interest groups such as Phyllis Schlafly's Eagle Forum battled NOW and other women's groups over ratification of the ERA.
      (2) NOW remains committed to enacting the protection the ERA would have constitutionally guaranteed by advocating the *enactment of many individual statutes.*

I. Consumers and public interest lobbies.

1. **Public interest lobbies** (representing groups that champion causes or ideas "in the public interest") are organizations that seek a "collective good," by which everyone should be better off—regardless of whether they joined in the lobbying.
2. Consumer groups.
   a. The consumer movement was spurred by Ralph Nader, who was propelled to national prominence by his book, *Unsafe at Any Speed*, which attacked the safety of General Motors' Corvair. Nader successfully sued General Motors for invasion of privacy after the GM hired a private detective to dig into his background and follow him around. He used the proceeds from the damage settlement to launch the first major consumer group in Washington, D.C.
   b. Consumer groups have won many legislative victories in recent years, including the creation in 1973 of the Consumer Product Safety Commission (authorized to regulate all consumer products and to ban particularly dangerous ones).
3. Other public interest groups include groups that speak for whose who cannot speak for themselves, such as children, animals, and the mentally ill; good-government groups such as Common Cause; religious groups; and environmental groups.

VII. UNDERSTANDING INTEREST GROUPS

A. Interest groups and democracy.
   1. The problem of interest groups in America today remains much the same as James Madison defined it over 200 years ago.
      a. A free society must allow for the *representation of all groups*, yet groups are usually more concerned with their own *self-interest* than with the needs of society as a whole.
      b. For democracy to work well, it is important that self-interested groups not be allowed to assume a dominant position.
   2. Madison's solution was to create an open system in which *many groups would be able to participate*, Groups with opposing interests would *counterbalance* each other.
      a. *Pluralist theorists* believe that a rough approximation of the public interest emerges from this competition.
      b. *Elite theorists* point to the proliferation of business PACs as evidence of more interest group corruption in American politics than ever. They particularly note that wealthier interests are greatly advantaged by the PAC system.
      c. *Hyperpluralist theorists* maintain that whenever a major interest group objects strongly to proposed legislation, policymakers will

bend over backwards to try to accommodate it. They argue that this behavior has made it increasingly difficult to accomplish major policy change and has thus led to policy gridlock.

B. Interest groups and the scope of government.
   1. The power of special interest groups through PACs and other means has implications for the *scope of government.*
   2. Most special interest groups strive to maintain established programs that benefit them—and thus promote government with a broader scope. Both President Carter and President Reagan remarked at the end of their time in office that their attempts to cut waste in federal spending had been frustrated by interest groups.
   3. Conversely, one can make the argument that the growth of the scope of government in recent decades accounts for a good portion of the proliferation of interest groups. As the federal government has become involved in more areas, more interest groups have risen to influence policy.

KEY TERMS AND CONCEPTS

Actual group: a group composed of those in the potential group who are members of the interest group.

Amicus curiae briefs: friend of the court briefs filed by interest groups to inform the court of their position and to state how their welfare would be affected by a ruling.

Class action lawsuits: a technique used by interest groups which allows groups of people with similar complaints to combine their grievances into a single suit.

Collective good: something of value which cannot be withheld from individuals in the potential group.

Electioneering: helping sympathetic candidates get into office.

Elite theory: argues that because only a few groups have enough power to influence policy, power is concentrated into a few interlocking power centers.

Free-rider problem: a situation where individuals let others work to secure a collective good and then enjoy the benefit without contributing anything to the group effort.

Hyperpluralist theory: argues that too many groups are getting what they want at the expense of the unrepresented and that this behavior leads to incoherent public policy.

Interest group: organizations where people with similar policy goals enter the political process to achieve those goals.

Lobbying: a communication by someone other than a citizen acting on his or her own behalf, directed to a governmental decision-maker with the hope of influencing his or her decision.

Olson's law of large groups: suggests that the larger the group, the more difficult it will be to secure enough of the collective good to encourage participation.

Pluralist theory: argues that interest group activities provide additional representation and compete against each other to influence political outcomes.

Political Action Committees: a legal means for groups to participate in elections by contributing money.

Potential group: a group composed of all people who share some common interest.

Public interest lobbies: organizations which seek a collective good which does not only benefit their membership.

Right to work laws: a law which outlaws union membership as a condition of employment.

Selective benefits: these benefits are goods that a group can restrict to those who are members.

Single-issue group: groups which have very narrow interests, shun compromise, and single-mindedly pursue goals.

Subgovernments: exclusive relationships composed of interest groups leaders, government agency personnel, and members of congressional committees who perform mutually beneficial services for each other at the public's expense.

Union shop: a rule established to prevent free-riders by requiring new employees to join the union where one has been granted bargaining rights.

TEACHING IDEAS: CLASS DISCUSSION AND STUDENT PROJECTS

- Ask your class to distinguish between the problems of *honest lobbying* and *dishonest lobbying*. Suggest that they read the beginning segment of the chapter in preparation for this discussion.

- As a library assignment, have your class look up early news reports detailing Ralph Nader's fight with General Motors. Ask for an assessment of how they think the public (and Congress) would react to a similar situation today, contrasted with the original reaction. If Nader's *Unsafe at Any Speed* is still available in your library, place it on reserve so that interested students can examine it.

- Ask students what groups they belong to. Are any of these interest groups? Have students who belong to an interest group describe what it is, why they joined, and what benefits they receive from group membership. Then assign students to identify what groups represent their interests as students. Does it matter whether they are members of those groups or not? (Alternatively, you might ask students to query their parents about their group memberships.)

- This exercise reinforces the Olson theory on large groups and the free-rider problem. Ask students to make a list of all their group associations, including groups on campus. Have them separate the groups into formal membership associations and informal group sympathies. In addition, have students classify their groups into large and small groups. Then have them list the reasons why they joined some groups and have not joined the others. Have them do a simple cost benefit analysis of both their formal and informal associations. Stress the problems of collective action and the use of selective goods to maintain membership. If they cannot list any material benefit, ask them to identify the nonmaterial reasons for their formal associations. (Alternatively, you might ask students to query their parents about their group memberships.)

- This exercise provides a reading and writing connection. Have students keep a file using articles by or about interest groups downloaded from the Internet. Tell them to identify one area or topic in which the federal government has a legislative interest, and then try to locate as many groups as possible that provide information on the topic and their activities as possible. What groups did students consider to be interest groups? Why or why not? Have students write a brief essay describing the variety of groups they found on the Web, who the groups represent, and the variety of activities that the groups reported engaging in. If students do not have access to the Internet, the same exercise could be conducted using newspaper and magazine articles.

- Have students investigate a federal candidate of their choice by using FECA data on PAC contributions available on the Internet. Who contributed to "their" candidate? What is the typical size of contributions? Do these data provide any surprising findings? Students could also be asked to investigate the candidate's challenger, and compare differences in the sources and levels of funding.

- Assign each student a different interest group, drawing from the list in Table 11.1 and supplementing it with equality, environmental and public interest lobbies. Ask students to document the formation of their group, with particular attention paid to the free-rider problem, the use of selective incentives and patrons (government and private individuals). For a writing assignment, have students write a three-page essay on these issues.

BACKGROUND READING

Baumgartner, Frank R. and Beth L. Leech. Basic Interests: The Importance of Groups in Politics and in Political Science. Princeton, New Jersey: Princeton University Press. 1998.

Berry, Jeffrey. The Interest Group Society. 3rd ed. NY: Addison-Wesley. 1996.

Berry, Jeffrey M. The New Liberalism: The Rising Power of Citizen Groups. Washington, D.C.: Brookings. 1999.

Cigler, Allan J. and Burdett A. Loomis, eds. Interest Group Politics. 5th. ed. Washington, DC: Congressional Quarterly Press. 1998.

Kollman, Ken. Outside Lobbying: Public Opinion and Interest Group Strategies. Princeton: Princeton University Press. 1998.

Lowi, Theodore. The End of Liberalism. NY: Norton. 1979.

Petracca, Mark P. ed. The Politics of Interests: Interest Groups Transformed. Boulder, CO: Westview Press. 1992.

Salisbury, Robert H. Interests and Institutions. Pittsburgh: University of Pittsburgh Press. 1992.

Schlozman, Kay L. and John T. Tierney. Organized Interests and American Democracy. NY: Harper & Row. 1986.

Smith, Hedrick. The Power Game: How Washington Works. NY: Random House, Inc. 1988.

Sorauf, Frank. J. Inside Campaign Finance: Myths and Realities. New Haven: Yale University Press. 1994.

MEDIA SUGGESTIONS

Influences and Interests. Part of the "We the People" series. A Films Incorporated video series on Congress. A thirty minute film examining interest group influence on members of Congress.

Lobbying Congress. Part of the "We the People" series. A thirty-minute film on lobbying Congress. Films Incorporated.

Organizing America: The History of Trade Unions. 1994. This film examines the formation of collective action among workers in America as a force of social change. Insight Media.

Religious Fundamentalism. 1996. This film examines the rise of religious fundamentalism as organized interests and analyzes its impact on American political life. Films for the Humanities and Sciences.

The Religious Right. This program analyzes the impact of the conservative religious right on contemporary Republican policies. Films for the Humanities and Sciences.

The Unelected. Part of the Power Game series from PBS. This 1990 video examines the influence of power lobbies and the media on Capitol Hill politics.

CHAPTER TWELVE: CONGRESS

PEDAGOGICAL FEATURES

LEARNING OBJECTIVES

After studying this chapter, students should be able to:

- Describe the essential roles and functions of a senator and representative.
- List the characteristics of a "typical" member of Congress.
- Identify the advantages of *incumbency* in the congressional election process.

- Examine the role of money in congressional elections—where it comes from, how it is used, and what influence or effect it has.

- Summarize both the advantages and disadvantages of the growing influence of PACs.

- Contrast organizational style and procedures in the House of Representatives with those of the Senate.

- Identify the major leadership positions in the House and Senate and summarize the functions of each office.

- Review the four types of congressional committees and explain how they control the congressional agenda and guide legislation.

- Determine the significance of legislative procedures like the *filibuster* and *oversight.*

- Outline the process by which a bill would move through the legislative process, from introduction to the point where it is sent to the president.

- Contrast three theories of the role of a legislator: *trustee*, *instructed delegate*, and *politico*.

- Appraise the influence of lobbyists and interest groups on the legislative process.

- Identify both representative and unrepresentative aspects of Congress.

- Examine the effect that the U.S. Congress has had on the *scope* of government.

CHAPTER OVERVIEW

INTRODUCTION

The framers of the Constitution conceived of Congress as the center of policy-making in America. Although the prominence of Congress has fluctuated over time, in recent years Congress has been the true center of power in Washington. In addition to its central role in policy making, Congress also performs important roles of representation.

Congressional tasks become more difficult each year. At the same time, critics charge Congress with being responsible for enlarging the scope of government, and public opinion is critical of the institution. Why would individuals want to serve in Congress? And are the critics' claims correct?

THE REPRESENTATIVES AND SENATORS

Despite public perceptions to the contrary, *hard work* is perhaps the most prominent characteristic of a member of Congress' job. The typical representative is a member of about six committees and subcommittees; a senator is a member of about ten. There are also attractions to the job. Most important is *power*: members of Congress make key decisions about important matters of public policy. They also receive a substantial salary and "perks."

The Constitution specifies only that members of the House must be at least twenty-five years old, American citizens for seven years, and must be residents of the states from which they are elected. Senators must be at least thirty years old, American citizens for nine years, and must be residents of the states from which they are elected.

Members come mostly from occupations with high status and usually have substantial incomes. Law is the dominant prior occupation, with other elite occupations also well represented. Women and other minorities are substantially underrepresented. Although members of Congress obviously cannot claim **descriptive representation** (representing their constituents by mirroring their personal, politically relevant characteristics), they may engage in **substantive representation** (representing the interests of groups).

CONGRESSIONAL ELECTIONS

The most important fact about congressional elections is that **incumbents** usually win. Not only do more than 90 percent of the incumbents seeking reelection to the House of Representatives win, but most of them win with more than 60 percent of the vote. Even when challengers' positions on the issues are closer to the voters' positions, incumbents still tend to win. Voters are not very aware of how their senators and representatives actually vote.

Even though senators have a better-than-equal chance of reelection, senators typically win by narrower margins than House members. One reason for the *greater competition in the Senate* is that an entire state is almost always more diverse than a congressional district and thus provides more of a base for opposition to an incumbent.

Despite their success at reelection, incumbents have a strong feeling of vulnerability. They have been raising and spending more campaign funds, sending more mail to their constituents, traveling more to their states and districts, and staffing more local offices than ever before.

Members of Congress engage in three primary activities that increase the probability of their reelections: advertising, credit claiming, and position taking. Most congressional **advertising** takes place between elections and takes the form of *contact with constituents*. **Credit claiming** involves *personal and district service*, notably through **casework** and the **pork barrel.** Members of Congress must also engage in **position taking** on matters of public policy when they vote on issues and when they respond to constituents' questions about where they stand on issues.

When incumbents do face challengers, they are likely to be weak opponents. Seeing the advantages of incumbency, potentially effective opponents often do not want to risk challenging members of the House. However, an incumbent tarnished by scandal or corruption becomes vulnerable. Voters *do* take out their anger at the polls. Redistricting can also have an impact. Congressional membership is reapportioned after each federal census, and incumbents may be redistricted out of their familiar base of support. When an incumbent is not running for reelection and the seat is **open**, there is greater likelihood of competition. Most of the turnover of the membership of Congress is the result of vacated seats, particularly in the House.

Candidates spend enormous sums on campaigns for Congress. In the 1998 Senate elections, the average winner spent over $4.7 million. In the 1998 House elections, the average winning candidate spent more than $740,000. Spending is greatest when there is no incumbent and each party feels it has a chance to win. In open seats, the candidate who spends the most usually wins.

Although most of the money spent in congressional elections comes from individuals, 30 percent (about $200 million) of the funds raised by candidates for Congress in 1996 came from the nearly 4000 **Political Action Committees (PACs).** In 1996, incumbents in both houses received $157 million from PACs, challengers received $21 million, and the rest went to candidates for open seats. PACs seek *access* to policymakers. Thus, they give most of their money to incumbents, who are already heavily favored to win. Critics of PACs are convinced that PACs are not trying to elect but to buy influence.

Prolific spending in a campaign is no guarantee of success. Money is important for challengers, however. The more they spend, the more votes they receive. Money buys them name recognition and a chance to be heard. In contests for open seats, the candidate who spends the most usually wins.

The high reelection rate of incumbents brings stability and policy expertise to Congress. At the same time, it also may insulate them from the winds of political change.

HOW CONGRESS IS ORGANIZED TO MAKE POLICY

Making policy is the toughest of all the legislative roles. Congress is *a collection of generalists trying to make policy on specialized topics.* The complexity of today's issues requires more specialization. Congress tries to cope with these demands through its elaborate committee system.

The House and Senate each *set their own agenda.* Both use committees to narrow down the thousands of bills introduced. The House is much larger and *more institutionalized* than the Senate. Party loyalty to leadership and party-line voting are more common than in the Senate. One institution unique to the House is the **House Rules Committee**, which reviews most bills coming from a House committee before they go to the full House. Each bill is given a "rule," which schedules the bill on the calendar, allots time for debate, and sometimes even specifies what kind of amendments may be offered. The Senate is *less disciplined* and *less centralized* than the House. Today's senators are more equal in power than representatives are. Party leaders do for Senate scheduling what the Rules Committee does in the House. One activity unique to the Senate is the **filibuster**. This is a tactic by which opponents of a bill use their right to unlimited debate as a way to prevent the Senate from ever voting on a bill.

Much of the leadership in Congress is really *party leadership.* Those who have the real power in the congressional hierarchy are those whose party put them there. Power is no longer in the hands of a few key members of Congress who are insulated from the public. Instead, power is widely dispersed, requiring leaders to appeal broadly for support.

Chief among leadership positions in the House of Representatives is the **Speaker of the House**. This is the only legislative office mandated by the Constitution. Today the Speaker presides over the House when it is in session; plays a major role in making committee assignments, which are coveted by all members to ensure their electoral advantage; appoints or plays a key role in appointing the party's legislative leaders and the party leadership staff; and exercises substantial control over which bills get assigned to which committees. The Speaker's principal partisan ally is the **majority leader** – a job that has been the main stepping stone to the Speaker's role. The majority leader is responsible for scheduling bills in the House. Working with the majority leader are the party's **whips**, who carry the word to party troops, counting votes before they are cast and leaning on waverers whose votes are crucial to a bill. The Constitution makes the vice president of the United States the president of the Senate; this is the vice president's only constitutionally defined job. The Senate majority leader – aided by the majority whips – is a party's workhorse, corralling votes, scheduling the floor action, and influencing committee assignments. The majority leader's counterpart in the opposition, the minority leader, has similar responsibilities.

The structure of Congress is so complex that it seems remarkable that legislation gets passed at all. Its bicameral division means that bills have two sets of committee hurdles to clear. Recent reforms have decentralized power, and so the job of leading Congress is more difficult than ever. Congressional leaders are not in the strong positions they occupied in the past. Leaders are elected by their fellow party members and must remain responsive to them.

Most of the real work of Congress goes on in committees and subcommittees. **Committees** *dominate congressional policy-making* at all stages. They regularly hold hearings to investigate problems and possible wrongdoing, and to investigate the executive branch. Committees can be grouped into four types: **standing committees** (by far the most important), **joint committees**, **conference committees**, and **select committees.**

More than *11,000 bills are submitted by members every two years*, which must be sifted through and narrowed down by the committee process. Every bill goes to a standing committee; usually only bills receiving a favorable committee report are considered by the whole House or Senate. New bills sent to a committee typically go directly to **subcommittee**, which can hold **hearings** on the bill. The most important output of committees and subcommittees is the **"marked-up"** (revised and rewritten) bill, submitted to the full House or Senate for consideration. Members of the committee will usually serve as *"floor managers"* of the bill when the bill leaves committee, helping party leaders secure votes for the legislation. They will also be *cue-givers* to whom other members turn for advice. When the two chambers pass different versions of the same bill, some committee members will be appointed to the conference committee.

Legislative **oversight**—the process of *monitoring the bureaucracy and its administration of policy*—is one of the *checks* Congress can exercise on the executive branch. Oversight is handled primarily through hearings. Members of committees constantly monitor how a bill is implemented.

Although every committee includes members from both parties, a majority of each committee's members—as well as its chair—come from the majority party. **Committee chairs** are the most important influence on the committee agenda. They play dominant—though no longer monopolistic—roles in scheduling hearings, hiring staff, appointing subcommittees, and managing committee bills when they are brought before the full House. Until the 1970s, committee chairs were always selected through the **seniority system**; under this system, the member of the majority party with the longest tenure on the committee would automatically be selected. In the 1970s, Congress faced a revolt of its younger members, and both parties in each house permitted members to *vote* on committee chairs. Today, seniority remains the *general rule* for selecting chairs, but there have been notable exceptions.

The explosion of *informal groups* in Congress has made the representation of interests in Congress a more direct process (cutting out the middleman, the lobbyist). In recent years, a growing number of **caucuses** have dominated these informal groups. Also increasing in recent years is the size of, and reliance of members of Congress on, their personal and committee staffs, along with staff agencies such as the *Congressional Research Service*, the *General Accounting Office* and the *Congressional Budget Office.*

THE CONGRESSIONAL PROCESS

Approximately 5500 **bills** are introduced annually or 11,000 in each two-year session of Congress. Most bills are quietly killed off early in the legislative process. In both chambers party leaders involve themselves in the legislative process on major legislation earlier and more deeply, using special procedures to aid the passage of legislation. In the House, special rules from the Rules Committee have become powerful tools for controlling floor consideration of bills and sometimes for shaping the outcomes of votes. Often party leaders from each chamber negotiate among themselves instead of creating conference committees. Party leaders also use *omnibus* legislation that addresses numerous and perhaps unrelated subjects, issues, and programs to create winning coalitions. In the Senate, leaders have less leverage and *individual* senators have retained great opportunities for influence. As a result, it is often more difficult to pass legislation in the Senate.

Presidents are partners with Congress in the legislative process, but all presidents are also Congress' adversaries in the struggle to control legislative outcomes. Presidents have their own *legislative agenda*, based in part on their party's platform and their electoral coalition. The president's task is to persuade Congress that his agenda should also be Congress' agenda.

Presidential success rates for influencing congressional votes vary widely among presidents and within a president's tenure in office. Presidents are usually most successful early in their tenures and when their party has a majority in one or both houses of Congress. Regardless, in almost any year, *the president will lose on many issues*.

Parties are *most cohesive* when Congress is *electing its official leaders*. For example, a vote for the Speaker of the House is a straight party-line vote. On other issues, the party coalition may not stick together. Votes on issues like civil rights have shown deep divisions within each party. Differences between the parties are sharpest on questions of social welfare and economic policy.

There are a variety of views concerning how members of Congress should fulfill their function of *representation.* The eighteenth-century English legislator Sir Edmund Burke favored the concept of legislators as **trustees**, using their best judgment to make policy in the interests of the people. The concept of representatives as **instructed delegates** calls for representatives to mirror the preferences of their constituents. Members of Congress are actually **politicos**, combining the trustee and instructed delegate roles as they attempt to be both representatives and policymakers.

The most effective way for constituents to influence congressional voting is to elect candidates who match their policy positions, since winners of congressional elections tend to vote on roll calls pretty much as they said they would. On some controversial issues, it is perilous for a legislator to ignore constituent opinion. Representatives and senators have recently been concerned about the many new **single-issue groups** that will vote exclusively on a candidate's position on a single issue rather than on the member's total record.

Lobbyists—some of them former members of Congress—represent the interests of their organizations. They also can provide legislators with crucial information, and often can give assurances of financial aid in the next campaign. There are more than 14,000 individuals in Washington representing nearly 12,000 organizations. The bigger the issue, the more lobbyists are involved in it. Until 1995, lobbyists were regulated primarily by the **Federal Regulation of Lobbying Act** (1946). Paid lobbyists whose principal purpose is to influence or defeat legislation must register and file reports with the secretary of the Senate and the clerk of the House. A 1995 law passed by Congress requires anyone hired to lobby members of Congress, congressional staff member, White House officials, and federal agencies to report what issues they were seeking to influence, how much they were spending on the effort, and the identities of their clients. Congress also placed severe restrictions on the gifts, meals, and expense-paid travel that public officials may accept from lobbyists.

UNDERSTANDING CONGRESS

The central legislative dilemma for Congress is combining the faithful *representation of constituents* with the making of *effective public policy*. Supporters see Congress as a forum in which many interests compete for a spot on the policy agenda and over the form of a particular policy. Critics wonder if Congress is so responsive to so many interests that policy is too uncoordinated, fragmented, and decentralized. Some observers feel that Congress is so representative that it is incapable of taking decisive action to deal with difficult problems.

In a large democracy, the success of democratic government depends on the quality of representation. Congress clearly has some undemocratic and unrepresentative features: its members are an American elite; its leadership is chosen by its own members; voters have little direct influence over the people who chair key committees or lead congressional parties. There is also evidence to support the view that Congress is representative: Congress does try to listen to the American people; the election does make a difference in how votes turn out; which party is in power affects policies; linkage institutions do link voters to policymakers. If Congress is responsive to a multitude of interests and those interests desire government policies to aid them in some way, does the nature of Congress predispose it to continually increase the scope of the public sector? Members of Congress vigorously protect the interests of their constituents. At the same time, there are many members who agree with Ronald Reagan that government is not the answer to problems but rather *is* the problem. These individuals make careers out of fighting against government programs (although these same senators and representatives typically support programs aimed at aiding *their* constituents). Congress does not impose programs on a reluctant public; instead, it responds to the public's demands for them.

CHAPTER OUTLINE

I. INTRODUCTION

A. The framers of the Constitution conceived of Congress as the *center of policy-making* in America.
   1. Although the prominence of Congress has fluctuated over time, in recent years Congress has been the true center of power in Washington.
   2. Congress' tasks become more difficult each year. The movement of legislation through the congressional labyrinth has never been more complicated, and just finding time to debate the issues has become increasingly difficult.
   3. Some critics charge Congress with being the source of government expansion.

II. THE REPRESENTATIVES AND SENATORS

A. The job.
   1. Despite public perceptions to the contrary, *hard work* is perhaps the most prominent characteristic of a member of Congress' job.
      a. The typical representative is a member of about six committees and subcommittees; a senator is a member of about ten.
      b. Members are often scheduled to be in two places at the same time.
   2. There are also *attractions* to the job.
      a. The most important is *power*. Members of Congress make key decisions about important matters of public policy.
      b. Members of Congress receive substantial salary and perquisites ("perks").
   3. Despite the salaries, the perks, and the thousands of staff members, Congress is relatively inexpensive. Per citizen, Americans annually spend about the equivalent of the cost of a hamburger, fries, and cola on running the nation's legislature.

B. The people.
   1. There are 535 members of Congress—100 in the Senate (2 from each state) and 435 in the House of Representatives.
   2. The Constitution specifies only that members of the House must be at least twenty-five years old, American citizens for seven years, and must be residents of the states from which they are elected. Senators must be at least thirty years old, American citizens for nine years, and must be residents of the states from which they are elected.
   3. Members come mostly from occupations with high status and usually have substantial incomes. Law and business are the dominant prior occupations, with other elite occupations also well represented.
   4. Representation of minorities.

a. Less than ten percent of voting members of the House are African-American (compared with about 12 percent of the total population), and most of them are elected from overwhelmingly black constituencies.
b. There are fewer than twenty Hispanics in the House.
c. Women are the most underrepresented demographic group in Congress; more than half of the population is female, but only thirteen senators and fifty-nine voting representatives are female.

5. Although members of Congress obviously cannot claim **descriptive representation** (representing their constituents by mirroring their personal, politically relevant characteristics), they may engage in **substantive representation** (representing the interests of groups).

III. CONGRESSIONAL ELECTIONS

A. Who wins?

1. **Incumbents** are those already holding office. The most important fact about congressional elections is that *incumbents usually win.* Even in a year of great political upheaval such as 1994, in which the Republicans gained eight seats in the Senate and fifty-three seats in the House, 92 percent of incumbent representatives won their bids for reelection.
2. House of Representatives.
   a. Not only do more than 90 percent of the incumbents seeking reelection to the House of Representatives win, but most of them win with more than 60 percent of the vote.
   b. Even when challengers' positions on the issues are closer to the voters' positions, incumbents still tend to win.
   c. Thus, the most important resource to ensure an opponent's defeat is simply to be the incumbent.
3. Senate.
   a. Even though senators have a better-than-equal chance of reelection, senators typically win by narrower margins than House members.
   b. One reason for the *greater competition in the Senate* is that an entire state is almost always more diverse than a congressional district and thus provides more of a base for opposition to an incumbent.
   c. Senators have less personal contact with their constituents and receive more coverage in the media than representatives do (and are therefore more likely to be held accountable on controversial issues).

   d. Senators tend to draw more visible challengers who are already known to voters and who have substantial financial backing.
4. Despite their success at reelection, incumbents have a strong feeling of vulnerability; thus, they have been raising and spending more campaign funds, sending more mail to their constituents, traveling more to their states and districts, and staffing more local offices than ever before.

B. The advantages of incumbents.
1. Voters are not very aware of how their senators and representatives actually vote.
2. Stories of presidential **coattails** (the theory that other candidates could ride into office by clinging to presidential coattails) do not seem to hold up in practice.
3. Members of Congress do not gain or lose very much from the fluctuations of the economy.
4. Members of Congress engage in three primary activities that increase the probability of their reelections: advertising, credit claiming, and position taking.
   a. Most congressional **advertising** takes place between elections and takes the form of *contact with constituents*: members concentrate on staying visible, and trips to the home district (or state) are frequent.
   b. **Credit claiming** involves *personal and district service.* There are two ways members of Congress can *service the constituency*: casework and the pork barrel.
      (1) **Casework** is helping constituents as individuals, such as cutting through bureaucratic red tape.
      (2) The **pork barrel** refers to expenditures on federal projects, grants, and contracts for cities, businesses, colleges, and institutions. Because credit claiming is so important to reelection, members of Congress rarely pass up the opportunity to increase federal spending in their state or district.
   c. Members of Congress must also engage in **position taking** on matters of public policy when they vote on issues and when they respond to constituents' questions about where they stand on issues. The positions they take may make a difference in the outcome of an election, especially if the issues are on matters salient to voters and their stands are out of line with those of a majority of their constituents (especially in the Senate, where issues are likely to play a greater role than in House elections).
5. Weak opponents.

a. Incumbents are likely to face weak opponents.
b. Seeing the advantages of incumbency, potentially effective opponents often do not want to risk challenging members of the House.

C. The role of party identification.
1. Although party loyalty at the voting booth is not as strong as it was a generation ago, it is still a good predictor of voting behavior.
2. Most members of Congress represent constituencies in which their party is in the majority.

D. Defeating incumbents.
1. An incumbent tarnished by scandal or corruption becomes vulnerable. Voters *do* take out their anger at the polls.
2. Congressional membership is reapportioned after each federal census, and incumbents may be redistricted out of their familiar base of support. The majority party in the state legislature is more likely to move two of the opposition party's representatives into the same district than two of its own.
3. In 1994 a major political tidal wave spawned by angry voters defeated thirty-five incumbents in the House and two incumbents in the Senate.

E. Money in congressional elections.
1. Candidates spend enormous sums on campaigns for Congress. In the 1998 Senate elections, the average winner spent over $4.7 million. In the 1998 House elections, the average winning candidate spent more than $740,000.
2. Spending is greatest when there is no incumbent and each party feels it has a chance to win.
3. Critics of **Political Action Committees (PACs)** offer substantive criticism of the present system of campaign finance. [see Chapter 11]
   a. Although most of the money spent in congressional elections comes from individuals, 30 percent (about $200 million) of the funds raised by candidates for Congress in 1996 came from about four thousand **Political Action Committees (PACs)**.
   b. In 1997-98, incumbents in both houses received $157 million from PACs, challengers received $21 million, and the rest went to candidates for open seats.
   c. Each PAC is *limited to an expenditure of $5000 per candidate* (most give less), but some organized interests *circumvent the limitations* on contributions by creating or contributing to several PACs.

   d. PACs seek *access* to policymakers. Thus, they give most of their money to incumbents, who are already heavily favored to win. Critics of PACs are convinced that PACs are not trying to elect but to buy influence.
4. Spending a lot of money in a campaign is no guarantee of success. In 1998 Alfonse D'Amato spent more than $23 million to retain his Senate seat in New York and lost.
5. Money *is important for challengers.* Money buys them name recognition and a chance to be heard.
6. When an incumbent is not running for reelection and the seat is **open**, there is greater likelihood of competition.
   a. Most of the turnover of the membership of Congress is the result of vacated seats, particularly in the House.
   b. In open seats, the candidate who spends the most usually wins.

F. Stability and change.
   1. As a result of incumbents usually winning reelection, there is some stability in the membership of Congress. This provides the opportunity for representatives and senators to *gain some expertise* in dealing with complex questions of public policy. It also *insulates* them from political change and makes it more difficult for citizens to "send a message to Washington" with their votes.
   2. Some reformers have proposed *term limitations* laws for senators and representatives.

IV. HOW CONGRESS IS ORGANIZED TO MAKE POLICY

A. *Making policy* is the toughest of all the legislative roles. Congress is *a collection of generalists trying to make policy on specialized topics.* The complexity of today's issues require more *specialization.* Congress tries to cope with these demands through its *elaborate committee system.*

B. American bicameralism.
   1. A **bicameral legislature** is one divided into two houses. The U.S. Congress and every American state legislature except Nebraska's are bicameral. Each state is guaranteed two senators in the U.S. Congress, with representation in the House of Representatives based on population.
   2. The framers of the Constitution thought the Senate would protect elite interests. They gave the House (which they expected to be closest to the masses) the power of initiating all revenue bills and of impeaching officials; they gave the Senate the responsibility for ratifying all treaties, for confirming important presidential nominations, and for trying impeached officials.

3. The House and Senate each *set their own agenda.* Both use committees to narrow down the thousands of bills introduced.
4. House of Representatives
   a. The House is much larger and *more institutionalized* than the Senate.
   b. Party loyalty to leadership and party-line voting are more common than in the Senate.
   c. *Debate can be ended* by a simple majority vote.
   d. One institution unique to the House is the **House Rules Committee**, which reviews most bills coming from a House committee before they go to the full House. Each bill is given a "rule," which schedules the bill on the calendar, allots time for debate, and sometimes even specifies what kind of amendments may be offered. Members are appointed by the Speaker of the House.
5. Senate.
   a. The Senate is *less disciplined* and *less centralized* than the House. Today's senators are more equal in power than representatives are.
   b. Party leaders do for Senate scheduling what the Rules Committee does in the House.
   c. The **filibuster** permits *unlimited debate* on a bill. In practice, this sometimes means that opponents of a bill may try to "talk it to death." At the present time, sixty members present and voting can halt a filibuster by invoking **cloture** (closure) on debate.

C. Congressional leadership.
1. Much of the leadership in Congress is really *party leadership.* Those who have the real power in the congressional hierarchy are those whose party put them there.
2. Power is no longer in the hands of a few key members of Congress who are insulated from the public. Instead, power is widely dispersed, requiring leaders to appeal broadly for support.
3. House leadership.
   a. The **Speaker of the House** is second (after the vice president) in the line to succeed a president who resigns, dies in office, or is impeached.
      (1) At one time, the Speaker had almost autocratic powers. Many of the powers were removed from the Speaker's control in 1910 and given to committees; some of the powers were later restored.
      (2) *Formal powers* of the Speaker today include: presides over the House when it is in session; plays a major role in making

committee assignments; appoints or plays a key role in appointing the party's legislative leaders and the party leadership staff; exercises substantial control over which bills get assigned to which committees.

(3) The Speaker also has a great deal of *informal power* both inside and outside Congress.

b. The Speaker's principal partisan ally is the **majority leader**. The majority leader is responsible for rounding up votes on party legislation and for scheduling bills in the House.

c. Party **whips** work with the majority leader to round up votes and to report the views and complaints of the party rank-and-file back to the leadership.

d. The *minority party* is also organized (with a **minority leader** and **whips**), and is prepared to take over the key posts if it should win a majority in the House.

4. Senate leadership.

a. The Constitution names the vice president as **president of the Senate**. Vice presidents typically have little power or influence in the Senate, except in the rare case when their vote can break a tie.

b. The **Senate majority leader**—aided by the majority whips—is the position of real power and authority in the Senate. He rounds up votes, schedules the floor action, and influences committee assignments.

5. Congressional leadership in perspective.

a. The structure of Congress is so complex that it seems remarkable that legislation gets passed at all. Its *bicameral division* means that bills have two sets of committee hurdles to clear. Recent reforms have *decentralized power*, and so the job of leading Congress is more difficult than ever.

b. Congressional leaders are not in the strong positions they occupied in the past. Leaders are elected by their fellow party members and must remain responsive to them.

c. Party leadership—at least in the House—*has* been more effective in recent years. Following the Republican takeover in 1995, Speaker Newt Gingrich began centralizing power and exercising vigorous legislative leadership.

D. The committees and subcommittees.

1. Most of the real work of Congress goes on in committees.

a. Committees *dominate congressional policy-making.*

b. They regularly hold hearings to investigate problems and possible wrongdoing, and to investigate the executive branch.

c. They *control the congressional agenda and guide legislation* from its introduction to its send-off for the president's signature.

2. Committees can be grouped into four types: *standing committees* (by far the most important), *joint committees*, *conference committees*, and *select committees*.
   a. **Standing committees** are *permanent subject-matter* committees, formed to handle bills in different policy areas. Each chamber has its own committees and subcommittees. In the 103rd Congress, the typical representative served on two committees and four subcommittees, while senators averaged three committees and seven subcommittees each.
   b. **Joint committees** are study committees that exist in a few policy areas, with membership drawn from both the Senate and the House.
   c. **Conference committees** are formed to work out the differences when different versions of a bill are passed by the two houses. Membership is drawn from both houses.
   d. **Select committees** are *temporary* committees appointed for a specific ("select") purpose, such as the Senate select committee that looked into Watergate.
3. The committees at work: legislation and oversight.
   a. More than *11,000 bills are submitted by members every two years*, which must be sifted through and narrowed down by the committee process. Every bill goes to a standing committee; usually only bills receiving a *favorable committee report* are considered by the whole House or Senate.
   b. New bills sent to a committee typically go directly to **subcommittee**, which can hold **hearings** on the bill. The most important output of committees and subcommittees is the **"marked-up"** (revised and rewritten) bill, submitted to the full House or Senate for consideration.
   c. Members of the committee will usually serve as "*floor managers*" of the bill when the bill leaves committee, helping party leaders secure votes for the legislation. They will also be *cue-givers* to whom other members turn for advice. When the two chambers pass different versions of the same bill, some committee members will be appointed to the conference committee.
   d. Legislative **oversight**—the process of *monitoring the bureaucracy and its administration of policy*—is one of the *checks* Congress can exercise on the executive branch.
      (1) Oversight is handled primarily through hearings. Members of committees constantly monitor how a bill is

implemented. The process enables Congress to exert pressure on executive agencies, or even to cut their budgets in order to secure compliance with congressional wishes.

(2) Congressional oversight occasionally captures public attention, such as congressional investigations into the Watergate scandal and the 1987 Iran-Contra affair.

(3) Congress keeps tabs on more routine activities of the executive branch through its committee *staff members*, who have *specialized expertise* in the fields and agencies that their committees oversee (and who maintain an extensive network of formal and informal *contacts* with the bureaucracy).

4. Getting on a committee.
   a. Just after election, new members write to the party's congressional leaders and members of their state delegation, indicating their committee preferences. Each party in each house has a slightly different way of picking its committee members, but party leaders almost always play a key role.
   b. Members seek committee assignments that will help them achieve three goals: reelection, influence in Congress, and the opportunity to make policy in areas they think are important.
   c. Although every committee includes members from both parties, *a majority of each committee's members*—as well as its *chair*—come from the majority party.
5. Getting ahead on the committee: chairs and the seniority system.
   a. **Committee chairs** are the most important influencers of the committee agenda. They play dominant—though no longer monopolistic—roles in scheduling hearings, hiring staff, appointing subcommittees, and managing committee bills when they are brought before the full House.
   b. Until the 1970s, committee chairs were always selected through the **seniority system**—the member of the majority party with the longest tenure on the committee would automatically be selected.

      (1) Chairs were so powerful that they could single-handedly "bottle up" legislation in committee.

      (2) The system also gave a decisive edge to members from **"safe" districts**, where members were seldom challenged for reelection.
   c. In the 1970s, Congress faced a revolt of its younger members.

      (1) Both parties in both houses permitted members to *vote* on committee chairs.

(2) Today, seniority remains the *general rule* for selecting chairs, but there have been notable exceptions.
(3) These and other reforms have somewhat reduced the clout of the chairs.

E. The mushrooming caucuses: the informal organization of Congress.
   1. The explosion of *informal groups* in Congress has made the representation of interests in Congress a more direct process (cutting out the middleman, the lobbyist).
   2. In recent years, a growing number of caucuses have dominated these traditional informal groups. A **caucus** is a grouping of members of Congress sharing some interest or characteristic, such as the Black Caucus, the Hispanic Caucus, the Congresswomen's Caucus, and the Sunbelt Caucus. Caucuses include regional groupings, ideological groupings, and economic groupings.
   3. The proliferation of congressional caucuses (more than 100 f them in the 106th Congress) gives members of Congress an informal, yet powerful, means of shaping the policy agenda. Composed of legislative insiders who share similar concerns, the caucuses exert a much greater influence on policy-making than most citizen-based interest groups can.

F. Congressional Staff.
   1. Most staff members work in the personal offices of individual members. The average representative has 17 assistants and the average senator has 44. In total, about 11,500 individuals serve on the personal staffs of members of Congress. Nearly one-half of these House staffers and nearly one-third of the Senate personal staff work in members' offices in their constituencies, not in Washington. This makes it easier for people to make contact with the staff.
   2. The committees of the House and Senate employ another 2,500 staff members. These staff members organize hearings, research legislative options, draft committee reports on bills, write legislation, and, keep tabs on the activities of the executive branch.
   3. Congress has three important staff agencies that aid it in its work.
      a. The first is the *Congressional Research Service* (CRS), administered by the Library of Congress. The CRS employs nearly 750 researchers, many with advanced degrees and highly developed expertise.
      b. The *General Accounting Office* (GAO), with more than 3,500 employees, helps Congress perform its oversight functions by reviewing the activities of the executive branch to see if it is following the congressional intent of laws and by investigating the efficiency and effectiveness of policy implementation.

c. The *Congressional Budget Office* (CBO) employs more than 230 people. Its principal focus is on analyzing the president's budget and making economic projections about the performance of the economy, the costs of proposed policies, and the economic effects of taxing and spending alternatives.

V. THE CONGRESSIONAL PROCESS

A. Approximately 5500 bills are introduced annually. A **bill** is a *proposed law*, drafted in precise, legal language.
   1. Anyone can draft a bill, but only members of the House or Senate can formally submit a bill for consideration. The White House and interest groups are common *sources* of bills.
   2. Most bills are quietly killed off early in the legislative process.
   3. Legislators often use **riders** to pass a bill that does not have enough support on its own to pass.

B. Presidents and Congress: partners and protagonists.
   1. Presidents are *partners* with Congress in the legislative process, but all presidents are also Congress' *adversaries* in the struggle to control legislative outcomes.
   2. Presidents have their own *legislative agenda*, based in part on their party's platform and their electoral coalition. Political scientists sometimes call the president the **chief legislator**; the president's task is to persuade Congress that his agenda should also be Congress' agenda.
   3. Presidents have many resources with which to influence Congress. They may try to influence members directly, but more often will leave White House lobbying to the congressional liaison office and work primarily through regular meetings with the party's leaders in the House and Senate.
   4. Rather than *creating* the conditions for important shifts in public policy, an effective president is a *facilitator* who works at the margins of coalition building to recognize and exploit opportunities presented by a favorable configuration of political forces.
   5. Presidential success rates for influencing congressional votes vary widely among presidents and within a president's tenure in office. Presidents are usually *most successful early in their tenures* and when their party has a majority in one or both houses of Congress. Regardless, in almost any year, *the president will lose on many issues*.

C. Party, constituency, and ideology.
   1. Party influence.

a. Parties are *most cohesive* when Congress is *electing its official leaders*. A vote for the Speaker of the House is a straight party-line vote. On other issues, the party coalition may not stick together. Votes on issues like civil rights have shown deep divisions within each party.
b. Differences between the parties are sharpest on questions of social welfare and economic policy.
c. In democracies with *parliamentary systems* such as Great Britain, almost all votes are *party-line votes*. Parties are considerably weaker in the United States. Party affiliation does influence votes of U.S. legislators, but in a typical year, a majority of Democrats and Republicans oppose each other less than half the time.
d. Party leaders in Congress are limited in their powers to obtain support from party members. They cannot remove a recalcitrant member from the party, although they do have some influence (such as committee assignments). Recently the parties—especially the Republicans—have been a growing source of money for congressional campaigns.

2. Constituency versus ideology.
   a. There are a variety of views concerning how members of Congress should fulfill their function of *representation.*
      (1) The eighteenth century English legislator, Sir Edmund Burke, favored the concept of legislators as **trustees**, using their *best judgment* to make policy in the interests of the people.
      (2) The concept of representatives as **instructed delegates** calls for representatives to *mirror the preferences of their constituents*.
      (3) Members of Congress are actually **politicos**, *combining the trustee and instructed delegate roles* as they attempt to be both representatives and policymakers.
   b. Winners of congressional elections tend to vote on roll calls pretty much as they said they would. The most effective way for constituents to influence congressional voting is to elect candidates who match their policy positions.
   c. On some controversial issues, it is perilous for a legislator to ignore constituent opinion. Representatives and senators have recently been concerned about the many new *single-issue groups* that will vote exclusively on a candidate's position on a single issue (such as gun control), and not on the member's total record.
   d. Members of Congress do pay attention to voters, especially on visible issues, but most issues do not interest voters. However, it

is difficult for legislators to *know what the people want*. On less visible issues, other factors (such as lobbyists and the member's individual ideologies) influence policy decisions.

D. Lobbyists and interest groups.
   1. **Lobbyists**—some of them former members of Congress—represent the interests of their organization. They also can provide legislators with crucial information, and often can give assurances of financial aid in the next campaign.
   2. There are more than 14,000 individuals in Washington representing nearly 12,000 organizations. The bigger the issue, the more lobbyists are involved in it.
   3. Lobbyists are regulated primarily by the **Federal Regulation of Lobbying Act** (1946) and a 1995 law. Paid lobbyists whose principal purpose is to influence or defeat legislation must *register* and *file reports* with the secretary of the Senate and the clerk of the House.
      a. Anyone hired to lobby members of Congress, congressional staff members, White House officials, and federal agencies must report what issues they were seeking to influence, how much they were spending on the effort, and the identities of their clients.
      b. In theory, the disclosure requirements would prevent shady deals and curb the influence of special interests.

VI. UNDERSTANDING CONGRESS

A. Congress and democracy.
   1. In a large democracy, the success of democratic government depends on the quality of representation.
   2. Congress clearly has some undemocratic and unrepresentative features: its members are an American elite; its leadership is chosen by its own members; voters have little direct influence over the people who chair key committees or lead congressional parties.
   3. There is also evidence to support the view that Congress is representative: Congress does try to listen to the American people; the election does make a difference in how votes turn out; which party is in power affects policies; linkage institutions do link voters to policymakers. Members of Congress are *responsive to the people, if the people make it clear what they want.*

B. Reforming Congress.
   1. Reformers have tried to promote a more open, democratic Congress. To a large degree, they have succeeded.

2. In the 1950s, the real power was at the top. Committee chairs were automatically selected by seniority, and their power on the committee was unquestioned.

C. Democratization.
   1. Lyndon Johnson started the reform process during his tenure as majority leader when he implemented the "*Johnson rule,*" which gave each senator a seat on at least one key committee. This reform allowed junior members more room at the top.
   2. By the 1970s, the reform movement tried to create more democracy by spreading power around. Chairs were elected by the majority party (some chairs were replaced), and the power of committee chairs was reduced. Subcommittees became the new centers of power in Congress.
   3. The proliferation of informal caucuses have tended to decentralize power in Congress, although recent reforms by the Republicans may change this.

D. Representativeness versus effectiveness.
   1. The central legislative dilemma for Congress is combining the faithful *representation of constituents* with the making of *effective public policy.*
   2. Supporters see Congress as a forum in which many interests compete for a spot on the policy agenda and over the form of a particular policy (as the founders intended).
   3. Critics wonder if Congress is so responsive to so many interests that policy is too uncoordinated, fragmented, and decentralized. Some observers feel that Congress is so representative that it is *incapable of taking decisive action* to deal with difficult problems.

E. Congress and the scope of government.
   1. Americans have contradictory preferences regarding public policy. They want to balance the budget and pay low taxes, but they also support most government programs. These *contradictory preferences* may help explain the pervasive ticket splitting in national elections which has frequently led to divided government.
   2. Big government helps members of Congress get reelected and even gives them good reason to support making it bigger. However, Congress does not impose programs on a reluctant public; instead, it responds to the public's demands for them.

KEY TERMS AND CONCEPTS

Bicameral legislature: a legislature which is divided into two chambers.

Bill: a proposed law, drafted in precise, legal language.

Casework: helping constituents as individuals cut through bureaucratic red tape to receive their rightful benefits.

Caucus: a grouping of members of Congress sharing some interest or characteristic.

Committee chairs: the most important influences of the congressional agenda by scheduling hearings, hiring staff, appointing subcommittees, and managing committee bills.

Conference committees: a special committee formed when each chamber passes a bill in different forms composed of members of each chamber who were appointed by each chamber's leaders to work out a compromise bill.

Filibuster: is unlimited debate, is unique to the Senate, and can only be ended by a vote for cloture by sixty members.

House Rules Committee: a committee unique to the House which is appointed by the Speaker of the House, reviews most bills coming from a House committee for a floor vote, and which gives each bill a rule.

Incumbents: people who already hold office.

Joint committees: special committees composed of members from each chamber.

Legislative oversight: the process of monitoring the bureaucracy and its administration of policy.

Majority Leader: The Speaker's principal partisan ally who is responsible for soliciting support for the party's position on legislation.

Minority Leader: is the minority party's counterpart to the majority party's leadership.

Pork barrel: list of federal projects, grants, and contracts available to cities, businesses, colleges, and institutions.

Select committees: appointed for a specific purpose.

Seniority system: a system used until the 1970s where majority party members who had served on their committees the longest, regardless of party loyalty, mental state, or competence, were automatically appointed chair of the committee.

Speaker of the House: is mandated by the Constitution, is next in line after the vice president to succeed a president who is unable to fulfill his/her term and who presides over the House.

Standing committees: committees formed in each chamber to handle bills in different policy areas.

Whips: The majority or minority leader's principle tool for securing support for legislation and who lobby partisans for support.

TEACHING IDEAS: CLASS DISCUSSION AND STUDENT PROJECTS

- Distribute several copies of the *Congressional Record* in your class. Ask students to look for the main features of the *Record*: the Proceedings of the House and Proceedings of the Senate, which contain an official account of the floor proceedings of each chamber; the "Extension of Remarks," which contains various documents (some of them extraneous) inserted by members; and the "Daily Digest," which contains a list of meetings and hearings of committees and subcommittees and summarizes the day's congressional activities. Point out the black dots known as "bullets" that are used to designate speeches that were not made in person. Solicit views from the class about the practice whereby members may revise or edit speeches that were made from the floor.

- Videotape several short segments of Congress in session and use them in class to discuss congressional functions. For example, you could show advise and consent hearings, a roll call vote, debate, and even a brief procedural segment. Alternatively, assign students to watch C-SPAN, and discuss the nature of the proceedings.

- Members of Congress can obviously not claim *descriptive representation* since they come primarily from occupations with high status and usually have substantial incomes. Moreover, women and minorities are underrepresented. Ask your class to consider whether the personal characteristics of members of

Congress are important. Can members of Congress effectively represent the concerns of their constituents when they do not share their constituents' economic and social backgrounds?

- Surveys consistently show a high level of dissatisfaction with Congress, yet voters continue to reelect members by extraordinary percentages (especially for the House of Representatives). Ask your class to consider possible reasons for what seems to be a contradiction. Is it simply the advantage of incumbency? Is the American public more satisfied with their *own* representatives than with Congress as an institution?

- As a library assignment or using the Internet, have students locate basic information about the responsibilities of their senator and representative—committee assignments, subcommittees, length of time in office, and major bills he or she has sponsored. In addition, ask them to evaluate their representative's website and/or recent copies of constituency newsletters to assess the policy positions taken by their representative. To what extent is there representative/student agreement? Why or why not?

- Ask your class to debate the relative merits of various roles of legislators—the legislator as *trustee*, as *instructed delegate*, or as *politico*. Does the particular issue under consideration have any effect on their views? How do they perceive the performance of their own representative?

- Tape some televised coverage of House proceedings off of C-Span. Then ask a Representative (or one of his/her staff) to visit the class to discuss the proceedings. This will provide for an interactive yet unintimidating discussion of House politics as well as give students insights into the legislative structure.

- For a reading and writing connection, have students write their members of Congress (both Senate and House) for a copy of their newsletters. Have students write an essay identifying the phrases and terminology used by their members to project the image that they are good representatives. In particular, have students compare and contrast the method of advertising used by Senators as compared to House members in the newsletters.

- To build on the above reading and writing connection, have students examine the most recent voting record of their members of Congress. These records are published by Congressional Quarterly. Have students first identify what issues are important to them and then have them examine how their members voted on policies addressing those issues. For an extended exercise, students may examine their members' voting career on those issues by researching past voting records. Further, students could also look at how their fellow members' partisans acted on those issues to get a better sense of where their representative stands.

BACKGROUND READING

Bond, Jon R. and Richard Fleisher. Polarized Politics: Congress and the President in a Partisan Era. Washington, D.C.: CQ Press. 2000.

Dodd, Lawrence C. and Bruce I. Oppenheimer, eds. Congress Reconsidered. 6th ed. Washington, DC: Congressional Quarterly Press. 1997.

Hall, Richard L. Participation in Congress. New Haven: Yale University Press. 1998.

Jacobson, Gary C. The Politics of Congressional Elections. 4th ed. New York: Addison-Wesley. 1996.

Krehbiel, Keith. Pivotal Politics: A Theory of U.S. Lawmaking. Chicago: University of Chicago Press. 1998.

Sinclair, Barbara. Unorthodox Lawmaking: New Legislative Processes in the U.S. Congress. Washington, DC: Congressional Quarterly Press. 1997.

Smith, Steven S. and Christopher J. Deering. Committees in Congress, 3rd ed. Washington, DC: Congressional Quarterly Press. 1997.

MEDIA SUGGESTIONS

The Battle for Congress: From Campaign Headquarters to Capitol Hill. A realistic portrayal of campaigning for Congress, focusing on the 1998 House race between Tom Bordonaro and Lois Capps (D-CA). Films for the Humanities & Sciences.

Congress. Part of the PBS video series The Power Game. An interesting yet critical look at the distribution of power in Congress.

Congress: We the People. A 26 part series by Annenberg/CPB dealing with various aspects of Congressional structure. Numbers 25 "The Power of the Purse" and 26 "An Assessment of Congress" are especially good. Each selection lasts 30 minutes.

A Day in the Life of Congress. Part of the Congress series distributed by Insight Media. This 1992 video provides a view of a typical day in the work of a member of Congress.

A Day in the Life of a Representative. This show follows two members of Congress through a typical day, raising questions about how much and what we can expect members of Congress to do. Films for the Humanities & Sciences.

Evolution of the Congress. 1996. This film examines the evolutionary changes in Congress as responses to the challenges of democratic government. Films for the Humanities and Sciences.

Political Partisanship vs. Serving the People. 1996. This film explores the problem of congressional gridlock and the role of partisanship in resolving or creating that problem. Films for the Humanities and Sciences.

Political Partisanship vs. Serving the People. This program examines the extent to which Congress provides representation to diverse interests in society, and also tackles current issues such as legislative gridlock and the role of partisanship in Congress. Films for the Humanities & Sciences.

Politics in Action, Chapter 5: The Legislative Process. Includes a case study on the Brady Bill as well as an animated film on how a bill becomes law.

Chapter Thirteen: The Presidency

Pedagogical Features

Learning Objectives

After studying this chapter, students should be able to:

- Describe the constitutional process of impeachment and explain why it is so difficult to remove a discredited president before the end of his term.

- Outline the procedures established in the Twenty-fifth Amendment to deal with presidential succession and presidential disability.

- Trace the evolution of the presidency from the limited office envisioned by the framers to the more powerful contemporary office.

- Identify the major offices and positions that serve as key aides and advisors to the president.

- Examine the ways in which the American system of separation of powers is actually one of *shared* powers.

- Identify the powers that lead us to refer to the president as *chief legislator*.

- Review methods by which presidents may improve their chances of obtaining party support in Congress.

- Summarize the constitutional powers that are allocated to the president in the realm of national security.

- Identify and review major roles and functions of the president such as chief executive, chief legislator, commander in chief, and crisis manager.

- Determine the role that public opinion plays in setting and implementing the president's agenda.

- Describe the methods used by presidents and their advisors to encourage the media to project a positive image of the president's activities and policies.

- Examine the impact that changing world events (such as the transition from the 1950s and 1960s to the era of Vietnam and Watergate) have had on public debate over whether a "strong" president is a threat or a support to democratic government.

CHAPTER OVERVIEW

INTRODUCTION

This chapter examines *how presidents exercise leadership* and looks at *limitations* on executive authority. Americans expect a lot from presidents (perhaps too much). The myth of the president as a powerhouse distorts the public's image of presidential reality.

Presidents operate in an environment filled with checks and balances and competing centers of power. Other policymakers with whom they deal have their own agendas, their own interests, and their own sources of power. To be effective, the president must have highly developed political skills to mobilize influence, manage conflict, negotiate, and build compromises. Political scientist Richard Neustadt has argued that presidential power is *the power to persuade*, not to command.

THE PRESIDENTS

Throughout *Government in America*, the authors have pointed out the American political culture's strong belief in limited government, liberty, individualism, equality, and democracy. These values generate a distrust of strong leadership, authority, and the public sector in general. Americans are of two minds about the presidency. On the one hand, they want to believe in a powerful president, one who can do good. On the other hand, Americans dislike a concentration of power. Although presidential responsibilities have increased substantially in the past few decades, there has been no corresponding increase in presidential authority or administrative resources to meet these new expectations. Americans are basically individualistic and skeptical of authority.

Most presidents reach the White House through the electoral process. About one in five presidents assumed the presidency when the incumbent president either died or (in Nixon's case) resigned. Almost one-third of twentieth-century presidents have been "accidental presidents." Once in office, presidents are guaranteed a four-year term by the Constitution, but the **Twenty-second Amendment**, passed in 1951, limits them to two such terms.

Removing a discredited president before the end of a term is a difficult task. The Constitution prescribes the process through **impeachment**, which is roughly the political equivalent of an indictment in criminal law. (The term "impeachment" refers to the formal accusation, *not* to conviction.) Only two presidents have been impeached. Andrew Johnson narrowly escaped conviction in 1868 on charges stemming from his disagreement with radical Republicans. In 1998, the House voted two articles of impeachment against President Clinton on party-line votes. The public clearly opposed the idea, however, and the Senate voted to acquit the president on both counts in 1999. In 1974, the House Judiciary Committee voted to recommend the impeachment of Richard Nixon as a result of the **Watergate** scandal. Nixon escaped a certain vote for impeachment by resigning.

The **Twenty-fifth Amendment** clarified some of the Constitution's vagueness about presidential **disability** and **succession**. The amendment permits the vice president to become acting president if the vice president and the president's cabinet determine that the president is disabled or if the president declares his own disability, and it outlines how a recuperated president can reclaim the office. Provision is also made for *selecting a new vice president* when the office becomes vacant. In the event of a vacancy in the office of vice president, the president nominates a new vice president, who assumes the office when both houses of Congress approve the nomination.

PRESIDENTIAL POWERS

The contemporary presidency differs dramatically from the one the framers of the Constitution designed in 1787. The executive office they conceived of had more limited authority, fewer responsibilities, and much less organizational structure than today's presidency.

The Constitution says remarkably little about presidential power: "The executive power shall be vested in a president of the United States of America."

Institutional balance was essential to delegates at the Constitutional Convention. There is little that presidents can do on their own. They share executive, legislative, and judicial power with the other branches of government.

Today there is *more to presidential power than the Constitution alone suggests*, and that power is *derived from many sources*. During the 1950s and 1960s it was fashionable for political scientists, historians, and commentators to favor a powerful presidency. Historians rated presidents from strong to weak – and there was no question that "strong" meant good and "weak" meant bad. By the 1970s, many felt differently. The Vietnam War was unpopular. Lyndon Johnson and the war made people reassess the role of presidential power. In his book *The Imperial Presidency,* historian Arthur Schlesinger, an aide of John Kennedy's argued that the presidency had become too powerful for the nation's own good. The role of the president changed as America increased in prominence on the world stage, and technology also helped to reshape the presidency. Presidents themselves have taken the initiative in developing new roles for the office. Various presidents enlarged the power of the presidency by expanding the president's responsibilities and political resources.

RUNNING THE GOVERNMENT: THE CHIEF EXECUTIVE

One of the president's most important roles is *presiding over the administration of government.* The Constitution merely tells the president to "take care that the laws be faithfully executed." Today, the federal bureaucracy includes 4.5 million civilian and military employees and spends more than $1.7 trillion annually.

One of the resources for controlling the bureaucracy is the presidential power to *appoint top-level administrators.* New presidents have about 300 high-level positions available for appointment (cabinet and subcabinet jobs, agency heads, and other non-civil service posts), plus 2000 lesser jobs. In recent years, presidents have paid close attention to appointing officials who will be *responsive to the president's policies.* Presidents also have the power to *recommend agency budgets* to Congress—the result of the **Budgeting and Accounting Act of 1921**.

Although the group of presidential advisors known as the **cabinet** is not mentioned in the Constitution, every president has had one. Today, thirteen secretaries and the attorney general head executive departments and constitute the cabinet. In addition, individual presidents may designate other officials (such as the ambassador to the United Nations) as cabinet members.

The **Executive Office of the President** (established in 1939) is a loosely grouped collection of offices and organizations. Some of the offices are created by legislation, while others are organized by the president. The Executive Office includes three major policy-making bodies—the National Security Council, the Council of Economic Advisors, and the Office of Management and Budget—plus several other units serving the president.

The **White House staff** includes the key aides the president sees daily—the chief of staff, congressional liaison people, press secretary, national security advisor, and a few other administrative political assistants. Presidents rely heavily on their staffs for information, policy options, and analysis. Each president organizes the White House to serve his own political and policy needs, as well as his decision-making style.

Despite heavy reliance on staff, it is *the president who sets the tone* for the White House. It is the president's responsibility to demand that staff members analyze a full range of options (and their likely consequences) before they offer the president their advice.

PRESIDENTIAL LEADERSHIP OF CONGRESS: THE POLITICS OF SHARED POWERS

The president is *a major shaper of the congressional agenda*, and the term **chief legislator** is frequently used to emphasize the executive's importance in the legislative process. Presidents' most useful resources in passing their own legislation are their party leadership, public support, and their own legislative skills.

The Constitution also gives the president power to **veto** congressional legislation. If Congress adjourns within 10 days after submitting a bill, the president can simply let it die by neither signing nor vetoing it. This process is called a **pocket veto.** The presidential veto is usually effective; only about 4 percent of all vetoed bills have been overridden by Congress since the nation's founding. Thus, even the threat of a presidential veto can be an effective tool for persuading Congress to give more weight to the president's views.

Party leadership in Congress is every president's principal task when countering the *natural tendencies toward conflict* between the executive and legislative branches. The primary obstacle to party unity is the lack of consensus among party members on policies, especially in the Democratic party. This diversity of views often reflects the diversity of constituencies represented by party members.

Although party leaders in Congress are predisposed to support presidential policies and typically work closely with the White House, they are free to oppose the president or to lend only symbolic support. Party leaders are not in a position to reward or discipline members of Congress on the basis of presidential support. The *parties are highly decentralized,* and national party leaders do not control nominations and elections.

One way for the president to improve the chances of obtaining support in Congress is to increase the number of fellow party members in the legislature. The phenomenon of **presidential coattails** occurs when voters cast their ballots for congressional candidates of the president's party because those candidates support the president. Most recent studies show a diminishing connection between presidential and congressional voting, however, and few races are determined by presidential coattails.

Presidents who have the *backing of the public* have an easier time influencing Congress. Members of Congress closely watch two indicators of public support for the president—*approval in the polls* and *mandates in presidential elections.*

Public approval is the political resource that has the most potential to turn a situation of stalemate between the president and Congress into one that is supportive of the president's legislative proposals. Widespread support gives the president leeway and weakens resistance to presidential policies, while lack of support strengthens the resolve of those inclined to oppose the president and narrows the range in which presidential policies receive the benefit of the doubt.

An electoral **mandate**—the perception that the voters strongly support the president's character and policies—can be a powerful symbol in American politics. It accords *added legitimacy and credibility* to the newly elected president's proposals. Merely winning an election does not provide presidents with a mandate. It is common after close elections to hear claims—especially from the other party—that there was "no mandate." Even large electoral victories carry no guarantee that Congress will interpret the results as mandates, especially if the voters also elect majorities in Congress from the other party.

Presidents influence the legislative agenda more than any other political figure. No matter what a president's skills are, however, the "chief legislator" can rarely exercise complete control over the agenda. Presidents are rarely in a position to create—through their own leadership—opportunities for major changes in public policy. They may, however, use their skills to exploit favorable political conditions to bring about policy change. In general, presidential legislative skills must compete with other, more stable factors that affect voting in Congress, such as party, ideology, personal views and commitments on specific policies, and constituency interests.

THE PRESIDENT AND NATIONAL SECURITY POLICY

Constitutionally, the president has the leading role in American defense and foreign policy (often termed *national security*). The Constitution allocates certain powers in the realm of national security that are exclusive to the executive. For example, the president alone extends *diplomatic recognition* to foreign governments (and the president can also terminate relations with other nations). The president has the sole power to negotiate *treaties* with other nations, although the Constitution requires the Senate to approve them by a two-thirds vote. Presidents negotiate **executive agreements** with the heads of foreign governments; unlike treaties, executive agreements do not require Senate ratification.

As the leader of the Western world, the president must try to lead America's allies on matters of economics and defense. Presidents usually conduct diplomatic relations through envoys, but occasionally they engage in personal diplomacy. As in domestic policy-making, the president must rely principally on *persuasion* to lead.

Because the Constitution's framers wanted *civilian control of the military*, they made the president the commander in chief of the armed forces. Although only Congress is constitutionally empowered to declare war and vote on the military budget, Congress long ago became accustomed to presidents making short-term military commitments of troops or naval vessels. In 1973 Congress passed the **War Powers Resolution** (over President Nixon's veto). It required presidents to consult with Congress, whenever possible, before using military force, and it mandated the withdrawal of forces after 60 days unless Congress declared war or granted an extension. Congress could at any time pass a concurrent resolution (which could not be vetoed) ending American participation in hostilities. All presidents serving since 1973 have deemed the law an unconstitutional infringement on their powers, and there is reason to believe the Supreme Court would consider the law's use of the **legislative veto** (the ability of Congress to pass a resolution to override a presidential decision) to be a violation of the doctrine of separation of powers. In recent years, presidents have committed U.S. troops to action without seeking congressional approval.

Questions continue to be raised about the relevance of America's 200-year-old constitutional mechanisms for engaging in war. Some observers are concerned that modern technology allows the president to engage in hostilities so quickly that opposing points of view do not receive proper consideration. Others stress the importance of the commander in chief having the flexibility to meet America's global responsibilities and to combat international terrorism.

As chief diplomat and commander in chief, the president is also the country's *crisis manager*. A **crisis** is a *sudden, unpredictable, and potentially dangerous event.* Most occur in the realm of foreign policy; quick judgments are often needed despite sketchy information.

With modern communications, the president can instantly monitor events almost anywhere. Because situations develop more rapidly today, there is a premium on rapid action, secrecy, constant management, consistent judgment, and expert advice. Since *Congress usually moves slowly*, the *president has become more prominent* in handling crises.

Although the president is the dominant force behind national security policy today, Congress also has a central constitutional role in making policy. The allocation of responsibilities for such matters is based upon the founders' apprehensions about the concentration and potential for abuse of power. The founders *divided the powers of supply and command.* Congress can thus refuse to provide the necessary authorizations and appropriations for presidential actions, while the chief executive can refuse to take actions favored by Congress. The role of Congress has typically been *oversight of the executive* rather than initiation of policy.

POWER FROM THE PEOPLE: THE PUBLIC PRESIDENCY

Perhaps the greatest challenge to any president is *to obtain and maintain the public's support.* Because presidents are rarely in a position to command others to comply with their wishes, they must *rely on persuasion.* The necessity of public support leads the White House to employ *public relations techniques* similar to those used to publicize products. Much of the energy the White House devotes to public relations is aimed at increasing the president's *public approval.* The reason is simple: the higher the president stands in the polls, the easier it is to persuade others to support presidential initiatives. Contrary to the conventional wisdom, citizens seem to focus on the president's efforts and stands on issues rather than on personality ("popularity") or simply how presidential policies affect them (the "pocketbook"). Job-related personal characteristics of the president, such as integrity and leadership skills, also play an important role in influencing presidential approval.

Commentators on the presidency often refer to it as a "bully pulpit," implying that presidents can *persuade or even mobilize the public* to support their policies if they are skilled enough communicators. Presidents frequently do attempt to obtain public support for their policies with speeches over the radio or television or speeches to large groups. All presidents since Truman have had *media advice* from experts on such matters as lighting, makeup, stage settings, camera angles, and even clothing.

Mobilization of the public may be the ultimate weapon in the president's arsenal of resources with which to influence Congress. The modern White House makes extraordinary efforts to control the context in which presidents appear in public and the way they are portrayed by the press. The fact that presidents nevertheless are frequently low in the polls is persuasive testimony to the *limits of presidential leadership of the public.*

THE PRESIDENT AND THE PRESS

The press has become the *principal intermediary between the president and the public*, and relations with the press are an important aspect of the president's efforts to lead public opinion. It is the mass media that provides people with most of what they know about chief executives and their policies.

Presidents and the press tend to come into conflict with each other. Presidents want to control the amount and timing of information about their administration, while the press wants immediate access to all the information that exists. The best known direct interaction between the president and the press is the presidential press conference. Despite their visibility, press conferences are not very useful means of eliciting information. Presidents and their staffs can anticipate most of the questions that will be asked and prepare answers to them ahead of time, reducing the spontaneity of the sessions. Moreover, the large size and public nature of press conferences reduce the candor with which the president responds to questions.

Bias is the most politically charged issue in relations between the president and the press. However, a large number of studies have concluded that the news media are not biased *systematically* toward a particular person, party, or ideology. To conclude that the news contains little explicitly partisan or ideological bias is not to argue that the news does not distort reality in its coverage of the president. Some observers believe that news coverage of the presidency often tends to emphasize the negative. On the other hand, one could also argue that the press is inherently biased *toward* the White House. A consistent pattern of favorable coverage exists in all major media outlets, and the president is typically portrayed with an aura of dignity and treated with deference. In fact, the White House can largely control the environment in which the president meets the press.

UNDERSTANDING THE AMERICAN PRESIDENCY

Concerns over presidential power are generally closely *related to policy views*. Those who oppose the president's policies are the most likely to be concerned about too much presidential power. Aside from acting outside the law and the Constitution, there is little prospect that the presidency will be a threat to democracy. The Madisonian system of checks and balances remains intact.

It is often said that the American people are *ideologically conservative and operationally liberal.* In the past generation, the public has chosen a number of presidents who reflected their ideology and congresses that represented their appetite for public service. It has been the president more often than Congress who has objected to government growth.

CHAPTER OUTLINE

I. INTRODUCTION

A. Americans expect a lot from presidents (perhaps too much). The *myth of the president as a powerhouse* distorts the public's image of presidential reality.
   1. To accomplish policy goals, the president must get other people to do things they otherwise would not do.
   2. The main reason presidents have trouble getting things done is that other policymakers with whom they deal have their own agendas, their own interests, and their own sources of power.
   3. Presidents operate in an environment filled with checks and balances and competing centers of power.

B. To be effective, the president must have highly developed *political skills* to mobilize influence, manage conflict, negotiate, and build compromises. Political scientist Richard Neustadt has argued that presidential power is *the power to persuade*, not to command.

II. THE PRESIDENTS

A. The *presidency* is a *highly personal office*: the personality of the individual who serves as president does make a difference.

B. Americans are of two minds about the presidency.
   1. They want to believe in a powerful president—one who can do good.
   2. Americans do not like concentrations of power; they are basically individualistic and skeptical of authority.

C. Characteristics of presidents.
   1. The Constitution simply states that the president must be a natural-born citizen at least 35 years old and must have resided in the United States for at least 14 years.
   2. All American presidents have been white, male, and (except for John Kennedy) Protestant. In other ways, there has been considerable diversity among recent presidents.

D. How they got there.
   1. Elections: the normal road to the White House.
      a. Most presidents reach the White House through the electoral process. [see Chapters 8 and 9]

b. Once in office, presidents are guaranteed a four-year term by the Constitution, but the **Twenty-second Amendment** (ratified in 1951) limits them to a maximum of *two terms or ten years*.
c. Only eleven of the forty-one presidents before Bill Clinton have actually served two or more full terms.

2. The vice presidency: another road to the White House.
   a. About one in five presidents assumed the presidency when the incumbent president either died or (in Nixon's case) resigned; in the twentieth century, almost one-third have been "accidental presidents."
   b. At one time, the selection of the vice president was of little importance. Today, the selection is primarily an effort to placate some important symbolic constituency.
   c. Once in office, vice presidents find that their main job is waiting.
      (1) Constitutionally, they are assigned the minor task of presiding over the Senate and voting in case of a tie.
      (2) Recent presidents have involved their vice presidents in policy discussions and important diplomacy.
3. Impeachment.
   a. Removing a discredited president before the end of a term is a difficult task. The Constitution prescribes the process through **impeachment**, which is roughly the political equivalent of an indictment in criminal law. (The term "impeachment" refers to the formal accusation, *not* to conviction.)
   b. The House of Representatives may impeach the president (and other civil officers) for "Treason, Bribery, or other high Crimes and Misdemeanors." Impeachment requires a simple majority vote of the House.
   c. If the House votes for impeachment, the accused president will be tried by the Senate.
      (1) The chief justice of the Supreme Court presides when a president is being tried; the vice president (as president of the Senate) will preside if a civil officer other than the president has been impeached.
      (2) The Senate may convict and remove the president by a two-thirds vote of the senators present.
   d. Impeachment charges are heard first by the House Judiciary Committee or by a select committee, which makes recommendations to the full House.
      (1) In 1974, the House Judiciary Committee voted to recommend the impeachment of Richard Nixon as a result of the **Watergate** scandal.

(2) Nixon escaped a certain vote for impeachment by resigning.

e. Andrew Johnson, Lincoln's successor, is the only president who has ever been impeached; he narrowly escaped conviction in 1868 on charges stemming from his disagreement with radical Republicans.

4. Presidential succession.
   a. The **Twenty-fifth Amendment** clarified some of the Constitution's vagueness about presidential **disability** and **succession.**
   b. The Amendment permits the vice president to become acting president if the vice president and the president's cabinet determine that the president is disabled or if the president declares his own disability, and it outlines how a recuperated president can reclaim the office.
   c. Provision is also made for *selecting a new vice president* when the office becomes vacant.
      (1) The president nominates a new vice president, who assumes the office when both houses of Congress approve the nomination.
      (2) This provision has been used twice: President Nixon named Gerald Ford as the new vice president after Spiro Agnew resigned in 1973, then President Ford named Nelson Rockefeller after Richard Nixon resigned in 1974.
   d. *Statutes* specify the *order of succession* following the president and vice president—from vice president, to the Speaker of the House, to the president *pro tempore* of the Senate, through the cabinet in chronological order according to when the department was created.

III. PRESIDENTIAL POWERS

A. The contemporary presidency differs dramatically from the one the framers of the Constitution designed in 1787. The executive office they conceived of had more limited authority, fewer responsibilities, and much less organizational structure than today's presidency.

B. Constitutional powers.
   1. The constitutional discussion of the presidency begins with these general words: "The executive power shall be vested in a president of the United States of America."
   2. The Constitution says little else about presidential authority, going on to list only a few powers.
   3. *Institutional balance* was essential to delegates at the Constitutional Convention.

   a. There is *little that presidents can do on their own.*
   b. They share executive, legislative, and judicial power with the other branches of government.
4. Powers derived from the Constitution.
   a. National security powers:
      (1) Commander in chief of the armed forces;
      (2) Make treaties with other nations, subject to the agreement of two-thirds of the Senate;
      (3) Nominate ambassadors, with the agreement of a majority of the Senate; and
      (4) Receive ambassadors of other nations, thereby conferring diplomatic recognition on other governments.
   b. Legislative powers:
      (1) Present information on the state of the union to Congress;
      (2) Recommend legislation to Congress;
      (3) Convene both houses of Congress on extraordinary occasions;
      (4) Adjourn Congress if the House and Senate cannot agree on adjournment; and
      (5) Veto legislation (Congress may overrule with a two-thirds vote of each house).
   c. Administrative powers:
      (1) "Take care that the laws be faithfully executed";
      (2) Appoint officials as provided for by Congress and with the agreement of a majority of the Senate;
      (3) Request written opinions of administrative officials; and
      (4) Fill administrative vacancies during congressional recesses.
   d. Judicial powers:
      (1) Grant reprieves and pardons for federal offenses (except impeachment); and
      (2) Appoint federal judges with the agreement of a majority of the Senate.

C. The expansion of power.
   1. Today there is *more to presidential power than the Constitution alone suggests*, and that power is *derived from many sources*.
   2. The role of the president changed as America increased in prominence on the world stage, and technology also helped to reshape the presidency. [see Chapter 3]
   3. Presidents themselves have taken the initiative in developing new roles for the office. Various presidents enlarged the power of the presidency by *expanding the president's responsibilities and political resources.*

IV. RUNNING THE GOVERNMENT: THE CHIEF EXECUTIVE

A. One of the president's most important roles is *presiding over the administration of government.*
   1. The Constitution merely tells the president to "take care that the laws be faithfully executed."
   2. Today, the federal bureaucracy includes 4.5 million civilian and military employees and spends more than $1.7 trillion annually.
   3. One of the resources for controlling the bureaucracy is the presidential power to *appoint top-level administrators.*
      a. New presidents have about 300 high-level positions available for appointment (cabinet and subcabinet jobs, agency heads, and other non-civil service posts), plus 2000 lesser jobs.
      b. In recent years, presidents have paid close attention to appointing officials who will be *responsive to the president's policies.*
      c. Presidents have also taken more interest in the *regulations* issued by agencies.
   4. Presidents have the power to *recommend agency budgets* to Congress—the result of the **Budgeting and Accounting Act of 1921.**

B. The Vice President.
   1. Usually chosen to symbolically reward an important constituency.
   2. Main job is to wait for "better" political opportunities.

C. The cabinet.
   1. Although the group of presidential advisors known as the **cabinet** is not mentioned in the Constitution, every president has had one.
   2. George Washington's cabinet consisted of just three secretaries (state, treasury, and war) and the attorney general. Presidents since Washington have increased the size of the cabinet by asking Congress to create new **executive departments.**
   3. Today, thirteen secretaries and the attorney general head executive departments (and constitute the cabinet). In addition, individual presidents may designate other officials (such as the ambassador to the United Nations) as cabinet members.

D. The executive office.
   1. The **Executive Office of the President** (established in 1939) is a loosely grouped collection of offices and organizations.
      a. Some of the offices are created by legislation (such as the Council of Economic Advisors), while others are organized by the president.
      b. The Executive Office includes three major policy-making bodies—the National Security Council, the Council of Economic

Advisors, and the Office of Management and Budget—plus several other units serving the president.

2. The **National Security Council (NSC)** is the committee that *links the president's key foreign and military policy advisors*. The president's special assistant for national security affairs and his staff provide the president with information and policy recommendations on national security, aid the president in national security crisis management, coordinate agency and departmental activities bearing on national security, and monitor the implementation of national security policy.
3. The **Council of Economic Advisors (CEA)** has three members, each appointed by the president, who *advise the president on economic policy*. They prepare the *Annual Report of the Council of Economic Advisors* and help the president make policy on inflation, unemployment, and other economic matters.
4. The **Office of Management and Budget (OMB)**, which is the successor to the Bureau of the Budget (BOB), has responsibility for *preparing the president's budget*. [see Chapter 14]
   a. Presidents use the OMB to *review legislative proposals* from the cabinet and other executive agencies so they can determine whether or not they want an agency to propose them to Congress.
   b. The OMB assesses the proposals' budgetary implications and advises the president on the proposals' consistency with the administration's overall program.

E. The White House staff.
   1. The **White House staff** includes the *key aides* the president sees daily—the chief of staff, congressional liaison people, press secretary, national security advisor, and a few other administrative political assistants.
   2. The full **White House Office**, an agency of the Executive Office of the President, consists of about 600 people (many of whom the president rarely sees) that provide the president with a wide variety of services ranging from advance travel preparations to answering the thousands of letters received each year.
   3. Presidents rely heavily on their staffs for *information, policy options, and analysis*.
   4. Each president organizes the White House to serve his own political and policy needs, as well as his decision-making style.
   5. Despite heavy reliance on staff, it is *the president who sets the tone* for the White House. It is the president's responsibility to demand that staff members analyze a full range of options (and their likely consequences) before they offer the president their advice.

F. The First Lady.
   1. Not an official government position.
   2. Historically, First Ladies have received a lot of attention, and occasionally been active in politics.
   3. More recently, First Ladies have been at the center of attention in policy-making matters and played important roles as advisors to their husbands.

V. PRESIDENTIAL LEADERSHIP OF CONGRESS: THE POLITICS OF SHARED POWERS

A. Chief legislator.
   1. The president is *a major shaper of the congressional agenda*, and the term **chief legislator** is frequently used to emphasize the executive's importance in the legislative process.
   2. The Constitution requires the president to report to Congress on the **State of the Union** and instructs the president to bring other matters to Congress' attention "from time to time."
   3. The Constitution gives the president the power to sign or to **veto** congressional legislation (a veto may be overridden by two-thirds of each house).
      a. He may also decide not to take any action at all.
      b. If Congress is still in session after ten working days, the bill will become law without his signature; if Congress adjourns within ten days after submitting a bill, taking no action will permit the bill to die without his signature (known as a **pocket veto**).
   4. The presidential veto is usually effective; only about *4 percent* of all vetoed bills have been overridden by Congress. Even the *threat* of a presidential veto can be an effective tool for persuading Congress.
   5. In 1996 Congress passed a law granting the president authority to propose rescinding funds in appropriations bills and tax provisions that apply to only a few people.
      a. The president has five days following his signing of tax or spending bills to propose rescissions, and the only way such provisions can become law is for Congress to pass them as separate bills, which would then be subject to a presidential veto.
      b. The law was immediately challenged in the courts as being an unconstitutional grant of power to the president, but the Supreme Court refused to hear the case in 1997.

B. Party leadership.
   1. Presidents' most useful resources in passing their own legislation are their *party leadership*, *public support*, and their own *legislative skills*.

2. **Party leadership** in Congress is every president's principal task when countering the *natural tendencies toward conflict* between the executive and legislative branches.
3. The bonds of party.
   a. For most senators and representatives, being in the same political party as the president creates a *psychological bond.*
   b. Presidents remain highly dependent upon their party to move their legislative programs.
   c. Representatives and senators of the president's party usually form the nucleus of coalitions supporting presidential proposals.
4. Slippage in party support.
   a. Presidents are forced to be active in party leadership and to devote their efforts to *conversion* as much as to *mobilization of members of their own party*: presidents can count on their own party members for support *no more than two-thirds of the time*, even on key votes.
   b. The primary obstacle to party unity is the lack of consensus among party members on policies, especially in the Democratic party. This diversity of views often reflects the diversity of constituencies represented by party members (illustrated by the frequent defection of Southern Democrats known as "boll weevils").
5. Leading the party.
   a. Although party leaders in Congress are *predisposed to support* presidential policies and typically work closely with the White House, they are *free to oppose* the president or lend only symbolic support.
      (1) Party leaders are not in a position to reward or discipline members of Congress on the basis of presidential support.
      (2) The White House provides many amenities to congressional party members in an attempt to create goodwill (such as "photo opportunities"), but there is little the president can do if party members wish to oppose the administration.
      (3) The *parties are highly decentralized*, and national party leaders do not control nominations and elections. [see Chapter 8]
   b. One way for the president to improve the chances of obtaining support in Congress is to *increase the number of party members in the legislature.*
      (1) The term **presidential coattails** refers to voters casting their ballots for congressional candidates of the president's party because those candidates support the president. Thus, the

symbolism was that the candidates would "ride into office on the president's coattails."

(2) However, most recent studies show a *diminishing connection* between presidential and congressional voting.

(3) In **midterm elections**—those held between presidential elections—the president's party typically *loses* seats; in 1994 the Democrats lost eight Senate seats and fifty-three House seats, losing control of both houses in the process. The 1998 election was an exception: the Democrats gained five seats in the House.

c. A major impediment to party leadership is the fact that the president's party often lacks a majority in one or both houses of Congress.

(1) The president usually has to solicit help from the opposition party.

(2) Although only a few votes may be obtained, that may be enough to bring the president the required majority.

C. Public support.

1. Presidents who have the *backing of the public* have an easier time influencing Congress. Members of Congress closely watch two indicators of public support for the president—*approval in the polls* and *mandates in presidential elections*.

2. Public approval.

a. Public approval is *the political resource that has the most potential* to turn a situation of stalemate between the president and Congress into one that is supportive of the president's legislative proposals.

(1) Widespread support gives the president leeway and weakens resistance to presidential policies.

(2) Lack of support strengthens the resolve of those inclined to oppose the president and narrows the range in which presidential policies receive the benefit of the doubt.

(3) Low ratings in the polls may create incentives to attack the president, further eroding an already weakened position.

b. Public approval gives the president leverage, not control; presidents' leadership resources do not allow them to dominate Congress.

3. Mandates.

a. An electoral **mandate**—the perception that the voters strongly support the president's character and policies—can be a powerful symbol in American politics. It accords *added legitimacy and credibility* to the newly elected president's proposals.

b. *Merely winning an election does not provide presidents with a mandate.*
   (1) It is common after close elections to hear claims—especially from the other party—that there was "no mandate" (as with Bill Clinton's election in 1992).
   (2) Even large electoral victories (such as Richard Nixon's in 1972 and Ronald Reagan's in 1984) carry no guarantee that Congress will interpret the results as mandates, especially if the voters also elect majorities in Congress from the other party.

D. Legislative skills.
   1. Presidents influence the legislative agenda more than any other political figure.
      a. No matter what a president's skills are, however, the "chief legislator" can rarely exercise complete control over the agenda.
      b. Presidents are rarely in a position to create—through their own leadership—opportunities for major changes in public policy. They may, however, use their skills to exploit favorable political conditions to bring about policy change.
   2. Presidential leadership skills include *bargaining, making personal appeals, consulting with Congress, setting priorities, exploiting "honeymoon" periods, and structuring congressional votes.*
      a. Bargaining—in the form of trading support on two or more policies or providing specific benefits for representatives and senators—occurs less often and plays a less critical role in the creation of presidential coalitions in Congress than is often implied.
      b. Presidents may improve their chances of success in Congress by making certain strategic moves.
         (1) It is wise for a new president to be ready to send legislation to the Hill during the first year in office in order to exploit the "honeymoon" atmosphere that typically characterizes this period.
         (2) It is important to establish *priorities* among legislative proposals.
   3. In general, presidential legislative skills must compete with other, more stable factors that affect voting in Congress, such as party, ideology, personal views and commitments on specific policies, and constituency interests.

VI. THE PRESIDENT AND NATIONAL SECURITY POLICY

A. Constitutionally, the president has the leading role in American defense and foreign policy (often termed **national security**).

B. Chief diplomat.

1. The Constitution allocates certain powers in the realm of national security that are exclusive to the executive.
   a. The president alone extends **diplomatic recognition** to foreign governments (and the president can also terminate relations with other nations).
   b. The president has the sole power to negotiate **treaties** with other nations, although the Constitution requires the Senate to approve them by a two-thirds vote.
   c. Presidents negotiate **executive agreements** with the heads of foreign governments; unlike treaties, executive agreements do not require Senate ratification.
2. As the leader of the Western world, the president must try to lead America's allies on matters of economics and defense.
   a. Presidents usually conduct diplomatic relations through envoys, but occasionally they engage in personal diplomacy.
   b. As in domestic policy-making, the president must rely principally on *persuasion* to lead.

C. Commander in chief.

1. Because the Constitution's framers wanted *civilian control of the military*, they made the president the commander in chief of the armed forces.
2. Today the president is commander in chief of nearly 1.5 million uniformed men and women, with commitments to defend nations around the globe.
3. The president commands a vast nuclear arsenal; *the football*—a briefcase that contains the codes to unleash our nuclear capabilities—is never more than a few steps from the president.

D. War powers.

1. Although only Congress is constitutionally empowered to declare war and vote on the military budget, Congress long ago became accustomed to presidents making short-term military commitments of troops or naval vessels.
2. In recent years, presidents have committed U.S. troops to action without seeking congressional approval (as in Korea and Vietnam).
3. As a reaction to disillusionment about American fighting in Vietnam and Cambodia, Congress passed the **War Powers Resolution** (1973) over President Nixon's veto.
   a. It required presidents to *consult with Congress*, whenever possible, *prior to using military force*, and it mandated the

withdrawal of forces after sixty days unless Congress declared war or granted an extension. Congress could at any time pass a *concurrent resolution* (which cannot be vetoed) ending American participation in hostilities.

b. All presidents serving since 1973 have deemed the law an unconstitutional infringement on their powers, and there is reason to believe the Supreme Court would consider the law's use of the **legislative veto** to end American involvement a *violation of the doctrine of separation of powers.*

c. Presidents have largely ignored the law and sent troops into hostilities.

4. Questions continue to be raised about the relevance of America's 200-year old constitutional mechanisms for engaging in war.
   a. Some observers are concerned that modern technology allows the president to engage in hostilities so quickly that opposing points of view do not receive proper consideration.
   b. Others stress the importance of the commander in chief having the flexibility to meet America's global responsibilities and to combat international terrorism.
   c. There has been much controversy over the issue of who should be able to commit the United States to war, but the public has overwhelmingly indicated a desire for Congress to be involved in the decision.

E. Crisis manager.
   1. As chief diplomat and commander in chief, the president is also the country's *crisis manager.*
   2. A **crisis** is a *sudden, unpredictable, and potentially dangerous event.*
      a. Most occur in the realm of foreign policy; quick judgments are often needed despite sketchy information.
      b. Crises are rarely the president's doing, but they can be the president's undoing if badly handled.
   3. Early in American history, there were fewer immediate crises.
      a. Communications could take weeks or even months to reach Washington.
      b. Likewise, officials' decisions often took weeks or months to reach those who were to implement them.
   4. With *modern communications*, the president can *instantly monitor events* almost anywhere.
      a. Because situations develop more rapidly today, there is a *premium on rapid action*, secrecy, constant management, consistent judgment, and expert advice.

      b. Since *Congress usually moves slowly*, the *president has become more prominent* in handling crises.

F. Working with Congress.
   1. Congress has a central constitutional role in making national security policy.
      a. The allocation of responsibilities for such matters is based upon the founders' apprehensions about the concentration and potential for abuse of power.
      b. The founders *divided the powers of supply and command*: Congress can thus refuse to provide the necessary authorizations and appropriations for presidential actions, while the chief executive can refuse to act (for example, by *not* sending troops into battle).
   2. Despite the constitutional role of Congress, the president is the dominant force behind national security policy.
      a. The role of Congress has typically been *oversight of the executive* rather than initiation of policy.
      b. Commentators on the presidency often refer to the *two presidencies* — one for domestic policy and the other for national security policy. By this they mean the president has more success in leading Congress on matters of national security than on matters of domestic policy.

VII. POWER FROM THE PEOPLE: THE PUBLIC PRESIDENCY

A. Perhaps the greatest challenge to any president is *to obtain and maintain the public's support.* Because presidents are *rarely in a position to command* others to comply with their wishes, they must *rely on persuasion*.

B. Going public.
   1. *Public opinion can be an important resource for presidential persuasion.*
   2. The necessity of public support leads the White House to employ *public relations techniques* similar to those used to publicize products.
      a. John Kennedy was the first president to regularly use public appearances to seek popular backing for his policies.
      b. Kennedy's successors (with the exception of Richard Nixon) have been even more active in making public appearances.
      c. The *integration of policy goals and public communications* is an especially prominent feature of the Clinton administration.

3. In America, the jobs of **head of state** (ceremonial) and **head of government** (executive authority) are combined.
   a. As head of state, the president is America's *ceremonial leader and symbol of government.*
   b. Ceremonial activities give presidents an important symbolic aura and a great deal of favorable press coverage, contributing to their efforts to build public support.

C. Presidential approval.
   1. The president's standing in the polls is monitored closely by the press, members of Congress, and others in the Washington political community: the higher the president stands in the polls, the easier it is to persuade others to support presidential initiatives.
   2. Presidents *frequently do not have widespread public support,* often failing to win even majority approval.
   3. Presidential approval is the product of many factors.
      a. Many people are predisposed to support the president.
         (1) Political *party identification* provides the basic underpinning of approval or disapproval.
         (2) Presidents usually benefit from a "honeymoon" with the American people after taking office.
      b. *Changes* in approval levels appear to be due primarily to the public's evaluation of how the president is handling policy.
         (1) *Contrary to conventional wisdom,* citizens seem to focus on the president's efforts and stands on *issues* rather than on personality or simply how presidential policies affect them.
         (2) Job-related personal characteristics of the president—such as integrity and leadership skills—also play an important role.
         (3) Sometimes public approval of the president takes sudden jumps, often stimulated by **"rally events"** that relate to international relations (illustrated by President Bush's 18-percentage-point rise immediately after the fighting began in the Persian Gulf War in 1991). Such occurrences usually have little enduring impact on a president's public approval.
   4. The modern White House makes extraordinary efforts to control the context in which presidents appear in public and the way they are portrayed by the press. The fact that presidents nevertheless are frequently low in the polls is persuasive testimony to the *limits of presidential leadership of the public.*

D. Policy support.
   1. Commentators on the presidency often refer to it as a "bully pulpit," implying that presidents can *persuade or even mobilize the public* to support their policies if they are skilled-enough communicators.
      a. Presidents frequently do attempt to obtain public support for their policies with speeches over the radio or television or speeches to large groups.
      b. All presidents since Truman have had *media advice* from experts on such matters as lighting, makeup, stage settings, camera angles, and even clothing.
   2. Despite these efforts, presidential speeches designed to lead public opinion have typically been rather unimpressive.
   3. The public is not always receptive to the president's message, and the public may misunderstand or ignore even the most basic facts regarding presidential policy.

E. Mobilizing the public.
   1. *Mobilization of the public* may be the ultimate weapon in the president's arsenal of resources with which to influence Congress.
      a. Mobilizing the public entails the double burden of obtaining both opinion *support* and political *action* from a generally inattentive and apathetic public.
      b. There are certain *risks* involved: if the president attempts to mobilize the public and fails, the lack of response speaks clearly to members of Congress.
   2. Perhaps the most notable recent example of the president mobilizing public opinion to put pressure on Congress was Ronald Reagan's televised plea for support of his tax-cut proposals, which resulted in a massive outpouring of phone calls, letters, and telegrams.
      a. Reagan's success appears to be a deviant case (even for Ronald Reagan).
      b. Despite high levels of approval for much of his presidency, Reagan was never again able to arouse many in his audience to communicate their support of his policies to Congress.

VIII. THE PRESIDENT AND THE PRESS

A. The press has become the *principal intermediary between the president and the public*, and relations with the press are an important aspect of the president's efforts to lead public opinion.
   1. It is the mass media that provides people with most of what they know about chief executives and their policies.

   2. The media also interprets and analyzes presidential activities, even the president's direct appeals to the public.
B. Presidents and the press *tend to conflict*.
   1. Presidents want to control the amount and timing of information about their administration.
   2. The press wants all the information that exists, without delay.
C. Because of the importance of the press to the president, the White House goes to great lengths to encourage the media to project a positive image of the president's activities and policies.
   1. The White House monitors the media closely.
   2. The president's **press secretary** conducts daily press briefings, giving prepared announcements and answering questions.
   3. Press secretaries and their staffs arrange private interviews with White House officials, photo opportunities, and travel arrangements for reporters when the president leaves Washington.
   4. The best-known direct interaction between the president and the press is the presidential **press conference**.
      a. Despite their high visibility, press conferences are *not very useful means of eliciting information*.
      b. Although press conferences may appear spontaneous, presidents and their staffs can anticipate most of the questions that will be asked and prepare answers to them ahead of time.
D. Most of the news coverage of the White House comes under the heading of "*body watch,*" which means that reporters focus on the most visible layer of presidents' personal and official activities rather than on the substance of policies or the fundamental processes operating in the executive branch.
E. *Bias* is the most politically-charged issue in relations between the president and the press.
   1. A large number of studies have concluded that the news media is not biased *systematically* toward a particular person, party, or ideology.
   2. Some observers believe that news coverage of the presidency often tends to emphasize the negative; George Bush's handling of the economy during the 1992 election campaign is an example.
F. One could also argue that the press is inherently biased *toward* the White House.
   1. A consistent pattern of favorable coverage exists in all major media outlets, and the president is typically portrayed with an aura of dignity and treated with deference.

2. The White House can largely control the environment in which the president meets the press (as when Marine helicopters revved as President Reagan approached them so that he "could not hear" reporters' questions).

IX. UNDERSTANDING THE AMERICAN PRESIDENCY

A. The presidency and democracy.
   1. Because the presidency is the single most important office in American politics, there has always been concern about *whether the president is a threat to democracy.*
   2. Concerns over presidential power are generally closely *related to policy views*: those who oppose the president's policies are the most likely to be concerned about too much presidential power.
   3. In an era of divided government, some observers are concerned that there is *too much checking and balancing* and *too little capacity to act* to meet pressing national challenges. However, the best evidence indicates that major policy change is *not* hindered by divided government—that it is as likely to occur when the parties share control as when party control of the executive and legislative branches is divided.

B. The presidency and the scope of government.
   1. Supporting an increased role for government is not inherent in the presidency; leadership can move in many directions.
   2. It is often said that the American people are *ideologically conservative and operationally liberal.*
      a. In the past generation, the public has chosen a number of presidents who reflected their ideology and congresses that represented their appetite for public service.
      b. It has been the president more often than Congress who has objected to government growth.

KEY TERMS AND CONCEPTS

Cabinet: the group of presidential advisors who head the executive departments.

Council of Economic Advisors: members advise the president on economic policy and prepare the Annual Report of the CEA.

Crisis: a sudden, unpredictable, and potentially dangerous event.

Impeachment: the political equivalent of an indictment for removing a discredited president.

Legislative veto: a clause which allows Congress to override the action of the executive.

National Security Council: a committee that links the president's key foreign and military advisors.

Office of Management and Budget: responsible for preparing the president's budget and assessing the budgetary implications of legislative proposals.

Pocket veto: this occurs when Congress adjourns within ten days after submitting a bill and the president takes no action to sign it or veto it.

Presidential coattails: where voters cast their ballots for congressional candidates of the president's party because those candidates support the president.

Twenty-fifth Amendment: passed in 1967, permits the vice-president to become acting president in the event that the president is temporarily disabled.

Twenty-second Amendment: passed in 1951, limits presidents to two terms.

Veto: sending the legislation back to Congress with reasons for rejecting it.

War Powers Resolution: passed in 1973, requires presidents to consult with Congress prior to using military force and mandates the withdrawal of forces after sixty days unless Congress declares war or grants an extension.

Watergate: a political scandal involving President Nixon's abuse of his powers.

TEACHING IDEAS: CLASS DISCUSSION AND STUDENT PROJECTS

- Commentators on the presidency often refer to it as a *"bully pulpit,"* implying that presidents can persuade or even mobilize the public to support their policies if only they are skilled enough communicators. Ask your class to try to determine the skills that are needed to make a president an *effective communicator*. How has the concept of the "bully pulpit" changed since Theodore Roosevelt referred to the idea?

- It is often said that the American people are ideologically conservative and operationally liberal. Have your class write short essays in which students explain why voters choose presidents and congresses that appear to reflect different policy positions. Is this a negative or a positive factor of the American form of government?

- Ask students to use the Internet to locate a recent presidential speech. Describe the speech's main points and its intended audience. Discuss whether the speech is consistent with the broad policies and values espoused by the president.

- For a class discussion, have students debate the different ways vice-presidents can be used to enhance the president's opportunities for advancing his agenda in Congress. In particular, have them examine the concept of a co-presidency or the abolition of the vice-presidency position. What would be the consequences?

- For a reading and writing connection, have students keep a clipping file of newspaper coverage of the president for at least one week. Have them categorize the articles into stories about the president's (domestic and international) roles and personality. Then have them assess the tone and nature of the coverage. Once they have analyzed their clippings, have them write an analytical essay concerning the presidential news coverage and bias in the media.

- Have students choose the State of the Union address delivered by one president, and determine the extent to which the president's speech successfully set the Congressional agenda. What factors enhanced the President's ability to lead Congress? What factors hampered his ability to lead?

BACKGROUND READING

Bond, Jon and Richard Fleisher. The President in the Legislative Arena. Chicago: University of Chicago Press. 1990.

Cameron, Charles. Veto Bargaining: Presidents and the Politics of Negative Power. New York: Cambridge University Press. 1999.

Campbell, Colin and Bert A. Rockman, eds. The Clinton Presidency: First Appraisals. Chatham, New Jersey: Chatham House. 1995.

Edwards, George C. III, et. al, eds. Researching the Presidency: Vital Questions, New Approaches. Pittsburgh: University of Pittsburgh Press. 1993.

Edwards, George C. III. At the Margins: Presidential Leadership of Congress. New Haven, CT: Yale University Press. 1989.

Jones, Charles O. The Presidency in a Separated System. Washington D.C.: Brookings Institution.

Kernell, Samuel. Going Public: New Strategies of Public Leadership. 3rd ed. Washington D.C.: CQ Press. 1997.

Neustadt, Richard E. Presidential Power and the Modern President. New York: Free Press. 1991.

Van Tassel, Emily Field and Paul Finkelman. Impeachable Offenses: A Documentary History from 1787 to the Present. Washington, D.C.: CQ Press. 1998.

MEDIA SUGGESTIONS

Executive Privilege and the Delegation of Power. Part of "The Constitution: That Delicate Balance" series from Films Incorporated examining the powers of the president.

Modern Presidency. A five-part video series distributed by Enterprise Media examining the problems and issues of the past five presidential administrations from Nixon to Bush.

Politics in Action, Chapter 4: Presidential Leadership. Includes clips of Roosevelt, Truman, Eisenhower, Kennedy, Johnson, Nixon, Carter, Reagan, Bush and Clinton.

Powers of the President: The Constitution and Congress. This show focuses on various issues relating to the Constitutional relationship between the president and congress, and includes interviews with former presidents Carter, Nixon and Ford. Films for the Humanities & Sciences.

The President vs. The Press. Hosted by Hedrick Smith, this program features interviews with editors, news correspondents, press secretaries and presidential advisors on the relationship between the president and the press. Includes some discussion of presidential character, as well as the effect that the press has on public opinion. Films for the Humanities & Sciences.

Role of the Chief Executive. 1994. This program examines the various roles of the President and analyzes the factors which have contributed to changes in presidential power and influence over time. Insight Media.

Role of the First Lady. A new program distributed by Films for Humanities and the Sciences which examines the traditional and perceived role of the first lady.

War Powers and Covert Action. Part of "The Constitution: That Delicate Balance" series from Films Incorporated examining the war powers and foreign policy role of the president.

CHAPTER FOURTEEN: THE CONGRESS, THE PRESIDENT, AND THE BUDGET: THE POLITICS OF TAXING AND SPENDING

PEDAGOGICAL FEATURES

LEARNING OBJECTIVES

After studying this chapter, students should be able to:

- Identify the major sources of federal revenue.
- Determine how *tax expenditures* benefit middle- and upper-income tax payers and corporations.
- Identify the major recipients of federal tax expenditures.
- Discuss how the *rise of the national security state* and the *rise of the social service state* are associated with government growth in America.
- Explain how political scientists sometimes use the term *incrementalism* to describe the spending and appropriations process.
- Explain the impact that "uncontrollable" expenditures and entitlements have on the federal budget.
- Identify the key players and decision makers in the budgetary process.
- Explain how public opinion is a key element in the budgeting process.
- Outline the steps involved in developing the president's budget.
- Outline the steps in developing the congressional budget process.
- Ascertain the importance of budget resolution, reconciliation, authorization, and appropriations.
- Evaluate the ways in which the budget affects the scope of government.

CHAPTER OVERVIEW

INTRODUCTION

The central political issue for many years has been how to pay for policies that most people support. The president and Congress have been caught in a *budgetary squeeze*: Americans want them to balance the budget, maintain or increase the level of government spending on most policies, and still keep taxes low. Thus, two questions become central to public policy: who bears the burdens of paying for government? Who receives the benefits?

THE GOVERNMENT'S SOURCES OF REVENUE

Probably no government policy affects as many Americans as tax policy. In addition to raising revenues to finance its services, the government can use taxes to make citizens' incomes more or less equal, to encourage or discourage growth in the economy, and to promote specific interests.

This section looks at the substance of the budget to see how the American government raises money and where that money is spent. The three major sources of federal revenues are the *personal* and *corporate income tax*, *social insurance taxes*, and *borrowing*. In 1913, the **Sixteenth Amendment** was added to the Constitution, explicitly permitting Congress to levy an income tax. Although corporate taxes once yielded more revenues than individual income taxes, today corporate taxes yield only about ten cents of every federal revenue dollar, compared with forty-eight cents coming from individual income taxes.

Today the **federal debt**—all of the money borrowed over the years and still outstanding—exceeds $5.5 trillion. Eleven percent of all federal expenditures go to paying off the debt. When the federal government wants to borrow money, the Treasury Department sells bonds, guaranteeing to pay interest to the bondholder. Citizens, corporations, mutual funds, and other financial institutions purchase the bonds. Most observers are concerned about the national debt. Many have called for a *balanced budget amendment*.

A **tax loophole** is presumably some tax break or tax benefit. The **IRS Code** is riddled with exemptions, deductions, and special cases. For example, H. Ross Perot (1992 presidential candidate) hired a former Internal Revenue Service commissioner in 1975 to aid him in having the tax code changed to benefit him to the tune of approximately $15 million.. The bill was killed on the House floor when the press reported that *only Perot* would benefit from the provision. Tax loopholes may offend Americans' sense of fair play, but they cost the treasury relatively little because they apply to only a few people.

Loopholes are really a type of **tax expenditure**, which represent *the difference between what the government actually collects in taxes and what it would have collected without special exemptions*. Tax expenditures are essentially monies that government could collect but does not because they are *exempted* from taxation.

Early in his administration, President Reagan proposed a massive tax-cut bill, which was passed by Congress in July 1981. Families with high incomes received significant tax reductions with the 1981 bill, but those at the lower end of the income ladder did not notice much change in their tax burden because social insurance and excise taxes (which fall disproportionately on the poor) *rose* during the same period. Many blamed the massive deficits of the 1980s and 1990s at least partially on the *1981 tax cuts*, as government continued to spend more but reduced its revenues.

The *Tax Reform Act of 1986* was one of the most sweeping alterations in federal tax policy in history. It eliminated or reduced the value of many tax deductions, removed several million low-income individuals from the tax rolls, and changed the system of fifteen separate brackets to just two generally lower rates (28 percent and 15 percent). In 1990, a third bracket of 31 percent was added for those with higher incomes. In 1993, President Clinton proposed, and Congress approved, a plan to raise the income tax rate to 36 percent for families with incomes over $140,000 and add an additional surcharge of 3.6 percent to those families with incomes over $250,000. Corporate income taxes and energy taxes also rose.

FEDERAL EXPENDITURES

Among the most important changes of the twentieth century is *the rise of large governments.* American governments—national, state, and local—spend an amount equal to one-third of the Gross Domestic Product (GDP). Expenditures of the national government alone equal over 20 percent of the GNP. Nevertheless, the United States actually has one of the *smallest* public sectors among Western nations relative to the size of the Gross Domestic Product (GDP).

Two conditions associated with government growth in America are the *rise of the national security state* and the *rise of the social service state.* After World War II, the **"cold war"** with the Soviet Union resulted in a permanent military establishment and expensive military technology. President Eisenhower coined the phrase **military-industrial complex** to characterize the close relationship between the military hierarchy and the defense industry that supplies its hardware needs. The Pentagon wants weapons systems and arms makers want contracts, so they tend to be mutually *supportive.* In the 1990s, *defense expenditures have decreased* in response to the lessening of tensions in Europe. The budget of the Department of Defense now constitutes only about one-sixth of all federal expenditures.

The **Social Security Act** (passed in 1935) was originally intended to provide a minimal level of sustenance to older Americans. Lyndon Johnson's **"Great Society"** initiatives in the mid-1960s greatly expanded America's social services network, adding **Medicare** and **Medicaid** to the Social Security system and creating many new programs designed to aid the poor. Today, more than 45 million Americans receive payments from the Social Security system.

Social Security is not the only social policy of the federal government that is costly. The rise of the social service state has contributed to America's growing budget in health, education, job training, and scores of other areas. *Liberals* often favor these programs to assist individuals and groups in society. *Conservatives* see them as a drain on the federal treasury.

The picture of the federal budget is one of constant, slow growth. Expenditures mandated by an existing law or obligation (such as Social Security) are particularly likely to follow a pattern of **incrementalism**, which means that the best predictor of this year's budget is *last year's budget plus a little bit more*—that is, an increment. More and more of federal spending has become "uncontrollable." An **uncontrollable expenditure** is one that is *mandated* under current law or by a previous obligation. About *two-thirds of the federal budget is uncontrollable*—based on expenditures that are determined not by how much Congress appropriates to an agency but by *how many eligible beneficiaries* there are for a particular program. Many expenditures are uncontrollable because Congress has in effect obligated itself to pay *X* level of benefits to *Y* number of recipients. Such policies are called **entitlements**.

THE BUDGETARY PROCESS

Public budgets are the supreme example of Harold Lasswell's definition of politics as "who gets what, when, and how." Budget battles are fought over contending interests, ideologies, programs, and agencies.

The distribution of the government's budget is the outcome of a very complex budgetary process involving thousands of policy choices and prompting a great deal of politics. Every political actor has a stake in the budget. The main actors in the budgetary process include interest groups, agencies, the Office of Management and Budget, congressional tax committees and budget committees, congressional subject-matter committees and appropriations committees, the General Accounting Office, and of course the president.

According to the Constitution, *all federal appropriations must be authorized by Congress*—a control sometimes called the **"power of the purse."** In 1921, Congress passed the *Budget and Accounting Act*, requiring presidents to propose an executive budget to Congress and creating the *Bureau of the Budget* to help them. In the 1970s, President Nixon reorganized the Bureau of the Budget and renamed it the **Office of Management and Budget (OMB)**. The OMB now supervises preparation of the federal budget and advises the president on budgetary matters.

The **Congressional Budget and Impoundment Act of 1974** was designed to reform the congressional budgetary process. The act established *a fixed budget calendar* in which a timetable mandated by law was set for each step in the budgetary process. In April of each year, both houses of Congress are expected to agree upon a **budget resolution** which binds Congress to a total expenditure level that should form the bottom line of all federal spending for all programs.

The congressional budget resolution often requests that certain changes be made in law, primarily to achieve savings incorporated into the spending totals and thus meet the budget resolution. First is budget **reconciliation**, a process by which program authorizations are revised to achieve required savings; it frequently also includes tax or other revenue adjustments. The second way that laws are changed to meet the budget resolution (or to create or change programs for other reasons) involves more narrowly drawn legislation. An **authorization bill** is an act of Congress that establishes a discretionary government program or an entitlement, or that continues or changes such programs. An additional measure, termed an **appropriations bill**, must be passed to fund programs established by authorization bills.

The new system was supposed to force Congress *to consider the budget (both projected expenditures and projected revenues) as a whole*. However, Congress has often failed to meet its own budgetary timetable, and presidents have made matters worse by submitting budget proposals containing large deficits. Moreover, in many instances Congress has not been able to reach agreement and pass appropriations bills at all and has instead resorted to **continuing resolutions** – laws that allow agencies to spend at the previous year's level.

In response to growing frustration at its inability to substantially reduce annual budget deficits, Congress enacted the Balanced Budget and Emergency Deficit Control Act (1985), better known as the *Gramm-Rudman-Hollings Act*. As amended in 1987, the act mandated maximum allowable deficit levels for each year until 1993—at which point the budget was supposed to be in balance. If Congress failed to meet the deficit goals, automatic across-the-board spending cuts (called *sequestrations*) were to be ordered by the president, although a number of programs were exempt from the process.

In 1990, Congress decided to shift the focus from controlling the size of the deficit (which was the trigger for sequestration) to controlling increases in spending (under which the sheer size of the deficit would not matter). While Congress shifted to keeping a lid on expenditures, it allowed events beyond its control—such as war or a recession—to increase the size of the deficit without penalty. The *bottom line was a bigger deficit*; yearly deficits continued to climb and have continued into the Clinton administration.

The results of the 1994 congressional elections once again altered the budgetary game. In 1995, the new Republican majorities in each house, determined to balance the budget within seven years, argued for substantial cuts in the rate of growth of popular entitlement programs. The president agreed with the goal of balancing the budget – but on his terms – and took his case to the voters in 1996. The outcome, as we have seen, was divided government. In 1997, the president and Congress agreed to a budget that was to be in balance – by 2002. Each political party claimed victory, but the path to a balanced budget was eased by the booming economy, which produced more tax revenues than either side had anticipated.

UNDERSTANDING BUDGETING

Almost all democracies have seen a substantial growth in government in the twentieth century. Economists Allen Meltzer and Scott Richard argue that *government grows in a democracy* because of the *equality of suffrage*. Poorer voters will always use their votes to support public policies that redistribute benefits from the rich to the poor. Indeed, the most rapidly growing expenditures are items like Social Security, Medicaid, Medicare, and social welfare programs (all of which benefit the poor more than the rich).

One often thinks of elites—particularly corporate elites—as being opposed to big government. However, Lockheed and Chrysler corporations have appealed to the government for large bailouts when times got rough. Corporations support a big government that offers them contracts, subsidies, and other benefits. Poor and rich voters alike have voted for parties and politicians who promised them benefits. Government often grows by responding to groups and their demands.

Conversely, some politicians compete for votes by promising *not* to spend money (such as Ronald Reagan). In contrast with other nations, Americans have chosen to tax less and spend less on public services than almost all other democracies with developed economies. Paradoxically, Americans want to spend but they do not want to pay taxes. Being a democracy, that is exactly what the government does—and the inevitable result is red ink. America's large budget deficits have been as much a constraint on government as they have been evidence of a burgeoning public sector.

CHAPTER OUTLINE

I. INTRODUCTION

A. The president and Congress have been caught in a *budgetary squeeze*: Americans want them to balance the budget, maintain or increase the level of government spending on most policies, and still keep taxes low.
   1. Because budgets are so important to almost all other policies, *the budgetary process is the center of political battles* in Washington and involves nearly everyone in government.
   2. The central political issue for many years has been how to *pay* for policies that most people support.
      a. Resources have been scarce because the national government has run up a large budget deficit *each year during the 1980s and the early 1990s*. (A budget **deficit** occurs when **expenditures** exceed **revenues.**)
      b. The total national **debt** rose sharply during the 1980s, increasing from less than one trillion dollars to $5.6 trillion dollars by 2000.

II. THE GOVERNMENT'S SOURCES OF REVENUE

A. Where it comes from.
   1. The three major sources of federal revenues are the *personal* and *corporate income tax, social insurance taxes*, and *borrowing.* Only a small portion comes from *excise taxes* (such as tax on gasoline) and other sources.
   2. Income tax
      a. The first peacetime **income tax** was enacted in 1894.
         (1) The tax was declared unconstitutional in *Pollock* v. *Farmer's Loan and Trust Co.* (1895).
         (2) The **Sixteenth Amendment** was added to the Constitution in 1913, explicitly permitting Congress to levy an income tax. Congress had already started one before the amendment was ratified, and the **Internal Revenue Service (IRS)** was established to collect it.
      b. Corporations also pay income taxes. Although *corporate taxes once yielded more revenues than individual income taxes*, today corporate taxes yield only about *eight cents of every federal revenue dollar, compared with forty-five cents coming from individual income taxes.*

3. Social insurance taxes.
    a. *Social Security taxes* come from both employers and employees.
    b. Unlike other taxes, these payments do not go into the government's general money fund; they are specifically earmarked for the **Social Security Trust Fund** to pay benefits.
    c. Social Security taxes have *grown faster than any other source* of federal revenue.
4. Borrowing.
    a. When the federal government wants to borrow money, the Treasury Department sells bonds, guaranteeing to pay interest to the bondholder.
    b. Today the **federal debt**—all of the money borrowed over the years and still outstanding—exceeds $5.5 trillion.
    c. Eleven percent of all federal expenditures go to paying off the debt.
    d. Government borrowing crowds out private borrowers.
    e. Concerns about the national debt have led to some calls for a **balanced budget amendment.**
    f. Unlike state and local governments and private businesses, the federal government does not have a *capital budget*, a budget for items that will serve for the long-term. These purchases are counted as current expenditures and run up the deficit.

B. Taxes and public policy.
1. Tax loopholes.
    a. A **tax loophole** is presumably some tax break or tax benefit.
        (1) The **IRS Code** is riddled with exemptions, deductions, and special cases.
        (2) In 1975, H. Ross Perot (1992 and 1996 presidential candidate) hired a former Internal Revenue Service commissioner to aid him in having the tax code changed to benefit him to the tune of approximately $15 million. (The bill was killed on the House floor when the press reported that *only Perot* would benefit from the provision.)
    b. Although loopholes may offend Americans' sense of fair play, they actually cost the federal government very little; loopholes are really *a type of tax expenditure.*
2. Tax expenditures.
    a. What *does* cost the federal budget a substantial sum is the system of **tax expenditures**, which represent *the difference between what the government actually collects in taxes and what it would have collected without special exemptions.*

(1) Tax expenditures are essentially monies that government could collect but does not because they are *exempted* from taxation.
(2) The Office of Management and Budget estimated that the total tax expenditures in the mid-1990s would be about a third of the total federal receipts.
(3) Individuals receive most of the tax expenditures, and corporations get the rest.

b. Tax expenditures amount to subsidies for some activity, such as deductions for contributions to charities, deductions by homeowners for mortgage interest, and business deductions of investment in new plants and equipment at a more rapid rate than they can deduct other expenses

c. On the whole, tax expenditures benefit middle- and upper-income taxpayers and corporations. Poor people (who tend not to own homes) cannot take advantage of most such provisions.

3. Tax reduction.

a. Early in his administration, President Reagan proposed a massive tax-cut bill, which was passed by Congress in July 1981.
(1) Over a three-year period, Americans would have their federal tax bills reduced 25 percent, corporate income taxes were also reduced, new tax incentives were provided for personal savings and corporate investment, and taxes were *indexed* to the cost of living.
(2) Families with high incomes received significant tax reductions with the 1981 bill, but those at the lower end of the income ladder did not notice much change in their tax burden because social insurance and excise taxes (which fall disproportionately on the poor) *rose* during the same period.

b. Many blamed the massive deficits of the 1980s and 1990s at least partially on the *1981 tax cuts*, as government continued to spend but reduced its revenues.

4. Tax reform.

a. When President Reagan first revealed his massive tax simplification plan in 1986, the president actually had more problems obtaining the support of his own party than from the Democrats.

b. The **Tax Reform Act of 1986** was one of the most sweeping alterations in federal tax policy in history.
(1) It eliminated or reduced the value of many tax deductions, removed several million low-income individuals from the

tax rolls, and changed the system of fifteen separate brackets to just two generally lower rates (28 percent and 15 percent).

(2) In 1990, a third bracket of 31 percent was added for those with higher incomes.

(3) In 1993, Congress agreed to President Clinton's proposal to raise the income tax rate to 36 percent for families with incomes over $140,000 and add an additional surcharge of 3.6 percent to those families with incomes over $250,000. Congress also increased the top corporate income tax and an energy tax.

III. FEDERAL EXPENDITURES: WHERE REVENUES GO

A. Federal expenditures.
   1. Comparisons over time are somewhat misleading because they do not take into account changes in the value of the dollar.

B. Among the most important changes of the twentieth century is *the rise of large governments*.
   1. The United States actually has one of the *smallest* public sectors among Western nations relative to the size of the Gross Domestic Product (GDP). **Gross Domestic Product** is Gross National Product minus the value of goods and services produced outside the country.
   2. American governments—national, state, and local—spend an amount equal to one-third of the Gross Domestic Product (GDP).
   3. Expenditures of the national government alone equal over 20 percent of the GNP.
   4. Two conditions associated with government growth in America are the *rise of the national security state* and the *rise of the social service state*.

C. The rise of the national security state.
   1. President Eisenhower coined the phrase **military industrial complex** to characterize the close relationship between the military hierarchy and the defense industry that supplies its hardware needs. The Pentagon wants weapons systems and arms makers want contracts, so they tend to be mutually *supportive*.
   2. After World War II, the "**cold war**" with the Soviet Union resulted in a permanent military establishment and expensive military technology.
      a. In the 1990s, *defense expenditures have decreased* in response to the lessening of tensions in Europe. [see Chapter 20]
      b. The budget of the Department of Defense now constitutes only about one-sixth of all federal expenditures.

   c. Payrolls and pensions constitute a large component of the defense budget, as does research, development, and **procurement** (purchasing) of military hardware.
3. The *cost of advanced technology* makes any weapon, fighter plane, or component more expensive than its predecessors, and **cost overruns** are common.

D. The rise of the social service state.
   1. The **Social Security Act** (passed in 1935) was originally intended to provide a minimal level of sustenance to older Americans.
   2. Lyndon Johnson's **"Great Society"** initiatives in the mid-1960s greatly expanded America's social services network, adding **Medicare** and **Medicaid** to the Social Security system and creating many new programs designed to aid the poor.
   3. Today, more than 45 million Americans receive payments from the Social Security system.
      a. The typical retired worker received nearly $825 a month in 2001.
      b. Disability insurance was included in the 1950s, which included workers who had not retired but were disabled.
      c. Medicare was added to the system in 1965, providing both hospital and physician coverage to the elderly.
   4. Essentially, money is taken from working members of the population and spent on retired members; but *demographic and economic realities* now threaten to dilute this intergenerational agreement.
      a. Economist Eli Ginzberg calculated that in 1945, fifty workers paid taxes to support each Social Security beneficiary.
      b. In 1990, about three workers supported each beneficiary.
      c. By the year 2040, fewer than two workers will be supporting each beneficiary.
   5. Social Security is not the only social policy of the federal government that is costly. The rise of the social service state has contributed to America's growing budget in health, education, job training, and scores of other areas.
      a. *Liberals* often favor these programs to assist individuals and groups in society.
      b. *Conservatives* see them as a drain on the federal treasury.
   E. The rise of the social service state and the national security state together are linked with much of American governmental growth since the end of World War II.

F. Why the increasing federal budget is so difficult to control.
   1. Incrementalism.
      a. **Incrementalism** means that the best predictor of this year's budget is *last year's budget plus a little bit more* (an increment).

b. There is *a never-ending call for budgetary reform.*

c. Causes of incrementalism.

   (1) The support of relevant interests for spending programs makes it difficult to pare the budget.

   (2) The budget is too big to review from scratch each year.

   (3) More and more of federal spending has become "uncontrollable."

2. "Uncontrollable" expenditures.

   a. An **uncontrollable expenditure** is one that is *mandated* under current law or by a previous obligation.

      (1) Uncontrollable expenditures result from policies that make some group automatically eligible for some benefit.

      (2) Congress has in effect obligated itself to pay a certain level of benefits to a particular number of recipients. Such policies are called **entitlements.**

   b. About *two-thirds of the federal budget is uncontrollable*—based on expenditures that are determined not by how much Congress appropriates to an agency but by *how many eligible beneficiaries* there are for a particular program.

   c. Although Congress *legally can* control such expenditures, it could do so only by changing a law or existing benefit levels.

      1. Cutting benefits or tightening eligibility restrictions would provoke a monumental outcry from millions of older voters.

   d. The biggest uncontrollable expenditure is the *Social Security system, including Medicare*, which costs more than $600 billion; other uncontrollable expenditures include veterans aid, agricultural subsidies, military pensions, civil service workers' retirement benefits, and interest on the national debt.

   e. In 1999, President Clinton made financing Social Security his highest priority. He proposed allocating much of the new budget surplus to Social Security and investing some of it in the stock market. Everyone agreed that saving Social Security was a high priority, but not everyone agreed with the president's solutions. As a result, no major changes occurred.

IV. THE BUDGETARY PROCESS

A. Budgetary politics.

1. The main actors in the budgetary process are:

   a. *Interest groups* - lobbying for a group's needs takes place in the agencies, with presidents, and before congressional committees;

   b. *Agencies* - the heads of agencies almost always push for higher budget requests, sending their requests to the Office of

Management and Budget and presenting themselves before congressional committees;

c. *Office of Management and Budget (OMB)* - the OMB is responsible to the president, but the director and staff of the OMB have considerable independence, making them major actors in the annual budget process;
d. *The president* - the president makes the final decisions on what to propose to Congress; the president unveils the proposed budget in early February and then tries to ensure that Congress will stick close to the recommendations;
e. *The Tax Committees in Congress* - the **House Ways and Means Committee** and the **Senate Finance Committee** write the tax codes, subject to the approval of Congress as a whole;
f. *The Budget Committees* and the *Congressional Budget Office (CBO)* - the CBO is the congressional equivalent of the OMB; the CBO and its parent committees—the Senate and House Budget committees—examine revenues and expenditures and propose resolutions to bind Congress within certain limits;
g. *The subject-matter committees* - congressional committees write new laws, which require new expenditures; committee members may use hearings to support larger budgets for them, or to question agency heads about waste or overspending;
h. *The Appropriations Committees* and their *subcommittees* - these committees take policies coming from the subject-matter committees and decide how much to spend; their subcommittees hold hearings on specific agency requests;
i. *The Congress as a whole* - Congress as a whole approves taxes and appropriations; members have a strong interest in delivering federal dollars to their constituents; and
j. *The General Accounting Office (GAO)* - the GAO audits, monitors, and evaluates what agencies are doing with their budgets.

B. The president's budget.
   1. Office of Management and Budget.
      a. In 1921, Congress passed the **Budget and Accounting Act**, requiring presidents to propose an executive budget to Congress and creating the *Bureau of the Budget* to help them.
      b. In the 1970s, President Nixon reorganized the Bureau of the Budget and renamed it the **Office of Management and Budget (OMB)**.
      c. The OMB now supervises preparation of the federal budget and advises the president on budgetary matters.

d. The director of the OMB is a presidential appointee requiring Senate approval.

2. Preparation of the budget: by law, the president *must submit a budget by the first Monday in February.*
   a. The process begins almost a year before, when the OMB communicates with each agency, sounding out its requests and tentatively issuing guidelines.
      (1) The OMB presents an analysis of the economic situation to the president, and they discuss the budgetary outlook and policies.
      (2) The OMB gives guidelines to the agencies, which in turn review current programs and submit to the OMB their projections of budgetary needs for the coming year.
      (3) The OMB reviews these projections and prepares recommendations to the president.
      (4) The president establishes guidelines and targets.
   b. By summer, the president has decided on overall policies and priorities and has established general targets for the budget.
      (1) The OMB conveys the president's decisions to the agencies.
      (2) The OMB advises and assists agencies in preparing their budgets.
   c. During the fall, the agencies submit formal, detailed estimates for their budgets.
      (1) Budget analysts at the OMB pare, investigate, weigh, and meet to consider agency requests.
      (2) The OMB holds hearings, reviews its assessment of the economy, and prepares budget recommendations for the president.
      (3) The president revises and approves the budget message and transmits the budget document to Congress.
   d. In the winter, the budget document is readied for final presidential approval.
      (1) Agencies revise their estimates to conform with the president's decisions.
      (2) The OMB again reviews the economy and then drafts the president's budget message and prepares the budget document.
      (3) The president revises and approves the budget message and transmits the budget document to Congress.

C. Congress and the budget.

1. According to the Constitution, *all federal appropriations must be authorized by Congress*—a control sometimes called the **"power of the purse."**
2. Reforming the process: the **Congressional Budget and Impoundment Act of 1974** was designed to reform the congressional budgetary process.
   a. The act established *a fixed budget calendar*: a timetable mandated by law was set for each step in the budgetary process.
   b. The *Budget Committees in each house* are supposed to *recommend target figures to Congress for the total budget size* by April 1 of each year. By April 15, *Congress is to agree on the total size of the budget*, which guides the *Appropriations Committees* in juggling figures for individual agencies.
   c. The **Congressional Budget Office (CBO)** *advises Congress* on the likely consequences of its budget decisions, *forecasts* revenues, and is a counterweight to the president's OMB.
3. Provisions of the 1974 act:
   a. In April of each year, both houses are expected to agree upon a **budget resolution** which would bind Congress to a total expenditure level that should form the bottom line of all federal spending for all programs.
   b. The congressional budget resolution often requests *that certain changes be made in law*. These changes are legislated in two separate ways:
      (1) Budget **reconciliation** *revises program authorizations* to achieve required savings.
         (a) It usually also includes tax or other revenue adjustments.
         (b) Reconciliation usually comes near the end of the budgetary process.
      (2) An **authorization bill** is an act of Congress that *establishes a discretionary government program or an entitlement*, or that *continues or changes* such programs.
         (a) Authorizations specify program goals, and set the maximum amount that discretionary programs may spend.
         (b) For entitlement programs, an authorization sets or changes eligibility standards and benefits.
         (c) An additional measure, termed an **appropriations bill,** must be passed to *actually fund* programs established by authorizations bills. The appropriations bills cannot

exceed the amount of money authorized for a program, but they may appropriate less than was authorized.

4. Results of the 1974 reforms.
   a. The new system was supposed to force Congress *to consider the budget (both projected expenditures and projected revenues) as a whole.*
   b. Congressional budgets have been in the red every year since the 1974 amendments, and the red ink has grown worse (not better). Presidents have made matters worse by submitting budget proposals containing large deficits.
   c. Congress has often failed to meet its own budgetary timetable.
   d. In many instances, Congress has not been able to reach agreement and pass appropriations bills at all. Instead of an appropriations bill, Congress has sometimes passed **continuing resolutions**—laws that allow agencies to spend at the previous year's level.
   e. On some occasions, appropriations bills have been lumped together in one enormous and complex bill (known as **omnibus bills**), which precludes adequate review by individual members of Congress and forces the president to either accept unwanted provisions or veto the funding for the entire government.
   f. The 1974 reforms have helped Congress view the entire budget early in the process.
   g. The problem is *not so much the procedure* as agreement over *how scarce resources should be spent.*
5. More reforms.
   a. Yearly deficits mushroomed during the Reagan administration (1981-1988).
   b. By 1985, Congress was desperate—President Reagan refused to consider tax increases to pay for federal spending and continued to submit budgets that contained huge deficits.
   c. In response to growing frustration at its inability to substantially reduce annual budget deficits, Congress enacted the *Balanced Budget and Emergency Deficit Control Act* (1985), better known as the **Gramm-Rudman-Hollings** Act.
   d. As amended in 1987, the act mandated maximum allowable deficit levels for each year until 1993—at which point the budget was supposed to be in balance. If Congress failed to meet the deficit goals, automatic across-the-board spending cuts (called **sequestrations**) were to be ordered by the president, although a number of programs were exempt from the process.
   e. In 1990, Congress decided to shift the focus from controlling the size of the deficit (which was the trigger for sequestration) to

controlling increases in spending (under which the sheer size of the deficit would not matter).

(1) Discretionary spending was divided into three categories—domestic, defense, and international.

(2) Spending for entitlement programs such as Medicare were placed on a "pay-as-you-go" basis.

(3) While Congress shifted to keeping a lid on expenditures, it allowed events beyond its control—such as war or a recession—to increase the size of the deficit without penalty. The *bottom line was a bigger deficit.*

(4) The 1974 Budget Act was intended to give Congress more control of overall budget priorities; but by segregating the budget into three separate categories, the 1990 law effectively *precluded Congress from shifting budget priorities across categories.*

(5) The new law also altered the balance of power between Congress and the White House, giving the Office of Management and Budget closer scrutiny of legislation as it is crafted and further limiting the role of the congressional Budget Committees.

(6) Under the act, the president has the authority to determine whether a supplemental spending is an emergency measure *exempt* from automatic spending cuts.

(7) Yearly deficits continued to climb and have continued into the Clinton administration.

(8) In 1995, the new Republican majorities in each house were determined to balance the budget within 7 years, arguing for substantial cuts in the rate of growth of such popular entitlements programs as Medicaid and the outright elimination of many other programs. The president agreed with the goal—but on his terms.

V. UNDERSTANDING BUDGETING

A. Democracy and budgeting.

1. Almost all democracies have seen a substantial growth in government in the twentieth century.
2. Economists Allen Meltzer and Scott Richard argue that *government grows in a democracy* because of the *equality of suffrage.*
   a. Poorer voters will always use their votes to support public policies that redistribute benefits from the rich to the poor.

b. The most rapidly growing expenditures are items like Social Security, Medicaid, Medicare, and social welfare programs (all of which benefit the poor more than the rich).
3. One often thinks of elites—particularly corporate elites—as being opposed to big government.
   a. However, Lockheed and Chrysler corporations have appealed to the government for large bailouts when times got rough.
   b. Corporations support a big government that offers them contracts, subsidies, and other benefits.
4. Poor and rich voters alike have voted for parties and politicians who promised them benefits.
   a. Policymakers spend money for things voters like (and will remember on election day).
   b. Citizens are not the unwilling victims of big government and its big taxes; they are at least co-conspirators.
5. Government also grows by responding to groups and their demands.
6. Some politicians compete for votes by promising *not* to spend money (such as Ronald Reagan).
7. Americans have chosen to tax less and spend less on public services than almost all other democracies with developed economics. [see Chapter 1]
   a. Americans want to spend but not pay taxes.
   b. Being a democracy, that is exactly what the government does—and the inevitable result is red ink.

B. The budget and the scope of government.
   1. In many ways, the budget *is* the scope of government—the bigger the budget, the bigger the government.
   2. The budget can be a force for reining in the government as well as for expanding its role.
   3. One could accurately characterize policy-making in the American government since 1980 as the "*politics of scarcity*" — scarcity of funds for programs like health care reform and education.
   4. America's large budget deficit is *as much a constraint on government as it is evidence of a burgeoning public sector.*

KEY TERMS AND CONCEPTS

Appropriations bill: bill passed annually to fund an authorized program.

Authorization bill: an act of Congress that establishes a discretionary government program or an entitlement, or that continues or changes such programs.

Budget: a policy document that allocates burdens (taxes) and benefits (expenditures).

Budget resolution: a bill setting limits on expenditures based on revenue projections, agreed to by both houses of Congress in April each year.

Congressional Budget Office (CBO): research agency of Congress, responsible to it for providing analyses of budget proposals, revenue forecasts and related information.

Continuing resolutions: laws that allow agencies to spend at the previous year's level.

Deficit: occurs when government spends more money than it receives in taxes in the fiscal year.

Entitlements: expenditures for which the total amount spent is not by Congressional appropriation, but rather by rules of eligibility established by Congress.

Expenditures: money spent by the government in any one year.

Federal debt: all of the money borrowed by the government over the years that is still outstanding.

House Ways and Means Committee: responsible for originating all revenue bills.

Income tax: the portion of money individuals are required to pay to the government from the money they earned.

Incrementalism: the best predictor of this year's budget is last year's budget plus a little bit more.

Medicare: in 1965, this program was added to Social Security to provide hospital and physician coverage to the elderly.

Reconciliation: revisions of program authorizations to make the final budget meet the limits of the budget resolution, usually occurring toward the end of the budgetary process.

Revenues: money received by the government in any given year.

Senate Finance Committee: responsible for writing the tax code.

Sixteenth Amendment: passed in 1913, permits Congress to levy an income tax.

Social Security Act (1935): passed to provide a minimal level of sustenance to older Americans.

Tax expenditures: revenue losses due to special exemptions, exclusions, and deductions.

Uncontrollable expenditures: result from policies that make some group automatically eligible for benefits.

TEACHING IDEAS: CLASS DISCUSSION AND STUDENT PROJECTS

- *Tax expenditures* are essentially monies that government could collect but does not because they are exempted from taxation. The Office of Management and Budget estimated that the total tax expenditures in 2001 would be more than $700 billion—about one-third of the total federal receipts (see Table 14.1). If this estimate is correct, the government could close its budget deficit by taxing things it does not currently tax, such as Social Security benefits, pension fund contributions, and charitable contributions. Ask your class to vote on whether such taxes should be adopted. Ask them to analyze political and social implications of the positions they take.

- For class discussion, have students debate the value of a balanced budget amendment. In particular, have them examine the costs and benefits of balancing the budget given that most of the budget expenditures are mandated. Insist that students identify which benefits and which obligations should be the first to go.

- For a reading and writing connection, have students identify and investigate the number of federal agencies they and their families received benefits from within the last five years. Then have them evaluate the importance of these services to their and their families' standard of living. Finally, have them identify what they would have to do if these services were no longer available to them.

- If teaching at a state institution, have students investigate the sources of funding of higher education in the state. What proportion of costs does their student tuition cover? Who pays for the rest? What justification is there for state subsidies of higher education, i.e., who benefits?

- Have students locate public opinion data on public support for government programs (i.e., spending questions), using data sources such as the National Elections Studies or General Social Survey available on the Internet. Have students assess the extent to which the public supports reducing expenditures in various areas, as well as the extent to which the level of support depends on the exact question wording used. Based on these aggregate patterns, do students believe that support for reductions in spending generally applies to all government spending—or only spending on programs that benefit others?

- Have students access a website that provides simulation of the federal budget or provides student with other budgetary tradeoff or analysis games. Develop a current "balanced" budget. Have students compare their decisions in class, debating the value of their expenditure and revenue choices. (See, for example, the budget game available at www.washingtonpost.com. Also, try searching for "federal balanced budget game" to see other current options.)

- Invite a staff member from a representative's office to brief the class about the current status of the federal budget. Who's involved? Who wants what out of the budget? If a representative or their staffer is not available, consider inviting a state senator or representative to discuss the same questions, as well as differences between the federal and state budgetary process.

BACKGROUND READING

Eisner, Robert. The Great Deficit Scares: The Federal Budget, Trade, and Social Security. Washington, DC: Brookings Institution. 1997.

Kettl, Donald F. Deficit Politics: Public Budgeting in Its Institutional and Historical Context. NY: MacMillan. 1992.

Pechman, Joseph A. Federal Tax Policy. 5th ed. Washington, DC: Brookings Institution. 1987.

Phillips, Kevin. The Politics of Rich and Poor: Wealth and the American Electorate. NY: Random House. 1990.

Schick, Allen, with the assistance of Felix LoStracco. The Federal Budget: Politics, Policy Process. 2000. Washington: Brookings Institution.

Tomkin, Shelley Lynne. Inside OMB: Politics and Process in the President's Budget Office. Armonk, NY: M.E. Sharpe. 1998.

Wildavsky, Aaron. The New Politics of the Budgetary Process. 2nd ed. NY: HarperCollins. 1992.

MEDIA SUGGESTIONS

Getting Out of Business: Privatization and the Modern State. A video program distributed by Films for the Humanities and Sciences which examines government benefits to industry through providing employment and infrastructure.

CHAPTER FIFTEEN: THE FEDERAL BUREAUCRACY

PEDAGOGICAL FEATURES

LEARNING OBJECTIVES

After studying this chapter, students should be able to:

- Identify common "myths" that surround the bureaucracy and either justify or refute them.

- Describe in what ways the permanent bureaucracy is broadly representative of the American people.

- Trace the development of the American bureaucracy from the "spoils system" to the "merit system."
- Explain the two basic procedures through which most federal bureaucrats obtain their jobs.
- Identify and describe several theories of the functions and organization of bureaucracies.
- Describe the functions of the four basic types of federal agencies: cabinet departments, regulatory agencies, government corporations, and independent executive agencies.
- Understand what the textbook means when it says that bureaucracies are essentially *implementors* of policy, why implementation of policy can break down.
- Determine the importance of *administrative routine* and *administrative discretion.*
- Examine the conditions that are necessary for policy implementation to be effective.
- Contrast *command-and-control policy* of government regulation with an *incentive system* of regulation.
- Evaluate the effects that the movement toward *deregulation* has had on the American economy.
- Determine how presidents try to control the bureaucracy and how Congress tries to control the bureaucracy.
- Investigate the importance of *iron triangles* and issue networks.
- Explain the relationship between democratic theory and the operations of bureaucracies.

CHAPTER OVERVIEW

INTRODUCTION

Once Congress, the president or the Supreme Court makes a policy decision, it is most likely that bureaucrats must step in to implement those decisions. Since bureaucrats are typically less visible and are not elected to their positions, their actions and power are often subjects of considerable debate. This chapter describes who government bureaucrats are, the functions they perform and their relationships to the three branches of government designated in the constitution.

THE BUREAUCRATS

Bureaucrats are typically much less visible than the president or members of Congress. This section examines some myths about bureaucrats and shows who they are, how they got their jobs, and what they do.

There are approximately 3 million civilian bureaucrats (19 million if state and local public employees are included). Although Congress has ordered federal agencies to make special efforts to recruit and promote previously disadvantaged groups, *women and nonwhites are still clustered in the lower ranks.* As a whole, however, the permanent bureaucracy is more broadly representative of the American people than legislators, judges, or presidential appointees in the executive branch.

Bureaucrats do much more than simply follow orders: bureaucrats possess crucial information and expertise that make them partners with the president and Congress in making decisions about public policy. Those who compose the bureaucracy perform most of the vital services provided by the federal government. Despite all the complaints about bureaucracies, the vast majority of tasks carried out by governments at all levels are noncontroversial. Bureaucrats perform a wide variety of routine governmental tasks in a perfectly acceptable manner.

Until approximately 100 years ago, a person got a job with the government through the **patronage** system (a hiring and promotion system based on knowing the right people). Under this **"spoils system,"** nineteenth century presidents staffed the government with their friends and allies. Today, most federal agencies are covered by some sort of **civil service** system. The rationale for all civil service systems rests on the idea of *merit* and the desire to create a *nonpartisan* government service. The **Office of Personnel Management (OPM)** is in charge of hiring for most agencies of the federal government.

After serving a probationary period, civil servants are *protected.* It is difficult to fire a civil service employee after the probationary period: an employee can appeal his or her dismissal, which can consume weeks, months, or even years. Ensuring a nonpartisan civil service requires that workers have protection from dismissals that are politically motivated. At the very top of the civil service system are about 9000 members of the **Senior Executive Service**. These executives earn high salaries and may be moved from one agency to another as leadership needs change.

The other route to federal jobs involves recruiting from the *plum book*, which lists top federal jobs available for direct presidential appointment (often with Senate confirmation). Every incoming president launches a nationwide talent search to fill these positions (approximately 300 of them). Most will be "in-and-outers" who stay for a while and leave; they soon learn that senior civil servants know more, have been there longer, and will outlast them.

This chapter introduces students to three prominent theories about bureaucracy. The classic conception of bureaucracy was advanced by the German sociologist **Max Weber**, who stressed that the bureaucracy was a *"rational"* way for a modern society to conduct its business. To Weber, a **bureaucracy** depends upon certain elements, including a hierarchical authority structure, task specialization, and extensive rules which allow similar cases to be handled in similar ways. By contrast, some writers see bureaucracies as essentially *"acquisitive,"* busily maximizing their budgets and expanding their powers. Not only can bureaucracies be acquisitive, they can also be *monopolistic*. No matter how the bureaucracies behave, they will not lose their clients, so there is no competitive pressure to force them to improve service. Finally, there are those who view bureaucracies as *ambling and groping*, affected by chance. Cohen, March, and Olsen suggest that organizations operate by trial and error. Faced with a particular problem, members of an organization may pull an idea from the *"garbage can" of ideas* (one of the many ideas that may be floating around an organization) and use it.

HOW BUREAUCRACIES ARE ORGANIZED

In general, there are four types of bureaucracies: cabinet departments, regulatory agencies, government corporations, and independent executive agencies. Each of the fourteen **cabinet departments** is headed by a secretary (except the Department of Justice, which is headed by the attorney general); all are chosen by the president and approved by the Senate. Beneath the secretary are undersecretaries, deputy undersecretaries, and assistant secretaries. Each department manages specific policy areas, and each has its own budget and staff.

Each of the **independent regulatory agencies** has responsibility for some sector of the economy. Regulatory agencies make and enforce rules designed to protect the public interest; they also judge disputes over those rules.

Government corporations provide a service that could be handled by the private sector. They typically charge for their services, though often at cheaper rates than the consumer would pay a private sector producer.

The **independent executive agencies** are not part of the cabinet departments and generally do not have regulatory functions. They usually perform specialized functions.

BUREAUCRACIES AS IMPLEMENTORS

As policymakers, bureaucrats play three key roles: they are policy *implementors*; they *administer* public policy; and they are *regulators*. **Policy implementation** occurs when the bureaucracy carries out decisions of Congress, the president, and even the courts. Public policies are *rarely self-executing*: bureaucrats translate legislative policy goals into programs.

Policy implementation does not always work well, and bureaucrats usually take the blame when it does not. Reasons why implementation may break down include faulty program design, lack of clarity in the laws bureaucrats administer, lack of resources, the following of *standard operating procedures*, and dispersal of policy responsibility among several units of the bureaucracy.

Administrative discretion is the authority of administrative actors to select among various responses to a given problem. Discretion is greatest when rules do not fit a case; but even in agencies with elaborate rules and regulations—especially when more than one rule fits—there is still room for discretion. Michael Lipsky coined the phrase **street-level bureaucrats** to refer to those bureaucrats who are in constant contact with the public and have considerable discretion (including police officers, welfare workers, and lower court judges).

Implementation can be effective if goals are clear and the means to achieve the goals are unambiguous. The **Voting Rights Act of 1965** illustrates a program that was successfully implemented because its goal was clear: to register African-Americans to vote in southern counties where their voting rights had been denied for years. The means to achieve the goals were also clear: the act singled out six states in the Deep South in which the number of African-American registered voters was minuscule. The Justice Department was ordered to send federal registrars to each county in those states to register qualified voters. Implementation of this act helped bring the vote to some 300,000 African-Americans in less than a year.

BUREAUCRACIES AS REGULATORS

Government **regulation** is the use of governmental authority to control or change some practice in the private sector. This is the most controversial role of the bureaucracies, yet Congress gives them broad mandates to regulate activates as diverse as interest rates, the location of nuclear power plants, and food additives.

Until 1887, the federal government made almost no regulatory policies. Even the minimum regulatory powers of state and local governments were disputed. In 1887, Congress created the first regulatory agency, the **Interstate Commerce Commission (ICC)**, charged with regulating the railroads, their prices, and their services to farmers.

Most agencies charged with regulation first have to develop a set of rules (often called *guidelines*); guidelines are developed in consultation with (and sometimes with the agreement of) the people or industries being regulated. The agency must then apply and enforce its rules and guidelines, either in court or through its own administrative procedures.

Almost every regulatory policy was created to achieve some desirable social goal. Charles L. Schultze (chairman of President Carter's Council of Economic Advisors) is a critic of the current state of federal regulation, which he described as **command-and-control policy**: the government tells business how to reach certain goals, checks that these commands are followed, and punishes offenders. Schultze prefers an **incentive system**. Defenders of the command-and-control system of regulation compare it to preventive medicine; it is designed to minimize problems such as pollution or workplace accidents before they become too severe.

Government regulation of the American economy and society has grown in recent decades. The budgets of regulatory agencies, their level of employment, and the number of rules they issue are all increasing. Opponents of government regulation contend that the rapid increase in the number and scope of environmental regulations during the past two decades has stifled economic growth. Supporters of government regulation argue that such regulations are essential to protect the nation's air, land, and water (and the people who use it).

The idea behind deregulation – the lifting of government restrictions on business, industry, and professional activities – is that the number and complexity of regulatory policies have made regulation too complicated and burdensome. To critics, the problem with regulation is that it raises prices, distorts market forces, and – worst of all – does not work. Not everyone, however, believes that deregulation is in the nation's best interest. Many regulations have proved beneficial to Americans. As a result of government regulations, we breathe cleaner air, we have lower levels of lead in our blood, miners are safer at work, seacoasts have been preserved, and children are more likely to survive infancy.

UNDERSTANDING BUREAUCRACIES

In democratic theory, popular control of government depends on elections, but we could not possibly elect the 4.2 million federal civilian and military employees (or even the few thousand top men and women). However, the fact that voters do not elect civil servants does not mean that bureaucracies cannot respond to and *represent* the public's interests. Much depends on *whether bureaucracies are effectively controlled by the policymakers* that citizens do elect—the president and Congress.

One crucial explanation for the difficulty presidents and Congress face in controlling bureaucracies relates to the role of iron triangles and issue networks. When agencies, groups, and committees all depend on one another and are in close, frequent contact, they form **iron triangles** (or **subgovernments**). Iron triangles have dominated some areas of domestic policy-making by combining internal consensus with a virtual monopoly on information in their area. Iron triangles are characterized by *mutual dependency*, in which each element provides key services, information, or policy for the others (illustrated by the *tobacco triangle*). These subgovernments can add a strong decentralizing and fragmenting element to the policy-making process. Despite the fact that subgovernments often are able to dominate policy-making for decades, they are not indestructible; policies of the tobacco triangle, for one, have increasingly come under fire from health authorities.

The federal bureaucracy *has not grown over the past two generations*; in fact, the bureaucracy has *shrunk* in size relative to the population it serves. Originally, the federal bureaucracy had a modest role; but as the economy and the society of the United States changed, additional demands were made on government. Considering the more active role the bureaucracy is expected to play in dealing with social and economic problems, a good case can be made that the bureaucracy is actually too *small* for many of the tasks currently assigned to it (such as the control of illicit drugs or the protection of the environment).

CHAPTER OUTLINE

I. THE BUREAUCRATS

A. Bureaucratic agencies.

1. Each bureaucratic agency is created by Congress, which sets its budget and writes the policies it administers.
2. Most agencies are responsible to the president, whose administrative responsibilities are only vaguely hinted at in the constitutional obligation "to take care that the laws shall be faithfully executed."
3. How to manage and control bureaucracies is a central problem of democratic government.

B. Bureaucrats have been the scapegoats of American politics. Following are some of the most prevalent *myths* (and responses):

1. *Americans dislike bureaucrats.* Despite the rhetoric about bureaucracies, Americans are generally satisfied with bureaucrats and the treatment they get from them.
2. *Most federal bureaucrats work in Washington, D.C.* Only about seven percent of three million federal civilian employees work in Washington.
3. *Bureaucracies are growing bigger each year.* Almost all the growth in the number of public employees has occurred in *state and local* governments. As a percentage of America's total work force, *federal* government employment has actually been shrinking and now amounts to about three percent of all civilian jobs.
4. *Bureaucracies are ineffective, inefficient, and always mired in red tape.* Bureaucracy is simply a way of organizing people to perform work. Bureaucracies may be inefficient at times, but no one has yet demonstrated that government bureaucracies are more or less inefficient, ineffective, or mired in red tape than private bureaucracies.

C. Bureaucrats do much more than simply follow orders.

1. Bureaucrats possess crucial information and expertise that make them partners with the president and Congress in making decisions about public policy.
2. Those who compose the bureaucracy perform most of the vital services provided by the federal government.

3. Despite all the complaints about bureaucracies, the vast majority of tasks carried out by governments at all levels are noncontroversial.
4. Bureaucrats perform a wide variety of routine governmental tasks in a perfectly acceptable manner.
5. Because of their expertise, they inevitably have some discretion in carrying out policy decisions.

D. Federal employment.
1. The *Department of Defense (DOD)* employs about one-fourth of federal *civilian* workers in addition to the 1.5 million men and women in uniform. Altogether, the DOD makes up more than half of the federal bureaucracy.
2. The *Postal Service* accounts for an additional 25 percent of federal civilian employees.
3. The various *health professions* constitute nearly 10 percent; the *Department of Veterans Affairs* (clearly related to national defense) has more than 220,000 employees; and *all other functions of government* are handled by the remaining *20 percent* of federal employees.

E. Who they are and how they got there.
1. There are approximately three million civil bureaucrats (9 million if state and local public employees are included).
2. Although Congress has ordered federal agencies to make special efforts to recruit and promote previously disadvantaged groups, *women and nonwhites are still clustered in the lower ranks.*
3. As a whole, the permanent bureaucracy is more broadly representative of the American people than legislators, judges, or presidential appointees in the executive branch.
4. The diversity of employees in bureaucratic jobs mirrors the diversity of private sector jobs.

F. Civil Service: from patronage to protection.
1. Until approximately one hundred years ago, a person got a job with the government through the **patronage** system (a hiring and promotion system based on knowing the right people).
   a. Under this **"spoils system,"** nineteenth century presidents staffed the government with their friends and allies.
   b. In a tragic irony of history, Charles Guiteau (a disappointed office seeker) actually helped end this system of federal appointments: frustrated because President James A. Garfield would not give him a job, Guiteau shot and killed the president.
   c. Vice President Chester A. Arthur (who then became president) surprised his critics by pushing for passage of the **Pendleton Civil Service Act** (1883), which created the federal Civil Service.

2. Today, most federal agencies are covered by some sort of civil service system.
3. The rationale for all **civil service** systems rests on the idea of *merit* and the desire to create a *nonpartisan* government service.
   a. The **merit principle** (using examinations and promotion ratings) is intended to produce administration by people with talent and skill.
   b. Creating a nonpartisan civil service means insulating government workers from the risk of being fired when a new party comes to power.
   c. The **Hatch Act** (1939, amended 1993) also prohibits those employees from *active participation* in partisan politics.
4. The **Office of Personnel Management (OPM)** is in charge of hiring for most agencies of the federal government.
   a. For each position that is open, the OPM will send three names to the agency (known as the *rule of three*).
   b. Once hired, a person is assigned a **GS (General Schedule) rating**, ranging from GS 1 to GS 18.
   c. After a probationary period, civil servants are *protected*; it is difficult to fire a civil service employee after the probationary period. An employee can appeal his or her dismissal, which can consume weeks, months, or even years. (The right of appeal must be exhausted before one's paycheck stops.)
      (1) Ensuring a nonpartisan civil service requires that workers have protection from dismissals that are politically motivated.
      (2) Protecting all workers against political firings may also protect a few from dismissal for good cause.
5. At the very top of the civil service system are about 9,000 members of the **Senior Executive Service**. These executives earn high salaries and may be moved from one agency to another as leadership needs change.
6. The other route to federal jobs: recruiting from the *plum book.*
   a. Congress publishes the *plum book*, which lists top federal jobs available for direct presidential appointment (often with Senate confirmation).
   b. Every incoming president launches a nationwide talent search to fill these positions (approximately 300 of them).
   c. Presidents look for individuals who combine executive talent, political skills, and policy views similar to those of the president.
   d. Some positions—especially ambassadorships—go to large campaign contributors.

e. Most will be political appointees, "in-and-outers" who stay for a while and then leave; they soon learn that senior civil servants know more, have been there longer, and will outlast them.
f. Most find it difficult to exercise real control over much of what their subordinates do: the security of the civil servants' jobs combined with the transience (and even ignorance) of their superiors contribute to the bureaucracy's resistance to change.

II. WHAT THEY DO: SOME THEORIES ABOUT DEMOCRACY

A. Three theories.

1. The Weberian model.
   a. The classic conception of bureaucracy was advanced by the German sociologist Max Weber, who stressed that the bureaucracy was a *"rational"* way for a modern society to conduct its business.
   b. To Weber, a **bureaucracy** depends upon certain elements.
      (1) It has a *hierarchical authority structure*, in which power flows from the top down and responsibility from the bottom up.
      (2) It uses *task specialization*, so that experts instead of amateurs perform technical jobs.
      (3) It develops extensive *rules*, which allow similar cases to be handled in similar ways.
   c. Bureaucrats work on the *merit principle*, in which entrance and promotion are on the basis of demonstrated abilities.
   d. Bureaucracies behave with *impersonality* so that all clients are treated impartially.
2. The acquisitive, monopolistic bureaucracy.
   a. Some writers see bureaucracies as essentially "*acquisitive,*" busily maximizing their budgets and expanding their powers.
   b. Conservative economist William Niskanen believes that bureaucracies are themselves largely responsible for the growth of modern governments.
      (1) Bureaucratic administrators are committed to the "products" they "sell" (such as national security, education, or public health), and their piece of the government's total budget pie is perceived as a good measure of how highly their product is valued.
      (2) Administrators take more professional pride in running a large, well-staffed agency than a small, unimportant one.
      (3) Bureaucracies may even combine with Congress to expand big government.

c. Not only can bureaucracies be acquisitive, they can also be *monopolistic*. No matter how the bureaucracies behave, they will not lose their clients, so there is no competitive pressure to force them to improve service.
    (1) There is usually no alternative to the local fire department or water supply system; certainly, there is no alternative to the national defense system.
    (2) Only the wealthy really have an alternative to the local school system, the Social Security system, or Medicare.
d. Many conservative (and some liberal) critics of bureaucracy have favored *privatizing* some bureaucratic services to cut back on their monolithic and monopolistic power.

3. Garbage cans and bureaucracies.
    a. One view of bureaucracies sees them as *ambling and groping*, affected by chance.
    b. Cohen, March, and Olsen suggest that organizations operate by trial and error.
        (1) Faced with a particular problem, members of an organization may pull an idea from the *"garbage can" of ideas* (one of the many ideas that may be floating around an organization) and use it.
        (2) Organizations are not necessarily trying to find solutions to problems; just as often, *solutions are in search of problems* (as when a department gets a new computer and then discovers how many tasks it has that need computerizing).

III. HOW BUREAUCRACIES ARE ORGANIZED

A. In general, there are four types of bureaucracies: *cabinet departments, regulatory agencies, government corporations*, and *independent executive agencies*.

B. The cabinet departments.
    1. Each of the fourteen **cabinet departments** is headed by a secretary (except the Department of Justice, which is headed by the attorney general); all are chosen by the president and approved by the Senate.
        a. Beneath the secretary are undersecretaries, deputy undersecretaries, and assistant secretaries.
        b. Each department manages specific policy areas, and each has its own budget and staff.
    2. The real work of a department is done in the **bureaus** (sometimes designated by other names such as *service*, *office*, or *administration*).
    3. From the 1970s until 1995, the Department of Health and Human Services was the largest federal department in dollars spent (although

the Department of Defense still had more employees). The Social Security Administration became an independent agency in 1995, spending one-third of the federal budget on the massive programs of Social Security and Medicare.

C. The regulatory agencies.
   1. Each of the **independent regulatory agencies** has responsibility for some sector of the economy.
      a. Regulatory agencies make and enforce rules designed to protect the public interest; they also judge disputes over those rules.
      b. Their powers are so far-reaching that they are sometimes called "*the fourth branch of government*" (a term that has also been applied to other institutions, such as the mass media).
   2. They are sometimes called the "alphabet soup" of American government because most such agencies are known by their initials: ICC (Interstate Commission), FRB (Federal Reserve Board), NLRB (National Labor Relations Board), FCC (Federal Communications Commission), FTC (Federal Trade Commission), SEC (Securities and Exchange Commission).
   3. Each of the agencies is governed by a small commission, appointed by the president for fixed terms of office and confirmed by the Senate; regulatory commission members cannot be fired by the president.
   4. Critics often point to the **"capture" theory**—the view that the close connection between the regulators and the industries they regulate has meant that the agencies have become the "captives" of industry.

D. The government corporations.
   1. **Government corporations** provide a service that could be handled by the private sector.
   2. They typically charge for their services, though often at cheaper rates than the consumer would pay a private sector producer.
   3. Examples include the Tennessee Valley Authority (TVA), Amtrak, and the Federal Deposit Insurance Corporation (FDIC); the U.S. Postal Service is the largest of the government corporations.

E. The independent executive agencies.
   1. The **independent executive agencies** are not part of the cabinet departments and generally do not have regulatory functions; they usually perform specialized functions.
   2. Their administrators are typically appointed by the president and serve at his pleasure.
   3. Examples include the General Services Administration (GSA), National Science Foundation (NSF), and National Aeronautics and Space Administration (NASA).

IV. BUREAUCRACIES AS IMPLEMENTORS

A. As policymakers, bureaucrats play three key roles: they are policy *implementors*; they *administer* public policy; and they are *regulators*.

B. Policy **implementation** occurs when the bureaucracy carries out decisions of Congress, the president, and even the courts.
   1. Public policies are *rarely self-executing*: bureaucrats translate legislative policy goals into programs.
   2. Congress typically announces the goals of a policy in broad terms, sets up an administrative apparatus, and leaves the bureaucracy the task of working out the details of the program.

C. Three elements of implementation:
   1. Creation of a new agency or assignment of responsibility to an old one;
   2. Translation of policy goals into operational rules of thumb; development of guidelines; and
   2. Coordination of resources and personnel to achieve the intended goals.

D. Reasons why implementation may break down (policy implementation does not always work well, and bureaucrats usually take the blame when it does not):
   1. *Faulty program design* - a policy or program may be defective in its basic theoretical conception.
   2. *Lack of clarity* - bureaucracies are often asked to implement unclear laws; members of Congress can thus escape the messy details, and blame for the implementation decisions can be placed elsewhere.
   3. *Lack of resources* - as big as bureaucracy may appear, it frequently lacks the staff (along with the necessary training, funding, supplies, and equipment) to carry out the tasks it has been assigned to do; agencies may also lack the authority to meet their responsibilities.
   4. *Administrative routine* - much of administration involves a routine in which bureaucrats follow **standard operating procedures (SOPs)** to help them make numerous everyday decisions.
      a. SOPs bring uniformity to complex organizations.
      b. Justice is better served if rules are applied uniformly.
      c. Uniformity also makes personnel interchangeable.
      d. Routines are essential to bureaucracy (but they also become frustrating to citizens, who term them **"red tape"** when they do not appear to appropriately address a situation, and may become obstacles to action).

5. *Administrators' dispositions* - paradoxically, bureaucrats operate not only within the confines of routines but often with considerable *discretion to behave independently.*
   a. **Administrative discretion** is the authority of administrative actors to select among various responses to a given problem.
   b. Discretion is greatest when rules do not fit a case; but even in agencies with elaborate rules and regulations—especially when more than one rule fits—there is still room for discretion.
   c. Michael Lipsky coined the phrase **street-level bureaucrats** to refer to those bureaucrats who are in constant contact with the public and have considerable discretion (including police officers, welfare workers, and lower court judges).
   d. How bureaucrats exercise discretion depends on their dispositions about the policies and rules they administer; although bureaucrats may be indifferent to the implementation of many policies, others will be in conflict with their policy views or personal or organizational interests.
   e. Controlling the exercise of discretion is a difficult task: it is not easy to fire bureaucrats in the Civil Service, and removing appointed officials may be politically embarrassing to the president.
   f. The government relies heavily on rules to limit the discretion of implementors; however, these rules often end up creating new obstacles to effective and efficient governing.
6. *Fragmentation* - responsibility for a policy is sometimes dispersed among several units within the bureaucracy.
   a. This diffusion of responsibility makes the coordination of policies both time-consuming and difficult.
   b. Sometimes those who are supposed to administer a law receive contradictory signals from different agencies.
   c. Hyperpluralism and the decentralization of power make it difficult to reorganize government.
      (1) Bureaus have strong support from interest groups and interest groups try to forge common links with bureaucracies and congressional committees.
      (2) These iron triangles tend to decentralize policy-making, thereby contributing to hyperpluralism.

E. A case study: the Voting Rights Act of 1965.
   1. Implementation can be effective if goals are clear and the means to achieve the goals are unambiguous.

2. The **Voting Rights Act of 1965** was successfully implemented because its goal was clear: to register African-Americans to vote in southern counties where their voting rights had been denied for years.
    a. The act singled out six states in the Deep South in which the number of African-American registered voters was minuscule.
    b. The Justice Department was ordered to send federal registrars to each county in those states to register qualified voters.
    c. Congress outlawed literacy tests and other tests previously used to discriminate against African-American registrants.
3. Implementation of this act helped bring the vote to some 300,000 African-Americans in less than a year.

V. BUREAUCRACIES AS REGULATORS

A. Regulation in the economy and in everyday life.
1. Government **regulation** is the use of governmental authority to control or change some practice in the private sector.
2. This is the most controversial role of the bureaucracies, yet Congress gives them broad mandates to regulate activities as diverse as interest rates, the location of nuclear power plants, and food additives.
3. Everyday life itself is the subject of bureaucratic regulation; almost all bureaucratic agencies—not merely the ones called independent regulatory agencies—are in the regulatory business.
4. Most government regulation is clearly in the public interest. For example, the U.S. Department of Agriculture is charged with regulating the quality of meat products.

B. Regulation: how it grew, how it works.
1. Until 1887, the federal government made almost no regulatory policies.
    a. Even the minimum regulatory powers of state and local governments were disputed.
    b. In 1877, the Supreme Court upheld the right of government to regulate the business operations of a firm (*Munn* v. *Illinois*).
    c. In 1887, Congress created the first regulatory agency, the **Interstate Commerce Commission (ICC)**, charged with regulating the railroads, their prices, and their services to farmers.
2. Most agencies charged with regulation first have to *develop a set of rules* (often called *guidelines*); guidelines are developed in consultation with (and sometimes with the agreement of) the people or industries being regulated.
3. The agency must then apply and enforce its rules and guidelines, either in court or through its own administrative procedures.

a. Sometimes it waits for complaints to come to it (as the Equal Employment Opportunity Commission does).
b. Sometimes it sends inspectors into the field (as the Occupational Safety and Health Administration does).
c. Sometimes it requires applicants for a permit or license to demonstrate performance consistent with congressional goals and agency rules (as the Federal Communications Commission does).

4. All regulation contains these elements:
   a. a grant of power and set of directions from Congress;
   b. a set of rules and guidelines by the regulatory agency itself; and
   c. some means of enforcing compliance with congressional goals and agency regulations.

C. How should we regulate?
   1. Almost every regulatory policy was created to achieve some desirable social goal.
   2. Charles L. Schultze (chairman of President Carter's Council of Economic Advisors) is a critic of the current state of federal regulation, which he described as **command-and-control policy**: the government tells business how to reach certain goals, checks that these commands are followed, and punishes offenders. Schultze preferred an **incentive system.**
   3. Defenders of the command-and-control system of regulation compare it to preventive medicine; it is designed to minimize pollution or workplace accidents before they become too severe.

D. Government regulation of the American economy and society has grown in recent decades.
   1. The budgets of regulatory agencies, their level of employment, and the number of rules they issue are all increasing—and did so even during the Reagan administration.
   2. Opponents of government regulation contend that the rapid increase in the number and scope of environmental regulations during the past two decades has stifled economic growth.
   3. Supporters of government regulation argue that such regulations are essential to protect the nation's air, land, and water (and the people who use it).

E. Toward deregulation.
   1. The idea behind **deregulation** is that the number and complexity of regulatory policies have made regulation too complex and burdensome.
   2. Critics of regulation have a number of accusations against the regulatory system.
      a. It raises prices.

   b. It hurts America's competitive position abroad.
   c. It does not always work well.
3. In 1978, the Civil Aeronautics Board (CAB) began to deregulate airline prices and airline routes; in 1984, the CAB formally disbanded.

F. Critics of deregulation
1. Critics of deregulation point to severe environmental damage resulting from lax enforcement of environmental protection standards during the Reagan administration.
2. Many observers attribute at least a substantial portion of the blame for the enormously expensive bailout of the savings and loan industry to the deregulation of it in the 1980s.

VI. UNDERSTANDING BUREAUCRACIES

A. Bureaucracy and democracy.
1. In democratic theory, popular control of government depends on elections, but we could not possibly elect the five million federal civilian and military employees (or even the few thousand top men and women).
2. The fact that voters do not elect civil servants does not mean that bureaucracies cannot respond to and *represent* the public's interests.
3. Much depends on *whether bureaucracies are effectively controlled by the policymakers* that citizens do elect—the president and Congress.
   a. Presidents try to impose their policy preferences on agencies, using some of the following methods:
      (1) Appoint the right people to head the agency: putting their people in charge is one good way for presidents to influence agency policy.
      (2) Issue orders: presidents can issue **executive orders** to agencies; or presidential aides can pass the word that "the President was wondering if . . ."
      (3) Tinker with an agency's budget: the Office of Management and Budget is the president's own final authority on any agency's budget (but each agency has its own constituents within and outside of Congress, and it is *Congress* that appropriates funds).
      (4) Reorganize an agency: although President Reagan promised to abolish the Department of Energy and the Department of Education, he never succeeded—largely because each was in the hands of an entrenched bureaucracy, backed by elements in Congress and strong constituent groups.

b. Congress exhibits an ambivalent relationship with the bureaucracies:
   (1) On the one hand, members of Congress may find a big bureaucracy congenial (big government provides services to constituents).
   (2) On the other hand, Congress has found it hard to control the government it helped create.
c. Measures Congress can take to oversee the bureaucracy:
   (1) Influence the appointment of agency heads: even when senatorial approval of a presidential appointment is not required, members of Congress may be influential.
   (2) Tinker with an agency's budget: the congressional *power of the purse* is a powerful weapon for controlling bureaucratic behavior.
   (3) Hold hearings: committees and subcommittees can hold periodic hearings as part of their oversight job.
   (4) Rewrite the legislation or make it more detailed: Congress can write new or more detailed legislation to limit bureaucratic discretion and make its instructions clearer.

4. There is one other crucial explanation for the difficulty presidents and Congress face in controlling bureaucracies: iron triangles and issue networks.
   a. When agencies, groups, and committees all depend on one another and are in close, frequent contact, they form **iron triangles** (or **subgovernments**). [see Chapter 10]
   b. Iron triangles have dominated some areas of domestic policy-making by combining internal consensus with a virtual monopoly on information in their area.
   c. Iron triangles are characterized by *mutual dependency*, in which each element provides key services, information, or policy for the others (illustrated by the *tobacco triangle*).
   d. These subgovernments can add a strong decentralizing and fragmenting element to the policy-making process.
   e. Despite the fact that subgovernments often are able to dominate policy-making for decades, they are not indestructible; policies of the tobacco triangle, for one, have increasingly come under fire from health authorities.

B. Bureaucracy and the scope of government.
   1. The federal bureaucracy *has not grown over the past two generations*; in fact, the bureaucracy has *shrunk* in size relative to the population it serves.

2. Originally, the federal bureaucracy had a modest role; but as the economy and the society of the United States changed, additional demands were made on government. [see Chapter 3]
3. Considering the more active role the bureaucracy is expected to play in dealing with social and economic problems, a good case can be made that the bureaucracy is actually too *small* for many of the tasks currently assigned to it (such as the control of illicit drugs or the protection of the environment).

KEY TERMS AND CONCEPTS

Administrative discretion: authority of administrative actors to select among various responses to a given problem, especially when rules do not fit or more than one rule applies.

Bureaucracy: implementors of policy.

Civil service: promotes hiring on the basis of merit and establishes a nonpartisan government service.

Command-and-control policy: regulatory strategy where government sets a requirement and then enforces individual and corporate actions to be consistent with meeting the requirement.

Deregulation: the withdrawal of the use of governmental authority to control or change some practice in the private sector.

Executive orders: executive orders are regulations originating in the executive branch.

Government corporations: provide services that could be handled by the private sector and generally charge cheaper rates than a private sector producer.

GS (General Service) rating: assigned to each job in federal agencies, this rating helps to determine the salary associated with the position.

Hatch Act: passed in 1940, prohibits government workers from active participation in partisan politics.

Incentive system: regulatory strategy that rewards individuals or corporations for desired types of behavior, usually through the tax code.

Independent executive agencies: executive agencies which are not cabinet departments, not regulatory commissions, and not government corporations.

Independent regulatory agency: has responsibility for a sector of the economy to protect the public interest.

Iron triangles: refers to the strong ties between government agencies, interest groups and congressional committees and subcommittees.

Merit principle: using entrance exams and promotion ratings for hiring workers.

Office of Personnel Management (OPM): responsible for hiring for most agencies.

Patronage: a hiring and promotion system based on knowing the right people.

Pendleton Act: passed in 1883, it created the federal Civil Service.

Policy implementation: the stage of policymaking between the establishment of a policy and the results of the policy for individuals.

Regulation: the use of governmental authority to control or change some practice in the private sector.

Senior Executive Service: the very top level of the bureaucracy.

Standard operating procedures: detailed rules written to cover as many particular situations as officials can anticipate to help bureaucrats implement policies uniformly.

Street-level bureaucrats: bureaucrats who are in constant contact with the public.

TEACHING IDEAS: CLASS DISCUSSION AND STUDENT PROJECTS

- Have each student select one of the independent regulatory agencies and write a brief essay on the history and powers of the agency. Ask students to focus on the "capture" theory and try to determine how well—or how poorly—the theory fits the agency the student selected.

- Ask students to research current law and policies regarding the relationships between former government officials and government bureaucrats. Should these now-private citizens be able to use their former positions in order to obtain access for lobbying activities? Have your class propose changes to current federal policies on such lobbying activities.

- If yours is a fairly small community, have each student prepare a "service directory" of local government agencies. They will probably be surprised to find how many government offices and services are available even in small-town areas.

- For class discussion, have students debate the value of a professional bureaucracy. In particular, have them examine the costs and benefits of the patronage system as compared to those of the merit system in terms of responsibility and accountability to the people bureaucrats serve.

- For a reading and writing connection, have students conduct interviews with civil service employees at three different local bureaucratic agencies, preferably at the same levels. Have the student design a set of survey questions about the qualifications of the job and what kind of preparation a person would need to secure that kind of job. Encourage students to explore the popular myths about bureaucrats. In addition, have students ask questions about how much discretion each respondent has and how much interest groups and political appointees place on them. Then have students write an essay comparing and contrasting the respondents answers with the material in the text as well as with each other.

- Have students investigate the qualifications for a job in a federal agency of their choice using the government documents section of the library or government agency websites. Starting with the top appointed position to the street-level civil service positions, have them detail the qualifications stated in the government literature. Then have them examine, from biographical resources, who fills those positions now. Have students write an essay comparing the standards set with the qualifications of those in office. In particular, ask them whether they think merit standards have been met, at least in the civil service positions.

- Ask students to evaluate the organization and efficiency of your university. How is it organized? Who is employed in what types of positions? Who are the bureaucrats and how efficiently do they perform their jobs? Do these bureaucrats have the same challenges in implementing policy that federal bureaucrats face? Have students prepare brief reports or presentations on their findings.

BACKGROUND READING

Aberbach, Joel D. Keeping a Watchful Eye. Washington, DC: Brookings Institution. 1990.

Derthick, Martha and Paul J. Quirk. The Politics of Deregulation. Washington, DC: Brookings Institution. 1985.

Gormley, William. T. Jr. Taming the Bureaucracy: Muscles, Prayers, and Other Strategies. Princeton, NJ: Princeton University Press. 1989.

Heclo, Hugh. Government of Strangers: Executive Powers in Washington. Washington, DC: Brookings Institution. 1977.

Johnson, Cathy Marie. The Dynamics of Conflict between Bureaucracies and Legislators. Armonk, NY: Sharpe. 1992.

Light, Paul C. The New Public Service. Washington, D.C.: Brookings. 1999.

Light, Paul C. Thickening Government: Federal Hierarchy and the Diffusion of Accountability. Washginton, DC: Brookings Institution.

Meier, Kenneth J. Politics and the Bureaucracy: Policymaking in the Fourth Branch of Government, 4th ed. New York: Harcourt Brace. 2000.

Peters, B. Guy. The Politics of Bureaucracy. 4th ed. NY: Longman. 1995.

Pressman, Jeffrey and Aaron Wildavsky. Implementation. 3rd ed. Berkeley, CA: University of California Press. 1984.

Selden, Sally Coleman. The Promise of Representative Bureaucracy. New York: M.E. Sharpe. 1997.

Wilson, James Q. Bureaucracy: What Government Agencies Do and Why They Do It. NY: Basic Books. 1991.

Wood, B. Dan and Richard W. Waterman. Bureaucratic Dynamics: The Role of Bureaucracy in a Democracy. Boulder, CO: Westview Press. 1994.

MEDIA SUGGESTIONS

Bureaucracy of Government. A video distributed by Films for the Humanities and Sciences examining the liberal and conservative commentary concerning the value and problems of bureaucracy.

Congress and the Bureaucracy. From the "Congress: We the People" series distributed by Films Incorporated. This program examines the symbiotic relationships which evolve between Congress and bureaucratic agencies.

CHAPTER SIXTEEN: THE COURTS

PEDAGOGICAL FEATURES

LEARNING OBJECTIVES

After studying this chapter, students should be able to:

- Clarify the reasoning behind calling the American judicial system an *adversarial* system.

- Identify the major actors in the judicial system and explain their functions and responsibilities.
- Differentiate between *original* and *appellate jurisdiction*, and between *civil* and *criminal law.*
- Describe the functions of federal district courts, courts of appeals, and the U.S. Supreme Court.
- Summarize judicial selection procedures for federal judges and justices.
- Discuss the backgrounds of judges and justices.
- Describe the role of the courts as *policymakers.*
- Distinguish between *judicial review* and *statutory interpretation.*
- Summarize procedure in the U.S. Supreme Court, including the "discuss list," oral argument, the conference, and opinion writing.
- Explain the importance of opinion writing at the Supreme Court level and describe the different types of opinions.
- Identify factors used by the Supreme Court in deciding which cases to accept for review.
- Analyze the contrasting positions of *judicial restraint* and *judicial activism.*
- Trace the historical evolution of the policy agenda of the Supreme Court.
- Examine the ways in which American courts are both democratic and undemocratic institutions.

CHAPTER OVERVIEW

INTRODUCTION

Although the scope of the Supreme Court's decisions is broad, the actual number of cases tried in our legal system are in lower federal or state and local courts. This means that a great deal of judicial policymaking occurs in courts other than the Supreme Court. This chapter describes how the court systems are structured, how judges are selected and the influence of the courts on the policy agenda in the United States.

THE NATURE OF THE JUDICIAL SYSTEM

The judicial system in the United States is an **adversarial** one in which the courts provide an arena for two parties to bring their conflict before an impartial arbiter (a judge). The system is based on the theory that justice will emerge out of the struggle between two contending points of view.

There are two basic kinds of cases, criminal and civil. In *criminal law*, an individual is charged with violating a specific law; criminal law provides punishment for crimes against society (or public order). *Civil law* does not involve a charge of criminality; instead, it concerns a dispute between two parties and defines relationships between them. The vast majority of cases (both civil and criminal) involve state law and are tried in state courts.

Every case is a dispute between a *plaintiff* and a *defendant*—the former bringing some charge against the latter. The task of the judge or judges is to apply the law to the case; in some cases, a **jury** is responsible for determining the outcome of a lawsuit. **Litigants** (the plaintiff and the defendant) must have **standing to sue,** which means they must have a serious interest in the case. **Class action suits** permit a small number of people to sue on behalf of all other people similarly situated. Because they recognize the courts' ability to shape policy, interest groups often seek out litigants whose cases seem particularly strong. At other times groups do not directly argue the case for litigants, but support them instead with ***amicus curiae*** ("friend of the court") **briefs** that attempt to influence the Court's decision, raise additional points of view, and present information not contained in the briefs of the attorneys for the official parties to the case.

There are a number of limitations on cases that federal courts will hear. Federal judges are restricted by the Constitution to deciding **"cases or controversies."** Two parties must bring a case to them (a case involving an actual dispute rather than a hypothetical question). Courts may decide only **justiciable disputes**, which means that conflicts must be *capable of being settled by legal methods.*

THE STRUCTURE OF THE FEDERAL JUDICIAL SYSTEM

The Constitution is vague about the federal court system. Aside from specifying that there will be a Supreme Court, the Constitution left it to Congress' discretion to establish lower federal courts of general jurisdiction. In the Judiciary Act of 1789, Congress created a system of *constitutional courts* on the basis of this constitutional provision.

The basic judicial structure has been modified several times. At the present time, there are twelve federal courts of appeal, ninety-one federal district courts, and thousands of state and local courts (in addition to the Supreme Court).

Congress has also established some *legislative courts* (such as the Court of Military Appeals, the Court of Claims, and the Tax Court) for specialized purposes, based on Article I of the Constitution. These **Article I courts** are staffed by judges who have fixed terms of office and who lack the protections of judges on constitutional courts against removal or salary reductions.

Courts of **original jurisdiction** are those where a case is first heard, usually in which trials are held. Courts with **appellate jurisdiction** hear cases brought to them on appeal from a lower court. Appellate courts do not review the factual record, only the legal issues involved.

The 675 district court judges usually preside over cases alone, but certain rare cases require that three judges constitute the court. Jurisdiction of the district courts extends to federal crimes; civil suits under federal law; diversity of citizenship cases where the amount exceeds $50,000; supervision of bankruptcy proceedings; review of the actions of some federal administrative agencies; admiralty and maritime law cases; and supervision of the naturalization of aliens.

However, approximately *98 percent of all criminal cases in the United States are heard in state and local* court systems, not in federal courts. Even so, only a small percentage of the persons convicted in district courts actually have a trial. Most charged with federal crimes enter guilty pleas as part of a bargain to receive lighter punishment (*"plea bargaining"*). Most *civil suits* are also handled in *state and local* courts; the vast majority are *settled out of court* without a trial.

U.S. courts of appeal are *appellate* courts empowered to review final decisions of district courts; they also have the authority to review and enforce orders of many federal regulatory agencies. The United States is divided into *twelve judicial circuits,* including one for the District of Columbia. There is also a special appeals court called the **U.S. Court of Appeals for the Federal Circuit** (established in 1982), which hears appeals in *specialized cases*, such as those regarding patents, copyrights and trademarks, claims against the United States, and international trade.

About 90 percent of the more than 40,000 cases heard in the courts of appeal come from the district courts. Each court of appeals normally hears cases in panels consisting of three judges, but each may sit *en banc* (with all judges present) in particularly important cases Decisions are made by *majority vote* of the participating judges.

The U.S. **Supreme Court** is the only court specifically established within Article III of the Constitution. The size of the Court is not set in the Constitution, and it was altered many times between 1801 and 1869; the number has remained stable at nine justices since that time. All nine justices sit together to hear cases and make decisions.

The Supreme Court has *both original and appellate jurisdiction.* Very few cases arise under original jurisdiction, which is defined in *Article III* of the Constitution. Almost all the cases come from the appeals process; appellate jurisdiction of the Court is set by *statute.* Cases may be appealed from both federal and state courts. The great majority of cases come from the lower federal courts. Unlike other federal courts, it controls its own agenda.

THE POLITICS OF JUDICIAL SELECTION

Federal judges are constitutionally guaranteed the right to serve for life "during good behavior." Federal judges may be removed only by *impeachment*, which has occurred only seven times in two centuries. No Supreme Court justice has ever been removed from office, although Samuel Chase was tried (but not convicted by the Senate) in 1805.

Although the *president nominates* persons to fill judicial posts, the *Senate must confirm* each by majority vote. The customary manner in which the Senate disposes of state-level federal judicial nominations is through **senatorial courtesy**. Because of the strength of this informal practice, presidents usually check carefully with the relevant senator or senators ahead of time. The president usually has more influence in the selection of judges to the federal courts of appeal than to federal district courts. Individual senators are in a weaker position to determine who the nominee will be because the jurisdiction of an appeals court encompasses several states. Even here, however, senators of the president's party from the state in which the candidate resides may be able to veto a nomination.

Although on the average there has been an opening on the Supreme Court every two years, there is a substantial variance around this mean. Presidents have failed 20 percent of the time to get Senate confirmation of their nominees to the Supreme Court—a percentage much higher than that for any other federal position. When the **chief justice's** position is vacant, presidents usually nominate someone from outside the Court; but if they decide to elevate a sitting associate justice, he or she must go through a new confirmation hearing. Nominations are most likely to run into trouble under certain conditions. Presidents whose parties are in the minority in the Senate or who make a nomination at the end of their terms face a greatly increased probability of substantial opposition. Equally important, opponents of a nomination usually must be able to question a nominee's competence or ethics in order to defeat a nomination.

THE BACKGROUNDS OF JUDGES AND JUSTICES

Judges serving on federal district and circuit courts are not a representative sample of the American people. They are all lawyers, and they are overwhelmingly white males. Federal judges have typically held office as a judge or prosecutor, and often they have been involved in partisan politics.

Like their colleagues on the lower federal courts, Supreme Court justices share characteristics that qualify them as an elite group. All have been lawyers, and all but four have been white males. Typically, justices have held high administrative or judicial positions; most have had some experience as a judge, often at the appellate level; many have worked for the Department of Justice; and some have held elective office. A few have had *no* government service. The fact that many justices (including some of the most distinguished ones) *have not had any previous judicial experience* may seem surprising, but *the unique work of the Supreme Court* renders this background *much less important than it might be for other appellate courts.*

Partisanship is an important influence on the selection of judges and justices: only 13 of 108 members of the Supreme Court have been nominated by presidents of a different party. *Ideology* is as important as partisanship; presidents want to appoint to the federal bench people who share their views. Presidential aides survey candidates' decisions (if they have served on a lower court), speeches, political stands, writings, and other expressions of opinion. They also turn for information to people who know the candidates well. Presidents are typically pleased with the performance of their nominees to the Supreme Court and through them have slowed or reversed trends in the Court's decisions. Nevertheless, it is not always easy to predict the policy inclinations of candidates, and presidents have been disappointed in their nominees about one-fourth of the time.

THE COURTS AS POLICYMAKERS

The first decision the Supreme Court must make is *which cases to decide*: unlike other federal courts, the Supreme Court *controls its own agenda*. Approximately 7,500 cases are submitted annually to the U.S. Supreme Court (but only two percent are accepted for review).

The nine justices meet in *conference* every Wednesday afternoon and every Friday morning. The first task in conference is for the justices to consider the chief justice's *discuss list* and decide which cases they want to hear. Most of the justices rely heavily on their *law clerks* to screen cases. If four justices agree to grant review of a case (the "rule of four"), it can be scheduled for oral argument or decided on the basis of the written record already on file with the Court. The most common way for the Court to put a case on its docket is by issuing a ***writ of certiorari*** to a lower federal or state court—a formal document that orders the lower court to send up a record of the case for review.

An important influence on the Supreme Court is the **solicitor general**. As a presidential appointee and the third-ranking official in the Department of Justice, the solicitor general is in charge of the appellate court litigation of the federal government. By avoiding frivolous appeals and displaying a high degree of competence, they typically earn the confidence of the Court, which in turn grants review of a large percentage of the cases they submit.

The Supreme Court decides *very few cases*. In a typical year, the Court issues fewer than 100 *formal written opinions* that could serve as precedent. In a few dozen additional cases, the Court reaches a *per curiam decision*—a decision without explanation (usually unsigned); such decisions involve only the immediate case and have no value as precedent because the Court does not offer reasoning that would guide lower courts in future decisions.

The second task of the weekly conferences is to *discuss cases* that have been accepted and argued before the Court. Beginning the first Monday in October and lasting until June, the Court hears **oral arguments** in two-week cycles. Unlike a trial court, justices are familiar with the case before they ever enter the courtroom.

The Court will have received written **briefs** from each party. They may also have received briefs from parties who are interested in the outcome of the case but are not formal litigants (known as ***amicus curiae***—or "friend of the court"—briefs).

The chief justice presides in conference. The chief justices calls first on the senior associate justice for discussion and then the other justices in order of seniority. If the votes are not clear from the individual discussions, the chief justice may ask each justice to vote. Once a *tentative vote* has been reached (votes are not final until the opinion is released), an *opinion* may be written.

The written **opinion** is the legal reasoning behind the decision. The *content of an opinion may be as important as the decision itself.* Tradition requires that the chief justice—if he voted with the majority—assign the **majority opinion** to himself or another justice in the majority; otherwise, the opinion is assigned by the senior associate justice in the majority.

Concurring opinions are those written to support a majority decision but also to stress a different constitutional or legal basis for the judgment. ***Dissenting opinions*** are those written by justices opposed to all or part of the majority's decision. Justices are free to write their own opinions, to join in other opinions, or to associate themselves with part of one opinion and part of another.

The vast majority of cases are settled on the principle of ***stare decisis*** ("let the decision stand"), meaning that an earlier decision should hold for the case being considered. Lower courts are expected to follow the **precedents** of higher courts in their decision making. The Supreme Court may overrule its own precedents, as it did in *Brown v. Board of Education* (1954) when it overruled *Plessy v. Ferguson* (1896) and found that segregation in the public schools violated the Constitution.

Policy preferences do matter in judicial decision making, especially on the nation's highest court. When precedent is not clear, the law is less firmly established. In such cases, there is more leeway and judges become more purely political players with room for their values to influence their judgment.

Judicial implementation refers to how and whether court decisions are translated into actual policy, thereby affecting the behavior of others. The implementation of any Court decision involves many actors besides the justices, and the justices have no way of ensuring that their decisions and policies will be implemented.

The most contentious issue involving the courts is the role of *judicial discretion*; the Constitution itself does not specify any rules for interpretation. Some have argued for a jurisprudence of **original intent** (sometimes referred to as **strict**

constructionism). This view, which is popular with conservatives, holds that judges and justices should determine the intent of the framers of the Constitution and decide cases in line with that intent. Advocates of strict constructionism view it as a means of constraining the exercise of judicial discretion, which they see as the *foundation of the liberal decisions* of the past four decades. Others assert that the Constitution is subject to multiple meanings; they maintain that what appears to be deference to the intentions of the framers is simply *a cover for making conservative decisions.*

THE COURTS AND THE POLICY AGENDA

The courts both *reflect* and *help to determine* the national *policy agenda.* Until the Civil War, the dominant questions before the Court regarded the strength and legitimacy of the federal government and slavery. From the Civil War until 1937, questions of the relationship between the federal government and the economy predominated; the courts traditionally favored corporations, especially when government tried to regulate them. From 1938 to the present, the paramount issues before the Court have concerned personal liberty and social and political equality. In this era, the Court has enlarged the scope of personal freedom and civil rights, and has removed many of the constitutional restraints on the regulation of the economy. Most recently, environmental groups have used the courts to achieve their policy goals.

John Marshall, chief justice from 1801 to 1835, established the Supreme Court's power of **judicial review** in the 1803 case of *Marbury* v. *Madison* (the so-called *"midnight judges"* case). In a shrewd solution to a political controversy, Marshall asserted for the courts *the power to determine what is and is not constitutional* and thereby established the power of judicial review. By in effect reducing its own power—the authority to hear cases such as Marbury's under its original jurisdiction—the Court was able to assert the right of judicial review in a fashion that the other branches could not easily rebuke.

Few eras of the Supreme Court have been as active in shaping public policy as that of the Warren Court. The Court's decisions on desegregation, criminal defendants' rights, and voting reapportionment reshaped public policy and also led to calls from right-wing groups for Chief Justice Earl Warren's impeachment. His critics argued that the unelected justices were making policy decisions that were the responsibility of elected officials.

The Burger Court—which followed the Warren Court—was more conservative than the liberal Warren Court, but did not overturn the due process protections of the Warren era. The Court narrowed defendants' rights, but did not overturn the fundamental contours of the *Miranda* decision. It was also the Burger Court that wrote the abortion decision in *Roe* v. *Wade* (1973), required school busing in certain cases to eliminate historic segregation, and upheld affirmative action programs in the *Weber* case. When the Supreme Court was called upon to rule on whether President Nixon's White House (Watergate) tapes had to be turned over to the courts, it unanimously ordered him to do so (***United States* v. *Nixon***, 1974), and thus hastened his resignation.

The Rehnquist Court has not created a "revolution" in constitutional law. Instead, it has been slowly chipping away at liberal decisions such as those regarding defendants' rights, abortion, and affirmative action. The Court no longer sees itself as the special protector of individual liberties and civil rights for minorities; it has typically deferred to the will of the majority and the rules of the government.

UNDERSTANDING THE COURTS

Powerful courts are unusual; very few nations have them. The power of American judges raises questions about the compatibility of unelected courts with a democracy and about the appropriate role for the judiciary in policy-making.

In some ways, the courts are not a very democratic institution. Federal judges are not elected and are almost impossible to remove. Their social backgrounds probably make the courts the most elite-dominated policy-making institution. However, the courts are not entirely independent of popular preferences. Even when the Court seems out of step with other policymakers, it eventually swings around to join the policy consensus (as it did in the New Deal era).

There are strong disagreements concerning the appropriateness of allowing the courts to have a policy-making role. Many scholars and judges favor a policy of **judicial restraint** (sometimes called *judicial self-restraint*), in which judges play minimal policy-making roles, leaving policy decisions to the legislatures. Advocates of judicial restraint believe that decisions such as those on abortion and school prayer go well beyond the "referee" role they feel is appropriate for courts in a democracy. On the other side are proponents of **judicial activism**, in which judges make bolder policy decisions, even breaking new constitutional ground with a particular decision. Advocates of judicial activism emphasize that the courts may alleviate pressing needs, especially of those who are weak politically or economically.

Judicial activism or restraint should *not be confused* with *liberalism or conservatism.* In the early years of the New Deal, judicial activists were conservatives. During the tenure of Earl Warren, activists made liberal decisions.

The tenure of the conservative Chief Justice Warren Burger and several conservative nominees of Republican presidents marked the most active use of judicial review in the nation's history. The problem remains of reconciling the American democratic heritage with an active policymaking role for the judiciary. The federal courts have developed a doctrine of **political questions** as a means to avoid deciding some cases, principally those that involve conflicts between the president and Congress.

One factor that increases the acceptability of activist courts is *the ability to overturn their decisions*. The president and the Senate determine who sits on the federal bench (a process that has sometimes been used to reshape the philosophy of the Court). Congress can begin the process of amending the Constitution to overcome a constitutional decision of the Supreme Court, and Congress could even alter the appellate jurisdiction of the Supreme Court to prevent it from hearing certain types of cases. If the issue is one of **statutory construction** (in which a court interprets an act of Congress), the legislature routinely passes legislation that *clarifies existing laws*—and, in effect, overturns the courts.

CHAPTER OUTLINE

I. **THE NATURE OF THE JUDICIAL SYSTEM**
   A. The judicial system in the United States is an **adversarial** one in which the courts provide an arena for two parties to bring their conflict before an impartial arbiter (a judge).
      1. The system is based on the theory that justice will emerge out of the struggle between two contending points of view.
      2. In reality, most cases never reach trial because they are settled by agreements reached out of court.
      3. There are two basic kinds of cases, *criminal law* and *civil law*.
         a. In criminal law, an individual is charged with violating a specific law; criminal law provides punishment for crimes against society (or public order).
         b. Civil law does not involve a charge of criminality; instead, it concerns a dispute between two parties and defines relationships between them.
         c. The vast majority of cases (both civil and criminal) involve state law and are tried in state courts.
   B. Participants in the judicial system.

1. Federal judges are restricted by the Constitution to deciding *cases or controversies.*
2. Courts may decide only **justiciable disputes**, which means that conflicts must be *capable of being settled by legal methods*.
3. Every case is a dispute between a **plaintiff** and a **defendant**—the former bringing some charge against the latter.
4. **Litigants** (the plaintiff and the defendant) must have **standing to sue**, which means they must have a serious interest in a case (typically determined by whether or not they have sustained or are in immediate danger of sustaining a direct and substantial injury from another party or from an action of government).
   a. In recent years, there has been some broadening of the concept of standing to sue.
   b. **Class action suits** permit a small number of people to sue on behalf of all other people similarly situated (for example, a suit on behalf of all credit card holders of an oil company).

II. THE STRUCTURE OF THE FEDERAL JUDICIAL SYSTEM

A. The Constitution is vague about the federal court system: aside from specifying that there will be a Supreme Court, the Constitution left it to Congress' discretion to establish lower federal courts of general jurisdiction.
   1. In the **Judiciary Act of 1789**, Congress created a system of **constitutional courts** (also called **Article III courts**) on the basis of this constitutional provision. In addition to the Supreme Court, there are twelve federal courts of appeal, ninety-one federal district courts, and thousands of state and local courts.
   2. Congress has also established some **legislative courts** (such as the Court of Military Appeals, the Court of Claims, and the Tax Court) for specialized purposes, based on Article I of the Constitution. These **Article I courts** are staffed by judges who have fixed terms of office and who lack the protections of judges on constitutional courts against removal or salary reductions.

B. District courts.
   1. **District courts** are courts of *original jurisdiction.*
   2. They are *trial courts*—the only federal courts in which trials are held and in which juries may be impaneled.
      a. Approximately *98 percent of all criminal cases in the United States are heard in state and local* court systems, *not in federal* courts.
   3. The 576 district court judges usually preside over cases alone, but certain rare cases require that three judges constitute the court.

4. Jurisdiction of the district courts extends to: federal crimes; civil suits under federal law; diversity of citizenship cases where the amount exceeds $50,000; supervision of bankruptcy proceedings; review of the actions of some federal administrative agencies; admiralty and maritime law cases; supervision of the naturalization of aliens.

C. Courts of appeal.
   1. U.S. courts of appeal have **appellate jurisdiction**; *they are* empowered to *review final decisions of district courts*; they also have the authority to *review and enforce orders of many federal regulatory agencies.*
   2. The United States is divided into *twelve judicial circuits*, including one for the District of Columbia.
      a. About 90 percent of the more than 40,000 cases heard in the courts of appeal come from the district courts.
      b. Each court of appeals normally hears cases in panels consisting of three judges, but each may sit *en banc* (with all judges present) in particularly important cases.
      c. Decisions are made by *majority vote* of the participating judges.
   3. There is also a special appeals court called the **U.S. Court of Appeals for the Federal Circuit** (established in 1982), which hears appeals in *specialized cases*, such as those regarding patents, copyrights and trademarks, claims against the United States, and international trade.

D. The Supreme Court.
   1. The highest court in the federal system, the U.S. **Supreme Court** is also the only court specifically established within Article III of the Constitution.
      a. There are nine justices on the Court: eight associates and one chief justice.
      b. The size of the Court is not set in the Constitution, and it was altered many times between 1801 and 1869; the number has remained stable at nine justices since that time.
   2. Important functions include:
      a. resolving conflicts among the states;
      b. maintaining national supremacy in the law; and
      c. playing an important role in ensuring uniformity in the interpretation of national laws.
   3. All nine justices sit together to hear cases and make decisions (*en banc*). The first decision the Court must make is *which cases to decide*: unlike other federal courts, the Supreme Court *controls its own agenda.*

4. The Supreme Court has *both original and appellate jurisdiction.*
    a. Very few cases arise under original jurisdiction, which is defined in *Article III.*
    b. Almost all the cases come from the appeals process; appellate jurisdiction is set by *statute.*
    c. Cases may be *appealed* from *both federal and state courts.*
    d. The great majority of cases come from the lower federal courts.
5. Cases appealed from state courts:
    a. Cases appealed from state courts must involve "*a substantial federal question.*"
    b. Cases from state courts are heard only in the Supreme Court (not in the courts of appeal) and then only after the petitioner has exhausted all the potential remedies in the state court system.
    c. The Court will not try to settle matters of state law or determine guilt or innocence in state criminal proceedings.

III. THE POLITICS OF JUDICIAL SELECTION

A. Although the *president nominates* persons to fill judicial posts, the *Senate must confirm* each by majority vote.

B. Federal judges are constitutionally guaranteed the right to serve for life "during good behavior."
1. Federal judges may be removed only by *impeachment*, which has occurred only seven times in two centuries.
2. No Supreme Court justice has ever been removed from office, although Samuel Chase was tried but not convicted by the Senate in 1805.
3. Salaries of federal judges cannot be reduced (a stipulation that further insulates them from political pressures).

C. The lower courts: judicial selection procedures.
1. The customary manner in which the Senate disposes of state-level federal judicial nominations is through **senatorial courtesy**.
    a. Under this unwritten tradition (which began under George Washington in 1789), nominations for these positions are not confirmed when opposed by a senator of the president's party from the state in which the nominee is to serve.
    b. In the case of courts of appeal judges, nominees are not confirmed if opposed by a senator of the president's party from the state of the nominee's residence.
    c. Because of the strength of this informal practice, presidents usually check carefully with the relevant senator or senators ahead of time.

d. Typically, when there is a vacancy for a federal district judgeship, the one or two senators of the president's party from the state where the judge will serve suggest one or more names to the attorney general and the president; if neither senator is of the president's party, the party's state congresspersons or the other party leaders may make suggestions.
e. The Department of Justice and the Federal Bureau of Investigation then conduct competency and background checks on these persons, and the president usually selects a nominee from those who survive the screening process.

D. The Supreme Court.
1. Although on the average there has been an opening on the Supreme Court every two years, there is a substantial variance around this mean.
2. When the **chief justice's** position is vacant, presidents usually nominate someone from outside the Court; but if they decide to elevate a sitting associate justice (as President Reagan did with William Rehnquist in 1986), he or she must go through a new confirmation hearing.
3. Selection process.
    a. The president usually relies on the attorney general and the Department of Justice to identify and screen candidates for the Supreme Court.
    b. Sitting justices often try to influence the nominations of their future colleagues, but presidents feel no obligation to follow their advice.
    c. Senators play a much less prominent role in the recruitment of Supreme Court justices than in the selection of lower court judges.
    d. The ABA's Standing Committee on the Federal Judiciary has played a varied but typically modest role at the Supreme Court level; presidents have not generally been willing to allow the committee to prescreen candidates.
    e. Candidates for nomination usually keep a low profile.
4. Failure to confirm.
    a. Presidents have failed 20 percent of the time to get Senate confirmation of their nominees to the Supreme Court—a percentage much higher than that for any other federal position.
        (1) Thus, although home-state senators do not play prominent roles in the selection process, the Senate as a whole does.

(2) Through its **Judiciary Committee**, it may probe a nominee's background and judicial philosophy in great detail.

b. Nominations are most likely to run into trouble under certain conditions.
   (1) Presidents whose parties are in the minority in the Senate or who make a nomination at the end of their terms face an increased probability of substantial opposition.
   (2) Opponents of a nomination usually must be able to question a nominee's competence or ethics in order to defeat a nomination.
   (3) Opposition based on a nominee's ideology is generally not considered a valid reason to vote against confirmation (illustrated by the confirmation of Chief Justice William Rehnquist, who was strongly opposed by liberals).

IV. THE BACKGROUNDS OF JUDGES AND JUSTICES

A. Characteristics of district and circuit court judges.
   1. Judges serving on federal district and circuit courts are not a representative sample of the American people.
   2. They are all lawyers, and they are overwhelmingly white males.
   3. Federal judges have typically held office as a judge or prosecutor, and often they have been involved in partisan politics.

B. Characteristics of Supreme Court justices.
   1. Like their colleagues on the lower federal courts, Supreme Court justices share characteristics that qualify them as an elite group.
   2. All have been lawyers, and all but four (Thurgood Marshall, nominated in 1967, Sandra Day O'Connor, nominated in 1981, Clarence Thomas, nominated in 1991, and Ruth Bader Ginsburg, nominated in 1993) have been white males.
   3. Most have been in their fifties and sixties when they took office, from the upper-middle to upper class, and Protestants.
   4. Race and sex have become more salient criteria in recent years.
   5. Geography was once a prominent criterion for selection to the court, but it is no longer very important.
   6. At various times, there have been what some have termed a "Jewish seat" and a "Catholic seat" on the Court, but these guidelines are not binding on the president (and are not always followed).
   7. Typically, justices have held high administrative or judicial positions.
      a. Most have had some experience as a judge, often at the appellate level.

b. Many have worked for the Department of Justice, and some have held elective office.
c. A few have had *no* government service.
d. The fact that many justices (including some of the most distinguished ones) *have not had any previous judicial experience* may seem surprising, but *the unique work of the court* renders this background *much less important than it might be for other appellate courts*.

C. "Politics" and the selection process.
1. *Partisanship* is an important influence on the selection of judges and justices: only 13 of 108 members of the Supreme Court have been nominated by presidents of a different party.
2. Judgeships are considered very prestigious patronage plums; the decisions of Congress to create new judgeships are closely related to whether or not the majority party in Congress is the same as the party of the president.
3. *Ideology* is as important as partisanship; presidents want to appoint to the federal bench people who share their views.
    a. Presidential aides survey candidates' decisions (if they have served on a lower court), speeches, political stands, writings, and other expressions of opinion.
    b. They also turn for information to people who know the candidates well.
    c. Members of the federal bench also play the game of politics, and may try to time their retirements so that a president with compatible views will choose their successors.
4. Thus, presidents influence policy through the values of their judicial nominees, but this impact is limited by numerous legal and "extra-legal" factors beyond the chief executive's control.
    a. Presidents are typically pleased with their nominees to the Supreme Court, and through them have slowed or reversed trends in the Court's decisions (Franklin D. Roosevelt's nominees substantially liberalized the Court, whereas Richard Nixon's conservatized it).
    b. Nevertheless, it is not always easy to predict the policy inclinations of candidates, and presidents have been disappointed in their nominees about one-fourth of the time (President Eisenhower was displeased with the liberal decisions of both Earl Warren and William Brennan, and Richard Nixon was disappointed when Warren Burger wrote the Court's decision calling for immediate desegregation of the nation's schools).

V. THE COURTS AS POLICYMAKERS

A. *Deciding which cases to accept* is the first step in policy-making.
   1. Courts of original jurisdiction cannot very easily decide not to consider a case.
   2. The Supreme Court has control over its own docket.
   3. Approximately 7,500 cases are submitted annually to the U.S. Supreme Court.

B. Functions of weekly conferences:
   1. Establish an agenda.
      a. The nine justices meet in **conference** every Wednesday afternoon and every Friday morning.
      b. Conferences operate under the strictest secrecy, with only the justices in attendance.
      c. The justices consider the chief justice's *discuss list* and decide which cases they want to hear.
      d. Most of the justices rely heavily on their *law clerks* to screen cases.
      e. If four justices agree to grant review of a case (the "*rule of four*"), it can be scheduled for *oral argument* or decided *on the basis of the written record already* on file with the Court.
      f. The most common way for the Court to put a case on its docket is by issuing a **writ of *certiorari*** to a lower federal or state court—a formal document that orders the lower court to send up a record of the case for review.
      g. The **solicitor general** has an important influence on the Court.
         1. As a presidential appointee and the third-ranking official in the Department of Justice, the solicitor general is in charge of the appellate court litigation of the federal government.
         2. By avoiding frivolous appeals and displaying a high degree of competence, the solicitor general and a staff of about two dozen experienced attorneys typically have the confidence of the Court—which, in turn, *grants review of a large percentage of the cases* for which they seek it.
   2. Making decisions.
      a. The second task of the weekly conferences is to *discuss cases* that have been accepted and argued before the Court.
      b. Beginning the first Monday in October and lasting until June, the Court hears **oral arguments** in two-week cycles.
      c. Unlike a trial court, justices are familiar with the case before they ever enter the courtroom.
         1. The Court will have received written **briefs** from each party.

   2. They may also have received briefs from parties who are interested in the outcome of the case but are not formal litigants (known as ***amicus curiae***—or "friend of the court"—briefs).
  - d. In most instances, the attorneys for each side have only a half-hour to address the Court during oral argument.
  - e. The chief justice presides in conference.
    1. The chief justices calls first on the senior associate justice for discussion and then the other justices in order of seniority.
    2. If the votes are not clear from the individual discussions, the chief justice may ask each justice to vote.
    3. Once a *tentative vote* has been reached (votes are not final until the opinion is released), an *opinion* may be written.

C. Opinion writing.
  1. The *content of an opinion may be as important as the decision itself.*
     - a. The written **opinion** is the legal reasoning behind the decision.
     - b. Tradition requires that the chief justice—if he voted with the majority—assign the **majority opinion** to himself or another justice in the majority; otherwise, the opinion is assigned by the senior associate justice in the majority.
  2. Drafts of the opinion are circulated for comments and suggestions; substantial revisions may be made.
  3. Justices are free to write their own opinions, to join in other opinions, or to associate themselves with part of one opinion and part of another.
     - a. **Concurring opinions** are those written to support a majority decision but also to stress a different constitutional or legal basis for the judgment.
     - b. **Dissenting opinions** are those written by justices opposed to all or part of the majority's decision.
  4. The vast majority of cases are settled on the principle of ***stare decisis*** ("let the decision stand"), meaning that an earlier decision should hold for the case being considered.
     - a. All courts rely heavily upon such **precedent**—the way similar cases were handled in the past—as a guide to current decisions.
     - b. Lower courts are expected to follow the precedents of higher courts in their decision-making.
     - c. The Supreme Court may overrule its own precedents, as it did in ***Brown* v. *Board of Education*** (1954) when the Court overruled ***Plessy* v. *Ferguson*** (1896) and found that segregation in the public schools violated the Constitution.

   d. When precedent is not clear, the law is less firmly established; here there is more leeway and judges become more purely political players with room for their values to influence their judgment.
   e. Policy preferences do matter in judicial decision making, especially on the nation's highest court.

D. The Supreme Court decides *very few cases*.
   1. In a typical year, the Court issues fewer than 100 *formal written opinions* that could serve as *precedent*.
   2. In a few dozen additional cases, the Court reaches a **per curiam decision**—a decision without explanation (usually unsigned); such decisions involve only the immediate case and have no value as precedent because the Court does not offer reasoning that would guide lower courts in future decisions.
   3. Once announced, copies of a decision are conveyed to the press as it is being formally announced in open court.
   4. The decisions are bound weekly and made available to every law library and lawyer in the United States.

E. Implementing court decisions.
   1. Even Supreme Court decisions are *not self-implementing*; they are actually **"remands"** to lower courts, instructing them to act in accordance with the Court's decisions.
   2. Court decisions carry legal (even moral) authority, but courts do not possess a staff to enforce their decisions.
   3. **Judicial implementation** refers to how and whether court decisions are translated into actual policy.
   4. Charles Johnson and Bradley Canon suggest that implementation of court decisions involves several elements:
      a. There is an *interpretation population*—heavily composed of lawyers and other judges—who must correctly sense the intent of the original decision in their subsequent actions.
      b. The *implementing population* includes those responsible for putting the decision into effect; judicial decisions are more likely to be smoothly implemented if implementation is concentrated in the hands of a few highly visible officials.
      c. Every decision involves a *consumer population* (those affected by the decision); the consumer population must be aware of its newfound rights and stand up for them.

F. The debate over original intentions.
   1. The most contentious issue involving the courts is the role of *judicial discretion*; the Constitution itself does not specify any rules for interpretation.

2. Some have argued for a jurisprudence of **original intent** (sometimes referred to as **strict constructionism**).
   a. This view, which is popular with conservatives, holds that judges and justices should determine the intent of the framers of the Constitution and decide cases in line with that intent.
   b. Advocates of strict constructionism view it as a means of *constraining the exercise of judicial discretion*, which they see as the *foundation of the liberal decisions* of the past four decades.
3. Others assert that the Constitution is subject to multiple meanings; they maintain that what appears to be deference to the intentions of the framers is simply *a cover for making conservative decisions*.

VI. THE COURTS AND THE POLICY AGENDA

A. The courts both *reflect* and *help to determine* the national *policy agenda*.
   1. Until the Civil War, the dominant questions before the Court regarded the strength and legitimacy of the federal government and slavery.
   2. From the Civil War until 1937, questions of the relationship between the federal government and the economy predominated; the courts traditionally favored corporations, especially when government tried to regulate them.
   3. From 1938 to the present, the paramount issues before the Court have concerned personal liberty and social and political equality
      a. In this era, the Court has enlarged the scope of personal freedom and civil rights, and has removed many of the constitutional restraints on the regulation of the economy.
      b. Most recently, environmental groups have used the courts to achieve their policy goals.

B. John Marshall and the growth of judicial review.
   1. John Marshall, chief justice from 1801 to 1835, established the Supreme Court's power of judicial review in the 1803 case of *Marbury* v. *Madison*.
   2. In the election of 1800, Democrat Thomas Jefferson defeated Federalist John Adams.
      a. Adams allegedly stayed at his desk until nine o'clock on his last night in office, signing commissions for Federalist judges.
      b. Secretary of State John Marshall failed to deliver commissions to Marbury and sixteen others; when the omission was discovered, Jefferson and the new secretary of state, James Madison, refused to deliver the commissions.
      c. Marbury and three others sued Madison, asking the Supreme Court to issue a **writ of *mandamus*** (a court order to require

performance of an act) ordering Madison to give them their commissions.

d. They took their case directly to the Supreme Court under the Judiciary Act of 1789, which gave the Court original jurisdiction in such matters.

e. Ironically, the new chief justice was Adams' secretary of state (and himself one of Adams' "*midnight appointments*"), John Marshall.

3. In ***Marbury* v. *Madison*** (1803), Marshall and his colleagues argued that Madison was wrong to withhold Marbury's commission.
   a. However, the Court also found that the Judiciary Act of 1789 contradicted the words of the Constitution about the Court's *original jurisdiction*; thus, Marshall dismissed Marbury's claim, saying that the Court had no power to require that the commission be delivered.
   b. In this shrewd solution to a political controversy, Marshall asserted for the courts *the power to determine what is and is not constitutional* and established the power of **judicial review**.
   c. By in effect reducing its own power—the authority to hear cases such as Marbury's under its original jurisdiction—the Court was able to assert the right of judicial review in a fashion that the other branches could not easily rebuke.

C. The "nine old men".
1. When Franklin Roosevelt entered the White House, the Court was dominated by conservatives who viewed federal intervention in the economy as unconstitutional and tantamount to socialism.
2. At President Roosevelt's urging, Congress passed dozens of laws designed to end the Great Depression; but the Supreme Court declared the acts unconstitutional.
3. In 1937, Roosevelt proposed what critics called a **"court-packing plan."**
   a. Referring to the Court as the **"nine old men"** (a reference both to the advanced ages of the justices and to their political philosophies), he proposed that Congress expand the size of the Court.
   b. Since Congress can set the number of justices, this move would have allowed him to appoint additional justices sympathetic to the New Deal.
4. Although Congress never passed the plan, two justices (Chief Justice Charles Evans Hughes and Associate Justice Owen Roberts) began switching their votes in favor of New Deal legislation—a transformation that was called the **"switch in time that saved nine."**

D. The Warren Court (1953-1969).
   1. Few eras of the Supreme Court have been as active in shaping public policy as that of the Warren Court.
      a. In 1954, the Court held that laws requiring segregation of the public schools were unconstitutional (*Brown* v. *Board of Education*).
      b. The Court expanded the rights of criminal defendants in numerous areas.
      c. It ordered states to reapportion their legislatures according to the principle of "*one person, one vote.*"
   2. The Court's decisions on desegregation, criminal defendants' rights, and voting reapportionment led to calls from right-wing groups for Chief Justice Earl Warren's impeachment; critics argued that the unelected justices were making policy decisions that were the responsibility of elected officials.
E. The Burger Court (1969-1986).
   1. Warren's retirement in 1969 gave President Nixon his opportunity to appoint a "strict constructionist" as Chief Justice; he chose Warren E. Burger.
   2. The Burger Court was more conservative than the liberal Warren Court, but did not overturn the due process protections of the Warren era.
      a. The Court narrowed defendants' rights, but did not overturn the fundamental contours of the *Miranda* decision.
      b. It was also the Burger Court (not the Warren Court) that wrote the abortion decision in *Roe* v. *Wade* (1973), required school busing in certain cases to eliminate historic segregation, and upheld affirmative action programs in the *Weber* case. [see Chapter 5]
      c. When the Supreme Court was called upon to rule on whether President Nixon's White House (Watergate) tapes had to be turned over to the courts, it unanimously ordered him to do so, in ***United States* v. *Nixon*** (1974)—and thus hastened his resignation.
F. The Rehnquist Court (1986-present).
   1. The Rehnquist Court has not created a "revolution" in constitutional law; instead, it has been slowly chipping away at liberal decisions such as those regarding defendants' rights, abortion, and affirmative action. [see Chapters 4 and 5]
   2. The Court no longer sees itself as the special protector of individual liberties and civil rights for minorities; it has typically deferred to the will of the majority and the rules of the government.

VII. UNDERSTANDING THE COURTS

A. The courts and democracy.
   1. In some ways the courts are not a very democratic institution.
      a. Federal judges are not elected and are almost impossible to remove.
      b. Their social backgrounds probably make the courts the most elite-dominated policy-making institution.
   2. However, the courts are not entirely independent of popular preferences.
      a. Even when the Court seems out of step with other policymakers, it eventually swings around to join the policy consensus (as it did in the New Deal).
      b. The Court is not as insulated from the normal forms of politics as one might think.
         (1) The Court was flooded with mail during the abortion debate, subjected to demonstrations and protests, and bombarded with *amicus curiae* briefs.
         (2) Although it is unlikely that members of the Supreme Court cave in to interest group pressures, they are certainly aware of the public's concern about issues, and this becomes part of their consciousness as they decide cases.
      c. Courts can also promote *pluralism*; interest groups often use the judicial system to pursue their policy goals, forcing the courts to rule on important social issues.

B. What courts should do: the scope of judicial power.
   1. There are strong disagreements concerning the appropriateness of allowing the courts to have a policy-making role.
   2. Many scholars and judges favor a policy of **judicial restraint** (sometimes called *judicial self-restraint*), in which judges play minimal policy-making roles, leaving policy decisions to the legislatures.
   3. Advocates of judicial restraint believe that decisions such as those on abortion and school prayer go well beyond the "referee" role they feel is appropriate for courts in a democracy.
   4. On the other side are proponents of **judicial activism**, in which judges make bolder policy decisions, even breaking new constitutional ground with a particular decision.
   5. Advocates of judicial activism emphasize that the courts may alleviate pressing needs, especially of those who are weak politically or economically.

6. It is important *not to confuse judicial activism or restraint with liberalism or conservatism.*
    a. In the early years of the New Deal, judicial activists were conservatives.
    b. During the tenure of Earl Warren, activists made liberal decisions.
    c. Although the public often associates judicial activism with liberals, the tenure of the conservative Chief Justice Warren Burger and several conservative nominees of Republican presidents marked the most active use of judicial review in the nation's history.

C. How the court sets limits on the cases it will hear.
1. The federal courts have developed a doctrine of **political questions** as a means to avoid deciding some cases, principally those regarding conflicts between the president and Congress.
2. Judges attempt, whenever possible, to avoid deciding a case on the basis of the Constitution; they show a preference for less contentious "technical" grounds.
3. The courts employ issues of *jurisdiction*, *mootness* (whether a case presents an issue of contention), *standing*, *ripeness* (whether the issues of a case are clear enough and evolved enough to serve as the basis of a decision), and other conditions to avoid adjudication of some politically-charged cases.
4. Federal courts have been much more likely to find state laws rather than federal laws unconstitutional.

D. Other factors that limit judicial activism.
1. One factor that increases the acceptability of activist courts is *the ability to overturn their decisions.*
    a. The president and the Senate determine who sits on the federal bench.
    b. Congress can begin the process of amending the Constitution to overcome a constitutional decision of the Supreme Court; thus, the Sixteenth Amendment (1913) reversed the decision in *Pollock* v. *Farmer's Loan and Trust Co.* (1895), which prohibited a federal income tax.
    c. Congress could alter the appellate jurisdiction of the Supreme Court to prevent it from hearing certain types of cases (an alteration that has not occurred since 1869, although some in Congress threatened to employ the method in the 1950s regarding some matters of civil liberties).
    d. If the issue is one of **statutory construction** (in which a court interprets an act of Congress), the legislature routinely

passes legislation that *clarifies existing laws*—and, in effect, overturns the courts.

2. Thus, the description of the judiciary as the "ultimate arbiter of the Constitution" is hyperbolic; all the branches of government help define and shape the Constitution.

KEY TERMS AND CONCEPTS

Amicus Curiae briefs: friend of the court briefs by nonlitigants who wish to influence the Court's decision by raising additional points of view and information not contained by briefs prepared by litigants' attorneys.

Appellate jurisdiction: given to a court where cases are heard on appeal from a lower court.

Class action suits: cases which permit a small number of people to sue on behalf of all other people similarly affected.

Courts of appeal: courts which have the power to review all final decisions of district courts, except in instances requiring direct review by the Supreme Court.

District courts: the entry point for most federal litigation.

Judicial activism: theory that judges should make bolder policy decisions to alleviate pressing needs, especially for those who are weak politically.

Judicial implementation: how and whether court decisions are translated into actual policy.

Judicial restraint: theory that judges should play minimal role in policy making and leave policy decisions to the legislature.

Judicial review: the power of the courts to hold acts of Congress, and by implication the executive, in violation of the Constitution.

Justiciable disputes: cases that can be settled by legal methods.

Marbury v. Madison: the 1803 Supreme Court case that originated the notion of judicial review.

Opinion: a statement of the legal reasoning behind the decision.

Original intent: the theory that judges should determine the intent of the framers and decide in line with their intent.

Original jurisdiction: given to a court where a case is first heard.

Political questions: conflicts between the president and Congress.

Precedent: the way similar cases have been handled in the past is used as a guide to current decisions.

Senatorial courtesy: a tradition in which nominations for federal judicial positions are not confirmed when opposed by a senator of the president's party from the state in which the nominee is to serve or from the state of the nominee's residence.

Solicitor general: a presidential appointee who is in charge of the appellate court litigation of the federal government.

Standing to sue: litigants must have serious interest (sustained direct and substantial injury) from a party in a case.

Stare decisis: an earlier decision should hold for the case being considered.

Statutory construction: a procedure in which the legislature passes legislation that clarifies existing laws so that the clarification has the effect of overturning the court's decision.

Supreme Court: resolves disputes between and among states, maintains the national supremacy of law, ensures uniformity in the interpretation of national laws.

United States v. Nixon: 1974 Supreme Court decision that required President Nixon to turn White House tapes over to the Courts.

TEACHING IDEAS: CLASS DISCUSSION AND STUDENT PROJECTS

- Presidents have failed 20 percent of the time to get Senate confirmation of their nominees to the Supreme Court, a percentage much higher than any other federal position. Call on volunteers to analyze why this particular office should have a rate of rejection so much higher than for other offices.

- Check the court dockets for state and local courts in your vicinity. Distribute information on locations, time of court sessions, and types of cases pending. Each student should visit a session of court within the next two weeks and write a brief statement describing how the general courtroom atmosphere differed from what he or she may have expected.

- Assign groups of students to two panels. Hold a short debate on the opposing theories of *original intent* and *loose construction* of the Constitution. *You Are the Policymaker: The Debate over Original Intentions* could serve as the basis for allocating responsibilities among members of the panel.

- The Supreme Court has always insisted on maintaining complete secrecy over deliberations among the justices in conference. Therefore, there was great controversy when the Library of Congress released the papers of the late Justice Thurgood Marshall shortly after his death in 1993. Marshall's papers provide a rare look at behind-the-scenes maneuvering by the Court. Divide your class into several groups and have them review newspaper accounts of Marshall's files (May 1993). One or two groups should focus on key cases (particularly in the area of civil liberties) while another group should focus on the controversy over the decision to release the papers to the press.

- For an interesting class discussion, have students debate how democratic the Supreme Court is compared to other institutions. The discussion should integrate the material learned in other chapters about the role of representation and elections in enforcing accountability and responsibility in policy making.

- For a reading and writing connection, have students read memoirs and court papers from justices, attorneys, and others involved in the civil rights cases of the 1950s and 1960s. Why were these cases appealed to the courts? Were the courts acting in a democratic manner in their decisions? Why were the decisions made when they were? Did the composition of the court, the broader political context, or the specific legal strategy seem to influence the outcome the most?

- Have students read <u>The Brethren</u> and write brief essays on the myths of the judiciary, politics, or the legal system that it challenges.

- Assign the various court cases (federal and state) that arose as a result of the 2000 presidential election. Have each group brief each case (e.g. parties to the case, origin, issues, the decision, and the reasoning behind it). Then, in class discussion, have students evaluate the courts' decisions, and how democratic they were.

BACKGROUND READING

Abraham, Henry J. The Judiciary: The Supreme Court and the Governmental Process, 9th ed.. NY: Brown and Benchmark. 1994.

Baum, Lawrence. American Courts: Process and Policy. Boston: Houghton-Mifflin. 1998.

Baum, Lawrence. The Supreme Court. 6th ed. Washington, DC: Congressional Quarterly Press. 1998.

Bickel, Alexander M. The Least Dangerous Branch: The Supreme Court at the Bar of Politics. New Haven, CT: Yale University Press. 1986.

Epstein, Lee. Constitutional Law for a Changing America: Institutional Powers and Constraints. Washington D.C.: CQ Press. 1998.

Epstein, Lee. Contemplating Courts. Washington, D.C.: CQ Press. 1995.

Epstein, Lee and Jack Knight. The Choices Justices Make. Washington, D.C.: CQ Press. 1998.

Jacob, Herbert. Law and Politics in the United States. 2nd ed. Boston: Little, Brown. 1995.

Johnson, Charles A. and Bradley C. Cannon. Judicial Policies: Implementation and Impact. Washington, DC. Congressional Quarterly Press. 1998.

Wasby, Stephen. The Supreme Court in the Federal Judicial System. 4th ed. Chicago: Nelson-Hall. 1993.

MEDIA SUGGESTIONS

<u>An Introduction to the Federal Courts</u>. Part of the "Court System" series distributed by Insight Media. This 1991 program provides a general introduction to the structure and process of the judicial system.

<u>Congress and the Courts</u>. Part of the Congress: We the People Series distributed by Films Incorporated. Provides an examination of the structural relationship between Congress and the Supreme Court.

<u>Hill vs. Thomas</u>. This program, hosted by Lesley Stahl, provides diverse viewpoints on the Senate nomination hearings of Supreme Court justice Clarence Thomas. Films for the Humanities & Sciences.

<u>The Making of a Justice</u>. Part of the PBS series entitled "The Presidency and the Constitution." Examines the question of representativeness in the Supreme Court.

CHAPTER SEVENTEEN: ECONOMIC POLICY-MAKING

PEDAGOGICAL FEATURES

LEARNING OBJECTIVES

After studying this chapter, students should be able to:

- Recognize the dynamics of the interrelationship of *politics* and the *economy*.
- Identify the tools that are used by government in an attempt to control the economy.
- Summarize the key role of the Federal Reserve System in setting U.S. monetary policy.
- Recognize obstacles that make it difficult for politicians to manipulate the economy for short-run advantage to win elections.
- Contrast the views of liberals and conservatives with respect to government involvement in the economy.

- Describe the ways in which government both *benefits* and *regulates* areas of the economy such as business, labor, and agriculture.
- Summarize the development of U.S. consumer protection policy.
- Understand the relationship between democracy, the scope of government, and economic policy in America.

CHAPTER OVERVIEW

INTRODUCTION

Politics and economics are powerful, intertwined forces shaping public policies and public lives. The view that politics and economics are closely linked is neither new nor unique. Although the United States is often described as operating under a **capitalist** economic system, it is more accurately described as a **mixed economy**, a system in which the government, while not commanding the economy, is still deeply involved in economic decisions. Because voters are sensitive to economic conditions, the parties must pay close attention to those conditions when selecting their policies. Voters often judge officeholders by how well the economy performs. This chapter explores the economy and the public policies dealing with it.

GOVERNMENT AND THE ECONOMY

The problem of **unemployment** is one component of policymakers' regular economic concern. Measuring how many and what types of workers are unemployed is one of the major jobs of the Bureau of Labor Statistics (BLS) in the Department of Labor. Each 1 percent in the unemployment rate represents more than a million people out of work; adverse economic conditions are significantly associated with complex social problems. Unemployment impacts disproportionately upon minorities, who typically suffer unemployment rates two or three times higher than those of whites.

Some economists challenge the BLS's *definition* of the unemployment rate (the proportion of the labor force *actively seeking work* but unable to find a job). The unemployment rate would be higher if it included *"discouraged workers"*—people who have become so frustrated that they have stopped actively seeking employment. On the other hand, if the unemployment rate included only those who were unemployed long enough to cause them severe hardship, it would be much lower since most people are out of work for only a short time.

The problem of **inflation** is the other component of policymakers' regular economic concern. The **Consumer Price Index (CPI)** is the key measure of inflation. Some groups are especially hard hit by inflation (such as those who live on fixed incomes), while those whose salary increases are tied to the CPI (but who have fixed payments such as mortgages) may find that inflation actually increases their buying power.

People who are unemployed, worried about the prospect of being unemployed, or struggling with runaway inflation have an outlet to express some of their dissatisfaction – the polling booth. Ample evidence indicates that economic trends affect how voters make up their minds on election day, taking into consideration not just their own financial situation but the economic condition of the nation as well.

INSTRUMENTS FOR CONTROLLING THE ECONOMY

The impact of government on the economic system is substantial, but it is also sharply limited by a basic commitment to a free enterprise system. The time when government could ignore economic problems, confidently asserting that the private marketplace could handle them, has long passed. When the stock market crash of 1929 sent unemployment soaring, President Herbert Hoover clung to **laissez-faire** – the principle that government should not meddle with the economy. In the next presidential election, Hoover was handed a crushing defeat by Franklin D. Roosevelt. Government has been actively involved in steering the economy since the Great Depression and the New Deal.

Monetary policy and fiscal policy are two tools by which government tries to guide the economy. **Monetary policy** involves the *manipulation of the supply of money and credit* in private hands. An economic theory called **monetarism** holds that the supply of money is key to the nation's economic health. The main agency for making monetary policy is the Board of Governors of the **Federal Reserve System** ("the Fed"). The Fed has three basic instruments for controlling the money supply: setting *discount rates* for the money that banks borrow from the Federal Reserve banks; setting *reserve requirements* that determine the amount of money that banks must keep in reserve at all times; and exercising control over the money supply by *buying and selling government securities* in the market (*open market operations*).

Fiscal policy describes the *impact of the federal budget—taxing, spending, and borrowing—on the economy.* Fiscal policy is shaped mostly by the Congress and the president. Democrats tend to favor **Keynesian economic theory**, which holds that government must stimulate greater demand, when necessary, with bigger government (such as federal job programs). This theory emphasizes that government spending could help the economy weather its normal fluctuations, even if it means running in the red.

Since the Reagan administration, many republicans advocate **supply-side economics**, which calls for smaller government to increase the incentive to produce more goods. Ronald Reagan's economic advisors proposed this theory (which is radically different from traditional Keynesian economics), based on the premise that the key task for government economic policy is to *stimulate the supply* of goods, not their *demand.* Supply-side economists argued that incentives to invest, work harder, and save could be increased by cutting back on the scope of government. During his first administration, Reagan fought for and won massive tax cuts, mostly for the well-to-do. Instead of a fiscal policy that promoted bigger government, Americans got a policy that tried (but ultimately failed) to reduce the size of government.

OBSTACLES TO CONTROLLING THE ECONOMY

Some scholars argue that politicians manipulate the economy for short-run advantage to win elections; however, no one has shown that decisions to influence the economy at election time have been made on a regular basis. The inability of politicians to so precisely control economic conditions as to facilitate their reelection rests on a number of factors, including the decentralized nature of economic policy-making in the United States.

ARENAS OF ECONOMIC POLICY-MAKING

Government spends one-third of America's gross national product and regulates much of the other two-thirds—a situation that stimulates a great deal of debate. *Liberals* tend to favor active government involvement in the economy in order to smooth out the unavoidable inequality of a capitalist system. *Conservatives* maintain that the most productive economy is one in which the government exercises a hands-off policy of minimal regulation. *Liberal or conservative*, most interest groups seek benefits, protection from unemployment, or safeguards against harmful business practices.

Competition in today's economy is often about which corporations control access to, and the profits from, the new economy. In the old and the new economy,

Americans have always been suspicious of concentrated power, whether it is in the hands of government or business. In both the old economy and the new, government policy has tried to control excess power. The purpose of **antitrust policy** is to *ensure competition* and *prevent monopoly.* Antitrust legislation permits the Justice Department to sue in federal court to break up companies that control too large a share of the market. It also generally prevents restraints on trade or limitations on competition, such as price fixing. Enforcement of antitrust legislation has varied considerably.

Although business owners and managers complain about regulation, the government also sometimes comes to the *aid* of struggling businesses. When a crucial industry falls on hard times, it usually looks to the government for help in terms of subsidies, tax breaks, or loan guarantees (as the Chrysler Corporation did when it was close to bankruptcy).

The federal government is also involved in setting policies for consumer protection. The first major consumer protection policy in the United States was the **Food and Drug Act of 1906**, which prohibited the interstate transportation of dangerous or impure food and drugs. Today the **Food and Drug Administration (FDA)** has broad regulatory powers over the manufacturing, contents, marketing, and labeling of food and drugs. The **Federal Trade Commission (FTC)**, traditionally responsible for regulating trade practices, also jumped into the business of consumer protection in the 1960s and 1970s, becoming a defender of consumer interests in truth in advertising. "Consumerism" was awakened in the 1960s by consumer activists such as Ralph Nader, who argued that it was the government's responsibility to be a watchdog on behalf of the consumer. Budget cuts made during the 1980s left many independent regulatory agencies open to criticism from the consumer groups they were created to protect.

Throughout most of the nineteenth century and well into the twentieth, the federal government allied with business elites to squelch labor unions. Until the **Clayton Antitrust Act of 1914** exempted unions from antitrust laws, the federal government spent more time busting unions than trusts. Government enforced **"yellow dog contracts"**— contracts that forced workers to agree not to join a union as a condition of employment. In 1935, Congress passed the **National Labor Relations Act** (the *Wagner Act*), which guaranteed workers the right of **collective bargaining**—the right to have labor union representatives negotiate with management to determine working conditions—and set rules to protect unions and organizers. The **Taft-Hartley Act** of 1947 continued to guarantee unions the right of collective bargaining, but also prohibited various unfair practices by unions. Later public policies focused on *union corruption* with acts such as the *Labor-Management Reporting and Disclosure Act* of 1959 (also called the **Landrum-Griffin Act**).

UNDERSTANDING ECONOMIC POLICYMAKING

Some of the unjust aspects of a capitalist economy—which have caused revolutions in other countries—have been curbed in the United States; solutions to many of the problems of a free enterprise economy were achieved through the democratic process. As the voting power of the ordinary worker grew, so did the potential for government regulation of the worst aspects of the capitalist system.

On the other hand, it would be an exaggeration to say that democracy regularly facilitates an economic policy that looks after general rather than specific interests. One of the consequences of democracy for economic policy-making is that groups that may be adversely affected by an economic policy have many avenues through which they can work to block it. The *decentralized American political system* often works *against efficiency* in government.

Liberals and conservatives disagree about the scope of government involvement in the economy. Liberals focus on the imperfections of the market and what government can do about them; conservatives focus on the imperfections of government.

CHAPTER OUTLINE

I. POLITICS AND ECONOMICS

A. In the United States, the political and economic sectors are closely intermingled in a mixed economy, where the government, while not commanding the economy, is still deeply involved in economic decisions.

B. Policymakers worry constantly about the state of the economy, and voters often judge officeholders by how well the economy performs.

C. Measuring how many and what types of workers are unemployed is one of the major jobs of the **Bureau of Labor Statistics (BLS)** in the Department of Labor.

1. No one questions using a survey to determine the **unemployment rate**, but some economists do challenge the BLS's *definition* of this rate (the proportion of the labor force *actively seeking work* but unable to find a job).

D. Adverse economic conditions are significantly associated with complex social problems.
   1. An increase in unemployment is associated with increases in a variety of social problems such as the suicide rate, admissions to state mental hospitals, homicide rate, and deaths from cirrhosis of the liver (usually associated with alcoholism).
   2. Unemployment impacts disproportionately upon minorities, who typically suffer unemployment rates two or three times higher than those of whites.
E. The problem of **inflation** is the other half of policymakers' regular economic concern.
   1. The **Consumer Price Index (CPI)** is the key measure of inflation.
   2. Some groups are especially hard hit by inflation, such as those who live on fixed incomes.
   3. By contrast, people whose salary increases are tied to the CPI (but who have fixed payments such as mortgages) may find that inflation actually increases their buying power.
F. Elections and the economy.
   1. Evidence indicates that voters pay attention to economic trends in making up their minds on election day—and that they consider not just their own financial situation, but the economic condition of the nation as well.
   2. Roderick Kiewiet finds that voters who experience *unemployment* in their family are more likely to support Democratic candidates; concern over *inflation* has had less impact on voter choices.
G. Political parties and the economy.
   1. Because voters are sensitive to economic conditions, the parties must pay close attention to those conditions when selecting their policies.
   2. Democrats and Republicans do have different economic policies, particularly with respect to unemployment and inflation—a difference that reflects the voting coalitions that support the two parties.
      a. Democrats try to curb unemployment more than Republicans (though they risk inflation in so doing).
      b. Republicans are generally more concerned with controlling inflation (even at the risk of greater unemployment).

II. INSTRUMENTS FOR CONTROLLING THE ECONOMY

A. The impact of government on the economic system is substantial, but it is also sharply limited by a basic commitment to a free enterprise system.

1. When the **stock market crash of 1929** sent unemployment soaring, President Herbert Hoover clung to the ***laissez-faire*** principle that government should not meddle with the economy.
2. In the next presidential election, Hoover was handily defeated by Franklin D. Roosevelt, whose **New Deal** experimented with dozens of new federal policies to put the economy back on track.
3. Government has been actively involved in steering the economy since the Great Depression and the New Deal.
4. The American political economy uses two important *tools to guide the economy—monetary policy* and *fiscal policy.*

B. Monetary policy and the Fed.
1. **Monetary policy** involves the *manipulation of the supply of money and credit* in private hands.
   a. An economic theory called **monetarism** holds that the supply of money is the key to the nation's economic health.
   b. Monetarists believe that having too much cash and credit in circulation generates inflation.
2. The main agency for making monetary policy is the Board of Governors of the **Federal Reserve System** (otherwise known as "*the Fed*").
   a. Created by Congress in 1913 to regulate the lending practices of banks and thus the money supply, the Federal Reserve System is intended to be formally beyond the control of either the president and Congress.
   b. Its seven-member Board of Governors is appointed by the president (and confirmed by the Senate) for fourteen-year terms—a length of the time designed to insulate them from political pressures; the general finding is that the Fed actually is responsive to the White House, but at times the chief executive can be left frustrated by the politically insulated decisions of the Fed.
3. The Fed has three basic instruments for controlling the money supply.
   a. The Fed sets **discount rates** for the money that banks borrow from the Federal Reserve banks; by raising or lowering the rate that banks pay, these increased (or decreased) costs will be passed on to people who take out loans, and thus affect the amount of money in circulation.
   b. The Fed sets **reserve requirements** that determine the amount of money that banks must keep in reserve at all times; banks have less money to lend out when the reserve requirements are raised

and more money to lend when the reserve requirements are lowered.

c. The Fed can exercise control over the money supply by *buying and selling government securities* in the market (open market operations), thereby either expanding or contracting the money supply.

C. Fiscal policy: Keynesian versus supply-side economics.

1. **Fiscal policy** describes the *impact of the federal budget—taxing, spending, and borrowing—on the economy.*
2. Fiscal policy is *shaped mostly by the Congress and the president.*
3. Whether bigger government or smaller government best ensures a strong economy has become the central issue in economic policy-making.
4. On the side of big government, Democrats lean more toward **Keynesian economic theory**, which holds that government must stimulate greater demand, when necessary, with bigger government (such as federal job programs).
5. Many Republicans advocate **supply-side economics**, which calls for smaller government (such as tax cuts) to increase the incentive to produce more goods.
   a. Rather than public works programs to stimulate demand, Americans received tax cuts to stimulate supply.
   b. Instead of a fiscal policy that promoted bigger government, Americans received a policy that tried (but ultimately failed) to reduce the size of government.

III. OBSTACLES TO CONTROLLING THE ECONOMY

A. Some scholars argue that politicians manipulate the economy for short-run advantage to win elections; however, no one has shown that decisions to influence the economy at election time have been made on a regular basis.

B. The inability of politicians to so precisely control economic conditions as to facilitate their reelection rests on a number of factors (or "weak links").

1. Politicians—and even economists—do not understand the workings of the economy sufficiently well to always choose the correct adjustments to ensure prosperity.
2. Most policies must be decided upon a year or more before their full impact will be felt on the economy.
3. The American *capitalist system* presents a restraint on controlling the economy: because the private sector is much larger than the public sector, it *dominates the economy.*

4. The increasingly interdependent world activities of other nations can interfere with the American government's economic plans.
5. Fiscal policy is hindered by the *budgetary process*: most of the budget expenditures for any given year are "uncontrollable."
   a. Since most spending is already mandated by law, it is very difficult to make substantial cuts. [see Chapter 14]
   b. Benefits like Social Security are now *indexed*, meaning that they go up automatically as the cost of living increases.
6. Economic policy in the United States is decentralized: the president and Congress may not agree on taxes or spending, and neither may agree with the Fed.

IV. ARENAS OF ECONOMIC POLICYMAKING

A. *Government spends one-third of America's gross national product* and *regulates much of the other two-thirds*—a situation that provokes a great deal of debate.
   1. *Liberals* tend to favor active government involvement in the economy in order to smooth out the unavoidable inequality of a capitalist system.
   2. *Conservatives* maintain that the most productive economy is one in which the government exercises a hands-off policy of minimal regulation.
   3. *Liberal or conservative*, most interest groups seek benefits, protection from unemployment, or safeguards against harmful business practices.

B. Regulating business.
   1. The purpose of **antitrust policy** is to *ensure competition* and *prevent monopoly* (control of a market by one company).
   2. Government regulation of business is at least as old at the **Sherman Antitrust Act of 1890.**
   3. Benefiting business.
      a. Although business owners and managers complain about regulation, the government also sometimes comes to the *aid* of struggling businesses.
         (1) When a crucial industry falls on hard times, it usually looks to the government for help in terms of subsidies, tax breaks, or loan guarantees.
         (2) When Chrysler Corporation was close to bankruptcy—a failure that would have hurt thousands of workers and many American industries—the government guaranteed private loans that saved the automaker.

(3) In a few cases (Chrysler, Lockheed, and the nation's railroads), government loans or buyouts have made government an actual partner or owner in corporate America.

C. Consumer policy.
   1. The first major consumer protection policy in the United States was the **Food and Drug Act of 1906**, which prohibited the interstate transportation of dangerous or impure food and drugs.
   2. Today the **Food and Drug Administration (FDA)** has *broad regulatory powers over the manufacturing, contents, marketing, and labeling of food and drugs.*
      a. It is the FDA's responsibility to ascertain the safety and effectiveness of new drugs before approving them for marketing in America.
      b. One recent criticism of the FDA is that funding cuts have left it overburdened and seriously understaffed.
   3. "Consumerism" was awakened in the 1960s by consumer activists such as Ralph Nader, who argued that it was the government's responsibility to be a watchdog on behalf of the consumer.
      a. With broad public support, the 1960s and 1970s saw a flood of **consumer product legislation.**
      b. The **Consumer Product Safety Commission (CPSC)** has broad powers to ban hazardous products from the market.
   4. The **Federal Trade Commission (FTC)**—which has traditionally been responsible for regulating trade practices—also jumped into the business of consumer protection in the 1960s and 1970s; in 1968, Congress made the FTC the administrator of the new **Consumer Credit Protection Act** (which enforces "truth in lending").
   5. *Budget cuts* made during the 1980s left many independent regulatory agencies open to criticism from the consumer groups they were created to protect.

D. Labor and government.
   1. Throughout most of the nineteenth century and well into the twentieth, the federal government allied with business elites to squelch labor unions.
      a. The courts interpreted the antitrust laws as applying to unions as well as businesses.
      b. Until the **Clayton Antitrust Act of 1914** exempted unions from antitrust laws, the federal government spent more time busting unions than trusts.

c. Government enforced **"yellow dog contracts"**—contracts that forced workers to agree not to join a union as a condition of employment.

2. The major turning point in government policy toward labor took place during the New Deal.
   a. In 1935, Congress passed the **National Labor Relations Act** (often called the *Wagner Act*), which guaranteed workers the right of **collective bargaining**—the right to have labor union representatives negotiate with management to determine working conditions—and set rules to protect unions and organizers.
   b. The **Taft-Hartley Act** of 1947 continued to guarantee unions the right of collective bargaining, but also prohibited various unfair practices by unions.
      (1) It gave the president the power to halt major strikes by seeking a court injunction for an eighty-day "cooling off" period.
      (2) The law permitted states to adopt what union opponents call **right-to-work laws**—laws that forbid labor contracts from requiring workers to join unions in order to hold their jobs.
3. Later public policies focused on *union corruption* with acts such as the *Labor-Management Reporting and Disclosure Act* of 1959 (also called the **Landrum-Griffin Act**).
4. Unions have had two notable successes.
   a. Partly as the result of successful union lobbying, the government provides *unemployment compensation*.
   b. Since the era of the New Deal, government has *guaranteed a minimum wage* for hourly employees.

V. UNDERSTANDING ECONOMIC POLICY-MAKING

A. In America, solutions to many of the problems of a **free enterprise economy** were achieved through the democratic process.
   1. Some of the unjust aspects of a capitalist economy—which have caused revolutions in other countries—have been curbed in the United States.
   2. As the voting power of the ordinary worker grew, so did the potential for government regulation of the worst aspects of the capitalist system; political pressure grew for action to restrict unfair business practices and protect individual rights.
   3. The minimum wage and unemployment compensation are just two of many economic policies that contradict Karl Marx's assumptions of how a capitalist system inevitably exploits ordinary workers.

4. Likewise, the right to free enterprise is no longer interpreted as giving businesses the right to employ 10-year-olds or to force employees to work in unsafe conditions.

B. It would be an exaggeration to say that democracy regularly facilitates an economic policy that looks after general rather than specific interests.
   1. One of the consequences of democracy for economic policy-making is that groups that may be adversely affected by an economic policy have many avenues through which they can work to block it.
   2. The *decentralized American political system* often works *against efficiency* in government.

C. Economic policymaking and the scope of government.
   1. Liberals and conservatives disagree about the scope of government involvement in the economy.
   2. Liberals focus on the imperfections of the market and what government can do about them; conservatives focus on the imperfections of government.

KEY TERMS AND CONCEPTS

Antitrust policy: government regulation of business to ensure competition and prevent monopoly (control of a market by one company).

Capitalism: an economic system in which individuals and corporations own the principal means of production, through which they seek to reap profits.

Collective bargaining: the right of workers to have labor union representatives negotiate with management to determine working conditions.

Consumer price index (CPI): a government statistic that measures the change in the cost of buying a fixed basket of goods and services.

Federal Reserve System: created by Congress in 1913 to regulate the lending practices of banks and thus the money supply.

Federal Trade Commission (FTC): government agency responsible for regulating trade practices.

Fiscal policy: the government's decisions to tax, spend and borrow, as reflected in the federal budget.

Food and Drug Administration (FDA): government agency with broad regulatory powers over the manufacturing, contents, marketing and labeling of food and drugs.

Inflation: a government statistic that measures increases in the price of goods. Keynesian economic theory: named after English economist John Maynard Keynes, this economic philosophy emphasizes that government spending can help the economy weather its normal ups and downs, even if requiring deficit spending.

Keynesian economic theory: the theory emphasizing that government spending and deficits can help the economy weather its normal ups and downs. Proponents of this theory advocate using the power of government to stimulate the economy when it is lagging.

Laissez-faire: a belief that government should not intervene in the economy.

Mixed economy: a system in which the government, while not commanding the economy, is still deeply involved in economic decisions.

Monetarism: economic theory that suggests that the supply of money is key to the nation's economic health.

Monetary policy: government decisions regarding the money supply, including the discount rates for bank borrowing, reserve requirements for banks and trading of government securities.

National Labor Relations Act: passed by Congress in 1935, guarantees workers the right of collective bargaining; also known as the Wagner Act.

Right to work laws: laws forbidding labor contracts from requiring workers to join unions to hold their jobs.

Supply-side economics: economic philosophy that holds that the key task for government economic policy is to stimulate the supply of goods, not their demand.

Taft-Hartley Act: passed by Congress in 1947, prohibits various unfair practices by unions.

Transnational corporations: businesses with vast holdings in many countries.

Unemployment rate: a government statistic that measures how many workers are unemployed.

TEACHING IDEAS: CLASS DISCUSSION AND STUDENT PROJECTS

- *Monetary policy* is primarily set by appointed officials (the Fed) while *fiscal policy* is primarily established by elected officeholders (the president and Congress). Ask your class to consider whether the difference between elected and appointed policymakers appears to have an effect in setting our nation's economic policy.

- U.S. citizens frequently express concerns about the size of foreign investment in the United States (even though it still remains below that of most other economic powers). Survey your class to see what their reactions would be if other nations placed restrictions on *American* investments. An interesting class report could be based on U.S. resentment of French policies under Charles DeGaulle, at a time when the United States still had a positive international balance of payment and the French feared American intrusion into their economy and culture.

- As a library assignment, ask students to research some of the methodological issues surrounding our standard economic measures such as unemployment, inflation, and the consumer price index. In what ways are these measures biased? What don't they measure about the economy? Are there any alternative measures of economic health that should also be considered in economic policy-making?

- Have students examine the platform of the Republican and Democrat parties. Do the parties state particular economic goals? What policy positions do they espouse to reach those goals?

- Ask students to prepare briefs on current economic / regulatory issues being considered by Congress or regulatory agencies. Then have them research who supports regulatory change, the nature of such proposals, and who opposes the changes.

BACKGROUND READING

Morris, Irwin L. Congress, the President, and the Federal Reserve: The Politics of American Monetary Policymaking. Ann Arbor, Michigan: University of Michigan Press. 1999.

Tanzi, Vito, Ke-young Chu, and Sanjeez Gupta, eds. Economic Policy and Equity. Washington, DC: Brookings Institution. 1999.

MEDIA SUGGESTIONS

The Great Divide. This program focuses on the moral and ethical issues raised by the economic trend of the 1980s, with the rich getting richer and the poor getting poorer. Films for the Humanities & Sciences.

A Job for the World. Provides an overview of how world leaders have reacted to unemployment, underemployment and an unstable work environment. Films for the Humanities and Sciences.

Microsoft vs. the Justice Department: Playing Monopoly. Provides a background to the Microsoft anti-trust suit, focusing on legal arguments as well as public reactions to the dominance of Microsoft in the microcomputer market. Films for the Humanities & Sciences.

Minimum Wages. This film featuring Bill Moyers examines how global economic changes are changing the fortunes of the American working class. Films for the Humanities and Sciences.

Old Ways, New Game. This program focuses on the consequences of global competition for American workers and corporations, highlighting the effects of competition from Germany and Japan. Films for the Humanities and Sciences.

Politics in Action, Chapter 6: The Global Political Economy. Provides an overview of the debate over NAFTA.

CHAPTER EIGHTEEN: SOCIAL WELFARE POLICY-MAKING

PEDAGOGICAL FEATURES

LEARNING OBJECTIVES

After studying this chapter, students should be able to:

- Examine the related concepts of *income distribution* and *relative deprivation.*
- Summarize how liberals and conservatives disagree about the conduct and impact of public assistance programs.
- Identify the three major types of taxes and show how each can affect citizens' incomes.

- Summarize the effects that social welfare programs have had on the day-to-day living conditions of groups of Americans, such as the poor, the young, and the elderly.
- Differentiate between *entitlement* programs and *means-tested* programs.
- Indicate the role that entitlements play in the U.S. budgetary system.
- Identify the major American social welfare programs and the groups that benefit from them.
- Contrast social welfare policy in the United States with that of other major Western democracies.
- Trace the evolution of America's social welfare programs, with emphasis on the role of the Great Depression.
- Examine *intergenerational equality issues* that stem from the disparity in public dollars spent on the elderly as contrasted with public funds spent on children.
- Compare and contrast the views of recent presidents of both political parties toward social welfare expenditures.
- Explain why policy-making in the United States is very *incremental* in nature.
- Examine the relationship between social welfare policy and the scope of government.

CHAPTER OVERVIEW

INTRODUCTION

The vast differences in the wealth and income of citizens in the United States raise a host of questions related to why such differences exist and what the appropriate policy response should be. **Social welfare policies** attempt to provide assistance and support to specific groups in society.

THE SOCIAL WELFARE DEBATE

Many Americans equate social welfare exclusively with government moneys given to the poor. Yet the government gives far more money to the nonpoor than to people below the "poverty line." Some benefits (such as Medicare) may be provided regardless of financial need and are termed **entitlements**. Other benefits (such as food stamps and unemployment payments), are **means-tested,** provided selectively to those in particular need who meet specific eligibility criteria. This chapter emphasizes that these policies are determined as part of a political process, where some interests are represented more than others.

INCOME, POVERTY, AND PUBLIC POLICY

The concept of **income distribution** describes the share of national income earned by various groups in the United States. The distribution of income across segments of the American population is quite uneven. **Income** is the amount of money collected between any two points in time (such as a week or a year); **wealth** is the amount already owned (such as stocks, bonds, bank accounts, cars, and houses). Studies of wealth display even more inequality than those of income.

The sense of relative deprivation is becoming the common experience of a growing number of Americans. The census lists Americans' median family income in 1999 as $38,900, but there is also a great deal of poverty.

Poverty in America is concentrated among a few groups. Large percentages of some groups are poor, including African-Americans, Hispanics, young Americans, inner city residents, and rural residents.

The government spends one out of every three dollars in the American economy, and thus has a major impact on its citizens' wealth and income. In particular, there are two principal ways in which government can affect a person's income: government can *manipulate incomes through its taxing powers*, and government can *affect income through its expenditure policies*.

The best evidence indicates that the overall incidence of taxes in America is proportional, not regressive or progressive. This occurs because *regressive state and local taxes* are counterbalanced by more *progressive federal taxes*. Government *spending* policies can also affect a person's income. Benefits from government are called **transfer payments** because they transfer money from the general treasury to those in specific need. Government can also give an **"in-kind payment,"** something with cash value that is not cash itself (such as food stamps or a low-interest loan for college education).

THE EVOLUTION OF AMERICA'S SOCIAL WELFARE PROGRAMS

For centuries societies considered family welfare to be a private concern. With the growth of large, depersonalized cities and the requirements of the urban workforce, government was impelled to take a more active role in social welfare support.

A major change in how Americans viewed government's role in providing social welfare came during the Great Depression. After the onset of the Depression in 1929, many Americans began to think that governments must do more to protect their citizens against economic downturns. In 1935, the federal government responded to this change by passing the Social Security Act, one of the most significant pieces of social welfare legislation of all time. Other programs such as Medicare were added later.

The 1960s brought an outpouring of federal programs to help the poor and the elderly, to create economic opportunities for those at the lower rungs of the economic ladder, and to reduce discrimination against minorities. Many of these programs were established during the presidency of Lyndon B. Johnson (1963-1969), whose administration coined the term the "Great Society" for these policy initiatives.

The *entitlement programs*—aimed primarily at the elderly—had strong political support. Advocates of greater spending for *poverty programs* had a more difficult time. Poverty was closely tied to race issues in the minds of many people, and the poor were limited in their ability to form strong political bases from which to demand government help. Perhaps the *most important element for the success of both program types* was *strong presidential leadership.* President Johnson provided strong presidential commitment; he worked to rally the Congress, public opinion, and major interest groups behind him.

Likewise, it was the active leadership of a subsequent president (Ronald Reagan) that helped build coalitions to move American social welfare programs in a *different* direction. President Reagan chose to target poverty programs as one major way to *cut government spending.* This action served his own ideological beliefs of *less government* and *more self-sufficiency.* The president rallied public opinion and worked to create congressional coalitions to support these efforts. The Omnibus Budget Reconciliation Act (OBRA) of 1981 initiated many of the cuts President Reagan had sought, including substantial cuts in the AFDC program. Despite major changes, the basic outlines of the original programs persisted throughout the Reagan and Bush administrations.

In August 1996 President Clinton signed a welfare reform bill that was supported by congressional Republicans but was opposed by half of congressional Democrats. The major provisions of the bill included giving each state a fixed amount of money to run its own welfare program; requiring people on welfare to find jobs within two years or lose their benefits; and setting a lifetime maximum of five years on welfare. After welfare reform, they were known as **Temporary Assistance to Needy Families** (TANF), today's name for the means-tested aid for the poorest of the poor. TANF benefits like AFDC are small and declining. It is too early to assess the implications of these policy changes for social welfare.

THE FUTURE OF SOCIAL WELFARE POLICY

The long-term sustainability of entitlement programs, particularly Social Security and Medicare, is a matter of much current debate. Indeed, as it stands now, the Social Security program is living on borrowed time. At some point – about 2038 unless something changes – payouts will exceed income. The issue of Social Security awoke in the election of 2000, when Governor George W. Bush and the Republicans proposed diverting a small portion (the suggested figure was two percent) of Social Security contributions to private retirement funds.

The future of means-tested programs for the poor is another matter. Antipoverty programs have never been remotely as popular as programs for the elderly. The evidence that Social Security has lifted the elderly out of poverty is powerful. The evidence that antipoverty programs have lifted the poor out of poverty is mixed at best.

UNDERSTANDING SOCIAL WELFARE POLICY

In the social welfare policy arena, the competing groups are often quite unequal in terms of political resources. For example, the elderly are relatively well organized and often have the resources needed to wield significant influence in support of programs they desire. As a result, they are usually successful in protecting and expanding their programs. For the poor, however, influencing political decisions is more difficult. They vote less frequently and lack strong, focused organizations and money.

Although government benefits are difficult to enact, the nature of democratic politics makes it difficult to withdraw them once they are established. Tremendous pressures come from these supporters to keep or expand programs and to preserve them from elimination. These pressures persist even when the size and costs of programs seem to have grown beyond anything anyone might have originally envisioned.

Large government programs require large organizations to administer them. Past democratic conflicts and compromises in the social welfare policy area have given America a huge social welfare bureaucracy at all levels of government. The appropriate way to evaluate these administrative systems is not to focus on their scope or expense alone, but to weigh their scope and expense against the conduct of their mission, the goals and accomplishments of these programs, and the extent to which private non-governmental entities could realistically be depended on to help.

CHAPTER OUTLINE

I. INTRODUCTION

A. The United States is a diverse nation whose citizens and groups achieve different levels of material success. The fact that these differences exist raises important public policy questions.
   1. What are the economic differences and why do they exist?
   2. What roles should the government and the private sector play in helping those who are less fortunate?
   3. What are the most effective government policies?

B. **Social welfare policies** attempt to provide assistance and support to specific groups in society.

II. THE SOCIAL WELFARE DEBATE

A. Social Welfare Policies.
   1. Although social welfare programs have not ended poverty or reduced income inequality in America, these programs have produced substantial improvements in the day-to-day living conditions of many Americans.
   2. **Entitlement programs** like Social Security and Medicare are the largest and most expensive social welfare programs in America. [see Table 18.2, which summarizes the major social welfare programs]
      a. The elderly are receiving more and better treatment as a result of Medicare, and Social Security payments keep many senior citizens out of poverty.

3. **Means-tested programs** aimed specifically at the poor—such as Medicaid and food stamps—are funded at much lower levels than non-means tested entitlement programs for the elderly.
   a. Means-tested programs help a lot of poor Americans escape some of the ravages of poverty.
   b. Even though the expenditures for these poverty programs are substantially less than those provided for entitlement programs, they have raised many of the poor above the official poverty line.

III. INCOME, POVERTY AND PUBLIC POLICY

A. Who's getting what.
   1. The concept of **income distribution** describes the share of national income earned by various groups in the United States.
      a. The distribution of income across segments of the American population is quite uneven.
      b. During the 1960s and 1970s there was relatively little change in the distribution of income in America.
      c. The 1980s were a period when the rich got richer and the poor got poorer, with income and wages distributed more unequally among working people.
   2. **Income** is the amount of money collected between any two points in time (such as a week or a year); **wealth** is the amount already owned (including stocks, bonds, bank accounts, cars, and houses).
      a. Studies of wealth display even more inequality than those of income, with the top one percent of the wealth-holders currently possessing about 37 percent of all American wealth.

B. Who's at the bottom? Poverty in America.
   1. To count the poor, the U.S. Bureau of the Census has established the **poverty line**, which takes into account what a family would need to spend to maintain an "austere" standard of living (defined in 1998 as an annual income below $12,803 for a family of three).
   2. Poverty in America is concentrated among a few groups including African-Americans, Hispanics, young Americans, inner city residents, and rural residents.
   3. Because of the high incidence of poverty among unmarried mothers and their children, experts on poverty often describe the problem today as the **feminization of poverty**.

C. How public policy affects income.
   1. The government spends one out of every three dollars in the American economy, and thus has a major impact on its citizens' wealth and income.

2. In particular, there are two principal ways in which government can affect a person's income.
   a. Government can *manipulate income through its taxing powers.*
   b. Government can *affect income through its expenditure policies.*
3. Taxation.
   a. In general, there are three types of taxes; each can affect citizens' incomes in a different way.
      (1) A **progressive tax** takes a bigger bite from the incomes of the rich than from the poor (such as a progressive income tax that takes a higher percentage of income from the wealthy).
      (2) A **proportional tax** takes the same share from everyone, regardless of income or wealth (sometimes called a "flat rate" tax).
      (3) A **regressive tax** takes a higher percentage from the lower income levels than from the well-to-do (such as sales taxes, which are not overtly regressive but are regressive *in effect*).
   b. The best evidence indicates that the *overall incidence of taxes* in America is proportional, not regressive or progressive.
      (1) This occurs because *regressive state and local taxes* are counterbalanced by more *progressive federal taxes.*
      (2) At the national level, the wealthy are paying a good deal of the income taxes used to support many government policies, including poverty-related social welfare programs.
4. Government expenditures.
   a. The government can affect a person's income through its *spending* policies.
   b. Benefits from government are called **transfer payments** because they transfer money from the general treasury to those in specific need.
      (1) *Billions* of government checks are written every year, mostly to Social Security beneficiaries and retired government employees.
      (2) Government can also give an "*in-kind payment,*" something with cash value that is not cash itself (such as food stamps or a low-interest loan for college education).
   c. Income inequality.
      (1) It is clear that many are better off after these transfers than before (particularly the elderly); many of the poor have been raised above the poverty line by these cash and in-kind transfers.
      (2) There is little evidence that transfer programs have

significantly *redistributed* income in America or created greater income equality.

IV. THE EVOLUTION OF AMERICA'S SOCIAL WELFARE PROGRAMS

A. For centuries societies considered family welfare to be a private (not a public) concern.
  1. After the turn of the century, America and other industrialized societies recognized the breakdown in family-based support networks.
  2. With the *growth of large, depersonalized cities* and the requirements of the urban workforce, government was impelled to take a more active role in social welfare support.
  3. A major change in how Americans viewed government's role in providing social welfare came during the Great Depression.

B. The New Deal and the elderly.
  1. After the onset of the Great Depression in 1929, many Americans began to think that governments must do more to protect their citizens against economic downturns.
     a. External circumstances beyond the control of individuals or their families began to be seen as major contributions to poverty and need.
     b. In 1935, the federal government responded to this change by passing the **Social Security Act**—one of the most significant pieces of social welfare legislation of all time; other programs such as Medicare were added later.
     c. The *costs* were *shifted but not reduced*; what citizens had paid for directly they now paid for in taxes.
     d. Nationally, there has been *a redistribution of government benefits in favor of the elderly.*

C. President Johnson and the Great Society.
  1. The 1960s brought an outpouring of federal programs to help the poor and the elderly, to create economic opportunities for those at the lower rungs of the economic ladder, and to reduce discrimination against minorities.
  2. Many of these programs were established during the presidency of Lyndon B. Johnson (1963-1969), whose administration coined the term **The "Great Society"** for these policy initiatives.
     a. Johnson initiated antipoverty programs, community development programs, Medicare, school-aid schemes, job-retraining programs, and a host of other public programs.

b. During this period, government revenues were still growing and budget deficits were low (although the Vietnam War eventually drained funds from Johnson's Great Society).

3. Public reaction.
   a. The *entitlement programs*—aimed primarily at the elderly—had strong political support.
      (1) The elderly were a growing political constituency, important to both political parties.
      (2) Public opinion supported greater attention to the elderly.
   b. Advocates of greater spending for *poverty programs* had a more difficult time.
      (1) Poverty was closely tied to race issues in the minds of many people, and the worst aspects of racial discrimination and segregation were still quite fresh.
      (2) The ability of the poor and their supporters to form strong political bases from which to demand government help was limited.
      (3) On the positive side, minorities and the poor were becoming a more important constituency in the Democratic party.
   c. Perhaps the *most important element for the success of both program types* was *strong presidential leadership*.
      (1) President Johnson provided strong presidential commitment; he worked to rally the Congress, public opinion, and major interest groups behind him.
      (2) Likewise, it was the active leadership of a subsequent president (Ronald Reagan) that helped build coalitions to move American social welfare programs in a *different* direction.

D. President Reagan and limits to the Great Society.
   1. Unlike Presidents Nixon, Ford, and Carter—who largely accepted and even expanded some portions of the programs initiated by Johnson—President Reagan took a very different view.
      a. Public support for some welfare programs was eroding, particularly among members of the traditional Democratic coalition.
      b. The growing demands of defense spending and entitlement programs for the elderly had increased government deficits and threatened to stifle economic growth.
      c. The *vulnerability of the poor* had not changed: their group bases of support were still smaller than those of the elderly.
   2. Just as in the Johnson era, the major actor was the president.

a. President Reagan chose to target poverty programs as one major way to *cut government spending.*
b. This action served his own ideological beliefs of *less government* and *more self-sufficiency.*
c. The president rallied public opinion and worked to create congressional coalitions to support these efforts.

3. The **Omnibus Budget Reconciliation Act (OBRA) of 1981** initiated many of the cuts President Reagan had sought, including substantial cuts in the AFDC program.
   a. The growth rates of many programs were reduced, benefits were slashed, program burdens were shifted to the states, and many previously eligible recipients were removed from the rolls.
   b. Despite major changes, the basic outlines of the original programs persisted throughout the Reagan and Bush administrations.

E. In August of 1996, President Clinton signed a welfare reform bill that received almost unanimous backing from congressional Republicans was opposed by half of congressional Democrats.
   1. The major provisions of this bill were as follows:
      a. Each state would receive a fixed amount of money to run its own welfare programs;
      b. People on welfare would have to find work within 2 years or lose all their benefits; and
      c. A lifetime maximum of 5 years on welfare was set.
   2. Opponents of the bill expressed fears that these changes would push at least a million innocent children into poverty; proponents countered by asserting that millions would be lifted out of the culture of dependency and given the incentive to make something of their lives.

V. THE FUTURE OF SOCIAL WELFARE POLICY

A. Welfare reform over the past two decades has focused attention on:
   1. The long-term sustainability of entitlement programs, particularly Social Security and Medicare, is a matter of much current debate. Indeed, as it stands now, the Social Security program is living on borrowed time.
   2. At some point – about 2038 unless something changes – payouts will exceed income.
   3. The issue of Social Security awoke in the election of 2000, when Governor George W. Bush and the Republicans proposed diverting a small portion (the suggested figure was two percent) of Social Security contributions to private retirement funds.

B. The *evidence on how beneficial* the means-tested programs are is *mixed.*
   1. A major study by Charles Murray argued that not only did the social programs of the Great Society and later administrations fail to curb the advance of poverty, they actually made the situation worse.
   2. Murray maintained that these public policies discouraged the poor from solving their problems.
   3. Conversely, many scholars criticized Murray's argument and the decision to cut programs.
   4. Economists David Ellwood and Lawrence Summers showed that not only was spending for the poor relatively limited in these programs, but that economic growth and recessions were responsible for much of the movement into and out of poverty during the post-1965 period.

C. Social welfare policy elsewhere.
   1. American social welfare programs are more limited in scope than is the case in other democracies.
   2. Other national governments and their citizens often take a different approach to the problems of poverty and social welfare than does the United States (such as *comprehensive medical services* provided through a National Health Service).
      a. Americans tend to see poverty and social welfare needs as individual rather than governmental concerns, while European nations tend to support greater governmental responsibility for these problems.
      b. Europeans often have a more positive attitude toward government, while Americans are more likely to distrust government action in areas like social welfare policy.
   3. *Taxes commensurate with the benefits of social policy* are also commonplace in Western European nations, far exceeding those in the United States.

VI. UNDERSTANDING SOCIAL WELFARE POLICY

A. Democracy and social welfare.
   1. Sorting out the proper balance between *competition* and *compassion* is at the heart of policy disagreements about social welfare programs.
   2. In a democracy these competing demands are resolved by government decision makers.
      a. These decision makers are aligned with and pay allegiance to various groups in society.
      b. These groups include members of their legislative constituencies, members of their electoral coalitions, and members of their political party.

3. In the social welfare policy arena, the competing groups are often quite unequal in terms of political resources.
   a. The elderly are relatively well organized and often have the resources needed to wield significant influence in support of their programs.
   b. The poor vote less and lack strong focused organizations and money.
4. Although government benefits are difficult to enact, the nature of democratic politics makes it difficult to withdraw them once they are established.
   a. Policy-making in the United States is very *incremental* in nature, building on past policies.
   b. Tremendous pressures come from supporters to keep or expand programs and to preserve them from elimination.

B. Social welfare policy and the scope of government.
   1. Past democratic conflicts and compromises in the social welfare policy area have given America a huge social welfare bureaucracy at all levels of government.
   2. *Large government programs require large organizations to administer them.*
      a. The appropriate way to evaluate these administrative systems is *not to focus on their scope or expense alone*, but to *weigh* their scope and expense against the conduct of their mission, the goals and accomplishments of these programs, and the extent to which private non-governmental entities could realistically be depended on to help.
      b. With limited financial resources and a growing national debt, choices will be even more difficult to make in the future.

KEY TERMS AND CONCEPTS

Earned Income Tax Credit: a "negative income tax" that provides income to very poor individuals in lieu of charging them federal income taxes.

Entitlement programs: government benefits that certain qualified individuals are entitled to by law, regardless of need.

Feminization of poverty: the increasing concentration of poverty among women, especially unmarried women and their children.

Income distribution: the share of national income earned by various groups in the United States.

Income: the amount of money collected between any two points in time.

Means-tested programs: government programs available only to individuals below a poverty line.

Poverty line: official statistic indicating what a family would need to spend to maintain an "austere" standard of living.

Progressive tax: takes a higher percentage from the rich than from the poor.

Proportional tax: takes the same percentage from rich and poor.

Regressive tax: takes a higher percentage from the poor than from the rich.

Social welfare policies: attempt to provide assistance and support to specific groups in society.

Tax incidence: the proportion of income a particular group pays in taxes.

Temporary Assistance to Needy Families: once called "Aid to Families With Dependent Children," the new name for public assistance to needy families.

Transfer payments: benefits from government where money is transferred from the general treasury to those in need.

Wealth: the amount already owned.

TEACHING IDEAS: CLASS DISCUSSION AND STUDENT PROJECTS

- American social welfare programs are more limited in scope than is the case in other democracies. Divide your class into three or four research groups, and assign a country (including the United States) to each group. Ask each group to review current social welfare policies of the assigned nation. The group should focus on social welfare policies, but should also go beyond the "obvious" and look at advantages and disadvantages of the system. For example, what effect has the system had on the budget, and what is the level of taxation? One member of each group should be expected to give a brief presentation in class the following week outlining the research group's conclusions.

- *You Are the Policymaker: Should Welfare Recipients Be Allowed to Save for Their Children's Education?* asks students to assume the role of the policymaker and decide whether welfare mothers should be allowed to save for their children's education without losing welfare benefits. Ask your class to review this feature and then write a brief essay expounding the position they would take if they were the policymakers with authority to set rules for this type of case.

- One of the major policy accomplishments of President Clinton, working with a Republican-controlled Congress under House Speaker Newt Gingrich in the early 1990s was the reform of the social welfare system. Ask students to document the specific changes made to welfare programs in the United States. Then assign each student, or students working in groups, to use both the library and the Internet to determine how the states have responded to their new responsibilities. Is the new system better? In what ways?

- For a reading and writing connection, have students write an essay where they must identify and investigate the number of transfer payments they have benefited from either as direct payments or as benefits in-kind. Then have students evaluate the importance of each of these benefits to the successes or failures they have experienced personally. Finally, have students suggest what they would have to do if these services were not available to them when they needed help.

- Develop a writing assignment that requires students to interview a social welfare professional OR an individual currently or recently living in poverty. Have students describe the nature of poverty from either of these perspectives. How does it differ from what they expected?

- Have students develop a working budget for a family of three living at the poverty line. Conduct a class discussion which contrasts these budgets with students' current lifestyles.

BACKGROUND READING

Aaron, Henry J. and Robert D. Reischauer. Countdown to Reform: The Great Social Security Debate. Washington, D.C.: Brookings

Bane, Mary Jo and David Ellwood. Welfare Realities: From Rhetoric to Reform. Cambridge, MA: Harvard University Press. 1996.

Cook, Fay Lomax, and Edith J. Barrett. Support for the American Welfare State. NY: Columbia University Press. 1992.

Derthick, Martha. Policymaking for Social Security. Washington, DC: Brookings. 1979.

Gramlich, Edward M. Is It Time to Reform Social Security? Ann Arbor, MI: University of Michigan Press. 1998.

Hacker, Jacob. The Road to Nowhere: The Genesis of President Clinton's Plan for Health Security. Princeton: Princeton University Press. 1999.

Harrington, Michael. The New American Poverty. NY: Penguin Books. 1985.

Lieberman, Robert C. Shifting the Color Line: Race and the American Welfare State. Cambridge: Harvard University Press. 1998.

Light, Paul. The Politics of Social Security Reform. NY: Random House. 1985.

Patterson, James T. America's Struggle Against Poverty, 1900-1994. Cambridge, MA: Harvard University Press. 1994.

Phillips, Kevin. The Politics of Rich and Poor: Wealth and the American Electorate in the Reagan Aftermath. NY: Random House. 1990.

Piven, Frances Fox, and Richard A. Cloward. Regulating the Poor. NY: Pantheon. 1971.

Schram, Sanford F. and Samuel H. Beer. Welfare Reform: A Race to the Bottom? Batimore: Johns Hopkins University Press. 1999.

Schwartz, John E. America's Hidden Success: A Reassessment of Twenty Years of Public Policy. 2nd. edition. 1987.

Stier, Haya and Marta Tienda. The Color of Opportunity: Pathways to Family, Welfare and Work. Chicago: University of Chicago Press. 2000.

MEDIA SUGGESTIONS

America in the Thirties: Creating the Safety Net. This program examines the origins of the New Deal programs and the psychological and legislative impact of presidential leadership by Franklin Roosevelt. Films for the Humanities and Sciences.

Welfare Reform: Social Impact. This show traces the history of welfare in the U.S., beginning with the Depression. Includes interview with Wisconsin Governor Tommy Thompson. Films for the Humanities & Sciences.

Working: The American Worker. 1996. Examines the efforts of workers to maintain steady incomes in an era of corporate downsizing. Films for the Humanities and Sciences.

CHAPTER NINETEEN: POLICY-MAKING FOR HEALTH CARE AND THE ENVIRONMENT

PEDAGOGICAL FEATURES

LEARNING OBJECTIVES

After studying this chapter, students should be able to:

- Ascertain the effect that the technological revolution has had on standards of health care, on the costs and access to medical care.

- Contrast the *costs* and the *results* of health care policies in the United States with those of other industrialized nations.

- Compare the role of government in medical care in the United States with that of other comparable countries.
- Identify government insurance programs in the United States and determine who benefits from these programs.
- Describe the main components of President Clinton's Health Security Act proposal and discuss why it died in Congress.
- Determine how issues of pollution affect political choices through their impact on business, economic growth, and jobs.
- Summarize legislative enactments in the United States that establish federal environmental policy.
- Ascertain the impact of technological issues on the scope of government.

CHAPTER OVERVIEW

INTRODUCTION

The increasing speed of technological advance creates special problems for government and for policymakers. Medical technologies have changed the basic approach to medical care; their cost has transformed the American medical system. The rapid growth of the American economy during the twentieth century has brought energy and pollution problems to the forefront of politics.

Not only does technological change affect how Americans live their lives, but it also changes the expectations they have for the scope of government. This chapter examines public policy in two technologically complex areas: health and the environment.

HEALTH CARE POLICY

The United States is one of the wealthiest countries in the world, and it spends a *higher proportion of its wealth on health care than any other country*. Health care already takes up one-seventh of America's GNP, and its costs will almost certainly continue to rise with increased technology. Nevertheless, health care statistics show that Americans *lag behind* other countries in some key health care categories, including life expectancy and the infant mortality rate.

Inequalities in health and health care are major problems in America: the world's highest-quality care is available to some citizens, but many poor and working Americans are relegated to an inferior health care system because access to health insurance is not universal in the United States. About 43 million Americans (about 16 percent of the population) lack health insurance altogether, including a disproportionate number of Hispanics and African Americans. Even among those who have insurance, coverage is often incomplete; especially for those with low-paying jobs, health insurance may not cover all of their health needs. About 85 percent of workers receiving health insurance are enrolled in **health maintenance organizations** (HMOs), a form of managed care.

As in many other areas of the economy, the role of government in health care is smaller in the United States than in other comparable countries. The United States lacks national health insurance or a national health service to provide health care directly to those who need it. Even so, 46 percent of the country's total health bill is paid for by government sources; the average for industrialized countries is about 75 percent.

Although national health insurance has never been adopted in the United States, Congress did recognize the special problems of elderly Americans by adopting **Medicare** in 1965. In contrast to Medicare, **Medicaid** is a *means-tested* program designed to provide health care for the poor; like other public assistance programs, it is funded by both the states and the national government.

The cost of medical care in a high-tech age raises difficult and complex issues. Many lifesaving procedures are extremely expensive, so allocating them involves complicated questions of public policy. One reason for uneven government and private health care policies is related to the *representation of interests*. Powerful lobbying organizations representing hospitals, doctors, and the elderly want Medicare to pay for the latest techniques. On the other hand, many groups are unrepresented in government; their health care needs may not be met simply because no well-organized groups represent them.

President Clinton's **Health Security Act proposal** required employers to provide health insurance for their employees or pay a premium into a public fund (which would also cover Medicaid and Medicare recipients). Most companies would have to buy coverage through "health alliances" that would collect premiums, bargain with health plans, and handle payments. Opponents labeled the plan as a government takeover of the health care system; they launched an aggressive advertising campaign against it. After a long and torturous battle, the plan died in Congress. More recently, states have reacted to criticisms of managed care by enacting some restrictions on HMOs. President Clinton has proposed, but not been able to get Congress to pass, legislation billed as "a patient's bill of rights," including among other things the right of a patient to see the doctor of one's choice, obtain access to reasonable emergency care without prior authorization and the right to sue a plan for malpractice.

THE ENVIRONMENT

Concern for the environment has increased greatly in the United States since the 1950s, when few environmental groups existed. Steadily increasing percentages of Americans are willing to see the government spend money to clean up the environment.

Issues of pollution affect political choices through their impact on business, economic growth, and jobs. Business and government battle over the impact of pollution control on economic development. One of the tradeoffs policymakers often face is the question of whether tougher pollution legislation will drive away commerce and industry. In 1977 Congress wrote some amendments to the Clean Air Act that require no degradation of air quality, regardless of how pristine or dirty the air of a community. These amendments discourage industry from relocating to areas with clean air.

The **National Environmental Policy Act (NEPA)**, passed in 1969, requires government agencies to complete an **environmental impact statement (EIS)** every time an agency proposes to undertake a policy that is potentially disruptive to the natural environment. The **Clean Air Act of 1970** charges the Department of Transportation (DOT) with the responsibility of reducing automobile emissions. The smaller size of American cars, the use of unleaded gasoline, and the lower gas consumption of new cars are all due in large part to DOT regulations. The **Water Pollution Control Act of 1972** was enacted in reaction to the tremendous pollution of northeastern rivers and the Great Lakes; since its passage, water quality has improved dramatically.

Endangered species are increasingly threatened by expanding human populations and growing economic demands. The **Endangered Species Act of 1973** requires the government to actively protect each of the hundreds of species listed as endangered, regardless of the economic effect on the surrounding towns or region. The act was later amended to allow exceptions in cases of overriding national or regional interest.

Modern American society depends on the availability of abundant energy. Today, 88 percent of the nation's energy comes from coal, oil, and natural gas. The most controversial energy source is nuclear power. The trade-offs between nuclear and other forms of energy emphasize many of the problems of politics in a high-tech age. Recently, policymakers have shown more interest in conservation, renewable energy supplies, and alternative fuels.

Before the environmental movement focused public attention on pollution of the environment, polluters created problems that are going to cost taxpayers billions to solve. In 1980 Congress reacted to increased pressure to deal with toxic waste by establishing a **Superfund**, created by taxes on chemical products. Workers find that the damage is often so serious that some sites may never be cleaned satisfactorily. Another serious environmental challenge is the disposal of nuclear wastes.

Cleaning up the environment is a *political question* because environmental concerns often conflict with equally legitimate concerns about foreign trade, economic growth, and jobs. One of the biggest changes in environmental policy-making in recent years is the increasing presence of new sectors of society joining interest groups to complain about pollution and to press for government action. There is currently a backlash against vigorous environmental protection; opponents argue that the effects of environmental regulations on employment, economic growth, and international competitiveness must be part of the policy-making equation.

Recently even more technologically- and politically-complex issues relating to energy, the environment and global warming have emerged. The U.S. relies heavily on fossil fuels, which are the biggest contributors to global warming, and has come under pressure from other nations to reduce its reliance on fossil fuels. Also, the U.S. faces increasing technological and political pressure to deal with the disposal of toxic and nuclear wastes. Widening opposition to potentially hazardous industrial facilities (such as toxic or nuclear waste dumps) has further complicated environmental policymaking in recent years. Local groups have often successfully organized resistance to planned development, rallying behind the cry "Not in My Back Yard."

UNDERSTANDING HEALTH CARE AND ENVIRONMENTAL POLICY

Technologically complex issues such as health, energy, and the environment pose many special problems in a democracy. This section discusses how democracies handle technological issues and considers the impact of these issues on the size of government.

High-technology issues make it especially difficult to include the public in a reasoned political debate. In the face of complex, high-tech issues such as nuclear power, many Americans rely on interest groups to provide technological expertise and to serve as advocates for the public interest. A tension exists between demands for government services and protections and a concern about the government providing those services and protections.

Given Americans' increasing concern about the environment, and the centrality of health care issues to the public as a whole, it is likely that these issues will remain salient in politics for some time. Government is, and will continue to be, at the center of public debate.

Americans do not hesitate to call for government to play a greater role in high-technology issues, and the scope of the federal government has grown in response to these demands. In the past three decades, concerns for environmental protection have placed additional demands on the federal government. At the same time, important forces rein in the federal government. Thus, there is tension between demands for government services and protections and concerns about how government will provide those services and protections.

CHAPTER OUTLINE

I. INTRODUCTION

A. The *increasing speed of technological advance* creates *special problems* for government and for policymakers.
   1. Medical technologies have changed the basic approach to medical care: their cost has transformed the American medical system.
   2. The rapid growth of the American economy during the twentieth century has brought environmental and health care problems to the forefront of politics.
   3. As Americans have become more concerned with environmental quality, government has been called upon again and again to impose new restrictions on activities in the private sector.

B. Not only does technological change affect how Americans live their lives, but it also changes the expectations they have for the scope of government.

II. HEALTH CARE POLICY

A. The health of Americans.

1. Americans are not the healthiest persons in the world. Statistics show that *the United States lags behind some other countries regarding the health of its citizens* in key categories such as life expectancy and infant mortality rates.
2. The health care system in the United States may help explain why the health of Americans does not measure up to that of citizens of some other countries.

B. The cost of health care.

1. Health care already takes up *one-seventh of America's GNP.*
2. The United States is one of the wealthiest countries in the world, and it spends a *higher proportion of its wealth on health care than any other country.*
3. There are many reasons for rapid increases in health care costs (currently around $1 trillion a year).
   a. New technologies, drugs, and procedures often add to the cost of health care by addressing previously untreatable conditions or by providing better (but more expensive) health care.
   b. Much of the money that Americans pay for health care goes to services like organ transplants, kidney dialysis, and other treatments that are not widely available outside of the United States.
   c. American health providers have overbuilt medical facilities; one-third of all hospital beds are vacant on any given day.
   d. Doctors and hospitals have few incentives to be more efficient; in fact, with the rise in medical malpractice suits doctors may be ordering extra tests to ensure than they cannot be sued (an approach that is sometimes called *defensive medicine*).

C. Access to health care.

1. Access inequalities.
   a. *Inequalities in health and health care* are major problems in America: the world's highest-quality care is available to some citizens, but many poor and working Americans are relegated to an inferior health care system because access to health insurance is not universal in the United States.
   b. About *43 million Americans lack health insurance* altogether.
      (1) These people receive less health care, do not see health care professionals regularly, and when they do, they typically receive poorer quality care than those with insurance.
      (2) Hispanics and African-Americans are less likely to have health insurance than whites.

(3) The majority of uninsured are full-time workers.

2. One of the most recent innovations in seeking to increase access is the development of managed care, which now represents 85 percent of workers receiving health insurance.
   a. **Health maintenance organizations** provide medical care, negotiate with physician groups and try to monitor most aspects of care to control unnecessary use.
   b. Managed care tends to focus on prevention rather than treatment and by designating a single doctor as a patient's primary care provider.

D. The role of government in health care.
1. American health care is provided for by both government and private sources.
   a. As in many other areas of the economy, the role of government in health care is smaller in the United States than in other comparable countries.
   b. The United States lacks national health insurance or a national health service to provide health care directly to those who need it.
   c. America has *the most private medical care system in the developed world.*
      (1) Even so, 46 percent of the country's total health bill is paid for by government sources; the average for industrialized countries is about 75 percent.
      (2) The government also subsidizes employer-provided health insurance with tax breaks, the benefits of which go disproportionately to affluent, highly paid workers.
   d. A great deal of medical research is financed through the *National Institutes of Health (NIH).*
   e. The federal government pays for much of the nation's medical bill through the Medicare program for the elderly, the Medicaid program for the poor, and health care for veterans.
   f. Who pays for Americans' health care?
      (1) Americans often think that insurance companies pay most health care costs, but the government is actually more heavily involved than the private insurance industry.
      (2) Private insurance companies cover about one-third of the cost, and Americans pay one-fifth of their health care costs out of their own pockets.
   g. Government insurance programs.
      (1) Harry S. Truman was the first president to call for **national health insurance**—a compulsory insurance program to finance all Americans' medical care; the idea was strongly

opposed by the American Medical Association, which called this program *socialized medicine*.

(2) Although national health insurance has never been adopted in the United States, Congress did recognize the special problems of elderly Americans by adopting **Medicare** in 1965.

   (a) Part A of Medicare provides hospitalization insurance.

   (b) Part B (which is voluntary) permits older Americans to purchase inexpensive coverage for doctor fees and other expenses.

(3) **Medicaid** is a *means-tested* program designed to provide health care for the poor; like other public assistance programs, it is funded by both the states and the national government.

E. Policy-making for health care.

1. The cost of medical care in a high-tech age raises difficult and complex issues.
   a. Many lifesaving procedures are extremely expensive, so allocating them involves complicated questions of public policy.
   b. Oregon has taken the lead on the issue of *rationing health care*, setting priorities for medical treatments under the Medicaid program.
2. One reason for uneven government and private health care policies is related to the *representation of interests*.
   a. Powerful lobbying organizations representing hospitals, doctors, and the elderly want Medicare to pay for the latest techniques.
   b. On the other hand, many groups are unrepresented in government; their health care needs may not be met simply because no well-organized groups represent them.
3. President Clinton's **Health Security Act proposal** was an effort to deal with the two greatest problems of health care policy: costs and access.
   a. Paying for the plan required employers to provide health insurance for their employees or pay a premium into a public fund (which would also cover Medicaid and Medicare recipients).
   b. Most companies would have to buy coverage through "*health alliances*" that would collect premiums, bargain with health plans, and handle payments.
   c. Opponents labeled the plan as a government takeover of the health care system; they launched an aggressive advertising campaign against it.
   d. After a long and torturous battle, the plan died in Congress.

4. Managed care has received more criticism as it has come to dominate the provision of health care in the U.S.
   a. Critics claim that managed care imposes stifling rules on network physicians, blocks sick patients from seeing specialists and delays or denies coverage for recommended treatments or medications—all to save money.
   b. Some states have responded by passing legislative restrictions on managed care, while President Clinton has proposed a "patient's bill of rights," which includes the right to see a doctor of one's choice; obtain access to reasonable emergency care without prior authorization from a plan, secure the right to appeal a plan's refusal to provide medical treatments, attain easier access to out of network doctors and the right to sue a plan for malpractice.
5. There are likely to be increasing calls for more government regulation over the costs of health care and some attempt to help those who fall through the cracks of the American health care system.

II. THE ENVIRONMENT

A. Economic growth and the environment.
   1. Issues of pollution affect political choices through their impact on business, economic growth, and jobs.
   2. Environmental controls figure prominently in the debate about local and state economic development.
      a. The *federal system* puts the states in competition with each other for economic advantage.
      b. Millions of dollars are spent by states and cities pushing for large investments.
   3. Business and government battle over the impact of pollution control on economic development.
      a. One of the trade-offs policymakers often face is the question of whether tougher pollution legislation will drive away commerce and industry.
      b. One possible offset to the cost of enforcing pollution legislation is that states can save money by reducing health risks to residents.
      c. In 1977 Congress wrote some amendments to the Clean Air Act that require no degradation of air quality, regardless of how pristine or dirty the air of a community. These amendments discourage industry from relocating to areas with clean air.
B. Public concern about the environment.
   1. Concern for the environment has increased greatly in the United States since the 1950s, when few environmental groups existed.

2. Steadily increasing percentages of Americans are willing to see the government spend money to clean up the environment.

C. Environmental policies in America.
1. The **National Environmental Policy Act (NEPA)**, passed in 1969, requires government agencies to complete an **environmental impact statement (EIS)** every time an agency proposes to undertake a policy that is potentially disruptive to the natural environment.
2. In practice, the filing of impact statements alerts environmentalists to proposed projects.
   a. Environmentalists can then take agencies to court for violating the act's procedural requirements if the agencies file incomplete or inaccurate impact statements.
   b. NEPA has been a very effective tool in preventing much environmental damage: the law does not give the environmental groups the right to stop any environmentally unsound activities, but it does give them the opportunity to delay construction so much that agencies simply give up.
   c. Agencies have often abandoned proposed projects to avoid prolonged court battles with environmental groups.
3. Environmental policies to protect air and water.
   a. The **Clean Air Act of 1970** charges the Department of Transportation (DOT) with the responsibility of reducing automobile emissions. The smaller size of American cars, the use of unleaded gasoline, and the lower gas consumption of new cars are all due in large part to DOT regulations.
   b. The **Water Pollution Control Act of 1972** was enacted in reaction to the tremendous pollution of northeastern rivers and the Great Lakes; since its passage, water quality has improved dramatically.
      (1) The agency charged with administering these laws is the **Environmental Protection Agency (EPA).**
      (2) Created in 1970, the EPA is now the nation's largest federal regulatory agency.
      (3) In addition to the NEPA, the Clean Air Act, and the Water Pollution Control Act, the EPA is also charged with administering policies dealing with *toxic wastes* such as dangerous chemicals.
4. Endangered species are increasingly threatened by expanding human populations and growing economic demands.
   a. The **Endangered Species Act of 1973** requires the government to actively protect each of the hundreds of species listed as

endangered, regardless of the economic effect on the surrounding towns or region.

b. The act was later amended to allow exceptions in cases of overriding national or regional interest.

c. A cabinet-level committee was established to decide such cases; so far, it has granted few exemptions to the act.

D. Energy, the Environment and Global Warming.

1. Today, 88 percent of the nation's energy comes from coal, oil, and natural gas.
   a. The most controversial energy source is nuclear power.
   b. The trade-offs between nuclear and other forms of energy emphasize many of the problems of politics in a high-tech age.
   c. Recently, policymakers have shown more interest in conservation, renewable energy supplies, and alternative fuels.
2. Many scientists believe that the atmosphere is being changed due to our heavy reliance on fossil fuels, which contribute to a "greenhouse effect" when energy from the sun is trapped under the (polluted) atmosphere and warms the earth.
   a. There is no technology to control carbon emissions, so the only way to reduce greenhouse gases is to burn less fuel or find alternative sources of energy.
   b. At the end of 1997, 150 nations met in Kyoto, Japan, and signed a treaty that would require nations to reduce their emissions of greenhouse gases below 1990 levels by about 2010. Opponents fear that cutting greenhouse gases will cost a staggering sum. Due to the strong opposition to the treaty, President Clinton never submitted it to Congress.

E. Dealing with toxic wastes.

1. Before the environmental movement focused public attention on pollution of the environment, polluters created problems that are going to cost taxpayers billions to solve.
2. In 1980 Congress reacted to increased pressure to deal with *toxic waste* by establishing a **Superfund**, created by taxes on chemical products.
3. The Superfund law requires that those who polluted the land are responsible for paying to clean it up. The law has virtually eliminated haphazard dumping of toxic wastes.
4. Workers find that the damage from past dumping is often so serious that some sites may never be cleaned satisfactorily.
5. Cleaning up wastes left by private businesses (and by some government operations, such as the production of nuclear weapons) is going to take decades and cost billions of dollars.

a. The federal government spends more than $11 billion annually to restore lands spoiled by chemical and radioactive waste.
b. This is the fastest growing segment of the nation's environmental budget.
c. Another serious challenge is the disposal of nuclear wastes, some of which must be isolated for 10,000 years.

F. Making environmental policy.
1. Cleaning up the environment is a *political question* only because environmental concerns often conflict with equally legitimate concerns about foreign trade, economic growth, and jobs.
2. Oil has been at the center of many national and international crises, from the Persian Gulf to the *Exxon Valdez*.
3. One of the biggest changes in environmental policy-making in recent years is the increasing presence of new sectors of society joining interest groups to complain about pollution and to press for government action.
    a. The 1960s and 1970s saw an explosion in the size and number of environmental interest groups.
    b. The nature of environmental policy-making changed; issues that were once considered only from the point of view of jobs and economic growth are now much more controversial.
4. There is currently a backlash against vigorous environmental protection; opponents argue that the effects of environmental regulations on employment, economic growth, and international competitiveness must be part of the policymaking equation.
5. Widening opposition to potentially hazardous industrial facilities has further complicated environmental policy-making in recent years; local groups have often successfully organized resistance to planned development under the banner "Not In My Back Yard" (NIMBY).

III. UNDERSTANDING HEALTH CARE AND ENVIRONMENTAL POLICY

A. Democracy and health care and environmental policy.
1. High-technology issues make it especially difficult to include the public in a reasoned political debate.
2. In the face of complex, high-tech issues such as nuclear power, many Americans rely on interest groups to provide technological expertise and to serve as advocates for the public interest.
3. Individual citizens are unlikely to have the information or the resources to participate meaningfully because of the complexity of the debates.

B. Continued *growth in the scope of government* is expected in numerous areas of high-technology issues.

1. Americans do not hesitate to call for government to play a greater role in high-technology issues, and the scope of the federal government has grown in response to these demands.
2. At the same time, there are important forces reigning in the federal government.
3. A tension exists between demands for government services and protections and a concern about the government providing those services and protections.

KEY TERMS AND CONCEPTS

Clean Air Act of 1970: landmark legislation that charged the Department of Transportation with the responsibility of reducing automobile emissions.

Endangered Species Act of 1973: legislation that required the government to actively protect each of hundreds of species listed as endangered by the U.S. Fish and Wildlife Service, regardless of the economic effect on the surrounding towns or region.

Environmental impact statement (EIS): a description of the disruption to the environment that a business or government agency expects to result as a consequence of building projects; required by the National Environmental Policy Act of 1969:

Environmental Protection Agency (EPA): created in 1970, the government agency that is charged with administering various environmental laws.

Health maintenance organizations (HMO's): a form of network health plans that limits the choice of doctors and treatments.

Medicaid: government program designed to provide health care for the poor.

Medicare: government program designed to provide health care for the elderly.

National Environmental Policy Act: the centerpiece of federal environmental policy, passed in 1969, required the use of environmental impact statements by businesses and government.

National health insurance: compulsory health insurance program financing all Americans' medical care.

Superfund: established by Congress in 1980, a fund devoted to cleaning up toxic waste supported by taxes on toxic waste.

Water Pollution Control Act of 1972: passed by Congress to control pollution in the nation's rivers and lakes.

TEACHING IDEAS: CLASS DISCUSSION AND STUDENT PROJECTS

- Inequalities in health and health care are major problems in America. The textbook points out that altogether about 40 million Americans lack health insurance. Have your students carefully read the section in the text that covers President Clinton's Health Security Act proposal. Ask students to evaluate the proposal both from an economic standpoint and from a perspective of societal need. What changes have occurred in health policy and politics since the "failure" of Clinton's proposal? Document these changes by collecting newspaper articles on significant legislative and private sector initiatives.

- Ask your class to try to explain the contradiction between the high costs that Americans pay for health care (the highest costs in the world) and the fact that health care statistics show that Americans lag behind other countries in some key health care categories such as life expectancy and the infant mortality rate. Would your students make changes in the basic system, or are they satisfied with the process as it exists? Consider asking students to discuss these issues with members of their families or friends from different generations to see if individuals' experiences and evaluations differ by age group.

- Much of the acid rain caused by American industries actually falls in Canada; officials there estimate that more than 2000 lakes have "died" as a result of acid rain. Ask your class to consider the implications of internal policies that cross over international boundaries, as happens with pollution. Should Canadians have any recourse against American industry? What would your students' reactions be if the situation were reversed and Canadian industry polluted American waters?

- Have students investigate the quality of the environment in their local community. How clean is the air, the drinking water, lakes and rivers? Require the students to interview local officials for this information, as well as to document what they can through government records and local environmental groups.

- One of the most notable policy differences between Al Gore and George W. Bush in the 2000 presidential election campaign was their stance on the environment. Have students research the two candidates' proposed policies, and what Bush has done since taking office. Who has opposed or supported Bush's policy initiatives? Why?

BACKGROUND READINGS

Graig, Laurene. Health of Nations: An International Perspective on U.S/. Health Care Reform, 3rd ed. Washington, DC: Congressional Quarterly Press. 1999.

Rosenbaum, Walter A. Environmental Politics and Policy, 4th ed. Washington, DC: Congressional Quarterly Press. 1998.

Rovner, Julie. Health Care Policy and Politics A to Z. Washington, DC: Congressional Quarterly Press. 1999.

Vig, Norman J. and Regina S. Axelrod. The Global Environment: Institutions, Law and Policy. Washington, DC: Congressional Quarterly Press. 1999.

MEDIA SUGGESTIONS

The Great Health Care Debate. Featuring Bill Moyers, this film examines the failure of President Clinton's health care reform bill, highlighting the role of the media and special interest groups. Films for the Humanities and Sciences.

The Politics of Addiction. This program shows how the views of scientists, doctors, counselors and drug addicts are woven into public policies on drug addiction. Films for the Humanities and Sciences.

CHAPTER TWENTY: FOREIGN AND DEFENSE POLICY-MAKING

PEDAGOGICAL FEATURES

LEARNING OBJECTIVES

After studying this chapter, students should be able to:

- Understand how the instruments of foreign policy differ from those of domestic policy.

- List the major international and regional organizations and describe their roles in the realm of international relations.

- Determine how multinational corporations, groups, and individuals operate as actors in international relations.

- Identify the primary policymakers involved in foreign policy decision making.

- Delineate the major institutions of the U.S. national security establishment.

- Ascertain how the president and Congress share constitutional authority over foreign and defense policy.

- Briefly outline American diplomatic history from the period of isolationism to contemporary involvement in international relations.

- Contrast the policy of *détente* with prior policies such as containment and brinkmanship.

- Compare the general attitudes of liberals and conservatives toward defense expenditures and domestic policy expenditures.

- Summarize how domestic political concerns, budgetary limitations, and ideology all have a role in influencing decisions regarding the structure of defense policy.

- Outline the major agreements negotiated by the United States and other nations on arms limitations and nuclear reduction.

- Explain why the Middle East is such an important component of American foreign policy.

- Evaluate the roles that democracy and the scope of government play in the development of foreign policy and international relations.

CHAPTER OVERVIEW

INTRODUCTION

The end of the cold war in the early 1990s brought with it many questions regarding the future of international politics, from what the nature of threat is, to what new alliances are needed, to what the changing role of "superpowers" might be in the new global scene. This chapter reviews cold war policies and politics from a historical perspective as well as new issues concerning global inequality and human rights.

AMERICAN FOREIGN POLICY: INSTRUMENTS, ACTORS, AND POLICYMAKERS

Foreign policy involves making choices about relations with the rest of the world. The *instruments of foreign policy* are different from those of domestic policy. Foreign policies depend ultimately on three types of tools: military, economic, and diplomatic. Among the oldest instruments of foreign policy are war and the threat of war. Economic instruments are becoming weapons almost as potent as those of war. *Diplomacy* is the quietest instrument of foreign policy; it may involve meetings of world leaders at summit conferences, but more often involves quiet negotiations by less prominent officials.

Most of the challenges in international relations require the cooperation of many nations; thus, **international organizations** play an increasingly important role on the world stage. The **United Nations (UN)**, created in 1945, is the most important of the international organizations today. In addition to its peacekeeping function, the UN runs a number of programs focused on economic development and health, education, and welfare concerns. **Regional organizations** are organizations of several nations bound by a treaty, often for military reasons. For example, members of the **North Atlantic Treaty Organization (NATO)** agreed to combine military forces and to treat a war against one as a war against all. By contrast, the **European Union (EU)**, often called the **Common Market**, is an economic alliance of the major Western European nations; the EU coordinates monetary, trade, immigration, and labor policies.

More than one-third of the world's industrial output comes from **multinational corporations (MNCs)**, which are sometimes more powerful (and often much wealthier) than the governments under which they operate. **Groups** such as churches and labor unions have long had international interests and activities.

Even **individuals** are international actors; the recent explosion of tourism affects the international economic system.

The president is the main force behind foreign policy: as **chief diplomat**, the president negotiates treaties; as **commander-in-chief**, the president deploys American troops abroad. Presidents are aided (and sometimes thwarted) by a huge national security bureaucracy; Congress also wields considerable clout in the foreign policy arena. Other foreign policy decisionmakers include **diplomats** (such as the secretary of state and special assistants for national security affairs) and the **national security establishment** (including the Department of Defense, the Joint Chiefs of Staff, the National Security Council, and the Central Intelligence Agency).

AMERICAN FOREIGN POLICY: AN OVERVIEW

The United States followed a foreign policy of **isolationism** throughout most of its history. The **Monroe Doctrine** reaffirmed America's inattention to Europe's problems, but warned European nations to stay out of Latin America. In the wake of World War I, President Woodrow Wilson urged the United States to join the **League of Nations**; the Senate refused to ratify the treaty, indicating the country was not ready to abandon isolationism.

Pearl Harbor dealt the death-blow to American isolationism. At the end of World War II, the United States was the dominant world power, both economically and militarily; only the United States possessed nuclear weapons. The charter for the United Nations was signed in San Francisco in 1945, with the United States as an original signatory. NATO was created in 1949, affirming the mutual military interests of the United States and Western Europe.

All of Eastern Europe fell under Soviet domination as World War II ended. In 1946, Winston Churchill warned that the Russians had sealed off Eastern Europe with an "iron curtain." The United States poured billions of dollars into war-ravaged European nations through the Marshall Plan. Writing in *Foreign Affairs* in 1947 (under the pseudonym *"X"*), George F. Kennan proposed a policy of **"containment."** His containment doctrine called for the United States to isolate the Soviet Union and to "contain" its advances and resist its encroachments. The **Truman Doctrine** was developed to help other nations oppose communism.

The Soviet Union closed off land access to Berlin with the Berlin Blockade (1948-1949), which was countered by a massive *airlift* of food, fuel, and other necessities by the United States and its allies. The fall of China to Mao Zedong's Communist-led forces in 1949 and the development of Soviet nuclear capability seemed to confirm American fears. The invasion of pro-American South Korea by Communist North Korea in 1950 further fueled American fears. The Korean War began when President Truman sent American troops to Korea under United Nations auspices.

The **cold war** was at its height in the 1950s. Eisenhower's secretary of state, John Foster Dulles, proclaimed a policy of "brinkmanship" in which the United States was to be prepared to use nuclear weapons in order to *deter* the Soviet Union and Communist China from taking aggressive action. In the era of **McCarthyism**, domestic policy was deeply affected by the cold war and by anti-communist fears. With containment came a massive buildup of the military apparatus, resulting in the military-industrial complex (a phrase that was coined by President Dwight D. Eisenhower to refer to the interests shared by the armed services and defense contractors). Economist Seymour Melman wrote about Pentagon capitalism, linking the military's drive to expand with the profit motives of private industry. The 1950s ushered in an **arms race** between the Soviet Union and the United States; eventually, a point of mutual assured destruction (MAD) was reached in which each side could destroy the other.

In 1950, President Truman decided to aid the French effort to retain France's colonial possessions in Southeast Asia—the beginning of American involvement in Vietnam. In 1954, the French were defeated by the Viet Minh (led by Ho Chi Minh) in a battle at Dien Bien Phu. Although it was a party to agreements in 1954 among participants in Geneva, Switzerland, the United States never accepted the Geneva agreement to hold national elections in Vietnam in 1956; instead, it began supporting one non-Communist leader after another in South Vietnam.

Vietnam first became an election-year issue in 1964. Since Truman's time, the United States had sent *military "advisors"* to South Vietnam, which was in the midst of a civil war spurred by the Viet Cong (National Liberation Front). Senator Barry Goldwater was a foreign policy hard-liner who advocated tough action in Vietnam; President Lyndon Johnson promised that he would not "send American boys to do an Asian boy's job" of defending the pro-American regime in South Vietnam. Despite his election-year promise, Johnson sent in American troops when we were unable to contain the forces of the Viet Cong and North Vietnam with American advisors.

American troops and massive firepower failed to contain the North Vietnamese. At home, widespread protests against the war contributed to Johnson's decision not to run for reelection in 1968 and to begin peace negotiations. The new Nixon administration prosecuted the war vigorously, but also worked to negotiate a peace treaty with the Viet Cong and North Vietnam.

Even while the Vietnam War was being waged, President Nixon supported a new policy of ***détente***. Popularized by Nixon's national security assistant (and later secretary of state), Henry Kissinger, *détente* sought a *relaxation of tensions* between the superpowers, coupled with firm guarantees of mutual security. One major initiative that came out of *détente* was the **Strategic Arms Limitation Talks (SALT)**. These talks represented an effort by the United States and the Soviet Union to agree to scale down their nuclear capabilities, with each power maintaining sufficient nuclear weapons to deter a surprise attack by the other. President Nixon signed the first SALT treaty in 1972. A second SALT treaty (SALT II) was signed and sent to the Senate by President Carter in 1979, but the Soviet invasion of Afghanistan that year caused Carter to withdraw the treaty from Senate consideration; both he and President Reagan nevertheless insisted that they would be committed to its arms limitations.

The philosophy of *détente* was applied to the People's Republic of China as well as to the Soviet Union. President Nixon visited the People's Republic and sent an American mission there. President Carter extended formal diplomatic recognition in November 1978.

From the mid-1950s to 1981, the *defense budget had generally been declining* as a percentage of both the total federal budget and the gross national product (with the exception of the Vietnam War); the decline in defense spending became a major issue in Ronald Reagan's presidential campaign. During the campaign, Reagan said America faced a *"window of vulnerability"* because the Soviet Union was pulling ahead of the United States in military spending. President Carter's last budget had proposed a large increase in defense spending, and the Reagan administration proposed adding $32 billion on top of that. However, concern over huge budget deficits brought defense spending to a standstill in the second Reagan term.

Forces of change sparked by Soviet leader Mikhail Gorbachev led to a staggering wave of upheavals that shattered Communist regimes and the postwar barriers between Eastern and Western Europe. The *Berlin Wall* was brought down, and East and West Germany formed a unified, democratic republic. The former Soviet Union split into fifteen separate nations; non-Communist governments formed in most of them. On May 12, 1989, President Bush announced a new era in American foreign policy that he termed *"beyond containment."*

In 1989, reform seemed on the verge of occurring in China as well as in Eastern Europe. Thousands of students held protests on behalf of democratization in *Tiananmen Square* (the central meeting place in Beijing). However, on the night of June 3 the army violently crushed the democracy movement, killing hundreds—perhaps thousands—of protesters and beginning a wave of executions, arrests, and repression.

THE POLITICS OF DEFENSE POLICY

Defense spending comprises about one-sixth of the federal budget. Domestic political concerns, budgetary limitations, and ideology all have a role in influencing decisions regarding the structure of defense policy. The *end of the cold war* has not lessened the importance of national security policy. New and complex challenges have emerged to replace conflict with communism. As *military competition* with the East diminished with the end of the cold war, *economic competition* with the world increased.

At the core of defense policy is a judgment about what the United States will defend. Defense spending now makes up about one-sixth of the federal budget. Conservatives fight deep cuts in defense spending, pointing out that many nations retain potent military capability and insisting that America maintain its readiness at a high level. Liberals, on the other hand, maintain that the Pentagon wastes money and that the United States buys too many guns and too little butter. Whatever its cause, the lessening of East-West tensions has given momentum to significant reductions in defense spending, what some call the *peace dividend.* Changing spending patterns is not easy, however.

The structure of America's defense has been based on a large standing military force and a battery of strategic nuclear weapons. The United States has nearly 1.4 million men and women on active duty and nearly 900,000 million in the National Guard and Reserves. Cuts in defense spending have led to reduced numbers of active-duty personnel in the armed services.

To deter an aggressor's attack, the United States has relied on a triad of nuclear weapons: ground-based intercontinental ballistic missiles (ICBMs), submarine-launched ballistic missiles (SLBMs), and strategic bombers. These weapons, like troops, are costly (each Stealth bomber costs over a *billion* dollars), and they pose obvious dangers to human survival.

During the May 1988 Moscow summit meeting, President Reagan and President Gorbachev exchanged ratified copies of a new treaty eliminating **intermediate-range nuclear forces (INF)**. On November 19, 1990, the leaders of twenty-two countries signed a treaty cutting conventional arms in Europe. In 1991, the Warsaw Pact (the military alliance tying Eastern Europe to the Soviet Union) was dissolved. On July 31, 1991, Gorbachev and President Bush signed the *Strategic Arms Reduction Treaty*, following nine years of negotiations.

The democratization of Eastern Europe, the restructuring of the Soviet Union, and the deterioration of the Soviet economy substantially diminished Russia's inclination and potential to threaten the interests of the United States and its allies. In the fall of 1991, President Bush broke new ground with his decision to *unilaterally dismantle* some U.S. nuclear weapons; President Gorbachev followed suit shortly afterward. Presidents Bush and Yeltsin later signed an agreement to sharply reduce the U.S. and Russian nuclear arsenals.

Despite these changes, *high-tech weapons systems* will continue to play an *important role in America's defense posture.* The perception that space-age technology helped win the Gulf War in "100 hours" and with few American casualties provides support for high-tech systems.

THE NEW GLOBAL AGENDA

By whatever standards one uses, the United States is the world's mightiest power; but for Americans, merely being big and powerful is no guarantee of dominance. This is especially true since access to petroleum in the Middle East and global environmental issues have become increasingly important.

Although the United States has great military power, many of the world's issues today are not military ones. Interconnected issues of equality, economics, energy, and the environment have become important. Today's international economy is illustrated by **interdependency**. The health of the American economy depends increasingly on the prosperity of its trading partners and on the smooth *flow of trade and finance across borders.*

Since the era of the Great Depression, the world economy has moved away from high tariffs and protectionism toward lower tariffs and freer trade. President Bush signed the **North American Free Trade Agreement** in 1992 with Canada and Mexico; it was approved by Congress in 1993. In 1994 Congress approved the **GATT** agreement. Nontariff barriers such as *quotas*, *subsidies*, or *quality specifications* for imported products are common means of limiting imports today; such policies do save American jobs, but they also raise prices on products that Americans use.

For a number of years, America has experienced a **balance of trade deficit**; the excess of imports over exports *decreases the dollar's buying power* against other currencies, making Americans pay more for goods they buy from other nations.

On the plus side, this decline in the dollar also makes American products cheaper abroad, thereby increasing our exports. Since the late 1980s, the United States has actually experienced a balance of trade *surplus* with Western Europe; the trade deficit with Japan and other Asian countries has declined, but much more slowly.

Whereas the cold war meant continuous conflict between the Soviet Union and the West, world politics today includes a growing conflict between *rich nations* (concentrated in the northern hemisphere) and *poor nations* (concentrated in the southern hemisphere). The income gap between rich, industrialized nations and poor, underdeveloped ones is widening rather than narrowing. Not only are there wide gaps between rich and poor nations (**international inequality**), but there are also big gaps between the rich and poor *within* developing countries (**intranational inequality**). Although every nation has income inequality, *the poorer the nation, the wider the gaps between rich and poor.*

Presidents of both parties have pressed for aid to nations in the developing world—sometimes from humanitarian concern, sometimes out of a desire to stabilize friendly nations. **Foreign aid** has taken a variety of forms: sometimes it has been given in the form of grants, but it often has taken the form of credits and loan guarantees to purchase American goods, assistance with agricultural modernization, loans at favorable interest rates, and forgiveness of previous loans; preferential trade agreements have sometimes been granted for the sale of foreign goods here. A substantial percentage of foreign aid is in the form of military assistance and is targeted to a few countries that are considered to be of vital strategic significance. Foreign aid has never been very popular with Americans. Although the United States donates *more total aid than any other country*, it devotes a *smaller share of its GNP* to foreign economic development than any other developed nation.

Energy transfers offer convincing evidence that *world politics is a politics of growing dependency.* Massive oceangoing oil tankers (most sailing from OPEC nations) have made it possible to *import half of the oil Americans now use*, but they have also contributed to ruined fisheries and beaches from oil spills.

Almost every nation faces severe environmental problems. The formerly Communist nations of Central and Eastern Europe rank among the worst offenders. Underdeveloped nations almost always favor economic growth at the expense of the ecology. Recent concerns over the effects of fluorocarbons on the Earth's ozone layer have generated international studies and diplomatic discussions; Americans have bargained with other nations to restrict overfishing, limit pollution, and deal with deforestation of the tropical rain forests. Issues closer to home often get a different response: in 1992, President Bush refused to sign an international agreement on environmental protection, arguing that it would cost jobs in the United States and that it failed to protect patent rights of newly developing industries. However, President Clinton agreed to follow a specific timetable to reduce the threat of global warming and to sign a treaty protecting rare and endangered species.

Other important issues such as terrorism and nuclear proliferation have also become more important in an increasingly complex international environment.

UNDERSTANDING FOREIGN AND DEFENSE POLICY MAKING

The themes that have guided students' understanding of American politics throughout *Government in America*—democracy and the scope of government—also pertain to the topic of international relations. Treaty obligations, the nation's economic interests in an interdependent global economy, and other questions on the global agenda guarantee that the national government will be active in international relations. As the United States remains a superpower and continues to have interests to defend around the world, the scope of American government in foreign and defense policy will be substantial.

CHAPTER OUTLINE

I. INTRODUCTION

- A. The *end of the cold war* has not lessened the importance of national security policy.
  1. New and complex challenges have emerged to replace conflict with Communism.
  2. Many of the former Communist nations of Eastern and Central Europe are engaged in civil wars.
- B. As *military competition* with the East diminished with the end of the cold war, *economic competition* with the world increased.

II. AMERICAN FOREIGN POLICY: INSTRUMENTS, ACTORS AND POLICYMAKERS

- A. **Foreign policy** involves making choices about relations with the rest of the world.

1. Because the president is the main force behind foreign policy, the White House receives a highly confidential intelligence *briefing* every morning.
2. The *instruments of foreign policy* are different from those of domestic
policy.
   a. Foreign policies depend ultimately on three types of tools: *military*, *economic*, and *diplomatic*.
   b. Among the oldest instruments of foreign policy are *war and the threat of war*. The United States has often used force to *influence actions in other countries*.
   c. Today, *economic instruments* are becoming weapons almost as potent as those of war.
      (1) The control of oil can be as important as the control of guns.
      (2) Trade regulations, tariff policies, and monetary policies are among the economic instruments of foreign policy.
   d. *Diplomacy* is the quietest instrument of foreign policy.
      (1) Sometimes national leaders meet in summit talks.
      (2) More often, less prominent negotiators work out treaties handling all kinds of national contracts.

B. Actors on the world stage.
1. International organizations.
   a. More than 125 nations have emerged since 1945—nearly two dozen in the 1990s alone.
   b. Most of the challenges in *international relations* require the cooperation of many nations; thus, **international organizations** play an increasingly important role on the world stage.
   c. The **United Nations (UN)**, created in 1945, is headed by the **secretary general**, who usually comes from a neutral or nonaligned nation.
      (1) Its members agree to renounce war and respect certain human and economic freedoms.
      (2) The **UN General Assembly** is composed of about 175 member nations, each with one vote; the **Security Council**, with five permanent members and five chosen from session to session, is the seat of real power; the **Secretariat** is the executive arm of the UN and directs the administration of UN programs.
      (3) In addition to its peacekeeping function, the UN runs a number of programs focused on economic development and health, education, and welfare concerns.
2. Other international organizations.

a. The **International Monetary Fund** helps regulate the world of international finance; the **World Bank** finances development projects in new nations; and the **International Postal Union** helps get the mail from one country to another.
b. **Regional organizations** are organizations of several nations bound by a treaty, often for military reasons.
   (1) The **North Atlantic Treaty Organization (NATO)** was created in 1949; its members (the United States, Canada, most Western European nations, and Turkey) agreed to combine military forces and to treat *a war against one as a war against all.*
   (2) The *Warsaw Pact* was the regional security community of the Soviet Union and its Eastern European allies; the Warsaw Pact has been dissolved, and the role of NATO is changing dramatically as the cold war has thawed.
   (3) The **European Union (EU)**, often called the **Common Market**, is an *economic alliance* of the major Western European nations; the EU coordinates monetary, trade, immigration, and labor policies.

3. Multinational corporations, groups, and individuals.
   a. Much of the world's industrial output comes from **multinational corporations (MNCs)**, which are sometimes more powerful (and often much wealthier) than the governments under which they operate.
   b. **Groups** such as churches and labor unions have long had international interests and activities.
      (1) Environmental and wildlife groups such as Greenpeace have proliferated, as have groups interested in protecting human rights, such as Amnesty International.
      (2) Some groups are committed to the overthrow of particular governments and operate as terrorists around the world.
   c. **Individuals** are also international actors.
      (1) The recent explosion of tourism affects the international economic system.
      (2) Growing numbers of students are going to and coming from other nations; they are carriers of ideas and ideologies.
      (3) Immigrants and refugees place new demands on public services.

C. The policymakers.
   1. The president is the main force behind foreign policy: as **chief diplomat**, the president negotiates treaties; as **commander in chief**, the president deploys American troops abroad.

2. Presidents are aided (and thwarted) by a huge national security bureaucracy; Congress also wields considerable clout in the foreign policy arena.
3. Other foreign policy decision makers.
   a. The *diplomats*.
      (1) The **secretary of state** has traditionally been the key advisor to the president on foreign policy matters.
      (2) The 23,000 people working in the **State Department** are organized into *functional areas* and *area specialties*.
      (3) The top positions in the department and the highly select members of the **Foreign Service** are heavily involved in formulating and executing American foreign policy. (Presidents Nixon and Carter relied more heavily on their *special assistants for national security affairs* than on their secretaries of state.)
      (4) Many recent presidents have bypassed institutional arrangements for foreign policy decision making and have established more personal systems for receiving policy advice.
4. The *national security establishment*.
   a. The **Department of Defense (DOD)** was created after World War II when the Army, Navy, and Air Force were combined into one department.
   b. The commanding officers of each of the services, plus a chair, constitute the **Joint Chiefs of Staff**; Richard Betts carefully examined the Joint Chiefs' advice to the president in many crises, and found that the Joint Chiefs were *no more likely than civilian advisors to push an aggressive military policy*.
   c. The **secretary of defense** manages a budget larger than that of most nations and is the president's primary military advisor.
   d. American foreign military policies are *supposed to be coordinated*; the **National Security Council (NSC)** was formed in 1947 for this purpose.
      (1) Despite the coordinating role assigned to the NSC, conflict within the foreign policy establishment remains common.
      (2) The NSC staff has sometimes competed with—rather than integrated—policy advice from cabinet departments; it has also become involved in *covert operations*.
   e. The **Central Intelligence Agency (CIA)**, known as *"The Company,"* was created after World War II to *coordinate American information and data-gathering intelligence activities abroad* and to *collect, analyze, and evaluate its own intelligence*.

(1) The size of its budget and staff are secret; estimates put them at $3 billion and about 19,000 people.
(2) Most of its activities are *uncontroversial*, as the bulk of the material it collects and analyzes comes from readily available sources.
(3) The CIA also engages in **covert activities**.
   (a) One way the CIA collects information is by *espionage* (usually against foreign adversaries).
   (b) The CIA has a long history of involvement in other nations' internal affairs; it has trained and supported armies and has nurtured coups.
   (c) At times, the agency engaged in wiretaps, interception of mail, and the infiltration of interest groups *in the United States*; this violated the CIA's charter and damaged the agency's morale and external political support.
   (d) With the end of the cold war, there is less pressure for covert activities and a climate more conducive to *conventional intelligence gathering*. Currently, Congress requires the CIA to *inform relevant congressional committees* promptly of current and anticipated covert operations.

5. *Congress*.
   a. The president *shares constitutional authority* over foreign amd defense policy with Congress.
      (i) Congress has sole authority to *declare war*, *raise and organize the armed forces*, and *appropriate funds* for national security activities.
      (ii) The Senate determines whether *treaties* will be ratified and ambassadorial and cabinet *nominations* confirmed.
      (iii) The *"power of the purse"* and responsibilities for *oversight* of the executive branch give Congress considerable clout, and senators and representatives examine defense budget authorizations carefully.
   b. It is a common mistake to believe that the Constitution vests foreign policy solely in the president. Sometimes this erroneous view leads to perverse results, as with the **Iran-Contra affair**, when officials at high levels in the executive branch lied to Congress and others in an attempt to protect what they viewed as the president's "exclusive" powers.

III. AMERICAN FOREIGN POLICY: AN OVERVIEW

A. From isolationism to internationalism.
   1. The United States followed a foreign policy of **isolationism** throughout most of its history.
   2. The **Monroe Doctrine** reaffirmed America's inattention to Europe's problems, but warned European nations to stay out of Latin America.
   3. In the wake of World War I, President Woodrow Wilson urged the United States to join the **League of Nations**; the Senate refused to ratify the treaty, indicating the country was not ready to abandon isolationism.
   4. *Pearl Harbor* dealt the death-blow to American isolationism.
   5. The charter for the United Nations was signed in San Francisco in 1945, with the United States as an original signatory.

B. At the end of World War II, the United States was the dominant world power, both economically and militarily.
   1. Only the United States possessed nuclear weapons.
   2. The United States poured billions of dollars into war-ravaged European nations through the **Marshall Plan**.
   3. NATO was created in 1949, affirming the mutual military interests of the United States and Western Europe.

C. All of Eastern Europe fell under Soviet domination as World War II ended.
   1. In 1946, Winston Churchill warned that the Russians had sealed off Eastern Europe with an "**iron curtain.**"
   2. Writing in *Foreign Affairs* in 1947 (under the pseudonym "*X*"), George F. Kennan proposed a policy of "**containment.**" His containment doctrine called for the United States to isolate the Soviet Union and to "contain" its advances and resist its encroachments.
   3. The **Truman Doctrine** was developed to help other nations (particularly Greece) oppose Communism.
   4. The Soviet Union closed off land access to Berlin with the **Berlin Blockade** (1948-1949); it was countered by a massive *airlift* of food, fuel, and other necessities by the United States and its allies.
   5. The fall of China to Mao Zedong's Communist-led forces in 1949 and the development of Soviet nuclear capability seemed to confirm American fears.
   6. The invasion of pro-American South Korea by Communist North Korea in 1950 fueled American fears further.
      a. President Truman sent American troops to Korea under United Nations auspices.
      b. The **Korean War** (which lasted until July 23, 1953) was a chance to put containment into practice.
   7. The 1950s were the height of the **cold war**.

   a. Eisenhower's secretary of state, John Foster Dulles, proclaimed a policy of "**brinkmanship**" in which the United States was to be prepared to use nuclear weapons in order to *deter* the Soviet Union and Communist China from taking aggressive action.
   b. In the era of **McCarthyism** (named for Senator Joseph McCarthy, who made unsubstantiated accusations of disloyalty and breaches of security against both public officials and private citizens), domestic policy was deeply affected by the cold war and by anticommunist fears.
8. With containment came a massive buildup of the military apparatus, resulting in what some people called the **military-industrial complex**.
   a. The phrase was coined by President Dwight D. Eisenhower to refer to the interests shared by the armed services and defense contractors.
   b. Economist Seymour Melman wrote about **pentagon capitalism**, linking the military's drive to expand with the profit motives of private industry.
9. The 1950s ushered in an **arms race** between the Soviet Union and the United States; eventually, a point of **mutual assured destruction (MAD)** was reached in which each side could destroy the other.

D. The Vietnam War.
1. In 1950, President Truman decided to aid the French effort to retain France's colonial possessions in Southeast Asia.
2. During the 1950s, the **Viet Minh** (the Vietnamese Communist forces) began to receive military aid from the new Communist government in China.
3. In 1954, the French were defeated by the Viet Minh (led by Ho Chi Minh) in a battle at Dien Bien Phu.
4. Although it was a party to the 1954 agreements among participants in Geneva, Switzerland, the United States never accepted the Geneva agreement to hold national elections in Vietnam in 1956; instead, it began supporting one non-Communist leader after another in South Vietnam.
5. Vietnam first became an election-year issue in 1964.
   a. Since Truman's time, the United States had sent *military "advisors"* to South Vietnam, which was in the midst of a civil war spurred by the **Viet Cong** (National Liberation Front).
   b. Senator Barry Goldwater was a foreign policy hard-liner who advocated tough action in Vietnam; President Lyndon Johnson promised that he would not "send American boys to do an Asian

boy's job" of defending the pro-American regime in South Vietnam.

6. Despite his election-year promise, Johnson sent in American troops when we were unable to contain the forces of the Viet Cong and North Vietnam with American advisors.
   a. American troops (more than 500,000 at the peak of the *undeclared war*) and massive firepower failed to contain the North Vietnamese.
   b. At home, widespread protests against the war contributed to Johnson's decision not to run for reelection in 1968 and to begin peace negotiations.
7. The new Nixon administration prosecuted the war vigorously (in Cambodia as well as in Vietnam), but also worked to negotiate a peace treaty with the Viet Cong and North Vietnam.
   a. A peace treaty was signed in 1973, but no one expected it to hold.
   b. South Vietnam's capital, Saigon, fell to the North Vietnamese army in 1975.
   c. South and North Vietnam were reunited into a single nation, and Saigon was renamed Ho Chi Minh City.

E. The era of *détente*.
   1. Even while the Vietnam War was being waged, Richard Nixon supported a new policy of ***détente***.
      a. Popularized by Henry Kissinger, Nixon's national security assistant (and later secretary of state), *détente* sought a *relaxation of tensions* between the superpowers, coupled with firm guarantees of mutual security.
      b. Foreign policy battles were to be waged with diplomatic, economic, and propaganda weapons; the threat of force was downplayed.
   2. One major initiative coming out of *détente* was the **Strategic Arms Limitation Talks (SALT)**.
      a. These talks represented an effort by the United States and the Soviet Union to agree to scale down their nuclear capabilities, with each power maintaining sufficient nuclear weapons to deter a surprise attack by the other.
      b. President Nixon signed the first SALT treaty in 1972.
      c. A second SALT treaty (SALT II) was signed and sent to the Senate by President Carter in 1979, but the Soviet invasion of Afghanistan that year caused Carter to withdraw the treaty from Senate consideration; both he and President Reagan nevertheless insisted that they would be committed to its arms limitations.

3. The philosophy of *détente* was applied to the People's Republic of China as well as to the Soviet Union.
    a. President Nixon visited the People's Republic and sent an American mission there.
    b. President Carter extended formal diplomatic recognition in November 1978.

F. The Reagan rearmament.
1. From the mid-1950s to 1981, the *defense budget had generally been declining* as a percentage of both the total federal budget and the gross national product (with the exception of the Vietnam War).
    a. Ronald Reagan referred to the Soviet Union as the "*Evil Empire,*" he viewed the Soviet invasion of Afghanistan in 1979 as typical Russian aggression.
    b. During his presidential campaign, Reagan said America faced a "*window of vulnerability*" because the Soviet Union was pulling ahead of the United States in military spending.
2. President Carter's last budget had proposed a large increase in defense spending, and the Reagan administration proposed adding $32 billion on top of that. In the second Reagan term, concern over huge budget deficits brought defense spending to a standstill.
3. In 1983, President Reagan proposed the **Strategic Defense Initiative (SDI)**—renamed "Star Wars" by critics—to create a global "umbrella" of protection in space.

G. The final thaw in the cold war.
1. The cold war ended spontaneously—a situation that few could have predicted.
    a. Forces of change sparked by Soviet leader Mikhail Gorbachev led to a staggering wave of upheavals that shattered Communist regimes and the postwar barriers between Eastern and Western Europe.
    b. The *Berlin Wall* (the most prominent symbol of oppression in Eastern Europe) was brought down, and East and West Germany formed a unified, democratic republic.
    c. The former Soviet Union split into fifteen separate nations; non-Communist governments formed in most of them.
    d. On May 12, 1989, President Bush announced a new era in American foreign policy, one that he termed "*beyond containment.*" Bush declared that it was time to seek the integration of the Soviet Union into the community of nations.
2. In 1989, reform seemed on the verge of occurring in China as well as in Eastern Europe.

   a. Thousands of students held protests on behalf of democratization in *Tiananmen Square* (the central meeting place in Beijing).
   b. However, on the night of June 3 the army violently crushed the democracy movement, killing hundreds—perhaps thousands—of protesters and beginning a wave of executions, arrests, and repression.

IV. THE POLITICS OF DEFENSE POLICY

A. Defense spending.
   1. The central assumption of the current American defense policy is that the United States requires forces and equipment sufficient to fight two nearly simultaneous major regional wars.
   2. Defense spending comprises about one-sixth of the federal budget.
   3. Domestic political concerns, budgetary limitations, and ideology all have a role in influencing decisions regarding the structure of defense policy.
   3. Defense spending is a *political issue* entangled with *ideological disputes*.
      a. Conservatives oppose deep cuts in defense spending, pointing out that many nations retain potent military capability and insisting that America needs to maintain its high state of readiness.
      b. They credit the collapse of communism in Eastern and Central Europe to Western toughness and the massive increase in defense spending that occurred in the early 1980s.
      c. Liberals maintain that the Pentagon wastes money and that the United States buys too many guns and too little butter.
      d. They contend that Gorbachev and his fellow reformers were responding primarily to internal (not external) pressures; they believe the erosion of the Communist party's authority was well under way when Gorbachev rose to power and that it accelerated as *glasnost* called attention to the party's failures.
   5. Some scholars have argued that America faces a trade-off between defense spending and social spending.
      a. Evidence for the existence of such a trade-off is mixed.
      b. In general, defense and domestic policy expenditures appear to be independent of each other.
   6. The lessening of East-West tensions has provided momentum for significant reductions in defense spending (what some call the *peace dividend*).
      a. Some conservatives favor cutting defense spending in order to decrease the budget deficit.
      b. Some liberals want to allocate the funds to expanded domestic

programs.

c. Changing spending patterns is not easy: when assembly lines at weapons plants close down, people lose their jobs; these programs become political footballs.

d. Defense spending is decreasing, and the size of the armed forces is also being reduced.

B. Personnel.

1. The United States has nearly 1.4 million men and women on active duty and about 900,000 in the National Guard and Reserves; about 230,000 active duty troops are deployed abroad, mostly in Europe.

2. This is a very costly enterprise; many observers feel that America's allies—especially prosperous nations like Japan and Germany—should bear a greater share of common defense costs.

C. Weapons.

1. To deter an aggressor's attack, the United States has relied on a *triad of nuclear weapons*—ground-based **intercontinental ballistic missiles (ICBMs)**, submarine-launched **ballistic missiles (SLBMs)**, and **strategic bombers**.

2. Arms reduction.

a. During the May 1988 Moscow summit meeting, President Reagan and President Gorbachev exchanged ratified copies of a new treaty eliminating **intermediate-range nuclear forces (INF)**; Reagan became the first American president to sign a treaty to reduce current levels of nuclear weapons.

b. On November 19, 1990, the leaders of twenty-two countries signed a treaty cutting *conventional* arms in Europe.

c. In 1991, the Warsaw Pact (the military alliance tying Eastern Europe to the Soviet Union) was dissolved.

d. On July 31, 1991, President Gorbachev and President Bush signed the *Strategic Arms Reduction Treaty*, following *nine years of negotiations*.

3. The democratization of Eastern Europe, the restructuring of the Soviet Union, and the deterioration of the Soviet economy substantially diminished Russia's inclination and potential to threaten the interests of the United States and its allies.

a. In the fall of 1991, President Bush broke new ground with his decision to *unilaterally dismantle* some U.S. nuclear weapons; President Gorbachev followed suit shortly afterward.

b. Presidents Bush and Yeltsin signed an agreement to sharply reduce the U.S. and Russian nuclear arsenals.

4. Despite these changes, *high-tech weapons systems* will continue to play an *important role in America's defense posture*.

a. The perception that space-age technology helped win the Gulf War in "100 hours" and with few American casualties provides support for high-tech systems.

c. Producing expensive weapons also provides jobs for American workers.

V. THE NEW GLOBAL AGENDA

A. By whatever standards one uses, the United States is the world's mightiest power; but for Americans, merely being big and powerful is no guarantee of dominance.

1. Our economy is increasingly dependent on international trade.
2. Public opinion polls find that Americans are more likely to perceive threats to their security form *economic competition from allies* than from military rivalry with potential adversaries.
3. Political scientist Stanley Hoffman likened the United States' plight to that of Jonathan Swift's *Gulliver*, the traveler who was seized and bound by the tiny Lilliputians.

B. New issues and tools have emerged in the increasingly complex foreign affairs domain.

1. Economic sanctions are a new and powerful non-military penalty imposed on a foreign government in an attempt to modify its behavior.
2. Nuclear proliferation has become a more central issue, with the United States adopting a more assertive posture in attempting to deny nuclear weapons to rogue states.
3. Terrorism is the most troublesome issue in this new environment

C. The international economy.

1. Today's international economy is illustrated by **interdependency**.
2. The *International Monetary Fund (IMF)* is a cooperative international organization of 182 countries intended to stabilize the exchange of currencies and the world economy. The necessity of the IMF making the loans dramatically illustrates the world's economic interdependence.
3. The health of the American economy depends increasingly on the prosperity of its trading partners and on the smooth *flow of trade and finance across borders*.
   a. *Exports and imports* have increased ten-fold since 1970 alone; spending by foreign tourists bolsters U.S. travel, hotel, and recreation industries; American colleges and universities derive a significant portion of their revenue from foreign students.
   b. The *globalization of finances* has been even more dramatic than the growth of trade; worldwide computer and communications

networks instantaneously link financial markets in all parts of the globe.

4. At one time, **tariffs** (taxes added to the cost of imported goods) were the primary instruments of international economic policy.
   a. Tariffs are intended to raise the price of imported goods in order to *protect American businesses and workers from foreign competition.*
   b. Tariff making became a two-edged sword: high U.S. tariffs encourage *other nations to respond* with high tariffs on American products.
5. Since the era of the Great Depression, the world economy has moved away from high tariffs and *protectionism* toward lower tariffs and freer trade.
   a. President Bush signed the **North American Free Trade Agreement** in 1992 with Canada and Mexico; it was approved by Congress in 1993.
   b. In 1994, Congress also approved the even more important General Agreement on Tariffs and Trade **(GATT)** treaty.
6. Various circumstances combine to upset the **balance of trade** (the ratio of what a country pays for imports to what it earns from exports).
   a. For a number of years, America has experienced a balance of trade *deficit*; the excess of imports over exports decreases the dollar's *buying power* against other currencies, making Americans pay more for goods they buy from other nations.
   b. On the plus side, this decline in the dollar also makes American products cheaper abroad, thereby increasing our exports.
   c. Since the late 1980s, the United States has experienced a balance of trade *surplus* with western Europe; the trade deficit with Japan and other Asian countries has declined, but much more slowly.
   d. A poor balance of trade exacerbates *unemployment*; jobs as well as dollars are flowing abroad.
7. A *cheaper dollar* also makes the *cost of American labor more competitive.* More foreign-owned companies are now building factories in the U.S.

D. International inequality and foreign aid.
   1. Whereas the cold war meant continuous conflict between the Soviet Union and the West, world politics today includes a growing conflict between *rich nations* (concentrated in the northern hemisphere) and *poor nations* (concentrated in the southern hemisphere).
   2. The income gap between rich, industrialized nations and poor, underdeveloped ones is widening rather than narrowing.

3. Not only are there wide gaps between rich and poor nations **(international inequality)**, but there are also big gaps between the rich and poor *within* developing countries **(intranational inequality)**.
4. Although every nation has income inequality, *the poorer the nation, the wider the gaps between rich and poor.*
5. Presidents of both parties have pressed for aid to nations in the developing world—sometimes from humanitarian concern, sometimes out of a desire to stabilize friendly nations.
   a. **Foreign aid** has sometimes been given in the form of *grants*, but it often has taken the form of *credits and loan guarantees to purchase American goods*, *loans at favorable interest rates*, and *forgiveness of previous loans*; *preferential trade agreements* have sometimes been granted for the sale of foreign goods here.
   b. A substantial percentage of foreign aid is in the form of *military assistance* and is targeted to a few countries that are considered to be of vital strategic significance.
   c. Foreign aid programs have also assisted with *agricultural modernization, irrigation, and population control.*
   d. Foreign aid has never been very popular with Americans. Although the United States donates *more total aid than any other country*, it devotes a *smaller share of its GNP* to foreign economic development than any other developed nation.

E. The global connection, energy, and the environment.
   1. Massive oceangoing oil tankers (most sailing from OPEC nations) have made it possible to *import half of the oil Americans now use*, but they have also contributed to ruined fisheries and beaches from oil spills.
   2. *Energy transfers* offer convincing evidence that *world politics is a politics of growing dependency.*
      a. The less-developed nations have long depended on more industrialized nations.
      b. Recently the industrialized nations have themselves become dependent because of their growing need for imported energy sources.
   3. Almost every nation faces severe environmental problems.
      a. The formerly Communist nations of Central and Eastern Europe rank among the worst offenders.
      b. Underdeveloped nations almost always favor economic growth at the expense of the ecology.
      c. Recent concerns over the effects of fluorocarbons (found in many household products) on the Earth's ozone layer have generated

international studies and diplomatic discussions; Americans have bargained with other nations to restrict overfishing, limit pollution, and deal with deforestation of the tropical rain forests.

d. Issues closer to home often get a different response: in 1992, President Bush refused to sign an international agreement on environmental protection, arguing that it would cost jobs in the United States and that it failed to protect patent rights to newly developing industries; however, President Clinton agreed to follow a specific timetable to reduce the threat of global warming and to sign a treaty protecting rare and endangered species.

e. *Acid rain* has created difficulties between the United States and Canada, but global issues of the *world commons* have not yet become a major part of U.S. foreign policy.

VI. UNDERSTANDING FOREIGN AND DEFENSE POLICYMAKING

A. Foreign and defense policymaking and democracy.

1. Americans are usually more interested in domestic policy than foreign policy.
2. Public opinion plays an important part in American foreign and defense policy; as with other issues, policymakers are reluctant to make unpopular decisions.
3. The system of *separation of powers* plays a crucial role in foreign as well as domestic policy: the president does not act alone; Congress has a central role in matters of international relations. [see Chapter 12]
4. *Pluralism* is important to the development of American international economic policy: agencies and members of Congress—as well as their constituents—each pursue their own policy goals; even foreign governments hire lobbying firms.

B. Foreign and defense policymaking and the scope of government.

1. America's *global connections as a superpower* have many implications for how active the national government is in the realm of foreign policy and national defense.
2. Treaty obligations, the nation's economic interests in an interdependent global economy, and other questions on the global agenda guarantee that the national government will be active in international relations.
3. As the United States remains a superpower and continues to have interests to defend around the world, the scope of American government in foreign and defense policy will be substantial.

KEY TERMS AND CONCEPTS

Arms race: one side's weaponry motivates the other side to procure more weaponry.

Balance of trade: the ratio of what a country pays for imports to what it earns from exports.

Central Intelligence Agency (CIA): created after WWII to coordinate American information and data-gathering intelligence activities.

Cold war: where the U.S. and the Soviet Union were often on the brink of war.

Containment doctrine: called for the U.S. to isolate the Soviet Union to contain its advances by peaceful or coercive means.

Detente: a slow transformation from conflict thinking to cooperative thinking in foreign policy strategy designed to ease tensions between the superpowers and guarantee mutual security.

European Union (EU): often referred to as the Common Market, is an economic union to coordinate monetary, trade, immigration, and labor policies between major Western European Nations.

Foreign Policy: involves making choices about relations with the rest of the world.

Interdependency: actions reverberate and affect other people's actions.

Isolationism: a policy which directs the U.S. to stay out of other nations' conflicts.

Joint Chiefs of Staff: composed of commanding officers of each of the services, plus a chair, are the president's military advisors.

McCarthyism: persecution of prominent Americans and State Department officials accused of being Communists during the 1950s.

North Atlantic Treaty Organization (NATO): created in 1949 to combine military forces of the U.S., Canada, Western European nations, and Turkey.

Organization of Petroleum Exporting Countries (OPEC): organization comprised of oil producing countries in the Middle East.

Secretary of Defense: the president's main civilian defense advisor.

Secretary of State: a key advisor to the president on foreign policy.

Strategic Defense Initiative (SDI): also know as star wars, this plan proposed creating a global umbrella in space to destroy invading missiles.

Tariff: raises the price of an imported good to protect domestic business.

United Nations: an international organization created in 1945 where members agree to renounce war and respect human and economic freedoms.

TEACHING IDEAS: CLASS DISCUSSION AND STUDENT PROJECTS

- Reconciling covert activities with the principles of open democratic government remains a challenge for public officials. Does your class perceive any conflict between "democracy" and the need for "national security"? What types of limitations would your students place on covert activities? What type of distinction do they draw between activities of democracies and activities of nations like the former Soviet Union when it comes to national security?

- The feature *You Are the Policymaker: Defending Human Rights* challenges students to decide what they would have done after the Chinese army violently crushed the democracy movement by killing hundreds of protesters in Tiananmen Square; this was the beginning of a wave of executions, arrests, and repression. Ask your students to play the role of U.S. president. Their assignment is to decide if the United States should have continued normal relations with China, or if it should have taken some action against China. As a basis for class discussion, have your students read *A Question of Ethics* and review news reports from May and June of 1989.

- Public opinion polls find that Americans today are more likely to perceive threats to their security in economic competition from allies than from military rivalry with potential adversaries. As a library project, challenge your students to contrast the positions of the United States and Japan with regard to both defense expenditures and protective economic policies. Divide the class into several research groups for this project, and have them allocate some division of responsibility among themselves.

- For class discussion, have students debate the value of American involvement in U.N. peacekeeping efforts. In particular, have them examine the costs and benefits of this policy to American taxpayers. Ask them what exactly would they propose instead of American participation in these efforts.

- Have each student choose a country, and, using Internet, library, and government document sources, investigate the nature of foreign policy toward that country. What specific issues does the United States have an interest in? What policy instruments (foreign aid, diplomacy, military forces, etc.) is the United States using to accomplish those goals? Have students write a brief essay addressing these questions. If shared with the class, this writing exercise could also result in an interesting discussion highlighting the diversity of American interests around the world, and help students to develop more thoughtful positions on foreign and defense policy making.

- For a reading and writing connection, have students write an essay where they must identify and investigate the variety and quantity of goods and services they consume which are imported to the U.S. Then have students evaluate the cost differential for each good or service produced by American businesses which could substitute for those imports. Finally, have students justify the cost differential and explain why they would or would not support their original choices if given a opportunity to repurchase those goods and services.

BACKGROUND READING

Gilpin, Robert. The Political Economy of International Relations. Princeton: Princeton University Press. 1987.

Hilsman, Roger, Lauruua Gaughran and Patricia Wertsman. The Politics of Policymaking in Defense and Foreign Affairs. Englewood Cliffs, NJ: Prentice-Hall. 1992.

Kennedy, Paul M. The Rise and Fall of the Great Powers. NY: Vintage Books. 1989.

Mann, Thomas E. ed. A Question of Balance: The President, the Congress, and Foreign Policy. Washington, DC: The Brookings Institution. 1990.

Oye, Kenneth, et al. eds. Eagle in a New World. NY: HarperCollins. 1992.

Spanier, John. American Foreign Policy Since World War II. 14th ed. Washington, DC: CQ Press. 1997.

MEDIA SUGGESTIONS

America at War. This film examines American wars from World War II to the Persian Gulf. Films for the Humanities and Sciences.

The Road to War: American Decision Making During the Gulf Crisis. This film provides an in-depth analysis of how decisions were made in response to the Gulf crisis. Films for the Humanities and Sciences.

The United Nations: It's More Than You Think. 1991. This program examines the structure and functions of the U.N. Insight Media.

The Vietnam War. This program examines the origins of the Vietnam War, the role of American advisers, the escalation of the war, and the final evacuation of American troops. Films for the Humanities and Sciences.

CHAPTER TWENTY-ONE: THE NEW FACE OF STATE AND LOCAL GOVERNMENT

PEDAGOGICAL FEATURES

LEARNING OBJECTIVES

After studying this chapter, students should be able to:

- Discuss the new importance of state and local government.
- Identify provisions that are typically included in state constitutions.
- Outline the stages by which state constitutions may be amended.
- Describe and analyze the debate over direct democracy.
- Summarize the tasks that state legislatures perform.
- Assess legislative turnover and term limits.
- Summarize the tasks that state governors perform.
- Explain the significance of *fragmentation* of state executive authority.
- Describe the three-tier organization of state judicial systems and the functions each level performs.
- Evaluate the role of *grassroots democracy* in America.
- Identify and describe the three basic forms of municipal government.
- Identify the tasks performed by municipalities, school districts, county governments, townships, and special districts.
- Discuss how the fragmentation of local governments causes competition among them and makes it difficult for them to cooperate with one another.
- Summarize the sources of revenues and expenditures of state governments.
- Analyze the democracy and the scope of government at the state and local levels.

CHAPTER OVERVIEW

INTRODUCTION

In this chapter, we discuss subnational government with an eye toward two important characteristics: *revitalization* and *diversity*. Since the early 1960s, the states have become revitalized in their institutions, their personnel, and their role in the federal system. With the weight of the philosophical argument about where policymaking power should lie in the federal system swinging strongly toward the states for the past 30 years, the federal government has provided the states and localities with increasing control over policymaking.

STATE CONSTITUTIONS

State constitutions typically include provisions for separation of powers, legislative powers, executive powers, judicial powers, local governments, taxation and finance, and a bill of rights. States tend to have constitutions that are considerably longer than the U.S. Constitution; most are burdened with details that attempt to spell out government authority and limit government power.

Most states avoid the politically difficult process of writing a new constitution. Instead, most have adapted their governing documents by adding periodic amendments through a two-step process of *proposal and ratification.*

STATE ELECTIONS

Most top-level state policy-makers are elected to office, and recently greater attention has been given to state elections by voters. Most gubernatorial elections are held in non-presidential election years, and have become similar to presidential elections with their reliance on the mass media and money, and being candidate, rather than party, based.

State legislatures were **malapportioned** for much of the twentieth century, giving greater representation to rural areas than their population warranted. Following a succession of U.S. Supreme Court decisions in the mid-1960s (*Baker* v. *Carr*, 1962; *Reynolds* v. *Sims*, 1964), state legislative districts were redrawn to adhere to the principle of *"one-man, one-vote."* The result was an increase in urban state representatives and senators; a larger number of Republicans were elected in the South; and large states such as New York and California now have legislatures that are younger, better-educated, and more racially and ethnically diverse.

Legislative elections in the 1990s are less dependent on candidate personality and the mass media than are gubernatorial races, though they are becoming more like Congressional races. State legislatures are more closely divided today than in previous decades, and about half of the states have divided legislatures. *Divided government* exists when a single party does not control both chambers of the state legislature and the governor's office. After the 1998 elections, 26 states had divided government, approximately the same level as has been seen since the mid-1980s. Since 1990, 21 states have adopted term limits for state legislators, almost exclusively through direct democracy mechanisms. Elected state officials have become increasingly diverse with respect to race and gender.

GOVERNORS AND THE EXECUTIVE BRANCH

Like the president, governors are expected to wear *"many hats"* in their jobs. A governor directs a complex state government and the programs that it administers. Governors initiate much of the legislation that state legislatures will adopt, they help manage conflict, and they must work with a number of other elected executive officials to produce public policy.

Recent governors have often held previous experience as a statewide elected official or held a federal elective position. Various state-level reforms have enhanced the formal powers of some governors, with governors in seven states being ranked as very strong, eighteen governors ranked as strong, ten ranked as moderate, and governors in fifteen being ranked as weak.

Two of a governor's most important formal powers for controlling state government are the veto and the executive budget. Governors in forty-two states have a **line-item veto** that permits them to veto or amend portions of a budget bill or legislative language.

Governors also enhance their influence with more "personal powers." In sharp contrast to the political "hacks" who commonly served as governors earlier in this century, the modern governor is likely to be bright, experienced, and capable of managing the diverse problems of a state.

So many independent executives, commissions, and boards work within state governments that many politicians and scholars have called for major state government reorganization to allow governors more control and to increase efficiency generally. Such reorganization seldom results in cost saving and efficiency – benefits often promised by its proponents.

STATE LEGISLATURES

State legislatures are far more active, informed, representative and democratic today than they were forty years ago. Like Congress, state legislatures are responsible for a myriad of tasks as public representatives: making laws, appropriating money, overseeing the executive branch, approving the governor's appointments, and serving constituents. State legislatures also perform duties assigned to them by the U.S. Constitution, such as ratifying proposed amendments to the Constitution and redrawing congressional districts following each census and reapportionment.

Three types of *legislative professionalism* reforms have been passed over the past three decades: increasing the length of legislative sessions, increasing legislators' salaries, and increasing the professional staff available to legislators. Not all agree that these are positive changes. We may now be seeing the beginning of a "deprofessionalizing" trend in some states, as some harken back to the Jeffersonian ideal of the citizen legislature. Term limit laws are the most obvious manifestation of this, but recent laws in California limiting legislative staffing and in Colorado limiting the powers of the legislative leadership may also signal that the legislative professionalism movement is cyclical.

STATE COURT SYSTEMS

Most judicial business in the United States occurs in the state court systems. State courts have one hundred times the number of trials and hear five times more appeals than federal courts. States have generally organized their courts into a *three-tier system* of trial courts, intermediate courts of appeals, and a court of last resort, similar to the model of organization of the federal courts.

Trial courts are organized on a local basis. A single judge presides over each case, and citizens are called upon to serve as jurors and members of grand jury panels. It is at the trial court level that the *facts of the case* are considered, along with *due process guarantees* required for the accused under the U.S. Constitution.

Appeals may be made to an intermediate **court of appeals** in thirty-seven states (in other states, appeals go directly to the court of last resort). Appeals courts are organized on a regional basis in which judges work together in *panels* of three or more. Juries are not used in appellate courts; instead, judges read briefs and hear arguments prepared by lawyers that address legal issues such as whether the law was appropriately applied at the trial court level and whether due process of law was followed.

All states have a **court of last resort**, usually called a *supreme court*, that is the *final appellate level* in a state. The court of last resort hears both civil and criminal cases on appeal except in Oklahoma and Texas, which each have two top courts—one for civil appeals and one for criminal appeals. Supreme court decisions are significant *policy actions*; these courts are often called upon to practice judicial review of actions of the state legislature and the executive branch, to interpret laws and the state constitution, and to make judicial policy.

Popular *elections* are used to choose judges and justices for a limited term of office in some states; some states still use **partisan ballots** for judicial elections, but many have begun to choose judges on **nonpartisan ballots**. The most recent wave of judicial selection reforms in seventeen states was the adoption of a hybrid system of appointment and election known as the **Merit Plan**.

DIRECT DEMOCRACY

Constitutional initiative, **legislative initiative**, **referendum**, and **recall** are all tools of **direct democracy** introduced during the **Progressive Era**. Some observers feel that these tools often lead to *poorly crafted initiatives* and that they provide another avenue of *political influence for better financed, more privileged interest groups*.

STATE AND LOCAL GOVERNMENT RELATIONS

The intergovernmental relationship between states and their inferior local governments is important to understanding government as is the relationship between the national government and the states. It is not, however, nearly as ambiguous a relationship as that between the national and state governments. The basic relationship is that the local governments are totally subservient to the state government. According to **Dillon's Rule**, local government have only those powers that are explicitly given to them by the states. Many cities have managed to get state legislatures to grant them a degree of autonomy in their **local charter**.

LOCAL GOVERNMENTS

There are over 87 thousand governments in the United States, which has a strong tradition of **grassroots democracy.** Many Americans believe that public policy is best produced by governments that are *closest to the people*. Every U.S. citizen lives within the jurisdiction of a national government, a state government, and perhaps ten to twenty local governments. However, the vast number of governments is as much a burden as a boon to democracy.

Most city and school district governments are located in a **county** (called a *parish* in Louisiana and a *borough* in Alaska), and **county government** is the *administrative arm of state government in local areas*. County governments keep records of births, deaths, and marriages; establish a system of justice and law enforcement; maintain roads and bridges, collect taxes, conduct voter registration and elections; and provide for public welfare and education. County governments usually consist of an elected **county commission** that makes policy and a collection of *"row officers"* (such as a sheriff, prosecutor, county clerk, and assessor) who run county services; some *urban counties* now elect a county executive or appoint a county administrator.

Township governments are found in twenty states. Most have limited powers to assist with services in rural areas, but some function much like city governments. Townships can provide for public highways and local law enforcement, keep records of vital statistics and tax collections, and administer elections.

Municipalities (city governments) provide *most basic local programs and services*, such as police and fire protection, street maintenance, solid waste collection, water and sewer works, park and recreation services, and public planning. Many local communities in the United States were originally operated under the **"town meeting"** form of direct democracy, where all voting age adults in a community gathered once a year to make public policy. Since cities became too large for the town meeting style of governance, three *modern forms of municipal government* have been used: **mayor-council government** (with "weak" and "strong" variations), **council-manager government**, and **commission government.**

Most city council members and mayors are elected on a *nonpartisan ballot*. Traditionally, city council members represented a **district** or **ward** of the city—a practice that permitted the ward-based machine bosses to control elections. Reformers advocated **at-large** city elections, with all members of the city council chosen by voters across the city. An unintended consequence of at-large representation is that *minority group members have had difficulty gaining election* to the city council.

School districts are responsible for delivering education programs in 14,000 areas of the country; most school systems are run as independent local governments. In an **independent school district**, local voters within a geographically defined area are responsible for their own public education system. Within the guidelines of state policy and the parameters of state funding, locally elected school boards and appointed administrators deliver education services. One of the hottest debates in school policy today concerns how to *pay for* and *guarantee equity* in public education.

The United States also has 31,555 *independent, limited-purpose governmental units* (other than school districts) known as **special districts**. This classification includes a wide variety of local "districts" for parks, natural resources, fire protection, and libraries, as well as "public authorities," "boards," and government "corporations" that can be found in every state. Special districts represent *the fastest growing form of local democracy* during the past two decades and often result from the need of local governments to coordinate in a policy area.

Each governing body in a fragmented metropolis tends to look at problems from its *own narrow, partial perspective*. As a result, *local bodies fail to cooperate* with one another and plan effectively for the region's future needs. This fragmented nature of local governments leads to racial and class inequalities. With a few notable exceptions, prospects for increased cooperation among local governments remain dim. In many areas of the country, a **council of governments** (frequently referred to as a COG) exists wherein officials from various localities meet to discuss mutual problems and plan joint, cooperative action. These COGs are often formally very weak, being underfunded, poorly staffed, and lacking in any real legislative or taxing power.

STATE AND LOCAL FINANCE POLICY

The finances of state and local governments are a confusing array of responsibilities, revenues, and budgets. This situation is primarily due to different ways in which states and their local governments have allocated the functional responsibilities among local governments.

State government revenues are derived from a variety of sources. States receive the largest share of revenue (44 percent) from *taxes*, primarily sales taxes, income taxes, and motor vehicle and fuel taxes. The second largest source of state revenue is *aid from the federal government* (almost 23 percent), followed by revenue from *state insurance programs* (approximately 17 percent). Smaller revenue sources include charges for services, state-operated liquor stores, utilities, payments from local governments, and a number of miscellaneous sources.

Nearly 50 percent of state money goes to *operate state programs, construct state buildings, and provide direct assistance to individuals*; approximately 30 percent is allocated as *aid to local governments*. In fiscal year 1992, state governments allocated the bulk of their money to education (about 36 percent), followed by health and social services (about 14 percent) and public safely (just over 8 percent).

UNDERSTANDING STATE AND LOCAL GOVERNMENTS

States have been willing to decentralize their governing arrangement to permit the creation of grassroots-oriented local governments to address citizens' policy demands. The very existence of so many governments to handle so many different and needed services speaks to the *health of democracy*.

Yet state and local politics are *not perfectly democratic*: there is poor coverage in the media; there are low levels of citizen participation; business interests have substantial leverage in state and city affairs; and term limits can also have undemocratic aspects.

Growth in state and local government employment has exceeded that of the federal government for most of this century. Most of the growth has been associated with heightened demands of state and local residents for more government programs. Many state and local governments have tried to *reorganize their government structures* to get more effective government and more efficient use of taxpayers' dollars; in most cases, this process of reorganization has *not* resulted in smaller government.

Most state governments have experimented with *sunset legislation* in an effort to limit the scope of state government. However, as demands for services have grown, state and local governments have also had to grow in order to meet new challenges.

CHAPTER OUTLINE

I. INTRODUCTION

A. State and local governments, or **subnational governments**, touch our lives every day.
B. Since the early 1960s, the states have become revitalized in their institutions, their personnel, and their role in the federal system.
C. With the weight of the philosophical argument about where policymaking power should lie in the federal government swinging strongly toward the states for the past 30 years, the federal government has provided the states and localities with increasing control over policymaking.

D. A second characteristic important to understanding subnational government in the United States is diversity.
E. To understand this diversity among the states is to understand the politics and history of the United States better. This also raises the important questions of why these differences exist and what effects these differences have.

II. STATE CONSTITUTIONS

A. State constitutions are subordinate to the U.S. Constitution and the laws of the United States, but they take *precedence over state law.*
B. States tend to have constitutions that are considerably longer than the U.S. Constitution; most are burdened with details that attempt to spell out government authority and limit government power.
C. States may amend their constitutions through a two-step process of *proposal* and *ratification*.
    1. The most common method is **legislative proposal** (permitted in all fifty states), usually requiring approval by a vote of two-thirds of the legislature and then submission to state voters who may **ratify** the proposal by a simple majority vote.
    2. A second method is proposal by a **constitutional convention**.

III. STATE ELECTIONS

A. Most top-level state policy-makers are elected to office.
B. State elections used to be determined by national forces, but now they are more visible and voters pay more attention to them.
C. Gubernatorial elections have been *presidentialized*, becoming more personalized and resembling the mega-event of presidential elections.
    1. Most gubernatorial elections are in non-presidential-election years.
    2. Gubernatorial candidates must raise money and they do it by themselves rather than rely on party organizations.
    3. Gubernatorial elections have become less predictable over the past decade.
D. Races for state legislative offices are often decided based on forces beyond the candidates' control—the party identification of district voters and parties' candidates in the race for governor and president.
    1. Recently these races have become more like the electoral races for Congress.
E. State legislatures have become more competitive and more partisan; there is more divided government and many states have enacted term limits.
F. State elected officials are more diverse than ever.

IV. GOVERNORS AND THE EXECUTIVE BRANCH

A. The job of governor.
   1. Like the president, governors are expected to wear "*many hats*" in their jobs.
      a. A governor directs a complex state government and the programs that it administers.
      b. Governors initiate much of the legislation that state legislatures will adopt.
      c. They help manage conflict.
      d. They must work with a number of other elected executive officials to produce public policy.
   2. The powers of governors are not always commensurate with expectations that citizens have of them.
      a. State constitutions often grant only *weak powers* to governors, frequently dividing executive powers among many different administrative actors and agencies. In addition, extensive civil service and merit-based employment policies in most states further diminish the governor's power.
      b. Important formal powers include the **line item veto** and the executive budget. Forty-two governors have the item veto, which allows them to veto only parts of a bill while allowing the rest of it to pass into law.
      c. Governors supplement their formal powers with more "personal powers."
      d. Modernization in state governments has resulted in enhanced powers for governors, but it usually has not resolved the problem of *fragmentation of executive power*.
   3. Other executive officers include:
      a. attorney general—the state's legal officer, elected in 43 states;
      b. treasurer—the manager of the state's bank accounts, elected in 38 states;
      c. secretary of state—in charge of elections and record-keeping, elected in 36 states.
      d. auditor—financial comptroller for the state, elected in 25 states; and
      e. as well as, in some states, agricultural commissioner, and commissioners for land, labor, mines, and utilities, among others.

V. STATE LEGISLATURES

A. Between 1965 and 1985 many—but not all—state legislatures underwent a metamorphosis into more full-time, professional bodies, with several operating like state-level congresses.
   1. State legislatures serve the same basic function in the states as

Congress does in the federal government.
  a. make basic laws;
  b. appropriate money;
  c. oversee activities of executive branch; and
  d. serve constituencies.

B. *Legislative professionalism* reforms designed to improve the efficiency and effectiveness of the legislature in doing these jobs focus on the capacity of the legislature to perform its role with an expertise, seriousness and effort comparable to other actors.
   1. Legislative sessions have been lengthened.
   2. Legislative salaries have been increased.
   3. Professional staff available to legislators has been increased.
   4. Critics of legislative professionalism claim it leads to an overemphasis on re-election, inflated campaign costs and a lack of leadership.
   5. States with professional legislatures tend to be those with large and heterogeneous populations, and there is some evidence that professionalism leads to more liberal welfare policy and more divided government.

C. We may now be seeing the beginning of a "deprofessionalizing" trend in some states, as some harken back to the Jeffersonian ideal of the citizen legislature.

VI. STATE COURT SYSTEMS

A. Organization of state courts reflect two influences:
   1. model of organization established by federal courts; and
   2. judicial preferences of each state's citizens, as mànifested in state constitutions and statutes.

B. States have recently tried to organize a system in a way that parallels the federal system.
   1. State courts have one hundred times the number of trials and hear five times more appeals than federal courts.

C. States have generally organized their courts into a *three-tier system* of trial courts, intermediate courts of appeals, and a court of last resort.
   1. **Trial courts** are organized on a local basis.
      a. Judges often work in only one county and specialize in criminal, juvenile, or civil litigation.
      b. A single judge presides over each case.
      c. Citizens are called upon to serve as jurors and members of grand jury panels.
      d. It is at the trial court level that the *facts of the case* are considered, along with *due process guarantees* required for the accused under the U.S. Constitution.

2. Appeals may be made to an intermediate **court of appeals** in thirty-seven states (in other states, appeals go directly to the court of last resort).
   a. Appeals courts are organized on a regional basis in which judges work together in *panels* of three or more.
   b. No witnesses are called before appellate courts.
   c. Juries are not used in appellate courts; instead, judges read *briefs* and hear arguments prepared by lawyers that address legal issues such as whether the law was appropriately applied at the trial court level and whether due process of law was followed.
   d. **"Appeals of right"** involve cases that *must be heard and decided* by appellate courts based upon merit (mandatory appeals).
3. All states have a **court of last resort**, usually called a *supreme court*, that is the *final appellate level* in a state.

D. How judges are chosen varies across states.
   1. Eleven states select judges by partisan election ballot.
   2. Nineteen states select judges by non-partisan ballots.
   3. Seventeen states use a hybrid system of appointment and election known as the Merit Plan, where the governor appoints the states' judges from a list of persons recommended by the state bar or a committee of jurists and other officials.
      a. After a trial period, an election is held in which voters are asked whether the judge should be retained in office.
      b. There are repeated retention elections, but judges seldom lose.

VII. DIRECT DEMOCRACY

A. There are three main tools of direct democracy, a method of policy-making unique to sub-national governments.
   1. Eighteen states permit **popular initiative**, a direct democracy method to amend the constitution; proposed amendments may be placed directly before the voters (bypassing the legislature) when sufficient signatures are obtained on petitions.
   2. The **constitutional initiative**, a **Progressive Era** reform, is one of the tools of direct democracy that sought to place increased power directly with the people.
   3. Other Progressive Era reforms include the **legislative initiative**, the **referendum**, and the **recall**.

B. Problems of direct democracy.
   1. There is considerable *debate over the desirability* of rewriting and adding constitutional provisions through citizen-initiated amendments. Proposed constitutional amendments are often poorly drafted.

2. It is also unclear to what extent the initiative process empowers citizens or *merely gives new tools to better-financed, more privileged interest groups.*

VIII. STATE AND LOCAL GOVERNMENT RELATIONS

A. According to **Dillon's Rule**, local governments have only those powers that are explicitly given them by the states.
   1. The basis for this rule is the United States Constitution.
   2. Local governments can use informal political clout to make policy.
   3. Formal powers are gained through state legislatures granting a local charter—an organizational statement and grant of authority in which local governments are said to operate under **home rule**.

IX. LOCAL GOVERNMENTS

A. Many Americans believe that public policy is best produced by governments that are *closest to the people*, but the sheer number of local governments creates a complexity that may actually hurt democracy.
   1. The latest count from the U.S. Bureau of the Census revealed that there are *84,955 American governments*.
   2. Every U.S. citizen lives within the jurisdiction of a national government, a state government, and perhaps *ten to twenty* local governments.

B. Most city and school district governments are located in a **county** (called a *parish* in Louisiana and a *borough* in Alaska), and **county government** is the *administrative arm of state government in local areas.*
   1. County governments keep records of births, deaths, and marriages; establish a system of justice and law enforcement; maintain roads and bridges, collect taxes, conduct voter registration and elections; and provide for public welfare and education.
   2. Rural residents rely on county governments for services more often than city residents.
   3. County governments usually consist of an elected **county commission** that makes policy and a collection of "*row officers*" (such as a sheriff, prosecutor, county clerk, assessor) who run county services; some *urban counties* now elect a county executive or appoint a county administrator.

C. **Township** governments are found in twenty states.
   1. Most have limited powers to assist with services in rural areas, but some function much like city governments.
   2. Townships can provide for public highways and local law enforcement, keep records of vital statistics and tax collections, and administer elections.

3. Most *do not* have the power to pass local ordinances.

D. **Municipalities** (city governments) provide *most basic local programs and services*, such as police and fire protection, street maintenance, solid waste collection, water and sewer works, park and recreation services, and public planning.
   1. Citizen satisfaction with the delivery of services varies greatly.
   2. Many local communities in the United States were originally operated under the "**town meeting**" form of direct democracy, where all voting age adults in a community gathered once a year to make public policy.
   3. Since cities became too large for the town meeting style of governance, three *modern forms of municipal government* have been used.
      a. **Mayor-Council Government** - typically, local residents elect a mayor and a city council.
         (1) *Strong mayor* variety - city council makes public policy, while the mayor and city bureaucracy who report to the mayor are responsible for policy implementation; strong mayors have the power to veto actions of the city council.
         (2) *Weak mayor* variety - most power is vested in the city council, which directs the activities of the city bureaucracy; mayor serves as presiding officer for city council meetings and ceremonial head of city government.
         (3) Most mayor-council cities follow the weak mayor form; small cities of 10,000 or fewer residents are most likely to have a weak mayor charter.
      b. **Council-Manager Government** - voters choose a city council and may choose a mayor, who often acts as both presiding officer and voting member of the council; council is responsible for political or policy decisions; implementation and administration of the council's actions is placed in the hands of an appointed **city manager**.
      c. **Commission Government** - voters elect a panel of city commissioners who make public policy, but each is also elected as a commissioner of a *functional area of city government* (such as public safety); bureaucrats report to a single commissioner
   4. Most city council members and mayors are elected on a *nonpartisan ballot.*
      a. Traditionally, city council members represented a **district** or **ward** of the city—a practice that permitted the *ward-based machine bosses to control elections.*

b. Reformers advocated **at-large** city elections, with all members of the city council chosen by voters across the city.
   (1) These at-large representatives could not create public policies to benefit only their own neighborhoods since they were elected by all of the city's voters.
   (2) An *unintended consequence* of at-large representation is that *minority group members have had difficulty gaining election* to the city council.

E. **School districts** are responsible for delivering education programs in over 14,000 areas of the country; most school systems are run as independent local governments.
   1. In an **independent school district**, local voters within a geographically defined area are responsible for their own public education system.
   2. Within the guidelines of state policy and the parameters of state funding, locally elected school boards and appointed administrators deliver education services.
   3. One of the important debates in school policy today concerns how to *pay for* and *guarantee equity* in public education.
      a. Although the Supreme Court declared that states have a responsibility to eliminate discrimination in education policy (*Brown* v. *Education of Topeka*, 1954; *Swann* v. *Charlotte-Mecklenberg County Schools*, 1971), the United States continues to see inequities in the public school systems, with racial minorities still encountering poorly funded public education in many instances.
      b. This equality problem is combined with a *financial crisis* in many public school systems today.
      c. States have widely divergent school aid policies, with some providing a lot of aid to needy districts, and others not.
      d. Local revenue sources are disproportionately based upon the local property tax (a policy choice that results in wealthier districts having an abundance of resources while poorer districts are limited to relatively inadequate revenues).

F. The United States has 31,555 *independent, limited-purpose governmental units* (other than school districts) known as **special districts**.
   1. This classification includes a wide variety of local "districts" for parks, natural resources, fire protection, and libraries, as well as "public authorities," "boards," and government "corporations" that can be found in every state.
   2. Usually these districts provide only a single service.
   3. These governments are sometimes referred to as "invisible

governments" because there is limited knowledge and involvement of citizens in their policy-making process.

G. Fragmentation, cooperation, and competition.
   1. Each governing body in a fragmented metropolis tends to look at problems from its *own narrow, partial perspective.* As a result, *local bodies fail to cooperate* with one another and plan effectively for the region's future needs.
   2. Traditionally, special districts have been used to encourage regional cooperation.

H. Limits of local government.
   1. Constitutional limitations: Local governments have only the legislative, spending, and taxing authority that a state chooses to give them.
   2. Structural limitations: Extensive metropolitan fragmentation results in limitations on local government power.
   3. The use of special districts conflicts with a strong emphasis on small government and direct democracy.
   4. Conflicts of interest between urban and suburban citizens makes regional coordination difficult.
   5. **Council of governments** are informal organizations where officials from various localities meet to discuss mutual problems and plan joint, cooperative action.

X. STATE AND LOCAL FINANCE POLICY

A. State government revenues are derived from a variety of sources.
   1. States receive the largest share of revenue (44 percent) from *taxes*, primarily sales taxes, income taxes, and motor vehicle and fuel taxes.
   2. The second largest source of state revenue is *aid from the federal government* (slightly over 23 percent), followed by revenue from *state insurance programs* (17 percent).
   3. Smaller revenue sources include charges for services, state-operated liquor stores, utilities, payments from local governments, and a number of miscellaneous sources.

B. About 47 percent of state money goes to *operate state programs, construct state buildings, and provide direct assistance to individuals*; approximately 30 percent is allocated as *aid to local governments.*

C. Sources of local government revenues.
   1. The finances of local governments are a confusing array of responsibilities, revenues, and budgets.
   2. Local governments receive their revenues from three main sources—taxes, user charges, and intergovernmental aid.
   3. "Own-sources" taxes (mainly property taxes, sales taxes, and income taxes) and intergovernmental aid now each account for nearly 35

percent; charges on users of services (including libraries and recreation) account for abut 20 percent; municipally owned utilities and liquor stores bring in over eight percent.

D. Local government expenditures.
   1. Primary areas of services include public education (about 37 percent), health and social services (14.3 percent) and public safety (over eight percent).

XI. UNDERSTANDING STATE AND LOCAL GOVERNMENTS

A. Democracy at the state and local levels.
   1. States have been willing to decentralize their governing arrangement to permit the creation of grassroots-oriented local governments to address citizens' policy demands.
   2. Although nearly 85,000 local governments are found across the country, most of these units are effectively making public policy in a government that is closest to the people.
   3. The very existence of so many governments to handle so many different and needed services speaks to the *health of democracy*.
   4. Yet state and local politics are not perfectly democratic.
      a. There is poor coverage in the media.
      b. There are low levels of citizen participation.
      c. Business interests have substantial leverage in state and city affairs due to local governments competing for economic development.
      d. Term limits can also have undemocratic aspects.
      e. Judicial branch is invisible to most citizens.

B. The scope of state and local governments.
   1. Growth in state and local government employment has exceeded that of the federal government for most of this century; most of the growth has been associated with heightened demands of state and local residents for more government programs.
   2. Many state and local governments have tried to *reorganize their government structures* to get more effective government and more efficient use of taxpayers' dollars; in most cases, this process of reorganization has *not* resulted in smaller government.
      a. Most state governments have experimented with **sunset legislation** (periodic review of legislation to control the growth of government and eliminate unneeded agencies and programs).
      b. States have also empowered their legislatures to review executive branch regulations and rules.
   3. Modernization of subnational governments has not always been undertaken to reduce the size of governments: as demands for

services have grown, state and local governments have had to *grow* in order to meet new challenges.

KEY TERMS AND CONCEPTS

City manager: official appointed by an elected city council and given the responsibility of implementing policy decisions.

Council of governments: association of officials from various localities that facilitates discussion of mutual problems and planning joint, cooperative activities.

Dillon's rule: initially enunciated by Judy John Dillon, states that local governments have only those powers that are explicitly given to them by the states.

Direct democracy: a method of policy-making in the U.S. unique to sub-national governments where voters participate directly in policy-making.

Home rule: power of cities to write their own charters and to change them without permission from the state legislature.

Initiative: direct democracy technique that allows proposed constitutional amendments to be placed on a statewide ballot when enough signatures are obtained.

Item veto: power of governors to veto only certain parts of a bill while allowing the rest to pass into law.

Lieutenant governor: an executive officer of state government, often elected by voters; typically presides over the state senate.

Local charter: an organizational statement and grant of authority from the state to a local government.

Merit Plan: judicial selection process whereby the governor appoints the state's judges from a list of persons recommended by the state bar or a committee of jurists and other officials.

Recall: direct democracy technique that allows voters to remove an official from office prior to completion of an elected term.

Referendum: direct democracy technique that allows citizens to pass a bill originally proposed and approved in the state legislature.

Sub-national governments: state and local governments.

Term limits: restrictions on the number of terms state legislators are allowed to serve.

Town meeting: a form of direct democracy where all voting-age adults in a community gather annually to make public policy.

TEACHING IDEAS: CLASS DISCUSSION AND STUDENT PROJECTS

- Voters in a number of states have approved term limitations for their state legislators; some states also have term limitations for governors. Ask your class to write a brief essay supporting the idea of term limitations, then ask students to write a paragraph *refuting their own arguments*. (This process may be reversed, if you prefer, but students should not know in advance about the second half of the task.)

- Divide your class into research teams to examine the different ways by which states select judges. Students should look at both partisan and nonpartisan elections, at the Missouri Plan, and at variations of the Missouri Plan generally referred to as "merit selection."

- Compile a list of state and local government decision-making bodies that are open to the public in your area, such as city councils or commissions, county commissions, zoning or planning boards, school boards, and courts. As a class project, have each student sign up to attend a session or meeting of at least one government entity on your list.

- Have students review recent coverage of local government and politics in the local newspaper, identifying what major issues are being debated. If there is no local coverage (a point which you might want to discuss in class . . .), then have students visit local government offices and ask for meeting agendas, press releases or government reports that might convey what issues are currently on the agenda. Ask students to research the various groups that are represented in the policy discussion, what positions they take, and the resources and limitations that local government faces in dealing with the problem.

- Ask students to compile a list of government jurisdictions relevant to their home residences, identifying what services each unit provides. Have students present these lists in class, and discuss the advantages and disadvantages of this diversity in our democracy.

BACKGROUND READING

Beyle, Thad L. State and Local Government 1999-2000. Washington, DC: Congressional Quarterly Press. 1992.

Carey, John M., Richard G. Niemi and Lynda W. Powell. Term Limits in State Legislatures. Ann Arbor, MI: University of Michigan Press. 1999.

Gerber, Elisabeth R. The Populist Paradox: Interest Group Influence and the Promise of Direct Legislation. Princeton: Princeton University Press. 1999.

Harrigan, John J. Politics in States and Communities. New York: Addison-Wesley. 1999.

Hill, Kim Quaile. Democracy in the Fifty States. Lincoln, Nebraska: University of Nebraska Press. 1994.

Hovey, Harold A. State Fact Finder. Washington, DC: Congressional Quarterly Press. 1999.

Thompson, Joel E., Gary F. Moncrief and Herbert E. Alexander. Campaign Finance in State Legislative Elections. Washington, DC: CQ Press. 1997.

Media Suggestions

Can the States Do It Better? This film considers different viewpoints on whether, and what, state governments can accomplish more effectively than the national government, highlighting the historical conflicts between the states and the national government. Films for the Humanities and Sciences.

Can the States Do It Better? This program begins with the historical dispute between Thomas Jefferson and Alexander Hamilton regarding the relative powers of the federal and state governments, including issues as current as school vouchers and welfare reform. Films for the Humanities & Sciences.

The Law. This program provides an overview of how state governments affect virtually every aspect of our daily lives. Films for the Humanities and Sciences.

The Lawmakers. This film describes the various motivations and goals of individuals who choose to become legislators, including interviews with both state and national legislators. Films for the Humanities and Sciences.

Lawmaking. This program uses interviews with state legislators to describe the legislative process in the states. Films for the Humanities and Sciences.

Notes

Notes

Notes

Notes

Notes

Notes

Notes

Notes